In Her Own Right

IN HER OWN RIGHT

The Life of Elizabeth Cady Stanton

ELISABETH GRIFFITH

OXFORD UNIVERSITY PRESS
New York   Oxford

Oxford University Press

Oxford New York Toronto
Delhi Bombay Calcutta Madras Karachi
Petaling Jaya Singapore Hong Kong Tokyo
Nairobi Dar es Salaam Cape Town
Melbourne Auckland

and associated companies in
Beirut Berlin Ibadan Mexico City Nicosia

First published in 1984 by Oxford University Press, Inc.,
200 Madison Avenue, New York, NY 10016
First issued as an Oxford University Press paperback, 1985

Oxford is the registered trademark of Oxford University Press.

Library of Congress Cataloging in Publication Data
Griffith, Elisabeth.
Includes index.
1. Stanton, Elizabeth Cady, 1815–1902.
2. Feminists—United States—Biography.
3. Suffragettes—United States—Biography.
4. Women's rights—United States—History.   I. Title.
HQ1413.S67G74   1984   324.6′23′0924 [B]   83-25120
ISBN 0-19-503440-6
ISBN 0-19-503729-4 (pbk.)

Printing (last digit): 9
Printed in the United States of America

For my mother

Acknowledgments

Like detectives, historians search for clues, follow leads, examine documents, evaluate evidence, and investigate lives. The case of Elizabeth Cady Stanton sent me across the country in pursuit of correspondence by or about her and in search of lost relatives. I always expected to find a cache of hidden letters in some great-grandchild's attic, but I never did. Instead I discovered the generosity of librarians and scholars and the excitement of "getting the facts."

At the libraries and historical societies I visited, I was assisted by knowledgeable, courteous professionals. For their assistance and enthusiasm, I would like to thank the staffs at the Susan B. Anthony Memorial, Rochester, New York; the Boston Public Library, Department of Rare Books and Manuscripts; the Buffalo and Erie County Public Library; the Mabel Smith Douglass Library, Rutgers University; the Geneva (New York) Historical Society and Museum; the Houghton Library, Harvard University; the Huntington Library, San Marino, California; the Johnstown (New York) Public Library; the Library of Congress; the Missouri Historical Society, St. Louis; the New-York Historical Society; the New York Public Library; the Arthur and Elizabeth Schlesinger Library, Radcliffe College; the Seneca Falls (New York) Historical Society; the Sophia Smith Collection, Smith College; the Elizabeth Cady Stanton Foundation, Seneca Falls, New York; the Ernest Bird Library, Syracuse University; and Vassar College.

Equally helpful were the many people who answered my written requests, directed to the Columbia University Archives, New York; the Cornell University Archives and Alumni Office, Ithaca; the Friends Historical Society, Swarthmore College, Haverford, Pennsylvania; the Historical Society of Pennsylvania, Philadelphia; the Madison County (New York) Historical Society; the Minnesota Historical Society, St. Paul; the Stowe-Day Memorial Library and Historical Society, Hartford; the Clements Library at the University of Michigan, Ann Arbor; and the Yale University Alumni Records Office, New Haven. Individuals like Kenneth L. Brock, Archivist for the Emma Willard School; Virginia Mosley, Borough Historian of Tenafly, New Jersey; Charles Noxon of the Johnstown Historical Society; and Wilfred Rauber, Town and Village Historian of Dansville, New York, were both thorough and thoughtful in their responses. I especially want to thank my sister, Jane Griffith Bryan, head of the reference department of the Van Pelt Library at the University of Pennsylvania, who was never too busy to respond to my long-distance demands.

Unfortunately, too many of the people who helped me were never identified or introduced, like the woman at the public library in Greenwich, Connecticut, who answered my telephone query about the children of Stanton's granddaughter, whom the *New York Times* obituary reported to have died in Greenwich. She directed me to Stanton's great-granddaughter, Rhoda Barney Jenkins. "She lives just down the block," said the voice on the phone. When I called Mrs. Jenkins, she invited me and my tape recorder to spend the afternoon. That encounter began a friendship with a woman who resembles her famous foremother in many ways and who contributed her family memories and photographs to this book.

Another chance clue prompted an inquiry to the public librarian in Beaman, Iowa, who forwarded my letter to Barbara Wood McMartin, great-granddaughter-in-law of Stanton's sister Margaret. Mrs. McMartin, an energetic genealogist, helped trace the offspring of the rest of the Cady sisters. Also helpful were the court clerks in the County of New York (City) and Fulton County, New York.

The steadfast encouragement of my dissertation committee at American University invigorated this project. Their combined confidence in me and their demands on me strengthened this biography and honed my skills as a historian. Robert L. Beisner, the chairman of the committee, kept me on course and on schedule with good-humored patience; his skill as an editor challenged me to meet his standard of excellence. If Dr. Beisner was my mentor, Professor Valerie French was my role model. Her commitment to historical applications of psychological methodology convinced me to attempt a "psychobiography" of Stanton, and her informed questions forced me to probe more deeply and widely than I might have on my own. Alan Kraut contributed his expertise on abolition and nineteenth-century reform movements. Kay Mussell, head of the American Studies department, corrected my interpretations of women's history and sought to improve my craftsmanship as a writer.

This biography also benefited from the critical reading of John M. Cooper, Jr., of the University of Wisconsin, Madison, who had been my undergraduate adviser at Wellesley College; Anne Macdonald, head of the history faculty at the National Cathedral School in Washington, who nurtured both the book and its author; and Mary Grant, whose dissertation on Julia Ward Howe, an enemy of Stanton's, cemented our friendship. These friends deserve special thanks, as do the scholars who shared their insights or research with me: Margaret Hope Bacon, Ellen C. DuBois, Corinne Guntzel, Blanche Glassman Hersch, Kirk Jeffrey, Mary Kelley, Hanns Kuttner, Allan J. Lichtman, Edith Mayo, Carol Weissbrod, Judith Wellman, and Kathy Widom.

A Woodrow Wilson Grant for Research in Women's Studies, awarded in 1978, provided me with funds for travel and the purchase of *The History of Woman Suffrage*, as well as for photocopying and day care, all of which were necessary to the completion of this project.

I am even more indebted to Audrey Wolf, my agent, to Sheldon Meyer, my editor, to Ann Hofstra Grogg, my copy editor, and to Joan Fraser and Julia Goetz, friends and assistants, for sharing my enthusiasm for Mrs. Stanton. Finally, I want to thank my family for their encouragement and endurance: Anne and Katie, who almost completed their degrees before I did; my daughter Megan, whose joyful presence cheered me; and especially my husband, John Deardourff, who sustained me. All of us came to think of Mrs. Stanton as a member of our extended household.

McLean, Virginia   Elisabeth Griffith
December 1983

Contents

Introduction

Elizabeth Cady Stanton was the best known and most conspicuous advocate of women's rights in the nineteenth century. For almost fifty years she led the first women's movement in America. She set its agenda, drafted its documents, and articulated its ideology. Her followers grew from a scattered network of local reform groups into a national constituency of politically active women. Her statements and actions were recorded in the national press; her death in 1902 made international headlines. Newspapers called her "America's Grand Old Woman."

On November 12, 1895, six thousand people celebrated Stanton's eightieth birthday. The "Queen Mother" of American suffragists was enthroned on the stage of the Metropolitan Opera House. As usual, her rotound form was swathed in yards of black silk. White lace set off her carefully coifed thick white curls and bright blue eyes. Though no longer pretty, Mrs. Stanton radiated humor and intelligence. Behind her on the stage, under a canopy of evergreens, red carnations spelled out her name in a field of white chrysanthemums; dozens of roses banked her red velvet chair. Nearly immobile from overweight and old age, Mrs. Stanton surveyed her domain with delight. She sat through three hours of tributes and ovations from representatives of national and international women's groups. Mormon women from the Utah Territory gave her an onyx and silver ballot box; much to Stanton's amusement, it could not be opened. Finally, with the help of her children and two canes, she hobbled to the podium to acknowledge her audience of admirers. Too weak to speak for long, she could only remark, "I am well aware that all these public demonstrations are not so much tributes to me as an individual as to the great idea I represent—the enfranchisement of women."[1] The hall exploded with cheers for the cause and the crusader.

Stanton's feminism was not limited to suffrage. In an era of outspoken reformers, she was an innovative and radical thinker. She believed that women had been condemned to a subordinate status by entrenched attitudes based on Judeo-Christian tradition, patriarchal institutions, English common law, American statutes, and social customs. She frequently compared the position of women to that of slaves, and she worked to abolish both forms of bondage. In addition to suffrage she advocated coeducation, girls' sports, job training, equal wages, labor unions, birth control, cooperative nurseries and kitchens, property rights for wives, child custody rights for mothers, and reform of divorce laws. Stanton was the first person to enumerate every major advance achieved for women in the last century and many of the reforms still on the agenda in this century.

Stanton's talents were aptly suited to the role of agitator. Well educated and widely read, she had keen intelligence, a trained mind, and an ability to argue persuasively in writing and speaking. Her personality was magnetic. In conversation and correspondence she was witty and opinionated; in person she was funny, feisty, engaging. Her most remarkable trait was her self-confidence. It gave her the courage to take controversial stands without hesitation.

Elizabeth Cady Stanton's life was characterized by controversy. From the unusual academic and athletic achievements of her adolescence to her demand for female suffrage in 1848, to her declaration of a feminist ideology of independence, to her agitation for radical social change, to her attack on the Bible, her actions and attitudes provoked debate and dissension. Her politics, her prejudices, her rhetoric, her associates, her attire, even her child-raising practices alarmed many. Her behavior outraged the socially conservative element of the population, including her father. Eventually it offended her liberal allies as well, including her husband and her successors in the suffrage movement. Although she appeared to be a respectable matron, Stanton was accurately perceived to be a revolutionary—not a suitable role for a nineteenth-century woman.[2]

Having a revolutionary as an ally was a source of embarrassment to Stanton's colleagues. In the late 1860s Stanton's angry opposition to a reconstruction program that enfranchised black men but excluded black and white women created a schism in the ranks of suffragists. It resulted in the creation of rival organizations, the National and the American Woman Suffrage associations. The National Association, founded by Stanton, had a broad platform that addressed other women's issues in addition to demanding a constitutional amendment to enfranchise women. It was based in New York City and briefly defended by its own newspaper, the *Revolution*. The American Association, founded by Lucy Stone, her husband Henry Blackwell, and Julia Ward Howe, limited itself to suffrage. It focused on state referenda activity and allowed men to be members and officers. Boston based and socially conservative, the American published the *Woman's Journal* for fifty years. Even after the two groups merged into the National American Woman Suffrage Association (NAWSA) in 1890, Mrs. Stanton continued to irritate the conservative faction. Refusing "to sing suffrage evermore," she advocated unions for women workers, divorce reform, and birth control.[3] Two weeks after the public celebration of her eightieth birthday, Stanton published *The Woman's Bible,* an attack on traditional church teachings about the status of women.

Suffragists feared that Stanton's radical feminism and religious heresy would damn their chances for success. The concerns of NAWSA's leadership were not unfounded. As late as 1920 antisuffrage forces were recalling Stanton's allegedly antichurch, antifamily, prolabor stance.[4] To avoid the Stanton stigma, the younger women intentionally isolated and ignored her. In an effort to appear respectable and politically acceptable, they censured Stanton and canonized Susan B. Anthony. They provided "Aunt Susan" with a permanent seat on the executive committee, a secretary, and an annuity. After her death they turned her home into a shrine and named the Nineteenth Amendment after her, despite the fact that Stanton had proposed woman suffrage three years before she had met Anthony. Later generations, unaware of Stanton's role, put Anthony on a stamp and a coin. As a result, Elizabeth Cady Stanton, both notable and notorious in her own life, is better known as Susan B. Anthony's sidekick than as the instigator and ideologue of the first women's movement.

The substitution of Anthony for Stanton was a conscious strategy. In July 1923, on the seventy-fifth anniversary of Stanton's Seneca Falls suffrage resolution, Alice Paul led the National Woman's party to the site to introduce the Equal Rights Amendment. The ceremony was planned and the program printed without any reference to Stanton. Stanton's daughter, Harriot Blatch, insisted on paying tribute to her mother. She was the only speaker to mention Elizabeth Cady Stanton. The event concluded with a motorcade to nearby Rochester to lay a wreath at the Anthony memorial.[5] Fifty-four years later, in November 1977, when the national meeting to observe International Women's Year convened in Houston, Texas, it opened with the arrival of a torch that had been carried, by female runners, from Seneca Falls. Seated on the dais was Susan B. Anthony's grandniece and namesake. The heroine of Seneca Falls, Stanton herself, had been lost to history.

Efforts to reconstruct Stanton's life have been handicapped by the muddled state of the sources. Primary sources include letters, a diary, an autobiography and unpublished fragments, a political history, *The Woman's Bible,* speeches, articles, and newspaper columns. The correspondence of colleagues and family, newspaper reports, and the archives of the National and National American Woman Suffrage associations are also available. However, as Anthony frequently complained, Stanton was never very systematic about her record keeping. Research is further hampered by Stanton's handwriting. In her haste, she left many letters unfinished. One printer found her script so illegible that a speech about "males" became a diatribe against "mules."[6]

After Stanton's death in 1902, two of her children, Harriot Blatch and Theodore Stanton, began to collect her papers for publication. The planned work finally appeared in two volumes in 1922 as *Elizabeth Cady Stanton as Revealed in Her Letters, Diary and Reminiscences.* In an effort to whitewash their mother into respectability, they had rewritten her letters, destroyed her diary, and altered her autobiography. Having wreaked havoc with the primary sources, they then destroyed some of the documents. Those that remain are scattered. The most important collections are at the Library of Congress, Douglass College, and Vassar College.

The letters exist in various versions in various places. After the children had collected as many of the originals as they could locate, they each typed copies with carbons. The majority of the letters, with deletions, are included in the 1922 published collection. Harriot Blatch's originals and copies were divided between two sets of scrapbooks. One set was given to the Library of Congress in 1927. She gave the other to Vassar College in 1928, on the occasion of her fiftieth class reunion. After Theodore Stanton's death in 1925, his copies were left to Rutgers University and later deposited at Douglass College. This collection is more complete in content and scope than any other.

Family members recall that after the copies were made and the scrapbooks prepared, Mrs. Blatch burned the remnants.[7] But some additional letters must have survived because in 1939 she made them available to Alma Lutz, another Vassar alumna.* An officer of the National Woman's party, Miss Lutz was writing a biography of Stanton and collaborating on an autobiography of Mrs. Blatch.[8] Published without footnotes, these books quote materials not found elsewhere. Any Stanton biographer must compare the texts of the various copies of every letter to determine which most closely resemble the original in content and intention.[9]

Stanton's children also tampered with their mother's autobiography. In the 1922 version they deleted whole sections of the original, altered others,

---

* Alma Lutz (1890–1973) was a lifelong member of the National Woman's party, its national secretary, and a contributor to its paper, *Equal Times.* A graduate of Emma Willard and Vassar (1912), she wrote magazine and newspaper articles and biographies of Emma Willard and Anthony as well as Stanton.

and added approximately fifty pages. They purged any reference to marital friction, domestic discord, or political conflict.[10] Until 1971 the children's version was the only one available. Originally *Eighty Years and More* promised to be "the story of my private life as the wife of an earnest reformer, as an enthusiastic housekeeper, . . . and as the mother of seven children," but it was hardly introspective.[11] Even without the editorial interference of offspring, Stanton's autobiography is a suspect document. As a source, it is self-serving and often inaccurate. Like her maternal public image, Stanton self-consciously constructed an appealing autobiography, portraying herself as benign, amusing, undaunted, heroic, and praiseworthy. She admitted to no character flaws and few enemies. She omitted almost any mention of her mother, ignored her husband, misdated events, confused incidents, and forgot scandals.

Fortunately the records of Stanton's public life are more reliable. The first four volumes of the six-part opus, *The History of Woman Suffrage,* record her suffrage work and reprint her speeches.[12] The *History* is invaluable as an in-house record, unintentionally revealing both in what it includes and what it omits. It is essentially a cut-and-paste collection of meeting minutes, speech texts, newspaper clippings, and collegial recollections, lacking index, order, or analysis.

If potential biographers were undaunted by the difficulty of the search for evidence, they may have been deterred by the length and breadth of Stanton's life. She was active in reform politics for more than sixty years and had an opinion on every subject from bicycle riding for women (pro) to museum admission charges (con). As Theodore Tilton, an admiring journalist and her first biographer, observed in 1897, her life had many dimensions: "I have known you for more than forty years in more than forty characters — suffragist — journalist — lecturer — historian — traveler — prophetess — mater-familias — housekeeper — patriot — nurse — babytender — cook — milliner — lobbyist — parliamentarian — statistician — legislator — philosopher — tea-pourer — storyteller — satirist — kite-flyer —chessplayer . . . [and] theologian."[13]

Rather than grapple with such a long life and large personality, most historians have abandoned Stanton to journalists and writers of "juveniles." There is no thorough or documented "life and times" of Elizabeth Cady Stanton. The few scholars who are interested in her have limited their inquiries to an abbreviated life or have chosen to emphasize only one era or activity.[14] This biography intends to complete the factual record—to recall Stanton's contributions to women's rights, to investigate the nature of her collaboration with Anthony, to integrate her public and private lives. It will describe and analyze the steps Stanton took to forge her own independent self; it will examine her private feminist identity and her public feminist ideology; and it will suggest a hypothesis about what motivated her to behave as outrageously and courageously as she did.

It is typical of biographers to assume that subjects move from birth to death in a logical sequence, like characters in *Pilgrim's Progress*, following a course, advancing a cause, growing in grace. Not all lives have such a cohesive factor, but Stanton's did. What unifies Stanton's life is a feminist ethic of independence. She adopted this ethic first in every phase of her own life and then articulated it as an ideology of autonomy for other women. As Stanton matured, she rebelled against the restrictions on female activity that confronted her in every sphere. Her success in these conflicts caused her to value her feminist theories. She tried them out in her own behavior and then advocated them in print and speeches, urging independence for all women.

Rather than submit to what she believed to be outdated traditions, Stanton chose an alternative if less acceptable course. Caught up in a period of tumultuous social change, she sought to change the lives of American women. Denied a college education because she was female, she studied law informally and read voraciously. Influenced by the egalitarian preaching of the revival period, she undertook her own salvation through reform. Provoked by the political conservatism and arrogance of most churches, she created a theology based on an affectionate, androgynous God. Forbidden by her family to undertake reform activity, she married an abolitionist hero and became a militant reformer. Outraged by antifemale bias among liberal males, she challenged their leadership. Confined on all sides by male-imposed limits, she questioned the authority of paternal institutions. In the process she made herself physically, emotionally, intellectually, and financially independent, and sought to guarantee her legal and political equality as well.

Such "self-sovereignty" was the essence of Stanton's feminist theory. She summarized it in "The Solitude of Self," her last major speech, presented in January 1892 to two congressional committees and the annual meeting of the National American Woman Suffrage Association. She defined the "solitude of self" as the "individuality of each human soul," in both divine and democratic terms. Stanton argued that women must be treated as individuals without regard for the "incidental relations of life, such as mother, wife, sister, daughter." In reality women, like men, had only themselves to rely upon. She conceded that few women were ready for "self-dependence" because they had been overprotected by a patriarchal society. In order to achieve "self-dependence," women had to be emancipated from "all forms of bondage, . . . custom, dependence and superstition," both physical and psychological.[15]

Having freed herself from external and internal restraints, Elizabeth Cady

Stanton was unlike most of nineteenth-century American womanhood. She was not typical of white, middle-class, educated, married, Northern women, nor was she representative of female reformers. She was an uncommon woman. She had the intelligence, energy, vision, and courage to be a heroic character, and she was. She marshaled her superior qualities in a daily battle against entrenched institutions that denied women their social, economic, and legal independence. She was defeated again and again and again, but she continued the struggle with passionate impatience.

A compelling orator, a bold strategist, an unyielding opponent, and a generous ally, Stanton was a dynamic leader. After Stanton's death, journalist Ida Husted Harper extolled her as the principal philosopher, publicist, and politician of the first women's movement: "If the intellect of Elizabeth Cady Stanton had been possessed by a man, he would have had a seat on the Supreme Bench or in the Senate of the United States, but our country has no rewards for its great women."[16]

Elizabeth Cady Stanton was a great woman, and this is unabashedly a "great woman" biography. With the recognition in recent years that populations also contain soldiers, slaves, and shopkeepers, some of whom are women, the "great man" theories of history and the biographies they generated have fallen out of fashion. "Great woman" history, on the other hand, was rarely written.* But without adequate documentation of prominent women, the record is incomplete and comparisons are impossible. Not until the careers of America's first generation of feminists have been examined will scholars be able to generalize about these distinguished individuals. Such biographies will serve, in Barbara Tuchman's phrase, as a "prism" through which to view the political and social history of the last century in a new light.[17] Fortunately the rebirth of the women's movement in the late 1960s and the renaissance of women's history provide an opportunity for this generation to recover its foremothers from the nineteenth century. The most important of these was Elizabeth Cady Stanton.

Like many great men, Stanton thought of herself in historic and heroic terms. She expected to be recalled as a "foremother" rather than be forgotten.[18] She carefully constructed her dual public image as matriarch and revolutionary, equally expert on the domestic or political front. One of the most important aspects of her self-definition was her name. She insisted on being addressed by her full name, Elizabeth Cady Stanton, which she con-

* Initial efforts to record the lives of eminent American women were made in the 1890s, as the first generation of college-educated women sought to identify women of achievement in an earlier era. They established archives for research and wrote biographies of colonial and contemporary women, like Abigail Adams and Susan B. Anthony. Organizations like the Daughters of the American Revolution related their members to a past that provided proud models of accomplishment. The second surge of biographies came with the renaissance of women's history in the late 1960s.

sidered her own name, representing her own self. Except for letters to her children, she always signed all three names, even in correspondence with her closest friends. In return, Stanton was addressed less formally. To her best friend and cousin, Elizabeth Smith Miller, Stanton was "Johnson" to the other's "Julius" in a long standing imitation of a Christy minstrel team.[19] Anthony always called her "Mrs. Stanton," although she was addressed as "Dear Susan." To other intimates Stanton was "Libby." Her husband Henry sometimes called her "Lizzy Lee." Only her enemies, in an effort to remind her of her traditional domestic status, called her Mrs. Henry B. Stanton.*

Rather than defer to the prescribed form, Stanton combined her family and married names. The idea had been recommended by Henry's friend Theodore Weld, whom the couple visited shortly after their marriage in 1840. It did not become an established practice for another year. By 1847, before she had spoken out on any other women's issue, Mrs. Stanton was defending her right to her own name. As she explained in an argument with an acquaintance:

> I have very serious objections . . . to being called Henry. Ask our colored brethren if there is nothing to a name. Why are the slaves nameless unless they take that of their master? Simply because they have no independent existence. They are mere chattels, with no civil or social rights. Even so with women. The custom of calling women Mrs. John This and Mrs. Tom That and colored men Sambo and Zip Coon is founded on the principle that white men are the lords of all. I cannot acknowledge this principle as just; therefore I cannot bear the name of another.[20]

The emphasis on independence and individual rights and the extrapolation from her position to the position of other women would become characteristic of Stanton's developing feminist ideology. As well as defining the "self sovereign," she was defining herself. As Stanton concluded at the end of her life, "I became a very extraordinary woman, the first of the 'new women.' "[21]

---

* The question of how to address the female subjects of biography raises issues of style and substance. Biographers of great men never had to worry about what to call their protagonists, who had the same name all their lives. One's subject could age gracefully from "young John" to "Adams" to "the president" without confusing the reader. Biographers of great women have a more awkward nomenclature if their subject married, or married more than once. How should one address Elizabeth Cady Stanton? Using her first name or nicknames seems juvenile, too familiar, even disrespectful. Using her family name, Cady, is only appropriate for the period before her marriage, since she did not keep her name as Lucy Stone did. Using her full name is cumbersome but emphatic. For the most part this biography will refer to her as Stanton or Mrs. Stanton, following general newspaper practice. (The New York Times still insists on "Miss" or "Mrs." always; "Mr." is used only for "men of good standing," except on the sports pages.) Her husband Henry will be identified as Mr. Stanton or by using his first name. The younger Mr. Stantons, of whom there were five, will be distinguished as necessary. Other women will also be referred to by last names: Susan B. Anthony will be Anthony or Miss Anthony, rather than the more familiar Susan or "Aunt Susan."

In Her Own Right

I

Place and Privilege
1815–26

Elizabeth Cady Stanton was born into the first family of Johnstown, New York. Located forty miles northwest of Albany, the town of one thousand was the seat of Fulton County. It was an intellectual and industrial center in the early nineteenth century. The Cayadutta River at the north end of the village supplied power for factories making gloves and steel springs. Named for Sir William Johnson, an Englishman who had bought the site from the Indians before the Revolution, the town overlooked the Mohawk Valley. It was splendid in autumn and snowbound in winter.[1]

The Cady mansion, at the corner of Main and Market streets, dominated the east end of the town square. In position and proportion it equaled the church, the courthouse, and the jail. The first Cady home on the site, a two-story white frame colonial building, was Stanton's birthplace. That house was later torn down by her father and replaced with a "severely square grey brick mansion." A visitor described it in 1854 as "an elegant great house . . . [full of] beautiful things and tasteful environments." The impressive entry hall featured a divided staircase, and all the rooms were well proportioned and high ceilinged.[2] The house was large enough to accommodate the numerous children, law students, and servants in livery who made up the Cady ménage. At one time the Cadys employed twelve servants, including two black men and a boy, four nurses, a laundress, a cook with a drunken father, and assorted maids.[3]

Reigning over this large household was Elizabeth's mother, Margaret Livingston Cady. The Livingston name tied her to the old Dutch aristocracy in New York, although her parents were Canadians and only collaterally connected to their wealthy Hudson Valley relations. At the outbreak

of the Revolutionary War, her father, Col. James Livingston, raised a reg-
iment of Americans and fought at Quebec and Saratoga. The commander
of a battalion under Benedict Arnold, he frustrated the treason attempt of
Arnold and Gen. John André and fired on the *Vulture*. Returning to Saratoga after the war, he served on the first board of regents of the state
university and in the state assembly. His daughter Margaret, the sixth of
nine children, was born in 1785. In 1801, at age sixteen, she married Daniel Cady of Johnstown.*

Nearly six feet tall, a daring horsewoman, strong willed and self-reliant,
Margaret Livingston Cady was formidable. Twelve years younger and several inches taller than her husband, she was the only person in the household not in awe of him. She refused to move to a country estate and be
isolated from friends in town, she defied his ban on rocking chairs, and
she disagreed with his opposition to abolition and women's rights. She was
no less independent in the community. At one time Mrs. Cady insisted that
the votes of female parishioners be counted in the election of a new pastor.
According to her granddaughter, Mrs. Cady preferred "diplomacy to open
warfare." She expected "to mold people and circumstances" to get her own
way.[4]

Margaret Cady combined these dominant characteristics with an attractive demeanor. An acquaintance found her "very refined, a lady-like, loving, spirited woman; . . . [a] genteel mistress [with a] cordial smile [and]
gentle sweet voice." Her grandchildren remembered her as vibrant, interesting, and indulgent. She allowed them to read aloud while sitting on the
dining room sideboard, treated them to treasures from a special drawer,
and encouraged them to express and defend their opinions, as she did. One
of them concluded that Grandmother Cady was "freer and finer" without
her husband or family "weaving nets of convention about her."[5] No similarly vivid portrait of Margaret Cady ever appears in Stanton's autobiography.

In contrast to his wife, Daniel Cady was conventional in sentiment and
conservative in politics. He was a self-made man who, through cunning
and connections, had become one of the wealthiest landowners in the state.
Born in 1773, he farmed with his father in Canaan, New York. Appren-
ticed as a shoemaker, he was blinded in one eye in a cobbling accident; he
also tried school teaching and studied law before moving to Johnstown in
1799. Two years later he married Margaret Livingston. Her sister Elizabeth had married Peter Smith, John Jacob Astor's partner in the fur trade.
Cady became his brother-in-law's attorney and advised him on real estate
investments. As a result he had the means and opportunity to purchase land

---

* Genealogical sketches of the Livingston-Cady family and Cady-Stanton family appear in apps.
A and B.

throughout New York State. By the time Elizabeth was born, Daniel Cady was a wealthy landowner and a prominent citizen.

In 1808 Daniel Cady was elected to the state legislature. He served until 1814, when he was elected to Congress. Like most Federalists, he was overwhelmingly defeated in 1816. He ran again for Congress in 1832 and lost by thirty votes in the second Jackson landslide. In the interim his reputation as an expert in equity and real estate law attracted young men from across the country to clerk in his Johnstown office, including four of his five future sons-in-law. For many years he served as a circuit court judge, traveling with *"Coke on Littleton* in one of his saddlebags and a change of linen in the other."[6] In 1847 Judge Cady was elected associate justice of the New York Supreme Court for the Fourth District. Reelected for an eight-year term in 1849, he served until 1855, when he was eighty-two years old and deaf. He died in October 1859.

Short, intellectual, and austere, Daniel Cady was described by a guest as "a John Quincy Adams type of man," tough minded and taciturn. He was a strict Presbyterian who worried about salvation. He read legal texts in their original languages and owned an extensive library. In an era of reform enthusiasms, the only kind of improvements he discussed were the agricultural experiments that he practiced on his outlying farms. Although he became a rich man, he opposed the concentration of wealth in the upper class. To his even richer brother-in-law he declared, "It is not consistent with the well-being of society that a man and his posterity should for many generations go on rapidly accumulating property: should it be permitted . . . the great mass of mankind would become slaves."[7]

The Cadys had eleven children, five boys and six girls. Six of them died before adulthood, and no more than six children were alive at one time. The boisterousness of a big family was quieted by the deaths of so many children. The frequency of children dying in early nineteenth-century families did not diminish the tragedy. In 1814, the year he was elected to Congress, Daniel Cady lost two sons, first an eight-year-old and then an infant, both named for him. As the bereaved father confided to his brother-in-law, "Such is the fleeting nature of the treasures of this world—one moment they are objects of our warmest affections and at the next the source of bitterest anguish." In lieu of sons, Judge Cady devoted himself to his law clerks, sons-in-law, and grandsons. Three of his daughters named their sons Daniel Cady, and to each of them the judge willed a horse and a farm. To the first grandson to pass the bar examination, he promised his law library.[8]

Elizabeth was the Cadys' seventh child and middle daughter, born November 12, 1815. Her oldest sister, Tryphena, had been born in 1804 and named for Grandmother Cady. Family accounts depict the adult Tryphena as tall, handsome, and severe, a woman of "striking executive ability" who managed the family's investments and served as her father's executor. She was an active Presbyterian, the trustee of a private school, and a founder of the Woman's Homeopathic School and Hospital in New York. Married but childless, Tryphena was too fastidious and disapproving to warrant much affection from her numerous nieces and nephews. Although initially interested in temperance, she did not pursue other reforms. She "wept" over her sister's involvement with women's rights.[9] Yet Tryphena Cady Bayard was a strong-willed, independent, intelligent woman whose financial interests were exceptional among her contemporaries.

The next Cady daughter, Harriet, born in 1810, was the beautiful sister—petite, "delicate as a cameo," and so fragile that she never had any systematic schooling. As a result, she insisted on paying for the Vassar education of Stanton's daughters. Haddie married her cousin, Daniel Cady Eaton, a wealthy New York City merchant, and had two children. She attended the Seneca Falls women's rights meeting in 1848 and signed its Declaration of Sentiments, but her husband made her remove her name. During Elizabeth's bloomer period, the fashion-conscious Haddie was so humiliated that she refused to write or visit, and her ever upright husband sent furious letters to Seneca Falls. After her husband's death, Haddie lived with Tryphena.[10]

The two youngest daughters were closer to Elizabeth in age and interests. Margaret was born in 1817. Catherine's birth in 1819 was the first event Elizabeth claimed to remember. She recalled overhearing a neighbor bemoan the birth of another girl. Like Elizabeth, both Madge and Cate attended Emma Willard's seminary in Troy, New York, married men who had studied law with their father, bore five children, and participated in and contributed to the women's movement. Margaret's husband, Duncan McMartin, moved to Iowa after the Civil War and ran a two-thousand-acre experimental farm. Catherine's husband, Samuel Wilkeson, was a judge, a newspaper man, and an active Republican. The Wilkesons lived successively in Albany, Buffalo, Washington, and New York City.[11]

Of the Cadys' five sons, four died in childhood. Only Eleazar reached manhood. As Elizabeth recalled, her brother was "a fine manly fellow, the very apple of my father's eye." He graduated from Union College in 1826. A few weeks later, after a short illness, he died. He was twenty years old. The whole family was stunned. Judge Cady, who had been away from home, returned to find Eleazar dead. Heartbroken at the loss of his last son, the grief-stricken father kept an uninterrupted vigil by the casket. After the funeral he made daily, tearful visits to the grave. "It was easily seen," Elizabeth wrote later, "that while my father was kind to us all, the one son filled a larger place in his affections and future plans than the five daughters together."[12]

The loss of all of his sons must have been acutely painful to a father who had worked so hard to establish a name, a reputation, and an estate to pass on. Until passage of the New York State Married Women's Property Act in 1848, daughters could not inherit or hold property in their own right. Eventually all of the Cady daughters inherited sizable fortunes, but none could fulfill the expectations of achievement Judge Cady reserved for his sons.

Then over forty, Mrs. Cady had not been pregnant (or carried a pregnancy to term) for seven years. Nonetheless, she bore one more child. The infant, named Eleazar, died in 1828, before he was a year old. Exhausted by eleven births, depressed by the deaths of all her sons, defeated in her attempt to produce another son, Margaret Cady retired temporarily into ill health and inactivity.

The responsibility for the remaining girls was given to Tryphena. She also filled her mother's role by giving the family a son, in the form of a son-in-law. Within six months of Eleazar's death, she had married his classmate and close friend, Edward Bayard. He and his brother Henry, sons of a United States senator from Wilmington, Delaware, read law with Judge Cady. As Edward and Tryphena became acting parents for the younger children, he earned the family's affection. In the mid-1830s the Bayards moved to Seneca Falls, west of Syracuse, and later to New York City. Bayard gave up law for medicine and became one of the country's leading homeopaths.[13]

Not yet eleven years old when her only brother died, Elizabeth remembered the event vividly. Eleazar's death became the centerpiece of her childhood. In her recollection, the sound of funeral bells reverberate. The sudden loss of her beloved brother and the morbid graveyard visits of her father set off a preoccupation with dying that fueled two decades of religious inquiry.[14] Eleazar's death also resulted in dramatic changes in her life. Her father was incapacitated by his grief, her mother retired into pregnancy and depression, and the Bayards replaced her parents.

The impact of Eleazar's death on the preadolescent Elizabeth was decisive. In the midst of her grief, fear, and insecurity, Daniel Cady expressed his disappointment in daughters and his desire for sons. As Stanton remembered in her autobiography:

> I still recall . . . going into the large, darkened parlor to see my brother and finding the casket, mirrors, and pictures all draped in white, and my father seated by his side, pale and immovable. As he took no notice of me, after standing a long while, I climbed upon his knee, when he mechanically put his arm about me and, with my head resting against his

> beating heart, we both sat in silence, he thinking of the wreck of all his
> hopes in the loss of a dear son, and I wondering what could be said or
> done to fill the void in his breast. At length he heaved a sigh and said:
> "Oh, my daughter, I wish you were a boy!" Throwing my arms about his
> neck I replied, "I will try to be all my brother was."[15]

This melodramatic scene is recreated in every Stanton reminiscence.

At a time when Elizabeth was grief stricken and vulnerable, when she
wanted to comfort her bereaved father, when she sought his attention and
affection, these circumstances combined to encourage her to behave like
his son. She resolved to do everything she could to be "manly," which to
her meant becoming "learned and courageous." She decided "to study Greek
and learn to manage a horse." Her actions, and the reactions of the adults
who were important to her, did change her behavior. She learned, performed, and maintained new roles that affected the course of her life. "They
were resolutions never to be forgotten," she recalled, "destined to mold
my character anew."[16]

The Cadys' neighbor, Rev. Simon Hosack, tutored Elizabeth in Greek,
mathematics, and chess. Her brother-in-law Edward Bayard schooled her
in equestrian arts and philosophy. The law clerks teased her with legal riddles and challenged her to debate. Allowed to read whatever she wanted
in the Cady library, Elizabeth met the test. She succeeded in what were
then considered masculine fields: she won second place in the Johnstown
Academy Greek competition, she learned to jump four-foot fences, and she
became a skilled debater. More important, her intellect was ignited. Her
curiosity, wide-ranging reading, and analytic skills became lifelong habits.
Like her father, she enjoyed an independent intellectual life.

Of all the Cady daughters, Elizabeth was the one with the opportunity
and talent to succeed in these fields. Tryphena, just married, was twelve
years older and mathematically inclined. Harriet was too frail for sports
and uninterested in academics. Margaret and Catherine, nine and six years
old respectively in 1826, had the athletic potential but lacked the intellectual enterprise. Daniel Cady's expression of sorrow and frustration to Elizabeth—"I wish you were a boy!"—may not have been random. The choice
of Elizabeth may have been made in recognition of her superior talents, or
it may have been "self-selection" by his daughter. She wanted to fulfill his
ambitions as much as he wanted them fulfilled.

Judge Cady's reaction to Elizabeth's academic and athletic achievements
changed as she grew older. Initially permissive, he allowed her to undertake masculine activities. He did not forbid her to spend hours in the library or in his law office, to attend court sessions, or to ride any horse in
the stable. On occasion he actually encouraged her to compete and perform, and he took pride in the outcome. Interrupting her watercolors or

embroidery, he brought her lawbooks to study so that she would be able to participate in dinner table debates with his law clerks or guests. Yet when she won the Greek Prize, her father's only reaction was to reiterate his disappointment that she was not a boy.[17]

If Elizabeth had been a boy, her father would have been proud of her. But she was not a boy, and her father's reserve served to reinforce a sense of inadequacy based only on her gender. Having proved herself just as smart, able, and athletic as her brother, she resented the conclusion that she was not just as good as a boy. She longed for her father's approval but seldom received it. Yet her satisfaction in her own achievements, her pleasure in learning and riding, and her resentment that her successes were not appreciated by her father served to reinforce her commitment to these interests.

Judge Cady was caught between encouraging his daughter's intellectual potential and condoning uncustomary behavior in a young female. He allowed Elizabeth to go away to finishing school, but he forbade college. The more she did, the more she wanted to do, the more her father could no longer allow her to do. Her successes became embarrassments to him because they were inappropriate activities for daughters. Her interests were outside the "sexual sphere" of females, as defined by social conservatives, Presbyterians, *Godey's Lady's Book,* and the "cult of true womanhood." Within five years his permissiveness changed to prohibition. For the rest of his life he would criticize as unseemly behavior he had initially tolerated. As Elizabeth would recount to her friend Susan Anthony in 1855, "To think that all in me of which my father would have felt a proper pride had I been a man is deeply mortifying to him because I am a woman."[18]

Others in her extended family circle continued to encourage her untraditional achievements. Rev. Simon Hosack and Edward Bayard applauded her success. Hosack was especially important to her. His love and respect, she recalled, "cultivated in me a good deal of self-respect. I can remember beginning to think myself of some value from the way he used to prize me and talk to me." As a child, she visited him every day to give him a kiss and help him in his garden. When he died, the poor minister willed her his Greek texts.[19] The reactions of her mother have not been recorded. Elizabeth's attempt to win her father's approval coincided with the period of her mother's withdrawal from the family circle, but even in confinement Mrs. Cady served as a model. Because Stanton's descriptions of her parents and her relationship with each of them changed as she got older, it is difficult to assess their influence on her early development.

From her middle daughter's perspective, Margaret Cady was powerful, stern, and withdrawn. Confinement on account of pregnancy, the intervention of servants in child care and household management, and her depres-

sion after the deaths of both Eleazars removed Mrs. Cady from the adolescent Elizabeth. In Stanton's recollection of her childhood, her mother
functioned as a demanding and disapproving disciplinarian. "Whenever there
was a great deal of noise or confusion in the house or any mischief going
on my mother always imagined that I was at the head of it." Stanton remembered that to her mother "everything I liked and enjoyed was messy
or injurious; and . . . everything I disliked was just the thing."[20] Supposedly her mother, between pregnancies a horsewoman, even disapproved of
outdoor sports for her daughter. When she misbehaved, the recalcitrant
Elizabeth was sent to her father's office for discipline. According to Stanton's one-sided autobiography, Mrs. Cady emphasized domestic occupations. She expected her daughters to be housewives and trained them ac-
cordingly. Elizabeth had to clean her room, care for her clothes, practice
handwork, and learn to cook. Yet the Cadys' status and servants cushioned all the daughters from more onerous tasks. Mrs. Cady prepared them
for marriage and motherhood only within an upper-class cocoon.

Allusions to her mother in Stanton's autobiography are spare. Margaret
Cady is neither as vivid nor as affectionate in her daughter's memory as in
her grandchildren's. But in every description of her mother Stanton repeats
the adjective "queenly." The word encompasses the authority and superi-
ority of her mother's position in the Cady household and in the community. The connotation was not necessarily negative. "Queenly" was an adjective reserved for the powerful women Stanton came to admire: her mother,
the educator Emma Willard, the abolitionist Lucretia Mott, and in her old
age, herself.

Sovereignty was not the only characteristic mother and daughter shared.
In one typically brief autobiographical passage, Stanton recalled that her
mother, "a tall, queenly looking woman, was courageous, self-reliant, and
at her ease under all circumstances and in all places."[21] Other than height,
Stanton exhibited all of these traits, but she never directly acknowledged
their source in Margaret Cady. The self-confidence of mother and daughter, whether derived from social status or innate ability, was another common characteristic Stanton chose to ignore.

Despite their seemingly similar and sympathetic interests as adults, Elizabeth never gave her mother credit for providing a model of independence
in marriage or leadership in the community. Rather, Stanton repeatedly tried
to identify ways in which she resembled her father, despite the friction between them as adults. Indeed the only time Stanton directly affirmed her
mother's influence was to connect herself to her father. Stanton offered the
"prenatal influence" of her mother's interest in her father's congressional
campaign as the root of "the strong desire that I have always felt to participate in the rights and duties of government." So eager was Stanton to

associate herself with her father that she set the congressional election in 1815, the year of her birth, instead of 1814. She was quick to note the influence of other fathers on the lives of exceptional daughters.[22]

Despite Stanton's eagerness to portray her father as benevolent and supportive, the evidence indicates that he opposed her desire for higher education, her interest in reform, her marriage, and her public activities on behalf of women's rights. There is no doubt of his influence, but considerable doubt about how positive it was.

Stanton often repeated another childhood incident involving her father that she believed was as formative as Eleazar's death. Sitting in her father's office, Elizabeth heard the complaints of many weeping women. Her father had a client named Flora Campbell, who supplied the family with farm produce. When her husband died, his property passed to their son, who then treated his mother unkindly. Judge Cady had no remedy. Despite her tears, Mrs. Campbell's situation was neither illegal nor uncommon. Elizabeth realized "the cruelty of the laws"; "they kept me in a constant condition of wrath." She decided to get a scissors and cut every law unfair to women out of her father's statute books. When he discovered her plan, Judge Cady had to explain that such laws could only be changed by the legislature. He supposedly said, "As soon as you get old enough you can do that." Although Stanton frequently cited this incident as the stimulus for her reform career, it is unlikely that it occurred as she recalled it. In an unpublished, later account, she also noted that the event marked her first awareness of her father's fallibility and impotence.[23]

In writing about her childhood, Stanton chose to juxtapose her parents. She contrasts her tall, assertive, authoritarian mother with her diminutive, modest, and merciful father. After both of them were dead she confided to a contemporary biographer:

> My father was truly great and good—an ideal judge; and to his sober, taciturn and majestic bearing he added the tenderness, purity and refinement of a true woman. My mother was the soul of independence and self-reliance—cool in the hour of danger, and never knowing fear. She was inclined to a stern military rule of the household—a queenly and magnificent sway; but my father's great sense of justice, and the superior weight of his greater age . . . so modified the domestic government that the children had, in the main, a pleasant childhood.

Both parents were perceived as powerful people: her mother as "queenly," her father as "majestic." What is striking about the description is the opposition of traditionally masculine and feminine adjectives: he is gentle, she is brave; he is just, she is stern. Stanton's view of her parents is not corroborated by any other source. Her mother was powerful and commanding, but she was also charming, winsome, and high spirited. Judge Cady was retiring by nature, but other attorneys found him secretive, taciturn, wary, and "a most dangerous opponent."[24]

The image of her mother that prevails in most of Stanton's recollections is of a woman without warmth or humor or compassion, who lacked the standard female qualities, including subservience. Although Stanton claims to have been influenced more by her unassuming, intellectual father, as an adult she had much more in common with her mother. In both parents she had models of leadership and political style. Despite her own rhetoric and recollection, in reality, in example after example, Stanton patterned herself after her mother.

Stanton's early independent ambitions were undoubtedly if indirectly related to her mother's example. Not until her father began to criticize his adult daughter did Stanton begin to appreciate her mother's individuality or admit the strengths they shared. Unable to acknowledge her mother's influence when it either dominated or was withdrawn from her childhood, or while her father was alive, Stanton came to accept it as an adult. She began to view her mother as a silent but sympathetic ally. After Judge Cady's death the two women spent more time together. Mrs. Cady frequently cared for Stanton's children, enabling her daughter to travel and lecture. As a widow, Margaret Cady signed suffrage petitions, housed Elizabeth's reform friends, and contributed money to the cause. After her mother died, Stanton claimed that she had supported suffrage wholeheartedly. In her mother she had a female role model of unusual influence, yet it remained difficult for Stanton to acknowledge publicly or privately the role her mother had played.

Stanton's childhood, although punctuated by death and discipline, was not completely overcast. Elizabeth was a cheerful, active, resourceful girl, who enjoyed games, books, friends, and sports. The comfortable, conservative Cady household gave the children a sense of security and stability. Ostentation was avoided; dancing was forbidden. Breakfast was served at six, dinner at noon, supper at five, and a "piece [of pie]" at eight. The Cady daughters were dressed in red or blue flannel dresses (cotton in summer), with white neck ruffles, black alpaca aprons, and hand-knit stockings. Elizabeth rebelled against the restrictions of her confining, uncomfortable costume—she never chose to wear red as an adult—and against most of the rules. Neither parental discipline nor Presbyterian standards nor the "everlasting no, no, no!" of the nannies inhibited the Cady children from active childhoods.[25]

Within the restraints imposed, the children enjoyed the usual entertainments. They rode horseback, explored the hotel, jail, and courthouse, and attended apple harvests, quilting bees, school exhibitions, church fairs, and sleighing parties. Special holidays included the Fourth of July and county militia training days in September, which featured gingerbread, molasses candy, and a review of the troops at the racetrack. Elizabeth also remembered Christmas stockings stuffed with twenty-five cents, raisins, almonds, an apple, a fried cake, and a catechism of Old Testament stories illustrated with colored pictures.[26] The Cady money freed the children from all but minimal domestic chores, paid for tutors and music lessons, provided horses and sleds and the leisure to enjoy them. Their wealth ensured that every opportunity for education and enrichment could be afforded. Stanton's childhood also provided the examples, incentive, opportunity, skills, and successes necessary for her to learn and maintain new behaviors.

Stanton's conservative, secure childhood gave her unusual freedom and self-confidence. Her ability to enter the masculine sphere of sports, law offices, and higher education was not typical. American society in the early nineteenth century was sex segregated. Girls learned their roles and responsibilities from female relatives and friends; boys learned theirs from males. In the typical pattern, there were few areas in which men and women shared an activity or occupation either before or after marriage. Women shared the rituals of childbirth, nursing the sick, caring for the aged. They developed their own social events in sewing circles, quilting bees, and women's auxiliaries. As a result, women had the opportunity to become intimate friends.[27]

Elizabeth Cady participated in both feminine and masculine spheres. Whether on account of inattention, indifference, or design, she was allowed to try out a wide range of roles. She learned the domestic caretaking roles expected of women, and she tried some of the competitive, achievement-oriented roles enjoyed by men. At the time, male mentors were more visible and possibly more important than female role models. As an adult she practiced and found satisfaction in both traditional and untraditional behavior. She was a wife, mother, homemaker, nurse, seamstress, an intellectual, orator, author, reformer, and activist. Her unusual, upper-class childhood prepared her for untraditional roles and set a pattern for independent behavior.

2
Revival, Reform, and Romance
1827–39

Elizabeth Cady grew up in Jacksonian America. It was a turbulent era characterized by rapid growth and social change. The nation had extended its borders across the Mississippi and was filled with boundless optimism about its "manifest destiny" to control the continent. Settlers moved west to populate the plains, and more and more foreigners migrated to the land of promise. Canals, highways, and railroads tied the nation together. The availability of transportation and cheap labor spurred industrial development. Production moved out of homes and farms and into factories, changing the social order. Fewer employees lived with their employers; fewer husbands worked at home. Geographic and economic growth was paralleled by the extension of political rights. "Jacksonian democracy" meant universal manhood suffrage—for white men. The national mood was expansive, energetic, ambitious, and optimistic.

Conservative elements in the population would have added "worried" to those adjectives. Like a fast-growing adolescent, the United States outgrew its boundaries and the traditions and institutions that had governed it in the past. The rhetoric of equality contrasted sharply with increased class consciousness and economic distinctions. Women and slaves were not included in the egalitarian ethic. Churches and small communities could not easily solve the larger problems that accompanied economic growth and dislocation. The overthrow of traditional values and institutions generated a religious revival, which in turn inspired widespread interest in reform. Reformers organized to perfect mankind and man-made institutions. Societies to promote temperance, common schools, and church attendance, to improve prisons and insane asylums, and to end prostitution and slavery flourished.[1]

It was during the Jacksonian period, in the 1830s, that the "cult of true womanhood" was first articulated by ministers, ladies' magazines, and social conservatives. "True womanhood" was defined as domestic, maternal, religious, cultured, idle, and subservient. It sought to distinguish between ladies—the wives and daughters of the middle and upper classes—and all other women—immigrants, blacks, mill girls, and field hands. Ladies functioned only within the approved sphere of kitchen, nursery, and church. Unemployed female relatives became a status symbol for upwardly mobile males. With the rise of manufacturing, wives were no longer economic partners who turned raw materials into finished goods. Similarly, women were displaced from such traditional occupations as midwifery and undertaking. At the same time that opportunities for American men were expanding, the lives of American women became more restricted.[2]

Many of these trends were evident in upstate New York. The completion of the Erie Canal in 1825, stretching west from Albany to Buffalo for 363 miles, brought thousands of settlers into the region, mostly New Englanders and new immigrants. The availability of transportation and the development of steam power stimulated industry in the previously agrarian region. The first gristmills, distilleries, and packinghouses were joined by factories of every description. The population of the region swelled, and cities grew up along the waterway. Once middle class and homogeneous, farm settlements now had a wealthy class of bankers and merchants and a lower class of mill hands and mule drivers.

Intensive economic growth and the democratization of the political process in the Jacksonian era resulted in rapid change and social unrest. In this environment religious revival and reform were especially appealing. The first revival meetings were held around Oneida, near Syracuse. The enthusiasm spread west to Auburn and east to Troy. Because of the intensity of its revival experience, this area came to be known as the "burned-over district." In the decades following the completion of the Erie Canal, upstate New York produced Mormonism, spiritualism, millennialism, perfectionism, three third-party efforts, bloomers, and women's rights.[3]

The effect of these changes on Johnstown's first family was initially indirect. Elizabeth Cady Stanton's hometown lay twenty-five miles north of the canal and considerably east of the principal areas of reform activity. The village experienced some industrial expansion, population growth, and a decline in church membership. Judge Cady profited from the sale of his western holdings to canal developers and new settlers, and his law practice increased. The Cady family's social and economic position was secure, but not even the Cadys could shelter their household from what Judge Cady deemed the suspect enthusiasms sweeping the region. In the years of her adolescence, Elizabeth Cady would be exposed to the contagion of revival, reform, and romance, and would not recover.

The years following Eleazar's death in 1826 were full of changes for Elizabeth Cady. The most important was the advent of Edward Bayard. Elizabeth remembered him as "a southern gentleman, . . . a man of culture, of refined sensibilities, tall, graceful, extremely handsome, and very fond of children." A classmate of Eleazar's at Union College, a member of the politically prominent Delaware family, a clerk in Judge Cady's office, and Tryphena's husband, Bayard became the family's substitute son and brother. He filled the void left by the elder Cadys' withdrawal into grief— Judge Cady's absence and Mrs. Cady's retirement. The childless Bayards became acting parents for the three younger Cadys. "They selected our clothing, books, schools, acquaintances, and directed our reading and amusements," recalled Elizabeth. While Tryphena tried to maintain her mother's strict discipline, Bayard inaugurated "an era of picnics, birthday parties and endless amusements: the buying of pictures, fairy books, musical instruments and ponies, and frequent excursions with parties on horseback. . . . To me and my sisters he was a companion in all our amusements, a teacher in the higher departments of knowledge, and a counselor in all our youthful trials and disappointments." Because he had no children, Elizabeth later wrote, "his love centered on me." For the first time the children were allowed to travel beyond the village limits. Prompted by Bayard, they made "frequent journeys" to Saratoga, Utica, Peterboro, and the northern lake region. Spending her first night in a hotel in Schenectady, young Elizabeth was most impressed by the wallpaper.[4]

As Elizabeth's geographic sphere widened under Bayard's sponsorship, so did her intellectual scope. Having learned the rudiments at Maria Yost's dame school, Elizabeth attended the Johnstown Academy until she was fifteen. As she recalled, she "was the only girl in the higher classes of mathematics and the languages, yet in our [play] all the girls and boys mingled freely together. In running, sliding downhill, and snowballing we made no distinction of sex. . . . Equality was the general basis of our school relations."[5] Elizabeth was always at the top of her class. Her successful experience in these settings contributed to her self-esteem and accounted for her later advocacy of coeducation.

In addition to her classwork Elizabeth studied with Bayard, as she had with Rev. Hosack. Bayard "discoursed . . . on law, philosophy, political economy, history and poetry, and together we read novels without number; . . . our readings were varied with recitations, music, dancing and games." Provoking critical discussions on every subject, he taught her "how to think clearly and reason logically." According to her autobiography, they engaged in "intellectual fencing." It was Bayard who taught her to jump four-foot fences and to play chess.[6]

When Elizabeth graduated from the Johnstown Academy in 1830, she wanted to go to Union College, as her brother and Bayard had. At that time no college in the country admitted women.* She resented her automatic exclusion and her father's horror at the very idea. "My vexation and mortification knew no bounds," she later wrote. Her father saw no reason for any additional education. He suggested instead that she attend the circuit courts with him and enjoy the "balls and dinners." Or she could copy papers for his clerks and learn "how to keep house and make puddings and pies."[7] Elizabeth tried each of these alternatives but continued to press for more formal schooling. Finally Bayard persuaded Judge Cady to enroll her at the female seminary established by Emma Willard in Troy, New York.

Elizabeth Cady was fifteen years old when she entered the Troy Female Seminary on January 2, 1831, midway through the first term. In another example of autobiographical license, she claimed to have "already studied everything that was taught there except French, music, and dancing, so I devoted myself to these accomplishments." The record shows, however, that she took algebra, Greek, and music her first term, followed by twenty-two weeks of logic, botany, writing, geometry, and modern history. In the fall of 1831 her course work included criticism, arithmetic, chemistry, French, and piano. The standard course of study required religious and moral instruction, literature, human psychology, natural philosophy, domestic science, and optional ornamental accomplishments like singing and sketching.[8]

Judge Cady paid an annual tuition of three hundred dollars, plus extra charges for piano instruction and instrument rental. The catalog directed students to dress in calico or gingham dresses, "made in plain style." Parents were asked not to furnish "expensive laces, jewelry, . . . nor to leave [their daughters] the control of money."[9] By 1831 the seminary had an enrollment of more than a hundred boarding students and two hundred day students.

In retrospect, Elizabeth Cady heartily disliked the seminary. In contrast to her previous experience in coeducation, she was contemptuous of the "artificial relationships with boys" that resulted from single-sex isolation, and she disdained the "pretensions and petty jealousies" of the other girls. She also hated the repetition of "corned beef, liver, and bread pudding."

---

* Oberlin (1834) was the first institution to offer women a collegiate education; the first woman graduated in 1841. Lucy Stone and Antoinette Brown were Oberlin "coeds" during that decade. Mount Holyoke (1837) and Elmira College (1855) aspired to offer advanced courses in a single-sex setting.

Yet Stanton admired the school's head, Emma Hart Willard, whom she later described as "a splendid-looking woman, then in her prime [who] fully realized my idea of a queen."[10] Surprisingly, Stanton would become a loyal alumna. It may be that Elizabeth Cady's discontent at Emma Willard's female seminary resulted from the conflicting signals she received there about what were appropriate roles for educated women.

Emma Willard was the first educator to replace the traditional offerings of female academies with a rigorous program of instruction.* Although she called her school a "female seminary," she in fact aspired to make the classical and scientific curricula of men's colleges available to young women. She was the first woman to teach physiology, logic, and the enlightenment philosophy of natural rights to women. She was the first to urge the establishment of "normal schools" to train women teachers. She designed novel methods to present mathematics and history and wrote most of the textbooks used by her students. She was a militant advocate of women's education. Although she never supported wider political rights for women, she was active in antiprostitution campaigns and encouraged the achievements of other professional women, among them Dr. Elizabeth Blackwell, America's first female physician.[11]

Mrs. Willard was disarmingly feminine. Shrewdly, she made a conservative case for untraditional female education. When she petitioned the New York legislature in 1819 for state-sponsored teacher training schools for women, she assured its members that such a "school would differ from a school for men as women's character and duty differed from men's." The thrust of her argument, in tune with the "cult of true womanhood," was that better educated mothers would produce more virtuous citizens. She believed in "education for usefulness." Its purpose was "to bring its subjects to the perfection of their moral, intellectual, and physical nature: in order that [women] might be the greatest possible use to themselves and others." The legislature rejected Willard's plan, but the factory town of Troy, southwest of Albany, levied additional taxes of four thousand dollars to establish her school there in 1821.[12]

While Mrs. Willard stressed traditional if enlightened domestic roles for

---

* Emma Hart Willard (1787–1870) was born on a Connecticut farm into a family of sixteen children. Her father encouraged her appetite for education. She began teaching at age fifteen and soon began to explore academic opportunities for women. She was the head of a school in Vermont in 1807. Two years later she married John Willard, a physician and widower with four children. Their only child, John Hart Willard, was born in 1810. Denied the privilege of attending classes at Middlebury College, Mrs. Willard taught herself collegiate subjects and then taught her pupils. Inspired by her success, she presented her plan to the New York legislature. She ran the Troy Female Seminary singlehandedly after her husband's death in 1828. In 1838 she turned over its management to her son. After a disastrous second marriage ended in divorce, she returned to Troy and died there. In 1895 the Troy Female Seminary was renamed the Emma Willard School.

girl graduates, there remained a contradictory emphasis on academic achievement. Although the rationale for female education was based on maternal destiny, learning had unpredicted consequences. Emma Willard and other leaders of women's education gave the female graduate a breadth of interests, a mind attuned to serious study, and a self-consciousness based on gender.[13] These opposing pressures paralleled the confusing signals young Miss Cady had been receiving in Johnstown. She observed the contrast between a submissive, passive, and nonintellectual feminine ideal and the reality of an assertive, active, intelligent, and powerful female, personified by her mother and Emma Willard. Although Stanton purported to have been sensitive to feminist issues like the lack of women's legal status at this early date, she had not yet made a choice of roles. Edward Bayard, Rev. Hosack, Mrs. Willard, and occasionally even her parents applauded intellectual accomplishment, but none of them outwardly encouraged any but traditional roles for women.

Family members and teachers were not the only influential adults in Elizabeth Cady's life during this period. Equally important in her adolescence was her exposure to the preaching of Charles Grandison Finney during the Great Troy Revival of 1831. Strictly raised as a Presbyterian, Elizabeth had a gloomy view of a punitive God. Her perception was not altered by attending Episcopal services with "Black Peter," the family retainer, and being assigned to the Negro servants' pew. She had not formally joined a church or experienced conversion before going away to school. When carriage loads of her classmates attended the revival meetings in Troy, she went along and was spellbound. The experience, according to her recollection, "seriously influenced my character." "[One] of those intense revival seasons . . . swept over the city and through the seminary like an epidemic, attacking in its worst form the most susceptible. Owing to my gloomy Calvinist training in the old Scotch Presbyterian Church, and my vivid imagination, I was one of the first victims."[14] Finney's effect on the impressionable adolescent was not unusual. During the Great Revival, from 1830 to 1832, he made scores of converts wherever he preached.

Finney himself had undergone a dramatic conversion in 1821. He believed that he had seen Christ on a main street in Rochester, New York, and, like St. Paul, had wrestled with the Lord until he "could feel the impression, like a wave of electricity going through and through [him]." He immediately gave up his lucrative law practice and was ordained a minister. Finney began his first New York crusade in 1827 and was at the height of his power by 1831. He was vigorous, passionate, ruthless—the preeminent revivalist of the nineteenth century, a pivotal figure in the history of American Protestantism.[15]

Since the Revolution, a combination of factors had turned the population away from its earlier allegiance to organized churches. By 1820 the religious leadership was prepared to launch a conservative counterattack to win back the faithful.[16] The internal debates generated by the disestablishment of the Congregational Church of Connecticut in 1818 produced changes both in theological style and substance and spawned the Second Great Awakening. Influenced by Timothy Dwight and Nathaniel Taylor, the revivalists combined traditional methods with new ones. Prayer, confession, and Scripture study were taken outside the churches into tents and fields, where itinerant preachers would convert whole communities with fiery sermons and an unrelenting schedule of revival meetings.

Revival theology was Puritanism without predestination. Evangelical preachers abandoned the concept of an "elect." Instead they emphasized that an individual could choose to behave in such a manner that God would reward him with conversion. Each person had responsibility for the salvation of his own soul and that of others—drunks, prostitutes, sinners, and slaveholders, for example. What began as a conservative effort by church leaders to restore stability to American society and increase church attendance resulted in a popular phenomenon, a new theology, and the relocation of responsibility for sinners from the church to the community.[17]

Finney's style was irresistible. Stanton remembered him as a "tall, grave-looking man," who dressed in "unclerical gray." He dominated the pulpit with a resonant voice and dramatic gestures, "his great eyes rolling around the congregation and his arms flying about . . . like . . . a windmill."[18] He overpowered his listeners with his compelling personality and lawyer-like presentation. Meetings were held almost daily, disrupting the ordinary routine of the Troy community. Individual sinners were prayed for by name and put under devastating pressure to confess. Women were permitted to pray in public, an affront to the adherents of St. Paul and to conservatives like Daniel Cady, who considered such a public role for women indecent.

Finney's theology was as disturbing as his tactics. To the common people who flocked to barns, schoolhouses, and open-air meetings to hear him, Finney preached the revival doctrine of Christian perfectionism. He taught that man had free will to choose salvation and the responsibility to make that choice. He believed that every person, male or female, had to be confronted with a choice between salvation and damnation. Conversion was a reaffirmation of faith and an acceptance of an obligation to perfect oneself and one's community. Finney's God was just and benevolent; Finney's sinners could choose to be saved. As he repeated over and over, "All men may be saved if they will."[19]

The combination of Finney's strenuous style, congenial theology, and revival enthusiasm overwhelmed the fifteen-year-old Elizabeth Cady. Every day for six weeks she subjected herself to his preaching, until she found herself on the "anxious bench." Finally she confessed her sins and experienced "conversion." The result was not reassuring. Revival sapped her self-esteem and made her feel bad instead of good. She became ill and went home to Johnstown. As she recalled in her autobiography: "Fear of judgment seized my soul. Visions of the lost haunted my dreams. Mental anguish prostrated my health. Dethronement of my reason was apprehended by friends. . . . Returning home, I often at night roused my father from his slumber to pray for me, lest I should be cast into the bottomless pit before morning."[20]

Judge Cady, alarmed by Elizabeth's condition and shocked by the disgrace of a camp meeting conversion, forbade any further discussion of religion or mention of Finney until she had regained her composure. In June 1831 she traveled to Niagara Falls with her father and the Bayards. "My brother-in-law," she recalled, "explained . . . the nature of the delusions we had all experienced, the physical conditions, the mental processes, the church machinery by which such excitements are worked up." Bayard assigned novels by Sir Walter Scott, James Fenimore Cooper, and Charles Dickens, the rational philosophy of George Combe, and works about phrenology. Prodded by Bayard's good-humored skepticism, Elizabeth's "religious superstitions gave place to rational ideas based on scientific facts, and in proportion, as I looked at everything from a new standpoint, I grew more and more happy." With the attention of her father and Bayard, her pleasure in the journey, and a rational explanation of her frightening experience, her "mind was restored to its normal condition" and her girlhood gaiety returned.[21]

Despite her prompt recovery from conversion, Finney had made an indelible impression on Elizabeth Cady. Her experience initiated a decade of religious indecision. His preaching had called into question all her Calvinist training and helped her reject it. She accepted Finney's imperative that she had a choice to make, and in the end she chose skepticism. By encouraging her to be critical of Finney, Judge Cady and Bayard allowed her to treat theology analytically. Later she would reject religious authority of any kind. Her attack on the Bible in her old age concluded her religious quest and completed her definition of a coherent feminist ideology. The more immediate consequence of revival for her in the 1830s was to interest and involve her in the reform community.

The Great Revival created around Elizabeth Cady an environment conducive to reform. Led by men and women who had experienced revival conversions and were inspired by a commitment to perfect mankind, organizations for abolition, temperance, and Christian benevolence flourished in upstate New York. The significance of the inclusion of women as participants in revival and reform cannot be overlooked. Revival meetings were characterized by and criticized for the presence of women praying, testifying, confessing, and converting in public. Once converted, the women could not keep silent in the churches. Nor could they avoid the requirement of service on account of sex. Revival and reform activity for women raised issues of women's rights that would plague traditional and evangelical churches as well as the wider society for another century.

Ministers demanded that female activities be modest, unobtrusive, and "appropriate." Few realized that any activity would move women beyond their ordinary sphere and force a redefinition of the "cult of true womanhood" to include religious benevolence and community volunteerism as newly appropriate spheres of activity for ladies. Nourished by evangelical religion, female reform societies endowed their members with a sense of identity and purpose separate from their families. The societies provided women with organizational experience and political skills. As a small number of women attempted to act out the pious ideal in tract and mission societies or in temperance or abolition crusades, it became more difficult to sustain the myth of female subordination.[22] Rejection of religious authority and resentment of women's subordinate status were the long-term results for Elizabeth Cady and other nineteenth-century women in revival and reform circles.

The remainder of Elizabeth's education at Emma Willard's seminary was uneventful. She graduated in 1833 and returned to Johnstown. At seventeen, she was marriageable but unmarried. Her future was uncertain, and she had no plans. Because of her family's wealth, she was not forced to support herself by teaching, sewing, or factory work. She had only minor domestic responsibilities. For a brief period she joined a church auxiliary to finance the education of a young minister. As she recounted the story, the young women "sewed, baked, brewed and stewed things, had fairs, sociables and what not" to support the young man. When he graduated the women bought him a black broadcloth suit, high hat, and cane, and invited him to Johnstown to preach. He chose as the text of his sermon, "I suffer not a woman to speak in church." According to Stanton, she and the other young women walked out.[23] The tale is too pat to trust, but it illustrates Stanton's disdain for the patronizing treatment of female parishioners by male ministers.

Not all of Elizabeth Cady's activities were serious. For most of the 1830s she led the life of a belle. Vain about her curly brown hair and small feet, she was a pretty, petite, and vivacious young woman. Her letters report a whirl of parties, dances, hayrides, and horse races. She made rounds of visits to relatives. Her journal includes quotations about love from Lord Byron, Samuel Taylor Coleridge, John Dryden, and Scott. There are also autographs by girlfriends and an initialed inscription, "To Lib—the joyous laugh, the merry joke, the smile, the kind word." She loved to sing and accompany herself on the piano or guitar. She talked so much that one beau teased that she could not take a drive in silence. She accepted the challenge, put a straw dummy dressed in her cloak and bonnet in the carriage, and greeted the disconcerted young man on his return.[24] All her life she enjoyed practical jokes, games, dancing, and company.

Elizabeth Cady's was a typical upper-class girlhood. Less independent than adolescent males, "young ladies" lived in an intermediate and indeterminate stage between education and marriage or employment. Elizabeth shared the extended social life and limited domestic tasks of other young women of her social rank. Aside from her conversion, she does not appear to have experienced the introspection, brooding, alienation, or rebellion that made adolescence a period of stress for some young women.[25] Stanton saved a favorite photograph of herself at twenty, noting in a letter, "It looks so self-asserting and defiant that I love to look at it." Her description of a young friend in 1855 sounds like a self-portrait from her girlhood: "Full of life, energy and fun, she sings and plays delightfully, can dance and waltz like a fairy, has exquisite taste in dress and is a genius in the culinary department. A horsewoman, she is equal to Fanny Kemble; can drive and ride a horse, leap ditches and fences, is active and brave, and knows no fear of man or beast. On foot or horse she is unsurpassed."[26] While Miss Cady continued to investigate new ideas and read omnivorously, she was hardly a sedentary blue stocking.

After the Bayards moved to Seneca Falls, west of Syracuse, in 1834, Elizabeth visited them frequently. Edward Bayard's homeopathy practice disconcerted most of his family but increased his appeal for Elizabeth. Homeopathy emphasized the body's natural recuperative powers. It was the most popular alternative to standard medical practice in that period. Like phrenology and the Sylvester Graham diet, it was another optimistic outgrowth of the revival-reform era. Introduced to homeopathy by Bayard, Stanton would practice and advocate it for the rest of her life.

Elizabeth and her brother-in-law remained intimate friends. Ten years older than Elizabeth, Bayard had been her confidant and counselor for more than a decade. Then their relationship changed. Bayard, still married to Tryphena, proposed to Elizabeth. According to family sources, Bayard had fallen in love with Elizabeth and in 1838 urged that they run away. She refused him, and Bayard never allowed himself to be alone with her again. There is no record of her reaction, but she always referred to him in warm and generous terms. When Bayard died in 1889, Stanton wrote her daughter that she owed much of her childhood happiness to him. In a family scrapbook, her daughter wrote under his photograph, "Perhaps the most formative influence in the life of Elizabeth Cady."[27]

After 1838, Elizabeth Cady increased her visits to her cousin Gerrit Smith and his family in Peterboro, New York. The Smith household was dominated by enthusiasm for political reforms, especially abolition. Whereas Judge Cady forbade any discussion of abolition, Elizabeth's cousin Gerrit Smith was one of the most prominent and important abolitionists of the antebellum period. Smith introduced Elizabeth to all the current causes and celebrities.

Smith's mother was Margaret Cady's oldest sister, Elizabeth Livingston. His father, Peter Smith, was John Jacob Astor's partner and Daniel Cady's client. Born in Utica, New York, in 1797, Gerrit Smith had graduated from Hamilton College in 1818. His first wife died six months after they were married in 1819. He married Ann (Nancy) Fitzhugh in 1822 and fathered four children. His oldest daughter, Elizabeth Smith Miller, became Elizabeth Cady's best friend. When his father was declared incompetent, Gerrit Smith took over the family fortune and increased it. Eventually he owned land in Michigan, Virginia, Vermont, and in all but six counties of New York. One of the wealthiest men in the country, he was a philanthropist who contributed much of his money to reform causes. Gerrit Smith died in New York City in 1874, attended by Edward Bayard.[28]

Caught up in the revival spirit and encouraged by his beautiful and devout second wife, Smith experienced a conversion in 1825.[29] He rededicated himself, his money, and his nervous energy to benevolence. He supported the Sunday school movement, the American Bible Society, the Tract Society, the Home Missionary Society, prison reform, dress reform, equal rights for women, and the Greek and Irish revolutions; he was vice-president of the American Peace Society. He opposed capital punishment, drinking, smoking, and the eating of meat.

As an abolitionist he founded a seminary where Negro students could prepare for the ministry and a manual labor school for free blacks whom he brought to Peterboro. Originally an advocate of colonization, Smith became an "immediatist," demanding an immediate end to slavery after the antiabolition riots in Utica in 1835. He joined the American Anti-Slavery Society and served as president of the New York chapter from 1836 to 1839. His mansion was a station on the underground railroad. In response to violent public hostility to his position, he became even more radical and outspoken. Smith was one of the Secret Six who bought the arms for John Brown's raid on Harper's Ferry in 1859.[30]

As a leader of political abolitionists after 1840, Smith pursued a dismally unsuccessful political career. A founder of the Liberty party, he was defeated as its candidate for governor in 1840 and for president in 1848.

He was elected to Congress in 1852 but, frustrated by the resistance to abolition, he resigned after eighteen months. He was defeated again in 1858 in a second gubernatorial try as a Republican.

Six feet tall and weighing over two hundred pounds, with a mellow voice and full beard, Smith was erudite, urbane, gracious, and generous. But he was also, in the view of one biographer, a "strange, erratic individual . . . hypochondriac, compulsive, almost childlike, . . . given to unpredictable moods, now melancholy, now irascible, now charming and gregarious." Terrified of being found guilty of conspiracy after John Brown was hanged, Smith committed himself temporarily to an insane asylum.[31] Until political disagreements divided them in later years, Elizabeth Cady saw only the gentle, good-humored enthusiast.

Smith's sincere if unorthodox Christianity appealed to Elizabeth. His position on abolition had forced him to withdraw from the Presbyterian church because it did not condemn slaveholding as sinful. In 1843 he established a local nondenominational abolitionist church. A plaque engraved "God Is Love" hung over the Smiths' bedroom door: that sentiment set a tone of practical Christianity for their household. Although they owned the village of Peterboro, the Smiths lived simply. Stanton remembered that her cousin "would have nothing in his home which would make his humblest visitor feel out of place."[32] Throughout his life Smith worked for many religious reforms, ultimately refusing to accept the Bible as infallible truth. His individual Christianity presented Elizabeth with another foil for Finney.

At Peterboro in the late 1830s Elizabeth Cady met male and female abolitionist agents, runaway slaves, Oneida Indians, members of the old Dutch aristocracy, temperance advocates, politicians, reformers of every kind and conviction. "Every member of their household is an abolitionist, even to the coachman," she reported. Her visits made her receptive to the reform spirit. She was challenged to think about issues that were never discussed in her own home, and she thrived on the arguments and exchange of ideas. "It was in such company and varied discussions on every possible phase of political, religious and social life that I spent weeks every year. . . . The rousing arguments at Peterboro made social life seem tame and profitless elsewhere, and the youngest of us felt that the conclusions reached in this school of philosophy were not to be questioned." Even from the perspective of sixty years, Mrs. Stanton credited Gerrit Smith with giving her "a new inspiration in life and . . . new ideas of individual rights."[33]

Inspiration did not provoke action. Elizabeth Cady did not join any of Gerrit Smith's crusades. To do so would have required flaunting her father's social code at a time when she was still dependent on him. The contrast between the conservative opinions in Johnstown and the open-minded attitudes prevalent at Seneca Falls and Peterboro created another set of choices, as her education and conversion crisis had. In different ways both Bayard and Smith were active reformers. They approved and encouraged reform activity and attitudes in Elizabeth. But neither overcame the influence of her parents or proposed an alternative course for her to follow. Rather than make any choices, she accommodated herself to each environment and made no commitments. She was not yet ready to act on what she had absorbed.

Peterboro provided more than intellectual stimulation. Days of debate and "hot discussion" frequently ended with hayrides and dancing. As Stanton recalled, "[We] youngsters frequently put the lessons of freedom and individual rights [we] heard so much of into practice, and relieved [our] brains from the constant strain of argument on first principles by the wildest hilarity in dancing, all kinds of games, and practical jokes carried beyond all bounds of propriety."[34]

It was at Peterboro that Elizabeth Cady fell in love with Henry Stanton, a renowned abolitionist agent. Like Bayard, Henry Stanton was ten years older than she was. Like Finney, he was a forceful speaker. Like Smith, he was a celebrated abolitionist. In addition, he was tall, handsome, dynamic, and a genuine hero. He had faced down mobs and converted angry crowds. To her he was a "brave knight," vanquishing the forces of evil. The couple met in October 1839, when both were guests of the Smiths. For several weeks Henry spoke at Madison County antislavery gatherings; Elizabeth was in the audience, spellbound. Although she thought he was engaged to someone else, she accepted an invitation to go riding. On horseback, he unexpectedly proposed, and she accepted.[35] They were two magnetic personalities, passionately attracted to one another.

Born in 1805 to a Connecticut woolen manufacturer and a Mayflower descendant, Stanton had moved to upstate New York in 1826, after his father went bankrupt.* He worked first in a canal office and then for Thurlow Weed's newspaper. As a reward for helping elect Weed to the state assembly, Stanton was named deputy clerk for Monroe County (Rochester). In October 1830 Stanton heard Finney preach at the Rochester Revival and was converted. Recruited by his friend Theodore Weld, another Finney convert, Stanton decided to prepare for the ministry at the Lane Theological Seminary in Cincinnati.[36]

Under the weak leadership of Lyman Beecher, Lane Seminary soon be-

* Henry Brewster Stanton was born June 27, 1805, in Pachung, Conn., the second of six children and first son of Joseph and Susan Brewster Stanton. His youngest brother died during a cholera epidemic at the Lane Seminary. His distinguished ancestry included Revolutionary officers, members of Congress, an Indian negotiator, and several judges. Henry described his mother (1781–1853) as an "intelligent, high-spirited, and pious" woman who disdained "nerves." She moved to Rochester after Joseph's bankruptcy and death in 1827.

came a center of abolitionist controversy. Until the 1830s most antislavery sentiment in the United States favored the colonization of Negroes, returning slaves to Africa or elsewhere. The American Colonization Society, founded in 1817, was another agency in the moral reform network. The younger reformers, veterans of revivals, believed that slaveholding was sinful and pressed for "immediate" emancipation. The creation of the underground railroad, the publication of the *Liberator* by William Lloyd Garrison, the organization of the American Anti-Slavery Society, the nullification crisis, and Nat Turner's rebellion all increased the tension surrounding the abolition issue in the 1830s. When Lane students held a debate on the seizure of fugitive slaves in the summer of 1832, Henry Stanton was the only speaker to defend the North against the requirement of returning runaways to the South.[37]

At the same time, Theodore Weld, by then a Lane professor and a dedicated abolitionist, organized the students to work and "mingle" in the black community. The debate incident, coupled with Weld's "social intercourse" with Negroes, outraged and offended the trustees. They believed that the activities of the students might incite a riot in the city. In the fall of 1834 the trustees ordered the student antislavery society to disband and forbade any further activity or discussion. In response, Weld and Stanton led a walkout of fifty "Lane rebels." They founded their own institution at Oberlin, where they insisted on the admission of Negroes and women, a voice in faculty appointments, and the selection of Charles Grandison Finney as president.[38]

Neither Weld nor Stanton stayed on at Oberlin. Their antislavery activities had brought them to the attention of the American Anti-Slavery Society, and they were hired as agents. In May 1835 Stanton became one of the Band of Seventy, an abolition strike force like Finney's Holy Band of revival preachers. The abolitionists adopted many revival tactics: crisscrossing the Northeast, issuing tracts, collecting petitions, holding conventions, speaking outdoors, organizing whole communities, not moving on until they could leave a core of converts behind to promote their cause. An agent's existence was arduous, full of hardship and danger. During these years mobs pummeled Stanton with verbal and physical abuse that only reaffirmed his commitment to abolition.

As the Declaration of Sentiments of the American Anti-Slavery Society had announced, "We shall send forth agents to lift up the voice of remonstrance, of warning, of entreaty, and of rebuke." An eloquent speaker, a lucid writer, a skilled organizer, Henry Stanton soon distinguished himself. He was assigned to Massachusetts and joined the executive committee of the national society as secretary.[39] Initially a protégé of William Lloyd Garrison, Stanton eventually broke with his mentor over the necessity for political action and the role of women in abolition societies. Stanton advocated an elective strategy but opposed giving women voting rights within abolition societies because it would open the political abolitionists to ridicule.

In proposing marriage, Henry Stanton offered Elizabeth an alliance of affection and abolitionism. He assumed that she shared his political beliefs and would make abolition her life's work, because it was his. In Elizabeth, Henry had another convert. He thought he was rescuing her from "a giddy whirl of fashionable follies" and directing her energies into reform. "It pains me," he wrote to Gerrit Smith during their engagement, "to see a person of so superior a mind and enlarged heart doing nothing for the wicked world's salvation."[40] With the ardor of an evangelist, Henry offered Elizabeth a means to salvation and fulfillment. Like Bayard and Smith, he encouraged her to expand her role and to enlarge her sphere.

When Henry proposed, Elizabeth Cady was almost twenty-four years old. It had been seven years since she had left school. During that period her primary occupation had been visiting. Although she enjoyed the camaraderie of the law students, she did not marry one of them, as did her sisters. Perhaps there were already signs of her strong will and intellectual independence. Despite her cheerful manner and her father's money, she was older than most young women when they married. Had she not married Henry, there is no indication that she would have undertaken any other occupation. At Johnstown, Troy, and Peterboro, she had had opportunities to observe women as matriarchs, community leaders, teachers, administrators, religious converts, and social reformers, as well as in lower-class employments. Academic and athletic achievement had given her a sense of self-confidence. She was encouraged to undertake unusual activities for a girl, but no alternative occupations were suggested by her models or mentors. Like most of her peers, she sought occupation and identity in marriage rather than in independent action.

In Henry Stanton, Elizabeth found a combination of the elements she had found most appealing in the other men in her life. He was older, handsome, intelligent, engaging, eloquent, dominant, masculine, demanding, charming, and a good dancer. He was at the center of the circle of reformers at Peterboro. He was committed to a moral cause. And he was either not aware of or not alarmed by her strengths.

By marrying, Elizabeth Cady would escape girlhood and become an adult female. Socially, becoming a matron had higher status than remaining a spinster. Legally, she assumed a subordinate position. She was transferred from the protection of her father to the custody of her husband. Familiar as she was with law and custom, she did not anticipate that she might be entering bondage. She looked forward to marriage as an independent state, a shared adventure. Lingering at Peterboro in the autumn of 1839, the engaged couple planned the kind of life they would lead. Wrote Elizabeth Cady Stanton in retrospect, "It seemed to me that I never had so much happiness crowded into one short month."[41]

3
Marriage and Mrs. Mott
1840–47

Elizabeth Cady and Henry Stanton announced their engagement in October 1839, having known one another less than a month. To their surprise, the occasion was "not one of unmixed joy and satisfaction." Family and friends raised immediate objections. Gerrit Smith solemnly warned them that her father would never consent. According to her recollection, Smith suggested that Elizabeth announce her plans to Judge Cady by letter, so that she "might draw the hottest fire while still in safe harbor." Then he cautioned against marrying "without due consideration."[1] It was a measure of the reactions of their friends that even their chief ally had reservations about their decision.

To postpone the pending confrontation with her father, Elizabeth stayed on at Peterboro even after Henry had left to speak in Cleveland. When she did go home, she had to answer her father's objections alone. Henry joined her three weeks later, but he was not warmly received. Judge Cady opposed the union on political and financial grounds. Like other social conservatives, he had "a strong aversion to abolitionists and the whole antislavery movement," according to his daughter. He abhorred the idea of Elizabeth's marrying an antislavery agent. He distrusted a man who had defied traditional political loyalties and espoused radical social change. Judge Cady was also concerned about Henry's financial prospects. He lectured Elizabeth "on domestic relations from a financial viewpoint." As someone who had married above his social and economic station, opposing his daughter's engagement put Cady in an awkward position. He had also previously argued in favor of daughters being allowed to make their own marital choices.[2]

Judge Cady again relied on Edward Bayard to reinforce his position. Elizabeth's brother-in-law buttressed his personal objections to Henry with legal arguments. He reminded her of the legal disadvantages any marriage would entail. New York statutes, like those of every other state, offered little protection to married women and took away what limited rights they had enjoyed while single. Married women lost their legal individuality and became wholly subordinate to their husbands. Wives had no rights to inherit property, keep earnings, sign contracts, initiate suits, establish credit, or claim more than one-third of their husbands' estates. More devastating was their legal inability to have custody or control of their own children. Bayard did not need to remind Elizabeth of the deserted wives and disinherited widows who had appealed to her father for legal assistance in the past. She was already aware that marriage for some women resulted in hardship and heartache.[3]

There is no record of the reaction of Elizabeth's mother or sisters. She recalled that friends who had previously "paint[ed] the marriage relation in the most dazzling colors" now pointed out that it was "beset with dangers and disappointments." They warned that men were "depraved and unreliable." As a result of these pressures, her engagement was "a season of doubt and conflict—doubt as to the wisdom of changing a girlhood of freedom and enjoyment for I knew not what, and conflict because the step I proposed was in opposition to the wishes of my family."[4]

Heartened by tender missives from Henry, Elizabeth refused to change her mind. For four months of "anxiety and bewilderment," she refuted the objections of people she cared for. Then in late February 1840, while visiting the Bayards in Seneca Falls, she succumbed and broke her engagement. Her father, her cousin, and her brother-in-law together "outweighed my conscience and turned the sweetest dream of my life into a tragedy." In explaining her decision to Ann Smith, Elizabeth indicated that her action was not final. "We are still friends and correspond as before; perhaps when the storm blows over we may be dearer friends than ever."[5] She was not resigned to her decision and hoped to reverse it.

The engagement was an equally trying time for Henry, who had to juggle personal, political, and pecuniary concerns. He kept his betrothal secret from all but a few of his antislavery friends. Many would have agreed that it was time for him to get married. As one female abolitionist had observed, "If he were married to a woman of fine taste and some talent it would do him great good, for he needs constant polishing." For whatever motives, Henry wanted to marry Miss Cady. He knew her family opposed him. As he had confided to Gerrit Smith, he "dreaded the influence of Mr. Bayard" upon his fiancée.[6] When she broke their engagement, he agreed only to postpone their plans. He did not drop his suit.

Meanwhile Henry was caught up in the debate about overt political action that was splitting the American Anti-Slavery Society (AASS). By the spring of 1840 two factions had arisen. One group supported William Lloyd Garrison, the founder of the AASS and editor of the *Liberator*. The Garrisonians urged immediate emancipation but preferred "moral suasion" to political action as a tactic. Because they considered the Constitution a "slaveholders' document," some Garrisonians refused to vote. Henry Stanton, Gerrit Smith, Theodore Weld, and James G. Birney of Kentucky led the anti-Garrisonians. They preached practical political action and anticipated political solutions. They believed reformers had a moral and religious duty to vote, to establish alternative parties, and to nominate candidates. In April 1840 the political abolitionists called an assembly of antislavery men in Albany. Gerrit Smith casually named this rump group the Liberty party. Although it nominated Birney for president, it had little impact on the 1840 election.

In addition to political tactics, two questions of internal interest separated the factions—whether to criticize churches hostile to abolition and what the role of women members should be. Garrison and his followers took a radical position on each issue. They condemned proslavery churches and advocated women's rights within the society. They agreed that women should be able to vote, hold office, and serve as delegates, in addition to the speaking, traveling, and canvassing they already did. Neither of those positions was acceptable to the political abolitionists. They worried that such stands would alienate middle-class male voters, who might agree only on abolition.

The actual schism came in May 1840 at a national meeting of the American Anti-Slavery Society. The anti-Garrison minority was overwhelmingly defeated and walked out.[7] The renegades withdrew to found the rival American and Foreign Anti-Slavery Society. Henry Stanton was made executive secretary of the new group. Anticipating the split, the dissenters had already designated Henry to be a delegate to the upcoming World Anti-Slavery Convention. At the time of the walkout, he was en route to Europe.

When Elizabeth learned that Henry would be abroad for eight months, she insisted that they marry before the journey rather than after. As Henry explained in confidence to another abolitionist, "We thought of putting off the whole affair till my return—but, as the time draws near for my departure she will not consent to be left behind in the hands of her opposing friends and wishes to go with me that the storm may blow over while she is absent." Elizabeth's father threatened to disinherit her, according to Henry, but she had "wedded her soul to the cause at the call of duty." They decided to elope shortly before he sailed for London, keeping the plan a secret in fear that Judge Cady would whisk Elizabeth out of Henry's reach. As Henry concluded, "I am in a delicate predicament . . . my honor is at stake."[8]

The decision to marry put Henry under enormous financial pressure. He needed cash to purchase two ocean passages, at $120 each, and to pay their living expenses while abroad. In a letter to Elizabeth, clearly intended for her father, Stanton had laid out his financial position as of January 1840. He claimed to have supported himself since he was thirteen, paid for the education of two brothers, and saved three thousand dollars. Refuting the unspoken charge that he was marrying Elizabeth for her money, he wrote: "I have never received a dollar's gratuitous aid from anyone, though it has been frequently pressed upon me. I always declined it, because I knew it would relax my perseverance and detract from my self-reliance, and because I was aware that if I would be a man, I must build my own foundation with my own hands." Stanton dissembled. He had always worked but he had no career and no prospects. He had been a journalist, a county clerk, a theology student, and an agitator. After his break with Garrison, he had no job at all. He was owed two years' back salary. The new American and Foreign Anti-Slavery Society had no treasury to support him. In the remaining weeks of April 1840 Stanton badgered his friends to repay debts and subsidize his expenses. "I have had to screw and dodge and scamp to raise the wherewithal—and shall barely make out," he reported to his friend John Greenleaf Whittier. "I have made close calculations and shall but just rub and go."[9]

Having kept their plans secret for nearly a month, Henry and Elizabeth were married in Johnstown on May 1, 1840.[10] There was a last minute delay when Henry's packet from New York was stranded on a sand bar. Unable to make "the slightest preparation for a wedding or voyage," for fear of arousing suspicion about her plans, the bride wore a "simple white evening dress." Over the objections of the Presbyterian minister, they omitted the word "obey" from the vows. Although Elizabeth later claimed credit for this innovation ("I obstinately refused to obey one with whom I supposed I was entering an equal relation"), it may have been Henry's suggestion; he had witnessed the Welds take similar vows the previous year. Such an omission indicated that a woman could refuse to have intercourse with her spouse. A few friends were invited, but there is no record of whether Elizabeth's family attended.[11] The bride was twenty-four years old and undeterred; the groom was thirty-five and unemployed.

Following the ceremony the couple left at once for Peterboro. In inviting himself to visit the Smiths, Stanton had written, "We may come *in chains*— and much as you abhor thralldom, we shall totally dissent from any proposition of emancipation, immediate or gradual, present or prophetic!"[12]

As Henry's romantic metaphor unwittingly acknowledged, their affection would never be wholly separate from current events. After two nights at Peterboro, the newlyweds registered at the Waverly House in New York City. They made a short trip to Belleville, New Jersey, where Henry introduced Elizabeth to his best friend, Theodore Weld, his wife Angelina Grimké Weld, and her sister Sarah Grimké.* All of them except Elizabeth were renowned reformers. Weld and Stanton had both been Finney converts, Lane rebels, and Garrison agents. Now they were anti-Garrisonians. The South Carolina sisters had been the first women to speak to mixed audiences on antislavery.[13] But family cares and financial worries had forced the Grimké-Welds to withdraw from abolition activities.

The group also shared a commitment to the nutritional reforms of Sylvester Graham, an abolitionist and diet reformer.† Ralph Waldo Emerson called him "the poet of bran bread and muffins." In popular lectures Graham presented steps to improved health. He advocated eating vegetables and bran, avoiding caffeine and alcohol, sleeping on firm mattresses, bathing in cold water, wearing loose-fitting and lightweight clothing, exercising daily, keeping windows open, drinking water regularly, and being cheerful at meals. In his *Letters to Young Men* (1839), he advised limiting the frequency of intercourse to twelve times a year.[14] Elizabeth Stanton adopted the Graham regimen when she married Henry and followed many of its guidelines, except those governing food and sex.

The company at Belleville shared a Graham meal of rice, molasses, bread, milk, hominy, vegetables, and pie made without shortening. Undismayed

---

* Theodore Weld (1803–95) came from a family of ministers in upstate New York. In 1825 he joined Finney's Holy Band and converted to abolition in 1830. Although he retired from active antislavery and revival preaching after his marriage, he did organize a protest against the gag rule in Congress. Eventually the Grimké-Welds became schoolteachers and administrators, first in New Jersey and later in Massachusetts.

Angelina Grimké Weld (1805–79) and Sarah Grimké (1792–1873) were daughters of a Charleston slaveholder. Both emigrated to Philadelphia and became Quakers and abolitionists. In 1836 Angelina published *An Appeal to the Christian Women of the South* and became an antislavery agent. At first she spoke only to small groups of women, chaperoned by her sister. The novelty of a Southern lady preaching abolition drew men as well as women. In 1837 Angelina became notorious for addressing a "mixed" audience. The criticism of churchmen prompted the sisters to publish another pamphlet, *Letters on the Equality of the Sexes, and the Condition of Women* (1838). Angelina married Theodore Weld in 1838 and bore three children. Sarah lived with them for the rest of her life. Later the sisters joined the women's movement. B. Thomas, *Weld;* Katharine Lumpkin, *The Emancipation of Angelina Grimké* (Chapel Hill: Univ. of North Carolina Press, 1974); Gerda Lerner, *The Grimké Sisters from South Carolina: Pioneers for Woman's Rights and Abolition* (Boston: Houghton Mifflin, 1967).

† Sylvester Graham (1794–1851) was the father of Graham crackers. An orphan suffering from ill health, shuffled among relatives, he had a poor education. After his marriage he became a preacher and a temperance agent. His study of physiology and dietary habits led to a career as a popular lecturer. He marketed Graham flour, made from whole wheat, and established Graham boardinghouses.

by the menu, Elizabeth quickly became friends with the Grimké-Welds. Writing them from England she exclaimed, "Dear friends how much I love you!! What a trio! for me to love!" Her admiration was returned. As Angelina reported to the Smiths, "We are very much pleased with Elizabeth Stanton who spent several days with us, and I could not help wishing that Henry was better calculated to mold such a mind." Henry had no such qualms. Addressing Smith as "Cousin Gerrit," he wrote, "You know I need not say one word in praise of my newly acquired treasure . . . words cannot express to you my estimate of its value and excellence." [15]

Aware of Henry's delight in her company and pleased by her encounter with the Welds, the new Mrs. Stanton looked forward to an equally stimulating atmosphere among the abolitionists who gathered in London. The couple sailed for England on May 12, 1840, aboard the *Montreal*. They were joined by Henry's Liberty party colleague and presidential candidate, James Birney, a former slaveholder and a Weld recruit. He had a Southerner's conservative views about woman's place and was offended by Elizabeth's high spirits. He reprimanded her for addressing Henry by his first name in public and for being too friendly with the sailors. According to Mrs. Stanton, "Mr. Birney kept to himself like a clam in his shell all the time." Describing her first ocean voyage to Mrs. Weld she added, "Henry wishes me to say that he attributes his freedom from seasickness *to his strict observance of the Graham system*." [16]

The international antislavery meeting that the Stantons planned to attend had first been proposed by the editor of an American abolitionist periodical. The idea was taken up by the newly formed British and Foreign Anti-Slavery Society. It issued a call in October 1836 to "friends of the slave in every nation and of every clime." Realizing that "friends" might be construed as female, the British society revised its call in February 1840, asking that names of "gentlemen" representatives be forwarded. The purpose of the meeting was threefold: to exchange information on the results of British emancipation in the West Indies, to discuss the nature and extent of slavery and the slave trade in the free world, and to determine the best measures of achieving abolition and the welfare of the free Negro population. [17]

The Stantons arrived in London in early June. They boarded at Mark Moore's, at No. 6 Queen Street Place, with several other American delegates, including most of the women. Two American Female Anti-Slavery societies had sent representatives. From Boston came Emily Winslow, Abby Southwick, and Ann Green Phillips, who with her husband Wendell Phillips, another delegate, was also on her wedding trip. From Philadelphia came Lucretia Mott, Sarah Pugh, Mary Grew, Abby Kimber, and Elizabeth Neall.

Birney the southerner found the situation so intolerable that he moved out.

The question of whether or not to seat the American women as legitimate delegates provided the only excitement in an otherwise tame convention. The women knew that their rejection had been planned in advance by the anti-Garrison faction of American abolitionists, with which Henry Stanton was allied. Their exclusion was intended to reinforce the position of the new American and Foreign Anti-Slavery Society and the Liberty party. In an effort to challenge the exclusion of his wife and the other women, and to embarrass the political abolitionists, Wendell Phillips planned a parliamentary protest. Elizabeth Stanton knew little about this intrigue until she was caught up in it at her boardinghouse and on the convention floor.

The first World Anti-Slavery Convention opened on Friday, June 12, 1840, in Freemason's Hall on Great Queen Street. The venerable Thomas Clarkson presided. Birney was made one of the vice-presidents and Henry Stanton one of the secretaries. Henry Stanton made frequent speeches, including one urging British abolitionists to rely more on the press, churches, and economic coercion in their strategy.[18] Women delegates and guests were seated in a railed-off space on one side of the floor.

As delegate Mary Grew recorded in her diary, "The contest respecting the eligibility of women to seats was immediately commenced and sustained with great vigor during the remainder of the session." Wendell Phillips moved that a roster of all delegates with credentials from any antislavery body be prepared and adopted. Debate lasted for several hours. Birney and Mary Grew's father spoke against the motion. Members of the clergy reminded the delegates that participation by women would be "promiscuous" and inappropriate. Advocates responded that the women had been duly elected, had served the cause in America, and deserved to be seated. Finally Phillips's motion was defeated by a crushing majority. Permission for the women to remain at the business meetings was granted as a precedent-setting concession.[19]

Assured that the opponents had enough votes to defeat Phillips's motion, Henry Stanton had finessed the situation. He made a "very eloquent speech" in support of seating the women, and his wife and Garrison believed that he had voted yes on the motion. Others remembered the unrecorded tally differently. Both Birney and one of the women delegates recalled that Henry voted "emphatically" against seating the women.[20] Until his break with Garrison over political action by abolitionists, Stanton had supported women's participation in all antislavery activities. After 1840 he abandoned this position because women's rights were not "pragmatic" and undermined the ability of the political abolitionists to attract voters. In London he had nothing to lose by supporting the Phillips's motion, so he did. During his career as a political abolitionist he would seldom support women's rights in public.

On the whole, the first international antislavery convention was a timid affair. It failed to reach agreement on any of its goals. It is remembered primarily because it raised a question that would provoke a century and more of women's rights activity in America. It was significant in the life of Elizabeth Stanton because it focused her attention more narrowly on women's rights and introduced her to Lucretia Mott.

The antagonism to women evident in the debate aroused Elizabeth Cady Stanton more than the antislavery questions on the agenda. She was angry at the injustice of the situation and impatient with the hypocrisy of the abolitionists. The opposition of the most liberal leaders of the most radical movement of the era to a question of women's rights stunned her. She felt, she recalled: "humiliated and chagrined, except as these feelings were outweighed by contempt for the shallow reasoning of the opponents and their comical pose and gestures. . . . It was really pitiful to hear narrow-minded bigots, pretending to be teachers and leaders of men, so cruelly remanding their own mothers, with the rest of womankind, to absolute subjection to the ordinary masculine type of humanity."[21] She claimed later that her outrage at the London meeting ignited her interest in women's rights.

At the time everyone, not least of all Henry, was surprised that the new Mrs. Stanton sided with the Mott-Garrison faction. As a result of this vote, Garrison, Mrs. Mott, and Mrs. Stanton became mutual allies and admirers. When Garrison, arriving after the vote, chose to sit with the women, Henry's enemy became Elizabeth's hero. In turn, Garrison wrote to his wife that "Mrs. Stanton is a fearless woman and goes for women's rights with all her soul." Lucretia Mott confided to her diary, "Elizabeth Stanton growing daily in our affections."[22]

Lucretia Mott's diary also details the encounters and conversations with Elizabeth Stanton that became the basis of their enduring friendship. Although Mrs. Mott was twenty-two years older than Mrs. Stanton, they formed a lasting bond. Elizabeth praised Mott to Angelina Weld as a "peerless woman; . . . my soul finds great delight in her society." Together the women attended convention sessions, inspected schools and prisons, went shopping and sightseeing, dined out, and visited museums. "Wherever our party went," Mrs. Stanton remembered, "I took possession of Lucretia, much to Henry's vexation."[23] When Elizabeth heard Mrs. Mott preach in a Unitarian chapel, it was the first time she had ever heard a woman speak in public or give a sermon.

The diminutive Mrs. Mott combined the strengths of Margaret Cady and Emma Willard with a reform conscience. Both serene and vivacious, Lucretia Coffin Mott was a Quaker minister, abolitionist, and feminist. She was born in 1793 on Nantucket Island, to a China trade captain and his independent merchant wife. She grew up, she remembered, "so thoroughly imbued with women's rights that it was the most important question of my life from a very early day."[24] After a brief teaching career, she married James Mott in 1811, settled in Philadelphia, and bore six children. The death of her first son resulted in an increased interest in religion. In 1821 she was ordained as a Quaker minister. Although she always dressed and spoke in the modest Quaker mode, she grew more and more restless with the rigid demands of Quaker orthodoxy. When the Great Separation of 1827 divided Friends into orthodox and Hicksite sects, she and James joined Elias Hicks. They rejected evangelical tendencies and arbitrary control by the elders, believed in a direct relationship between God and conscience, and held that men and women had equal spiritual gifts. What was then considered heresy later became official Quaker doctrine.

Mrs. Mott's attitude about slavery was similarly progressive. From 1825 until Emancipation, she never knowingly used cotton cloth, cane sugar, or any other products of a slave economy. A proponent of immediate emancipation, she attended Garrison's convening meeting of the American Anti-Slavery Society and founded the Philadelphia Female Anti-Slavery Society in 1833. In 1837 she organized the Anti-Slavery Convention of American Women. Her outspoken political and religious views earned her the enmity of many, including Quakers.[25]

The impact on Elizabeth Cady Stanton of weeks of companionship and conversation with Lucretia Mott cannot be underestimated. At last Stanton had found a suitable female role model and a willing mentor.

> Mrs. Mott was to me an entire new revelation of womanhood. I sought every opportunity to be at her side, and continually plied her with questions. . . . She had told me of the doctrines and divisions among "Friends," of the inward light, of Mary Wollstonecraft, her social theories, and her demands of equality for women. I had been reading Combe's "Constitution of Man" and "Moral Philosophy," Channing's works, and Mary Wollstonecraft, though all tabooed by orthodox teachers, but I had never heard a woman talk what, as a Scotch Presbyterian, I had scarcely dared to think.

Under the tutelage of the older woman, Stanton searched for answers to her questions about religion and reform. "When I first heard from her lips that I had the same right to think for myself that Luther, Calvin and John Knox had, and the same right to be guided by my own convictions, I felt a new born sense of dignity and freedom," she remembered.[26] Conversations with Lucretia Mott gave Elizabeth Stanton greater confidence in her own opinions. Her independence and feminism were encouraged and congratulated.

On the day of the vote against seating the women delegates in London, Mrs. Mott and Mrs. Stanton left the hall together. The younger woman recalled their conversation. "As [we] walked home, arm in arm, commenting on the incidents of the day, we resolved to hold a convention as soon as we returned home, and [to] form a society to advocate the rights of women."[27] They did not take action immediately upon their return, but no action was taken until the two of them initiated it eight years later.

One of the differences between Elizabeth Stanton and Lucretia Mott was the roles played by their husbands. James Mott, a well-to-do Philadelphia merchant, was supportive. He accompanied his wife as she spoke, held her bonnet, and presided when a gentleman was required. In contrast, Henry expected Elizabeth to support and applaud him and his causes. To his credit, he did not seem alarmed or angry about her behavior in London, only occasionally "vexed." Within six weeks of their marriage, his wife had publicly aligned herself with his antagonist, William Lloyd Garrison, on an issue over which they had themselves divided. It was her first independent act as a married woman, and it was admired by her new friends.

After the London meeting adjourned in late June, Henry and Elizabeth began a five-month tour of Great Britain, Ireland, and France. In order to finance the trip, Henry had contracted to give a series of lectures on American abolition and to report on them for the *New York American* and the *National Era*. He gave forty lectures in thirty cities in England and attended two meetings in France. The trip enabled the couple to see the sights and meet with foreign reformers, but they were seldom alone. Henry was accompanied on his tour by Birney and Rev. John Scoble. The minister so offended Elizabeth's newfound feminism by criticizing her friend Lucretia Mott that she exclaimed, "In all my life I never did desire so to ring a man's neck as I did his."[28] Exasperated by Scoble's rudeness, Elizabeth returned to London and stayed by herself for ten days.

Startled by such outbursts of independent behavior, Henry reproved Elizabeth. He wished her demeanor to be more demure. As she admitted in a letter to her Cousin Gerrit: "[It] will do me no harm to be checked occasionally, and as we are among strangers and on such a mission we cannot be too serious. I feel that I am a little too gay, and much too ignorant on the subject of slavery for the circumstances in which I am placed. I hope Cousin Nancy will write me one of her long serious letters. Henry often wishes that I was more like her. I console him by telling him that Cousin Nancy was quite gay and frolicsome once." Yet her high spirits and intelligence won her many admirers among English reformers. "Mrs. Stanton is one in two thousand," wrote Richard Webb. "I have met very few women I consider equal to her. She is better than a whole third of that

portion of the Pledged Philanthropy which assembled in Freemasons' Hall."
His wife Hannah added, "Elizabeth Stanton (with whom we were highly
delighted) is a brave upholder of woman's rights."[29]

Finally escaping their reform companions for a walking tour of Scotland
in September, the Stantons felt "self-reliant and venturesome." After a round
of last-minute tea parties and departure calls, they sailed for the United
States in December 1840. Elizabeth remembered the North Atlantic crossing as "a cold, rough, dreary voyage." Henry, no longer a strict Grahamite, was confined to his berth, so she read novels, played chess, walked the
deck, and worried about their homecoming. She had begun the rapproche-
ment with her family while still in England, by writing frequent and affectionate letters.[30]

Arriving in New York City the day before Christmas, the Stantons stayed
for a week with Elizabeth's sister Harriet Eaton, where they had not been
welcome in May. Then they traveled by train and sleigh through twelve
feet of snow to Johnstown. There they were warmly greeted by the Cadys.
Henry still had no job and no prospects, but his wife was happy to be home
again. She reported to one of her friends that "Henry and I are quite undecided as to our future occupation and place of residence."[31]

The Stantons spent the winter visiting friends, chiefly the Smiths. Birney
was also a guest at Peterboro, so the men organized an impromptu abolition meeting in the Presbyterian church. But Henry realized that he could
neither support Elizabeth nor advance his political ambitions as an abolition agent. After a brief stopover in Seneca Falls with the Bayards, the
Stantons were back in Johnstown before the end of February. "Our trunks
unpacked, wardrobes arranged in closets and drawers, the excitement of
seeing friends over," Elizabeth recalled, "we spent some time in making
plans for the future."[32]

For both personal and political reasons, Henry decided to read law with
Judge Cady. Aware that his wife had risked severing her family ties to marry,
he wanted to repair the damage. He hoped to improve his relationship with
the Cadys and to enhance his political future. For fifteen months he clerked
for his father-in-law. The couple lived with the Cadys in Johnstown, following the pattern established by the older daughters and their husbands,
as would Elizabeth's younger sisters. As Elizabeth reported to Libby Smith,
"Papa seems quite contented with [Henry]." Henry did not abandon reform. He attended the first anniversary meeting of the Liberty party and
made an average of four political speeches a week during the summer of
1841. He was rewarded with a seat on the party's state central committee.[33]

Elizabeth was pleased with the arrangement. Freed from domestic responsibilities by her family's servants, she remembered these years as

"pleasant and profitable." She enjoyed the company of her sisters and "read law, history, political economy, with occasional interruptions to take part in some temperance or anti-slavery excitement." She taught a Sunday school class for black children, but resigned when her students were not allowed to participate in a church festival. She made her first speech, on temperance, to a group of women in Seneca Falls. She reported to a friend that she had infused it "with a homeopathic dose of women's rights as I take care to do in many private conversations."[34] She corresponded regularly with the women she had met in London, writing about politics, religion, and reform, occasionally penciling a recipe for calves' foot jelly or date bread on the envelope.

Henry's decision to study law and live with his in-laws was criticized by his former allies. They accused him of abandoning abolition and elevating himself to law and politics. Their wives were equally forthright, needling Elizabeth either for sharing Henry's politics or for not doing so. On abolition questions Mrs. Stanton genuinely agreed with Henry's anti-Garrisonian position. "Slavery is a political question, created and sustained by law and must be put down by law," she responded to Elizabeth Neall. As she explained to another correspondent, she had come to that conclusion independent of Henry.

> It may be that my great love for Henry may warp my judgment in favor of some of his opinions but I claim the right to look at his actions and opinions with the same freedom and impartiality that I do at those of any other man. Well, then, as I am not yet fully converted to the doctrine of no human government, I am in favor of political action and the organization of a Third Party is the most efficient way of calling forth and directing action. So long as we are to be governed by human laws, I should be unwilling to have the making and administration of these laws left entirely to the selfish and unprincipled part of the community.[35]

Mrs. Stanton continued to differ with Henry on women's rights and to admire Garrison for his "noble views" on women. She refused to attend antislavery meetings with her husband, she explained to another correspondent, "because I knew I would have no voice." In case there was any doubt about the source of her opinions, she added, "I do in truth think and act for myself deeming that I alone am responsible for the sayings and doings of E.C.S."[36]

A feminist thread runs throughout Stanton's post-London correspondence. She was aware of and annoyed by the treatment of women. To Lucretia Mott she admitted in 1841, "The more I think on the present condition of woman, the more I am oppressed with the reality of her degradation." It was at this time that she first insisted on being addressed by her full name, as a symbol of her individuality and independence.[37] She also established her habit of reading, analyzing, arguing, and defending her position on serious questions.

   Elizabeth Cady Stanton was still living at home when her first child, Daniel Cady Stanton (Neil), was born on March 2, 1842. Henry was absent on antislavery business. Two years later, in March 1844, Henry B. Stanton (Kit) was born at Judge Cady's townhouse in Albany. Their third son, Gerrit Smith Stanton (Gat), was born in Boston on September 18, 1845. The young mother read the latest opinions on child care, experimented with her infants, and discarded outdated methods. As she recalled in her autobiography, "Though uncertain at every step of my own knowledge, I learned another lesson in self-reliance."[38] Her innovations seemed to work; the boys thrived, and she enjoyed her role. Motherhood provided Elizabeth Cady Stanton with another means through which she felt successful and in charge.

   After weighing several opportunities in New York, Michigan, and Massachusetts, Henry Stanton had decided to practice law in Boston. He passed the Massachusetts bar in October 1842 and entered the office of Samuel Sewall. Henry had chosen Boston in order to challenge Garrison on his home ground. He hoped the city offered a congenial constituency for a future campaign. He was already well known among reformers, if not wholly admired. Garrisonians condemned him for pursuing politics "at the expense of principle." Henry had been active in the Liberty party's 1842 campaign in Massachusetts, in which it doubled its previous vote and elected several men to the legislature. He served as chairman of the party's state central committee in 1843 and kept alert for an elective opening for himself.[39]

   Spending so much time on politics did not reward Henry's pocketbook. As always, he admitted he had "pressing liabilities." In a rare reference to Elizabeth's attitude about his chronic poverty, Henry confessed to a friend, "My wife feels very bad, and is sometimes quite gloomy with the apprehension that we shall not get through the coming year." His colleagues assumed he was supported by her wealthy family, so Henry had to plead for repayment of debts owed him. He was forced to explain their position. "True, my father-in-law is worth some property; but he does not give his sons-in-law a dollar and will not till he dies, except to keep them from starving, thinking it better . . . to aid them indirectly by throwing business their way, and thus make them climb up as he did, by their own strength."[40] Henry struggled on, just barely making ends meet.

   Whether on account of their money problems or her second pregnancy, Elizabeth Stanton spent much of 1842 and 1843 in Albany with the Cady family. The judge had installed his extended family in a townhouse in the state capital, intending to establish the husbands of his two youngest daughters in the legal profession. The ménage included the Cady parents, three daughters, two sons-in-law, and two grandchildren. The Albany sojourns gave the middle Cady daughter an opportunity to live comfortably, share child care, and dabble in reform.

Although she always exaggerated her own role in retrospective accounts, Mrs. Stanton did lobby for the New York Married Women's Property Act. The first bill to ensure that married women could hold title to property in their own right, introduced in 1836, had failed for lack of interest. Renewed impetus for such a reform followed economic instability, when the panic of 1837 had demonstrated to many bankrupt businessmen the danger of losing their wives' property to their creditors. Fathers like Judge Cady, whose entire fortune would be inherited by married daughters, also had an interest in guaranteeing its safekeeping from errant sons-in-law. At first more men than women expressed an interest in the issue. When Ernestine Rose and Paulina Wright Davis circulated petitions urging reform of the old laws in 1840, only five women signed.* Concern increased in the 1840s. During Elizabeth Stanton's visits to Albany from 1843 to 1845, she joined other women in circulating petitions and, with her father's blessing, lobbied members of the legislature. The bill appealed to Mrs. Stanton's general interest in women's rights and her personal stake in property rights. It finally passed in 1848, the first of its kind in the country.[41]

During their separations Henry wrote frequently, complaining that Elizabeth did not. His letters were graceful, witty, sometimes passionate, always interesting. He addressed Elizabeth with such endearments as "my lovely Lee." Without her he felt "lonesome, cheerless, and homeless." Typically, he "forgot to leave cash." Henry's tone was not always affectionate. He admitted to "coldness and unkindness." Friends wondered among themselves what Elizabeth saw in Henry; one "personally would pick his eyes out if she were treated so badly." Sarah Grimké found them both lacking: "Henry greatly needs a humble, holy companion, and she needs the same."[42]

---

*Ernestine Potowski Rose (1810–92) was a Polish Jew. When she inherited property from her mother, her father, a rabbi, contracted to give it to an older husband as a dowry. She took him to court and won her claim and the inheritance. In 1827 she gave the money to her father, renounced her religion, and left Poland. She traveled around Europe, supporting herself. In 1836 she married William Rose, a silversmith and a disciple of Robert Owen, and emigrated to the United States. She became active in women's rights, free thought, and temperance.

Paulina Kellogg Wright Davis (1813–76) was a frontier child. Raised in western New York, she rebelled against orthodox Presbyterianism, underwent several revivals, and planned to become a missionary to Hawaii. Instead she married Francis Wright, a wealthy merchant, in 1833. Together they became active in abolition, temperance, and women's rights. After her husband died in 1845, leaving her independently wealthy, she lectured on female physiology and shocked her audience by using a manikin to demonstrate.

For six months in 1842 the Stantons and their first son had boarded in Boston with a Baptist minister who was married to a Cady relative, but Albany was a more comfortable and less expensive alternative. Finally Elizabeth's father came to their aid, again providing housing. Soon after the birth of their second child, Judge Cady gave the couple a house in Chelsea, an area overlooking the Back Bay. In June 1844 Elizabeth and her sons moved back to Boston.

The new house was newly furnished, and Elizabeth was delighted to be head of her own household at last. What she lacked in domestic experience she made up for in enthusiasm. She "studied up everything pertaining to housekeeping and enjoyed it all." She recorded daily expenses in a "little family book," supervised two servants and three children, inspired the laundress to have a whiter wash than the neighbors', filled the rooms with books and flowers, and experimented in the kitchen on the cook's day off. She recalled that the doctrine of separate spheres prevailed. "Mr. Stanton announced to me that his business would occupy all his time, and that I must take entire charge of the housekeeping." Rather than resent his lack of interest, she relished the responsibility. "It is a proud moment in a woman's life to reign supreme within four walls, to be the one to whom all questions . . . are referred."[43] She was finally fulfilling her mother's role, becoming a domestic monarch. Like motherhood, household management gave her another source of success and self-confidence.

The only drawback to domestic bliss was the servant problem. Mrs. Stanton remembered that Rose the cook, who had been "scientifically" selected by a phrenologist, burned the dinner and scalded the baby, prompting Henry to suggest that next time Elizabeth ask for references. Whenever "glaring blunders in the menu were exceedingly mortifying," she urged Henry to cover the defects with brilliant conversation.[44] Despite an unreliable kitchen staff, the Stantons entertained frequently. A list of their friends reads like a roster of reformers: Lydia Maria Child, Parker Pillsbury, Abby Kelley and Stephen Foster, Paulina Wright Davis, Samuel Sewall and his wife, Elizabeth Peabody, Maria Weston and her sisters, Oliver and Marianna Johnson, Joseph and Thankful Southwick, Frederick Douglass, Charles Hovey, Francis Jackson and his daughter, John Greenleaf Whittier, John Pierpont, Theodore Parker, Bronson Alcott, Ralph Waldo Emerson, James Russell Lowell, and Nathaniel Hawthorne. They even exchanged dinners with the Garrisons.

It was a stimulating life for Elizabeth. "I attend all sorts and sizes of meetings and lectures," she wrote a friend. "I consider myself in a kind of moral museum and I find that Boston affords as many curiosities in her way as does the British Museum in its." She had the leisure to read widely, to join "conversation clubs," and to attend lectures, sermons, concerts, antislavery bazaars, and meetings about peace, temperance, and prison reform. She visited Brook Farm and was impressed by the experiment in community living. "All sorts of new ideas are seething," she reported in a letter to her mother, "but I haven't either time or place even to enumerate them, and if I did you and my good father would probably balk at most of them."[45]

Despite an environment congenial to reformers, Elizabeth Cady Stanton did not distinguish herself in that circle. She lived in a community in which reform activity for women was expected and approved, but she participated only superficially. There is no record of leadership or even of membership in any reform society. Nor was there any shared reform activity with Henry. As the political abolitionists turned their energies to electoral strategy, women were automatically excluded.[46]

Throughout the 1840s Elizabeth Stanton and Lucretia Mott exchanged letters, most of them about religious subjects. On one occasion when they spent the day together in Boston, they discussed the possibility of holding a women's rights meeting there.[47] Why they did not pursue their London plan remains a question. Mrs. Mott was distracted at the time by the death of her mother, personal illness, and Quaker intrigues. Mrs. Stanton had the opportunity and interest but lacked incentive and experience. Perhaps without Mott she felt too immature to take the lead. Perhaps she was hesitant to ally with the Garrisonians on women's rights when Henry was contesting them on abolition tactics. Perhaps the need to discuss women's rights and wrongs seemed less imperative and less immediate in such a society than it would in another setting.

In Boston, Mrs. Stanton was more interested in religious questions than women's rights. She was pursuing a personal, mental independence from the Calvinist influences of her childhood. Encouraged and emboldened by Mrs. Mott, she investigated theological issues. She had, she wrote, a "hungering, thirsting condition for truth." In the 1840s Boston was the center of religious liberalism, and Theodore Parker was its leader. Among his admirers was Elizabeth Cady Stanton. To another Parker enthusiast she wrote in 1846: "I too have taken deep draughts from the same source and feel refreshed. I have heard a course of lectures from him and am now reading his discourses. . . . He finds my soul—he speaks to me or rather God (through him) to me."[48]

One of Emerson's neighbors in Concord, Theodore Parker combined Unitarianism, transcendentalism, and Christian perfectionism.* Like the revivalists, religious liberals rejected Calvinist determinism in favor of free

---

* Theodore Parker (1810–60) was the precocious offspring of distinguished Massachusetts forebears. After Harvard and a brief teaching career, he became a minister, graduating from Harvard Divinity School in 1834. His marriage to Lydia Cabot caused him to rethink his theology, making it more humane. He resigned from his first church and became active in improvement and antislavery, eventually becoming a member of the Secret Six.

will. They stressed individual responsibility for salvation and individual divinity. Parker preached God's presence in each person and His accessibility to men and women. He refused to take Scripture literally and suggested that God was an androgynous figure. His was an optimistic, romantic, humanistic creed that credited each individual conscience with the ability to intuit God's will. Parker's ideas freed Mrs. Stanton from the religious superstitions and fears of her youth. In his emphasis on the individual she found tacit approval for her own position, no matter what it was. Theodore Parker's liberal theology contributed to her self-esteem. Long before she achieved political rights or social equity, she had declared her religious independence.

At the time Elizabeth Cady Stanton turned thirty in Boston, she was content with her life. Her husband had begun to prosper, and she had three healthy children, a well-run house, and stimulating friends. She had undertaken a serious religious inquiry and felt comfortable with her conclusions. She enjoyed an active social life and occasionally dabbled in reform. Henry, however, was much less content. He had turned down the Liberty party's congressional nomination in 1844 because he thought he could not win it. When he polled fifteen hundred write-in votes, he regretted that he had not made the race.[49] After another unsuccessful electoral season, he began to search for a more hospitable district. He suffered chronic lung congestion in Boston and was increasingly unhappy. Finally, in 1847, Henry decided to leave Boston for Seneca Falls, New York.

4

Seneca Falls Sentiments
1848

The connection between Seneca Falls and Elizabeth Cady Stanton's independence is compelling. The combination of circumstances that followed her move to upstate New York converted her from high-minded housewife to feminist agitator. Discontented with the conditions of isolated housekeeping and encouraged by Lucretia Mott, Mrs. Stanton took action at last. In initiating and organizing what came to be known as the Seneca Falls Women's Rights Convention of 1848, Mrs. Stanton dared to try out in public the roles of feminist and reformer that she had privately admired.

Prior to 1848 Stanton had been observing and practicing different roles. The experiences of her privileged childhood, the expectations and rejections of her parents, her unusual education and extensive reading, the influence of male mentors, her exposure to revival and reform, her marriage to a political abolitionist, her introduction to female reformers, her friendship with Lucretia Mott, her grappling with patriarchy in religion and society, had all been factors in her development. Each episode allowed her to observe different behaviors and their results. Each observation enabled her to accept, reject, or modify various roles.

It must have been harder for her to anticipate what reactions some roles would evoke. In her experience female reformers had been ridiculed, condemned, disdained, ignored, and dismissed as ineffective. Yet the women themselves persevered and took pride in their contributions. Criticized by people Stanton no longer respected, these women were applauded by those she admired and by each other. The women themselves seemed to thrive, managing to combine public pursuits with more traditional occupations. They did not disintegrate under pressure. The high regard Stanton felt for

women reformers counterbalanced her father's disapproval, Edward Bayard's indifference, and Henry's political opposition to women as reformers. Stanton's reform efforts prior to 1848, on behalf of abolition, temperance, and women's property rights, were minor. They had not been opposed
by her husband, family, or friends. In the absence of opposition, the positive presence of Mrs. Mott freed Stanton to take the next step, to try out
the role of feminist reformer. Stanton accepted Mott's encouragement because what she had seen led her to believe that she could undertake the
part. She recognized that she had similar talents and an equal interest, and
she thought she could cope with any criticism her actions aroused.

Elizabeth Cady Stanton was thirty-one years old when she moved to
Seneca Falls in June 1847. She had been married for seven years and was
the mother of three lively boys, then five, three, and almost two years old.
Seneca Falls in the 1840s was a village of about four thousand inhabitants,
six churches, four hotels, one academy, and two dozen small factories and
mills. They produced cotton cloth, flour, paper, axes, leather, liquor, boats,
window sashes, and water pumps. The Cayuga and Seneca Canal linked
the town to the Erie Canal; the railroad connected it to Syracuse to the
east and Rochester to the west.[1]

The decision to leave Boston for this outpost in upstate New York had
been Henry's. The reason most frequently cited was his "delicate" health:
he was exhausted by Liberty party activities, suffered five-day headaches,
and was plagued by lung congestion. In a letter to Gerrit Smith, Henry
blamed his ill health on Boston's "repulsive" winters and "bracing" summers; he wished to escape the severe weather in New England for the "more
congenial climate in Central New York."[2] Anyone familiar with the seasons in New York's snow belt would find it more likely that Henry was
seeking a more hospitable political climate among New York abolitionists.
Having suffered the chill rebuff of Boston Garrisonians, Henry needed another district.

As a political abolitionist, Henry Stanton pursued a career in elective
politics. Although he devoted half of his adult life to politics, he was seldom successful. In New York he helped organize the Free Soil party in 1848.
He renounced it a year later to run for the state Senate as a Democrat, and
won. Reelected by only five votes in a special election in May 1851, Henry
Stanton was offered the lieutenant governorship in 1852. He turned the
Democrats down and never again held an elected position, but he remained active in abolition and, having switched parties again, in Republican affairs, for the rest of his life.[3]

Despite Judge Cady's disapproval of Henry's politics and his reluctance
to subsidize his sons-in-law, he once again provided the young couple with
a home. In a deed recorded on June 22, 1847, he gave Elizabeth and "her

heirs and assigns forever" a house and two acres at 32 Washington Street.*
It was a corner property on Locust Hill, commanding a view of the Seneca
River. Judge Cady also gave the Stantons a nearby farm.⁴ Although the
house was in Elizabeth's name, until passage of the Married Women's
Property Act of 1848 her property was legally Henry's.

The house had not been occupied for five years and needed wholesale
repair. Stanton's father challenged her, supposedly saying, "You believe in
woman's capacity to do and dare, now go ahead and put your house in
order." Mrs. Stanton left Henry in Boston, deposited her three children and
seventeen trunks in Albany, and proceeded to Seneca Falls. Whether her
recollection of her father's remark is accurate or apocryphal, it is significant that she recalled it as a challenge to her ability as a woman, and that
she felt she succeeded. She put carpenters, painters, paperhangers, and gar-
deners to work and supervised the addition of a kitchen and woodhouse.
As she recalled later, "Having left my children with my mother, there were
no impediments to a full display of my executive ability."⁵

She and Henry named the house "Grasmere," after Wordsworth's home,
which they had visited on their honeymoon. During their fifteen-year residence the house expanded with their family. As Stanton's daughter recalled in 1923, today "only a fraction of the house still stands, changed
. . . greatly [with its] wings clipped and its acres of shaded lawn and gardens cut to meet the needs of a growing neighborhood."⁶

As Elizabeth confided to her cousin Libby Miller, both the Stantons had
trepidations about leaving Boston. She was prepared to be "happy and
contented" in the country, but she worried that Henry would be "restless"
and "long for the strong excitement of city life."⁷ As it turned out, she was
the one who felt trapped and dislocated. In later life she always sang the
praises of rural life, claiming to have spent most of her life in the country,
but she preferred the city. So did Henry. After their move to Seneca Falls
he traveled frequently to Albany and Washington to register patents and
represent the interests of his new Seneca Falls clients. He attended political
functions, savoring the gossip and male camaraderie of those gatherings.
Dependent for income on his clients, the Stantons remained in Seneca Falls
even after Henry had abandoned elective politics and long after Elizabeth
wanted to leave.

As Henry flourished, Elizabeth floundered. Nothing in her experience as
privileged daughter or pampered bride had prepared her for the role of rural housewife. She was soon voicing discontent with the isolating, demean-
ing, and unrewarding character of her life and that of most of her neigh-

*Since 1980 Stanton's Seneca Falls house and the Wesleyan Chapel are a part of the Wom-
en's Rights National Historical Park.

bors. She was overworked and bored. Her dissatisfaction was still vivid in recollection.

> [Our] residence was on the outskirts of the town, roads often very muddy and no sidewalks most of the way. Mr. Stanton was frequently from home, I had poor servants, and an increasing number of children. The novelty of housekeeping had passed away, and much that was once attractive in domestic life was now irksome. I had so many cares. . . . My duties were too numerous and varied and none sufficiently exhilarating or intellectual to bring into play my higher faculties. I suffered with mental hunger, which, like an empty stomach, is very depressing. I had books, but no stimulating companionship. Cleanliness, order, the love of the beautiful and artistic all faded away in the struggle to accomplish what was absolutely necessary from hour to hour.[8]

For a woman who had been sheltered by servants and stimulated by social life in Boston, the change must have been dramatic. Stanton repeatedly admitted feeling lonely, depressed, angry, and exhausted, complaints that became the refrain of her Seneca Falls residence.

In the year following her move to Seneca Falls, Stanton was a lonely homemaker. Already overwhelmed by domestic drudgery, she despaired when the children caught malaria. The time-consuming homeopathic cure prolonged her nursing chores. Only slowly did she establish a domestic routine and settle into the Seneca Falls community. She was made intimately aware of woman's subordinate status in American society. Less able to articulate her discontent in 1848 than later, she recalled in her autobiography:

> The general discontent I felt with woman's portion as wife, mother, housekeeper, physician, and spiritual guide, the chaotic conditions into which everything fell without her constant supervision, and the wearied, anxious look of the majority of women impressed me with a strong feeling that some active measures should be taken to remedy the wrongs of society in general, and of women in particular. My experience at the World Anti-Slavery Convention, all I had read of the legal status of women, and the oppression I saw everywhere, together swept across my soul, intensified now by many personal experiences. . . . It seemed as if all the elements had conspired to impel me to some onward step. I could not see what to do or where to begin—my only thought was a public meeting for protest and discussion.[9]

While Stanton had so far met every challenge with resourcefulness, it is doubtful that her personal protest against woman's lot would have resulted in the 1848 convention without the encouragement and enthusiasm of Lucretia Mott and her friends. Stanton's nascent feminism had become an urgent commitment. But in order to turn ideology into reality, Stanton required a female mentor. In Mrs. Mott she had an attractive, successful, respected, and appealing model.

During the summer of 1848 Lucretia Mott and her husband traveled to upstate New York to attend the yearly New York meeting of Hicksite Quakers. On Thursday, July 13, Elizabeth Cady Stanton was invited to spend the day with Mrs. Mott at the home of Jane and Richard Hunt in Waterloo, three miles west of Seneca Falls. Mrs. Mott's sister, Martha Coffin Wright, and Mary Ann McClintock were also present. Sitting around the tea table in the sympathetic company of these women, Stanton "poured out . . . the torrent of my long-accumulating discontent with such vehemence and indignation that I stirred myself, as well as the rest of the party, to do and dare anything," a recollection still intense forty years later.[10] Whether persuaded by passion or pragmatism, the group decided to call a "convention" to discuss women's rights. Holding a meeting was a characteristic response among reformers; it gave them a means to state their grievance and identify sympathizers.

The five were not extraordinary women. All of them were married; all of them had children. All but Stanton were Garrisonian abolitionists and liberal Quakers. Mrs. Mott at fifty-four was the oldest; Mrs. Stanton at thirty-two was the youngest. Although Stanton and probably the others had attended various reform meetings, only Mrs. Mott had any previous experience as an organizer, delegate, or speaker. In terms of women's rights, the "chief movers and managers" of the first women's rights convention were all amateurs. As Stanton later summarized their situation in *The History of Woman Suffrage*, they "were neither sour old maids, childless women, nor divorced wives, as the newspapers declared them to be." They were motivated by the insults incident to sex, but "they had not experienced the coarser forms of tyranny resulting from unjust laws, or association with immoral and unscrupulous men." Rather, they had "souls large enough to feel the wrongs of others."[11]

For Martha Coffin Wright, the 1848 event was her first involvement in reform. Mrs. Mott's youngest sibling lived in Auburn, New York. A widow, she had married lawyer David Wright. The mother of seven children, she was noted for her warmth and humor. Mrs. Wright later became an officer of the National Woman Suffrage Association, a constant supporter of women's rights, and an adviser to Elizabeth Cady Stanton and Susan B. Anthony. Having been expelled from the Society of Friends for marrying out of meeting, Mrs. Wright was not a Quaker.[12] Like Stanton, she had little regard for organized religion.

Less is known about Jane Hunt and Mary Ann McClintock, both of whom, like Mrs. Mott, were Hicksite activists who believed that salvation required good works. Jane Master Hunt and her husband Richard lived in a sumptuous mansion in Waterloo, New York.* She was his fourth wife, the mother of three children and stepmother of three more. On the 1850 census her husband listed his occupation as "farmer" and placed his net worth at forty thousand dollars. Richard Hunt owned the Waterloo Woolen Mill and "Hunt's Block" in the commercial district and served as a bank director. According to some sources, it was he who first proposed the women's rights meeting.

Religious, business, and family ties accounted for the Hunts' link to the McClintocks. McClintock's sister Sarah had been Hunt's third wife, and he rented his store from Hunt. Mary Ann and Thomas McClintock lived much more modestly in Waterloo, where he was the druggist and minister of the Hicksite meeting for twenty-five years. The McClintock daughters, Mary Ann and Elizabeth, also attended the Seneca Falls convention and as adults became active suffragists.[13]

The Hicksite Quakers among the organizers had just returned from the yearly meeting a week earlier. The liberal Friends had had difficulty reaching consensus on two issues: how to minister to the Indian remnants in upstate New York and what qualified a member to participate in meetings. The question of equal rights among the Hicksites predisposed them to be responsive to Stanton's outburst.[14]

Having decided to convene a meeting to discuss the position of women, each of the five took an assignment. That same Thursday they convinced the minister of the Wesleyan Methodist Chapel in Seneca Falls to let them use his building, and they arranged for a newspaper announcement of their plans. The next day the *Seneca County Courier* published an unsigned call to a "convention to discuss the social, civil, and religious condition and rights of women," to be held July 19–20. The first day of the meeting, the blurb specified, was reserved "exclusively for women," who were "earnestly invited to attend."[15] The group then agreed to meet the next Sunday to set the agenda, draft a document for discussion and some resolutions, and decide on subjects for speeches.

When the women gathered around Mary Ann McClintock's parlor table, they did not know how to begin.† As Stanton recalled their dilemma in the *History*, "they felt as helpless and hopeless as if they had been suddenly asked to construct a steam engine." To get ideas the women perused

---

* Jane Master Hunt (1812–89) and Richard Hunt (1797–1856) chose to pursue Hicksite reforms rather than women's rights. Nor were Thomas McClintock (1801–76) and his wife Mary Ann prominent after 1848.

† The table, which also stood at the head of Stanton's casket during her funeral, is now on display at the Museum of American History, Smithsonian Institution, Washington, D.C.

"various masculine productions . . . but all alike seemed too tame and pacific for the inauguration of a rebellion." They finally decided to adopt the Declaration of Independence as their model. They substituted "all men" for the tyrant King George. The *History* records that the women had to make a "protracted search" to identify eighteen germane grievances.[16]

Mrs. Stanton prepared their document. It began with a paraphrase: "The history of mankind is a history of repeated injuries and usurpations on the part of man toward woman, having in direct object the establishment of an absolute tyranny over her." Their indictment charged that men had deprived women of legal rights, "profitable" employment opportunities and wages, opportunities in education and the professions, the right to divorce and to custody of their children. Men denied women "equal moral obligations" and undermined their "self-confidence." The first five points raised the suffrage question, demanding for women the "unalienable right to the elective franchise, . . . voting rights which are given to the most ignorant and degraded of men."[17]

Elizabeth Cady Stanton's ability to articulate these accumulated grievances attests to her enlarged empathy for "woman's portion." Although she was better off than most of her neighbors, she sometimes found that she had more in common with them in her daily life than with her own sisters. She could overcome her upper-class biases and ally herself more readily with women of other classes and conditions. Sympathy for other women and the ideals of romantic reform developed in her a republican spirit that coexisted with her tendency to elitism. Like other women, her social and economic status derived from her father and husband. Now she, too, demanded property rights, education, employment, equality under law, and the "sacred right to the elective franchise."

Finally satisfied with the composition, the women titled it "A Declaration of Rights and Sentiments." They borrowed the phrase from Garrison and the covenant of the American Anti-Slavery Association. Indeed, many of the ideas as well as the tactics of the first women's rights convention came from other reform sources. The strategy of meetings, declarations, speakers, and petitions had been established by reformers and revivalists in the 1830s, but the inclusion of economic and social injustices was the result of Mrs. Mott's conviction that every aspect of woman's sphere must be addressed.* Mott nurtured these sentiments in Stanton. Mrs. Stanton contended that few of Mrs. Mott's economic claims for women could be

---

* In a "Discourse on Women" (1849), Lucretia Mott argued that unequal education, wage differentials, job restrictions, and the denial of political rights were responsible for female bondage. She emphasized the connection between economic and political freedom. Equality in the marketplace would result in equality in other spheres.

achieved without the right to vote. In later years Stanton believed that ob-
taining equal employment and educational opportunities, as well as the right
to divorce, were as important and more immediate than suffrage.

The emphasis on political action was Mrs. Stanton's. The wife, daughter, and cousin of politicians and lawyers, she was convinced that social
problems required political solutions. Like the political abolitionists with
whom she was allied, Elizabeth Cady Stanton believed in using government to create legal remedies. Since women without voting rights had no
independent access to political power, she advocated suffrage. The combination of Mott's economic concerns and Stanton's political instincts made
the Declaration a comprehensive document.

Stanton's political philosophy was rooted in the theory of natural rights.
Like the abolitionists, Stanton applied eighteenth-century natural rights
doctrine to nineteenth-century sexual inequality.[18] Introduced to the theories of John Locke by Edward Bayard and Emma Willard, she had found
them useful and attractive. In Stanton's experience the enlightenment emphasis on the individual had been reiterated by the romantic movement and
radical Protestantism, by the revivalists and Theodore Parker. In contrast
to the thinking of most Americans in 1848, Stanton assumed that women
were individuals endowed with natural rights, the same natural rights possessed by American men. Not only did she claim that women naturally
merited equal rights, she also argued that men and women were equal. She
admitted different physical functions but asserted equal mental capacities.
To her, women were not appendages but individuals with independent rights.
Mrs. Stanton's rendering of the natural rights philosophy was evident in
the first three Seneca Falls resolutions:

> Resolved, That such laws as conflict, in any way, with the true and sub-
> stantial happiness of woman, are contrary to the great precept of nature
> and of no validity.

> Resolved, That all laws which prevent woman from occupying such a sta-
> tion in society as her conscience shall dictate, or which place her in a po-
> sition inferior to that of man, are contrary to the great precept of nature,
> and therefore of no force or authority.

> Resolved, That woman is man's equal—was intended to be so by the Cre-
> ator, and the highest good of the race demands that she should be rec-
> ognized as such.

Mrs. Mott, a Garrisonian abolitionist, and the other women had qualms
about the political nature of their Declaration. The older woman advised
against including the suffrage plank. She worried that it would make the
meeting and its sponsors "look ridiculous."[19] But Mott's affection for her

protégé was such that she acquiesced, perhaps expecting the meeting to strike the clause.

Henry Stanton, an anti-Garrisonian, also opposed the suffrage section. He claimed that Elizabeth would turn the proceedings into a "farce." Although he had helped draft some of the resolutions, he refused to attend the meeting and left town, perhaps to protect his own political credibility.[20] Family anecdote also reports that Judge Cady, alerted to her plan, rushed to Seneca Falls to determine her sanity.[21] Rather than allude to these incidents, Stanton implied that all of the husbands had supported their decisions. Three of the men attended the convention and signed the Declaration. Twice during the meeting Stanton insisted that the organizers were addressing general rather than personal questions. Her focus was on legal cases rather than on domestic wrongs. She seemed eager not to embarrass Henry any more than necessary and to avoid any suggestion that she was unhappily married.

Despite the reservations of Henry and Lucretia, the two most influential people in her life, Mrs. Stanton persevered. Having been previously convinced of the legitimacy of political action on behalf of abolition and of the justice of her claims on behalf of women, she was undeterred when others balked. Years later she claimed to have been spurred on by a remark made at a dinner party in Dublin in 1840. Daniel O'Connell, an Irish freedom fighter known as the "Great Liberator," had advised her always to demand more than she expected to get; eventually the outrageous would seem reasonable.[22] When the occasion arose for her to make such a demand, she asked that women be granted the right to vote.

Lucretia Mott had also worried about the turnout. Writing to Mrs. Stanton on July 16, she warned, "The convention will not be so large as it otherwise might be, owing to the busy time with the farmers' harvest." Yet according to one witness, on the morning of Wednesday, July 19, the roads approaching the Wesleyan Chapel were jammed with carriages and carts. When the organizers arrived they found a crowd gathering and the church locked, whether intentionally or inadvertently. Unable to locate a key, Mrs. Stanton had her nephew hoisted through a window.[23] More than a hundred men and women quickly filled the pews. Unsure about how to ask the men to leave, the organizers hastily decided to allow them to remain, even though they had planned to address only women on the first day.

Bold as they thought themselves, the women did not dare to preside over the meeting. As they had previously arranged, James Mott called the first session to order at eleven o'clock.[24] The McClintocks' daughter Mary Ann was appointed secretary, and Mrs. Stanton rose to state the object of the meeting: "We have met here today to discuss our rights and wrongs, civil and political." It was only her second public appearance, and one observer complained that she could hardly be heard.[25] Mrs. Mott urged the women to join freely in the debates. Then the Declaration of Sentiments was read by Stanton, reread paragraph by paragraph, amended and adopted. A lively debate on the propriety of having men sign the document ended in a favorable vote but was referred for reconsideration the next day. The first session adjourned at half past two.

The afternoon meeting was addressed by Mrs. Stanton and Mrs. Mott. The Declaration was read again, and a paper was circulated to obtain signatures. One hundred people signed: sixty-eight women, including Stanton's sister Harriet Cady Eaton, and thirty-two men, including the husbands of Mott, McClintock, and Hunt.[26] Postponing debate and discussion of the eleven resolutions, Mrs. Mott lightened the proceedings by reading a humorous newspaper article written by her sister Martha Wright. After an address by Elizabeth McClintock, the meeting finally adjourned. That evening Mrs. Mott, who was staying overnight at the Stantons', spoke to a larger audience on "The Progress of Reforms."

Promptly at ten o'clock on Thursday, July 20, James Mott called the third session to order. The minutes of the previous day were read, and Mrs. Stanton again read the Declaration. Discussion was animated. Finally the document was unanimously adopted and signed. The afternoon session was devoted to consideration of what the *Seneca County Courier* described as "the spirited and spicey resolutions."[27] Each was read and debated separately. Some elicited little discussion; others aroused heated debate. Partisans objected to such phrases as "corrupt customs" and "a perverted application of the Scriptures." But as the record states, "After some criticism, much debate, and some slight alterations [all] were finally passed by a large majority."

The most controversial was the ninth: "*Resolved,* That it is the duty of the women of this country to secure themselves their sacred right to the elective franchise." According to Mrs. Stanton in the *History,* opponents feared that a demand for voting would undermine the other, less controversial points. With a militant spirit, Stanton made bolder claims.

> Strange as it may seem to many, we now demand our right to vote according to the declaration of the government under which we live. We should not feel so sorely grieved if no man who had not attained the full stature of a Webster, Clay, Van Buren or Gerrit Smith could claim the right of elective franchise. But to have drunkards, idiots, horseracing rum-selling rowdies, ignorant foreigners, and silly boys fully recognized, while we ourselves are thrust out from all the rights that belong to citizens, is too grossly insulting to . . . be longer quietly submitted to. The right is ours. Have it we must. Use it we will. The pens, the tongues, the fortunes,

the indomitable wills of many women are already pledged to secure this right.

This is the first incidence of anti-male rhetoric by Stanton, and she tried to make amends for it later in the day. Despite her eloquence the resolution would not have succeeded without an able, masculine defense. Frederick Douglass, the former slave and publisher of the *North Star*, reiterated Mrs. Stanton's claim "that the power to choose rulers and make laws was the right by which all others could be secured." The resolution barely passed.

The final session was opened at seven Thursday evening by Thomas McClintock. In keeping with the accepted practice at "mixed" meetings— those attended by men and women—none of the five organizers had ever assumed the chair. Mrs. Stanton saw no reason to question the procedure. Neither Mrs. Hunt nor Mrs. Wright was noted as participating in speech or debate. Mr. McClintock called on Mrs. Stanton, who, in an odd turnabout, defended the "lords of creation" against the accusations she had leveled at them in the rhetoric of the Declaration, resolutions, and debate. Perhaps surprised by the vigor of her attack on male voters and eager to appear fair minded, Mrs. Stanton played devil's advocate. Unfortunately, no copy of her remarks remains.

Then Mr. McClintock read extracts from Blackstone's interpretation of women's status in English common law, and Mrs. Mott offered one more resolution: "*Resolved,* That the speedy success of our cause depends upon the zealous and untiring efforts of both men and women, for the overthrow of the monopoly of the pulpit, and for the securing to woman of equal participation with men in the various trades, professions, and commerce." The resolution was adopted. The McClintocks' daughter Mary Ann and Frederick Douglass made short speeches before the meeting closed with an hour-long appeal by Mrs. Mott. When the meeting finally adjourned, members of the audience had sat through eighteen hours of discussion. Their attention may have been indicative of the quality of the rhetoric, the general interest in reform, their practice in pews, or the curiosity of the spectacle.

In its report of the event the next day, the *Seneca County Courier* observed:

> This convention was novel in its character and the doctrines broached in it are startling to those who are wedded to the present usages and laws of society. The resolutions are of the kind called radical. Some of the speeches were very able—all the exercises were marked by great order and decorum. When the Declaration of Sentiments and Rights *[sic]* shall be printed and circulated, they will provoke much remark. Some will regard them with respect—others with disapprobation and contempt.

As the local paper predicted, when accounts of the meeting spread, they generated a critical response. Newspapers, as quasi-political organs, presented the case of the major parties: women were unfit for citizenship. Church leaders were equally offended by such unseemly demands and untraditional behavior. Conservative citizens rushed to defend traditional womanhood. The *Philadelphia Public Ledger and Daily Transcript* asserted that no lady would endorse voting rights. "A woman is nobody. A wife is everything. A pretty girl is equal to ten thousand men, and a mother is, next to God, all powerful. . . . The ladies of Philadelphia, therefore, under the influence of the most serious, sober second thoughts, are resolved to maintain their rights as Wives, Belles, Virgins and Mothers, and not as Women." In the *New York Herald,* editor George Gordon Bennett was equally sarcastic, charging that the Declaration was defective because women asked only to be doctors and ministers, not soldiers, sailors, or merchants.[28]

Very few newspapers cheered the effort. The *North Star,* edited by Frederick Douglass, argued that there was no reason to deny women the vote because "right is of no sex." The *Liberator,* edited by Garrison, used the appropriate headline, "Woman's Revolution." One of the few major papers to treat the question seriously was the *New York Tribune,* in which Horace Greeley found the demand unseemly but not unjust. "It is easy to be smart, to be droll, to be facetious in opposition to the demands of these Female Reformers; and in decrying assumptions so novel and opposed to established habits and usages, a little wit will go a great way. . . . However unwise and mistaken the demand, it is but the assertion of a natural right and as such must be conceded."[29]

Although the organizers had hoped to provoke public interest, the intensely negative response surprised them. They were caricatured as sexless old maids and radical heretics and branded as different from the majority of women. They were annoyed, offended, and put on the defensive by the misrepresentations of their critics. But as Mrs. Stanton shrewdly recognized, any publication of their demands was helpful. "There is no danger of the Woman Question dying for want of notice," she wrote to an offending editor. To Mrs. Mott she exclaimed: "Imagine the publicity given to our ideas by thus appearing in a widely circulated sheet like the *Herald.* It will start women thinking, and men, too, and when men and women think about a new question, the first step in progress is taken. The great fault of mankind is that it will not think."[30]

To assure that newspaper readers learned both sides of the argument, Mrs. Stanton wrote replies to negative editorials. A letter to the editor of the *Rochester National Reformer* refuted the doctrine of separate spheres as applied to political rights.

If God has assigned a sphere to man and one to woman, we claim the right ourselves to judge His design in reference to us, and we accord to man the same privilege. We think that a man has quite enough to do to find out his own individual calling, without being taxed to find out also where every woman belongs. . . . There is no such thing as a sphere for sex. Every man has a different sphere, in which he may or may not shine, and it is the same with every woman, and the same woman may have a different sphere at different times.[31]

Stanton had learned from observing Mrs. Mott that women could move from the kitchen to a pulpit to the nursery to a desk. The public and private events in Seneca Falls had helped her to extend and expand her own sphere. In addition to serving as an early indicator of the direction of Stanton's political philosophy, the Declaration of Sentiments asserted her own equality and independence.

So far Mrs. Stanton's ideas were much more radical than her actions. Two weeks after the Seneca Falls meeting, a second women's rights convention was held in the Unitarian church in Rochester. Without reliable help at home, Mrs. Stanton was apprehensive about attending a meeting out of town, but she did go. So did Mott, Mrs. McClintock, several Seneca Falls signers, and many others, including Susan B. Anthony's parents and sister Mary. The meeting was organized by Amy Post, a Quaker, abolitionist, and signer of the Declaration of Sentiments. She nominated Elizabeth McClintock as secretary and invited Mrs. Stanton to read the Declaration and to report on the salaries of household servants, a subject with which she was well acquainted. The resolution advocating suffrage was read and reintroduced in Rochester, as it would be at every successive women's rights convention. But when Mrs. Post urged that a woman named Abigail Bush be made the presiding officer, Mrs. Stanton objected. Stanton thought that breaking the precedent of male chairmen was "a hazardous experiment" and said so. But the majority of the large audience favored Mrs. Bush, and she took the gavel. Writing to Amy Post the next month, Mrs. Stanton admitted her chagrin. "I have so often regretted my foolish conduct," she said. "My only excuse is that woman has been so little accustomed to act in a public capacity that she does not always know what is due."[32] Stanton's action may have reflected her own lack of confidence. She was still defining her own public role and had not yet risked presiding at a meeting.

The organizers of Seneca Falls were equally unsure of what direction to follow. No definite strategy had been discussed or decided upon. The women pursued several courses at once. Some continued to organize meetings. Women in Ohio and Massachusetts soon followed the Seneca Falls pattern and expanded on the idea to hold national meetings of state delegates. Others advanced the cause less publicly. Unable to travel far from home, Mrs. Stanton wrote articles for newspapers, letters to other conventions, and private notes to friends to arouse them to action on behalf of women's rights. In September 1848 she asked Amy Post, "What are we next to do?" In answering her own question, Stanton suggested a simultaneous petition effort in several states, organized by a paid women's rights agent, but no agent was engaged and only sporadic petitioning was undertaken.[33] It would be twenty years before the effort begun at Seneca Falls would mature into a national organization, and seventy-two years before it would achieve success in the Nineteenth Amendment.

Yet the Seneca Falls convention was a personal success for Elizabeth Cady Stanton. The meeting and its Declaration had legitimized her complaints. It had challenged her to outline remedies. It had coalesced her thinking in terms of the equal capabilities of men and women and their natural rights. It had put Elizabeth Cady Stanton in the vanguard of the women's rights movement. As Lucretia Mott advised her shortly after the convention, "Thou art so wedded to this cause that thou must expect to act as pioneer in the work."[34]

Most important, the Seneca Falls convention had given Stanton an opportunity to perform as a feminist reformer. She had earned the praise of people she admired. Their approval enabled her to ignore the critics and to continue as an advocate for women's rights. Convinced of the truth and justice of her claims and confident of the acceptance of her female friends, she was not stopped by the opposition of press, pulpit, parents, or husband. "The opportunity of expressing myself fully and freely on a subject I felt so deeply about was a great relief," she recalled in her autobiography. As one of her children later commented, the meeting "cleared her mind."[35]

Stanton's response to the discontent she suffered in Seneca Falls set a pattern for future performance. Anguish turned to anger, which fired analysis, on which she took action. Her well-trained mind was able to dissect the causes of her discontent and to extrapolate from an individual complaint to a general problem. As she gained confidence as a speaker and writer, she would address these questions and present her solutions to larger and wider audiences.

Stanton realized that the issue was broader than the difficulties of individual women in isolated households, that it related to the status of women in American society. Women were placed in a subordinate position by custom and circumstance, and women acquiesced in their subordination. But not Elizabeth Cady Stanton. As Stanton acknowledged in retrospect, sharing the experience of dependent, passive, overworked women in an isolated upstate village brought home to her the reality of inequality in the lives of most women. Because she suffered some of these same hardships and observed others, she advanced along her feminist course.

Yet nothing had changed in her everyday existence as wife, mother, and homemaker. Indeed, as a result of the convention, Mrs. Stanton had taken on new responsiblilities without diminishing or delegating those domestic duties that had initially provoked her to act. But she had found a new source of stimulation. Feminism and her new female friends filled the gap left by the loss of her Boston social circle. Enthusiastic about her cause, she was more tolerant of household chores. In addition to child care and house-keeping, she was now occupied with writing and thinking about women's rights. As she said at the Rochester meeting in urging women to have in-dividual political rights: "Woman herself must do this work—for woman alone can understand the height, and the depth, the length and the breadth of her own degradation and woe. Man cannot speak for us—because he has been educated to believe that we differ from him so materially that he cannot judge of our thoughts, feelings, and opinions on his own."[36]

5
Bonds of Affection
1849–55

The Seneca Falls meeting marked the formal beginning of the women's rights movement in America and the informal beginning of Elizabeth Cady Stanton's career as a feminist leader. Yet, as the women's movement developed during the next decade, Mrs. Stanton was not among its most visible or outspoken leaders. The momentum for subsequent meetings came from others. Stanton did not take the initiative, and she rarely accepted invitations to participate. In the fall of 1848 Lucretia Mott invited Stanton to Philadelphia to help organize a women's rights meeting there. Stanton could not go that year, or any other.[1] In the years following her Seneca Falls Declaration, Mrs. Stanton remained, by circumstance and choice, a small-town housewife.

Nevertheless Stanton was filled with enthusiasm for the endeavor, and she did the most that she could at the moment. She began in small ways, by writing letters to editors and to friends. She responded to requests for her presence with letters to be read in her absence. She continued to read and study and reflect and write, so that she was always a source of new ideas, ideas that enlarged the scope of the women's movement from female suffrage to equal rights.

The challenge for Elizabeth Cady Stanton in the decade following the Seneca Falls convention was to find a way to meet the increased demands of her private and public lives. In this quest she was without a role model. No one in her acquaintance had combined mothering small children with nurturing social revolution. Lucretia Mott, Stanton's mother, and Gerrit Smith's wife had large household staffs or relatives to free them for community projects. Emma Willard, a widow with only one son, boarded at the seminary she founded. Only Mott traveled as widely as Stanton might aspire to. Among women in Stanton's age group, Angelina Grimké Weld had abandoned her reform work completely following marriage and maternity. The most active women had husbands who shared the same commitment to the same reform and few or no children.[2]

Like other housewives, Stanton was in charge of the shopping, cooking, preserving, sewing, schooling, and healing. She maintained high standards of housekeeping, entertained frequent guests, and became an active citizen of Seneca Falls, when she had time. When the children were ill or when she was nursing an infant, she had to curtail her activities and lower her standards of neatness. She was pummeled by the approval and disapproval of those dear to her, by their expectations, and her own ambitions. The tensions created by her unsuccessful but ongoing efforts to combine public and private roles characterized her residence in Seneca Falls.

Stanton's development during the two decades following the 1848 meeting parallels the organizational maturation of the first women's movement. Throughout the 1850s the movement was undefined and leaderless. While the younger women considered Lucretia Mott their leader, Mott refused to take over. With the exception of 1857, national meetings of delegates representing local groups were held annually from 1850 to 1861. A changing ad hoc executive committee struggled with financial crises and organizational problems. Women were a small contingent of American reformers, and, like the men, they spread their energies among various reforms—temperance, prostitution, foreign missions, abolition. As the conflict over slavery came to dominate antebellum politics, many of these women and men were diverted into antislavery activities. Finally the Civil War brought an end to women's rights meetings altogether. By the time women's rights advocates and organizations were able to reassert their claims, in 1865, Elizabeth Cady Stanton was ready to return to prominence.

It was more than two years after the 1848 meeting before Mrs. Stanton began to feel the strain of competing public and private roles. The anger and isolation that had provoked her participation in the first women's rights convention had been dissipated once she had expressed it in the demands of the Declaration of Sentiments. Having vented her frustration and voiced her protest, she regained her equanimity. As she later reflected in her autobiography, "With these new duties and interests, and a broader outlook on human life, my petty domestic annoyances gradually took a subordinate place,"[3] at least temporarily.

In addition to maintaining a wide-ranging correspondence, Stanton began to write anonymous articles for reform journals. One of these was published by her neighbor, Amelia Bloomer.* Mrs. Bloomer was the deputy postmaster of Seneca Falls, having been appointed by her husband, the postmaster and editor of the *Courier*. Her six-page monthly magazine, the *Lily*, first issued in January 1849, was a temperance organ.[4] Under the pseudonym "Sunflower," Stanton's first entry appeared a few months later. The piece, called "Henry Neil and His Mother," was an imaginary conversation between a mother and son on the evils of drink. By January 1850 "Sunflower" was a regular byline. Soon after, Mrs. Stanton was signing her own initials to articles such as "Why Women Must Vote" and "Lowell Girls." Stanton's pithy entries poked fun at what she called the "foibles and false traditions" that subordinated women. She was exploring ways to promote women's rights. These small steps ended her intellectual isolation, enhanced her self-confidence, prepared her for larger roles, and laid the groundwork for the growth of a women's rights movement.

When the Stantons celebrated their tenth anniversary in May 1850, they were both quite content. Elizabeth was satisfied with her domestic arrangements and the development of her three sons. She was engaged intellectually by women's rights questions and sustained by her correspondence with other feminists. Henry, ever handsome and charming, had been home for more than six months in 1849, a period longer than any in the coming decade. He reported to Gerrit Smith that he was busy gardening and grafting fruit trees for the two-acre orchard they had planted behind the house.[5] Henry had acquired more legal clients and had reissued the essays written on their European trip as *Sketches of Reforms* (1849). The work was favorably reviewed but accrued few profits.

Henry was also pleased with his political prospects. The same issue of the *Courier* that had reported on the Seneca Falls meeting carried the announcement that Henry B. Stanton had been chosen as a delegate to the New York Free Soil Convention.[6] Following the defeat of the Free Soil ticket, Henry changed parties for a third time and joined his fourth party. In the fall of 1849 he ran for the state Senate as a Democrat. He won his first election and began a two-year term. Even as a freshman member of the minority party, Henry distinguished himself. He was viewed as a politician of promise, if not principle, and was invited to address college commencements. He delighted in the intrigue and cronyism of Albany's cloakrooms, and his three-hundred-dollar Senate salary, added to legal fees and royalties, provided a comfortable income. But the couple's mutual satisfaction

* Amelia Jenks Bloomer (1818–94), born in Horner, N.Y., was a teacher before she married Dexter Bloomer in 1840 (without the word "obey"). In 1853 she moved to Ohio and in 1856 sold the *Lily*. After doing relief work during the Civil War, she became president of the Iowa Woman Suffrage Society and helped enact married women's property rights there.

would not survive the pressures of abolition politics and additional pregnancies.

Because efforts on behalf of suffrage and women's rights were still local and unorganized, Mrs. Stanton had no position and no assignments. The public criticism aroused by the Seneca Falls and Rochester meetings and the interest generated by the Free Soil election of 1848 temporarily distracted women's rights advocates and their allies. There was a delay before similar meetings were called in other places. The next was held almost two years later, in April 1850 in Salem, Ohio. Mrs. Stanton sent a letter to be read at the opening session.[7]

That same spring an American Anti-Slavery Convention in Boston closed with an announcement that those interested in having a women's rights convention meet in the lobby. Nine female abolitionists gathered, among them Lucy Stone, a recent graduate of Oberlin; Abby Kelley Foster, one of the first women lecturers; Paulina Wright Davis, a wealthy reformer; and Harriot Hunt, a self-educated doctor. These women formed a committee of correspondence and issued a call for a meeting to be held in Worcester, Massachusetts, on October 23, 1850. The call was signed by eighty-nine sponsors from six states, among them Elizabeth Cady Stanton and Henry B. Stanton.[8]

Over a thousand people attended the Worcester meeting. Mrs. Stanton, several months pregnant with her fourth child, intended to go but declined. Her letter to the convention outlined goals and set the agenda. She was appointed to the Central Committee, the Education Committee, and the Committee of Civil and Political Functions. The convention decided to collect suffrage petitions to present to eight state legislatures and put Mrs. Stanton in charge of western New York.[9] After that, each "national" convention held during the 1850s opened with a letter written by Elizabeth Cady Stanton.

Mrs. Stanton did not attend a national women's rights meeting until 1860. The discipline of the three older boys and the nurture of the four children she bore in the 1850s hampered her ability to travel and limited her participation in public life. But when she became pregnant in 1850, she did not anticipate that additional children would create conflicts for her. She apparently did nothing to prevent the pregnancies.

Stanton's later writings are ambivalent on the subject of birth control. Some indicate that she was ignorant of contemporary methods of contraception; others indicate that she was aware and approved of birth control, but did not practice it. During the early 1850s Elizabeth and Henry Stanton were still passionately attracted to each other and saw no reason to limit intercourse, although Stanton's refusal to vow to "obey" Henry at her marriage was assumed to mean that she might refuse if she chose. Their seven children were born over a seventeen-year span, on the average of one baby every two and a half years. When Henry was home for any period of time and if she was not breastfeeding, she became pregnant. Nor was she inhibited by the fear or pain of childbirth, which she rarely admitted. Rather, in contrast to her mother's constant, incapacitating confinements, Stanton reveled in her ability to bear children naturally and easily, usually assisted only by a midwife or female friend. Compared to her mother's eleven live births and possible miscarriages, Stanton produced a small family.

On February 10, 1851, Theodore Weld Stanton was born. To announce his arrival, his mother hung out a red flag; had he been a girl, the flag would have been white. Stanton had hoped for a daughter and was consoled by a humorous note from a neighbor: "Mrs. Stanton will please accept a bottle of temperance wine and drink to better luck next time." As Stanton reported the next day to her cousin Libby Miller:

> Laugh in your turn. I have actually got my fourth son! Yes, Theodore Stanton, after two long mighty flourishes of his royal crown, bounded upon the stage of life with great ease—comparatively!! He weighs 10½ pounds. I was sick but a few hours, and did not lie down until half an hour before he was born, but worked round as hard as I could all night to do the last things. At seven o'clock Sunday morning he was born. This morning I got up, bathed myself in cold water, and have sat by the table writing several letters.

"I am regarded as a perfect wonder," she boasted to Henry, who was in Albany. "Many people are actually impatiently waiting for me to die in order to make their theories good." She did have to postpone a trip to Albany to present the suffrage petitions she had collected. "Tell [your friends] they have one more year to live, as I shall not be there to annihilate them this season." [10] Nursing baby Theo, and then another baby, would delay her Albany appearance several seasons.

Henry was unable to come home to inspect his fourth son because of the press of state Senate business. The week Theodore was born, Henry had been caught in "a violent flareup" over the choice of a new United States senator. As a Democratic convert and a former Whig with third party and abolition ties, Henry was a pivotal figure in a body divided seventeen Whigs to fifteen Democrats. In recognition of his wife's political interest and his own self-importance, Henry reported every debate and roll call and enclosed copies of proposed bills for her to read. As promised, he had presented the women's rights petitions from western New York that she had collected. "Two Senators tried to throw ridicule upon them," Henry related. "I pounced upon them and they backed out." [11]

The next fight came over a Whig bill to enlarge the Erie Canal. The

Democrats viewed it as unnecessary and graft ridden, but it passed the House easily. To prevent the presence of the three-fifths quorum necessary to introduce the canal bill and so forestall its easy passage in the Senate, twelve members resigned, among them Henry Stanton. To fill the vacancies, a special election was ordered for May 28, 1851. The six senators whose districts were far away from the canal were successful. Of the six whose constituencies lay along the canal, only Henry Stanton was reelected. His margin was five votes. It was a "savage fight," Stanton recalled, in which the stump speakers in the field against him had been marshaled by his friend and relative Gerrit Smith.[12]

Henry Stanton's victory was so narrow that many supporters thought he had lost and sent him notes of condolence. His in-laws celebrated his defeat prematurely. Elizabeth Cady Stanton responded to these attacks with heat, writing to Libby Smith Miller:

> I have just received a letter from your father rejoicing over the supposed defeat of my husband last week Tuesday. We have had a crowing letter from Papa also. But he and Cousin Gerrit have "gone off" too soon. . . . I rejoice in the victory with my whole soul, for in spite of all my seeming liberality towards his opposers, I would sooner see every relative and friend I have on the face of the earth blown into thin air, and that old ditch running from Buffalo to Albany filled in with mud, than have had Henry mortified by a defeat in this election.

Three weeks later the canal bill passed the reconstituted Senate, twenty-two to eight. A year later, the State Court of Appeals found the bill unconstitutional.[13]

Henry's shrewdness and nerve had earned him new celebrity and the gratitude of New York Democrats. They were prepared to offer him the nomination for lieutenant governor in 1852. Henry rejected the offer and refused to run for reelection in the fall of 1851. As he self-righteously phrased it in his autobiography, "I could not afford to be a member, and I had no desire to support myself on the 'drippings of unclean legislation.' " He admitted to Charles Sumner, the Massachusetts abolitionist, that he had won the special election at the cost of neglecting his clients and family. Without steady legal fees he could not support his expanding household, and without his authority his older sons were creating havoc at home. Even Judge Cady felt constrained to remind his son-in-law of his paternal responsibilities. He warned Henry that he should not jeopardize domestic harmony in pursuit of public praise.[14]

The boys in question were hellions. In 1851 Daniel (Neil) was nine and almost as tall as his petite mother. His younger brother Henry (Kit) was seven and had a reputation for inventing both pranks and excuses. The smallest of the trio, Gerrit (Gat), was five and more manageable. All three were full of energy and mischief. Stanton referred to them as her "young savages." They were guilty of many misdemeanors that required swift justice or quick rescues. They leapt from rooftops and broke legs, slid down the lightning rod and cut hands, threw stones at Seneca Falls' shantytown residents, cursed, smoked, and drank. Once Neil shot an arrow into Gat's eye and locked Kit in the smokehouse. Another time Kit stranded baby Theo on a cork raft in the river; the next day he put the baby on top of the chimney.[15] It was no coincidence that Mrs. Stanton's first temperance article had been addressed to an imaginary delinquent named "Henry Neil."

Elizabeth Cady Stanton was a permissive parent. Although she claimed to have had a strict upbringing, her parents alternated between punishment and indulgence. Rather than reject her parents' pattern, she may have expanded upon it. Her children were not required to attend church. Occasionally she took them to the local Episcopal service because she enjoyed the music and the boys were fascinated by the minister's "nightgown." When he was home, Henry went to the Presbyterian church by himself. She refused to wake the children in the morning, believing that they should motivate themselves. When Theo was reluctant to practice the piano, she asked him to "be reasonable" and consider the benefits of self-discipline. She tried to distract or bribe the boys into good behavior. One of Henry's nephews recalled an incident in which Neil was promised an orange by his mother if he would return a toy to a younger brother. In Henry's absence Grandfather Cady alternated between threats of canings and promises of ponies.[16] Without a consistent approach and without their father's authority, the children's discipline deteriorated.

Preoccupied with the new baby, Elizabeth was unable to supervise the boys adequately. Initially dissatisfied with the schools in Seneca Falls, she had taught her children at home. Now she and Henry decided to send them away to school. In January 1852 the Stantons enrolled Neil and Kit in a progressive, coeducational boarding school established by Theodore and Angelina Grimké Weld. The Grimké-Welds were no longer active abolitionists. Impoverished, they had begun teaching in Belleville, New Jersey, and moved their school to a utopian community in Raritan. Gerrit Smith, Libby Miller, and Martha Wright also sent children there. The Welds found the Stanton boys, whom their parents candidly described as "miserable little underdeveloped vandals," difficult to handle. When the boys outgrew the Welds' school, they were entered in one closer to home, in Geneva, New York.[17]

At first the boys were homesick, and Elizabeth missed them as well. She wrote them frequently, closing her funny, affectionate letters, "a thousand kisses." Henry also wrote regularly, praising their progress, correcting their grammar, commenting on current events, preaching the standard virtues, and enclosing their allowance—sixty cents for Neil, forty cents for Kit. "Don't spend it for candy, tobacco or segars," he admonished, only half joking.[18]

Elizabeth admitted her inability to manage the boys, but she blamed it on the demands of the new babies rather than a flawed philosophy of child raising. With the exception of Neil, who remained a scoundrel—and her pet—his whole life, Stanton's children responded positively to her experiments in child raising. Based on her reading of Andrew Combe's book on child care and her own common sense, Stanton had abandoned many practices then accepted in America. She refused to allow her infants to be swaddled tightly and insisted that they be given water to drink, daily baths, fresh air, and sunshine. It was sometimes difficult to find servants who would carry out her edicts, so her caretaking chores increased. As she reported to Cousin Lib: "My baby [Theo] is very good and grows finely. I continue to be his wet as well as his dry nurse. It is easier to look after him myself than to train an ignorant girl to do so. I have invented a variety of ways to keep him quiet—that is, ways for him to keep himself quiet."[19]

Stanton was an affectionate, attentive, and demonstrative mother, always ready to join in games and songs. She welcomed neighborhood children, offering cake and milk, or, if the pantry was bare, "the grape arbor and the pump." She initiated a committee to improve the schools in Seneca Falls and organized a coeducational gymnasium for the older children. She encouraged independence and self-reliance in her offspring. In a letter to James Birney's wife she discussed her philosophy of child care.

> You say the baby wants to climb up stairs. Of course she does; nature wants another set of muscles brought into play. You must teach her how to go up and down with safety, how to take hold of the banisters. If you take very little pains, she will be delighted with her achievement. Most people try to fence off stairs and make children afraid of going up and down; then they are sure to fall. We must inspire them with confidence in themselves and show them how to do what they desire.[20]

Stanton's innovations in child care carried over into family health care. She and Henry had abandoned vegetarianism, added meat and butter to the menus, and on occasion drank wine. Skeptical of medical authorities, she continued to practice homeopathy. Sometime after Neil was born, perhaps during his birth, his shoulder had been dislocated. The two doctors Stanton consulted set it in restrictive bandages. The new mother's common sense dictated different treatment. So, as she told Henry, "with my usual conceit I removed [the bandages] . . . and turned surgeon myself." She designed a less confining sling and the shoulder healed. Previously encouraged by Edward Bayard to distrust "scientific quacks," she refused to be intimidated by masculine medical authority. With Elizabeth's home remedies the children survived malaria, whooping cough, mumps, and broken limbs, but she always worried. The only times she asked Henry to come home were when a child was sick.[21] Her remedies were famous in the neighborhood, and she was frequently called upon to serve as nurse or midwife. Henry's health improved with his political prospects; he was ill only following defeats.

With the exception of the difficulties of her last pregnancy and slow recovery in 1859, Mrs. Stanton enjoyed robust good health. Photographs from this period show her plump and vivacious, if sometimes a little haggard. One neighbor described her as "a handsome woman, with a most attractive face, winning smile and cordial manner, which instinctively won confidence." She enjoyed cooking and eating. Exercise included chasing the boys, cleaning, walking two miles before breakfast, and horseback riding. As she humorously reported to Libby Miller in 1853, she was thriving and would probably

> remain here to suffer and struggle for about half a century longer—barring accidents and God being willing. That is to say, it appears that my machinery is capable of running a long time. Of course, I may burst my boiler screaming to boys to come out of the cherry trees and to stop throwing stones, or explode from accumulated steam of a moral kind that I dare not let off, or be hung for breaking the pate of some stupid Hibernian for burning my meat or pudding on some company occasion. My babies, the boys and the Irish girls, as well as the generally unsettled condition of the moral, religious and political world, are enough to fret the pieces of the best constructed machinery.[22]

All of her relatives lived a long time, so Stanton's expectations of longevity were realistic.

Removal of the two older troublemakers and the addition of a housekeeper created temporary tranquillity at 32 Washington Street in 1852. Amelia Willard had joined their household in August 1851. A Quaker from Michigan, unrelated to Emma Willard, she stayed for thirty years. As Theodore Stanton would recall as an adult, Willard was his mother's "maid, cook, nurse, serving woman, housekeeper, and confidante." Stanton appreciated her good fortune, concluding in her autobiography, "But for this noble, self-sacrificing woman, much of my public work would have been quite impossible." Stanton described their peaceful domestic routine to her absent sons: "The boys are upstairs in bed and asleep. I sit in the dining room alone; Father has gone down to town to get the mail; and Amelia is in the kitchen mixing bread."[23]

As a middle-class matron, Stanton had the resources to find solutions to her domestic problems. When necessary, Amelia was aided by servant girls recruited from Seneca Falls' immigrant Irish. Mrs. Stanton invariably found them inadequate, untrained, and unreliable. When worse came to worst, another boy was sent to boarding school or she escaped to Johnstown to be pampered by her parents. On several occasions during the 1850s, usually when one or more of the children were seriously ill, she boarded up the house and went to the Cadys for four to eight weeks at a time.[24] Unable to afford the luxuries of her youth on Henry's income, Elizabeth accepted her mother's hospitality and the ministrations of family servants. While Stanton frequently disdained "ladies of fashion in bare-shouldered ballgowns," she enjoyed upper-class comforts. She liked to be taken care of. She had learned from her mother and Mrs. Mott to be good to herself. She liked to eat, rest, and dress well. She did not always have enough money for luxuries; she spent the resources she had first on servants, books, clothes, and lessons for the children, considering them necessities.

Mrs. Stanton's adoption of the bloomer costume in early 1851 was another attempt to make housekeeping easier and safer, as well as to protest "woman's clothes prison." The outfit consisted of long pants worn under a knee-length full skirt. It was created by Stanton's cousin, Libby Smith Miller, who arrived in Seneca Falls wearing "the shorts" in the winter of 1851. Mrs. Stanton, eight months pregnant with Theodore, immediately adopted an unsashed version of the outfit. She loved its practicality. It allowed her to climb stairs with her hands free to carry both a baby and a candle. Still enthusiastic two years later, she wrote its designer: "This dress makes it easier to do all these things—running from cradle to writing desk, from kitchen to drawing room, singing lullabies at one moment in the nursery and dear old Tom Moore's ditties the next moment on the piano stool. If I had long skirts, how could I accomplish all this?"[25] Soon her housekeeper, neighbors, and friends were wearing the outfit. It was called the "Turkish dress" until Amelia Bloomer published a sketch of it in the *Lily* in June 1852. She was besieged with requests for its pattern, which she printed in her newspaper. Circulation soared, and the outfit came to be known as the "bloomers."

Typically, Mrs. Stanton moved quickly from accepting the practicality of the short dress to advocating dress reform as a tenet in her feminist philosophy. She made the connection between the freedom of movement allowed by the bloomers and the movement to free women from other traditional constraints. She argued that custom had designed women's clothes to appeal to male passion rather than female necessity. Dependent on men for social status and financial support, women needed to be attractive and ornamental. Wearing five yards of skirt, plus hoops, petticoats, and corsets pleased men but kept women from moving easily, breathing comfortably, or engaging in healthy exercise. "Every vital organ is somewhat displaced by whale bone corsets," Stanton complained, and stopped wearing hers.

Hems dragged in muddy streets promoted disease and increased the time required to care for one's wardrobe. Because it was less time consuming, Stanton also favored short hair, although she was vain enough to insist on curls for herself. By adopting the bloomer style and advertising its convenience, Stanton hoped to set an example that would be widely copied. She urged that the outfit be made of "the richest materials, not gaudy, but . . . tasteful." She even had a short white ballgown made for dancing in Albany.[26]

The outfit suffered from design flaws, however. It was poorly proportioned and difficult to sit in, showing more pant leg than was considered proper. Its seeming immodesty undermined its popular appeal. Even Libby Miller found it awkward and uncouth. Stanton reported that her dress was "subject to the severest animadversions." Her father refused at first to invite her to Johnstown, and her sons begged her not to visit them at school "in costume." Henry did not oppose her wearing the bloomers, but he teased her about exposing her limbs to public scrutiny. He did not flinch when she wore the long pants throughout the special election campaign. Indeed, her costume became an election issue. "Some good Democrats said they would not vote for a man whose wife wore the Bloomers," Stanton reported to Libby Miller. Street urchins threw stones and "hissed and sung and screamed 'Breeches!' "[27]

Such opposition at first made Mrs. Stanton more stubborn, but she was surprised by its persistence. "How long will the heathen rage?" she wondered to Libby Miller. She worried that the controversy over dress would distract the public from other demands on behalf of women's rights, but she did not think the dress reformers could retreat. "Had I counted the cost of the short dress," she confessed, "I would never have put it on; however, I'll never take it off for now it involves a principle of freedom." Three months later she was drawing a parallel between the dilemma of the dress reformers and Aesop's fox, who, having cut off his tail, then tried to convince the other foxes to do likewise. "We can have no peace . . . until we cut off the great national petticoat." After two years of incessant ridicule, Mrs. Stanton stopped wearing the bloomers in public and urged other converts to "put down their hems" as well. Stanton continued to wear the short dress at home and to promote dress reform in public, but less urgently. Mrs. Miller wore a more graceful, ankle-length version of the dress for seven years; Mrs. Bloomer wore hers for eight. As Stanton concluded, "Such is the tyranny of custom, that to escape constant observation, criticism, ridicule, persecution, [and] mobs, one after another went back to the old slavery and sacrificed freedom to repose."[28]

Elizabeth Cady Stanton was wearing bloomers on the day she was introduced to Susan B. Anthony, one spring evening in March 1851. En route to a temperance meeting, Miss Anthony was in Seneca Falls as the house guest of Amelia Bloomer. Although Mrs. Stanton typically confused the date, she vividly recalled the event.

> How well I remember the day! George Thompson and William Lloyd Garrison having announced an anti-slavery meeting in Seneca Falls, Miss Anthony came to attend it. These gentlemen were my guests. Walking home after the adjournment, we met Mrs. Bloomer and Miss Anthony, on the corner of the street, waiting to greet us. There she stood, with her good earnest face and genial smile, dressed in gray delaine, hat and all the same color, relieved with pale blue ribbons, the perfection of neatness and sobriety. I liked her thoroughly, and why I did not at once invite her home with me to dinner I do not know. She accuses me of that neglect, and has never forgiven me.[29]

So began a friendship that endured for fifty years.

Susan Anthony had heard of Elizabeth Cady Stanton before they met. Her parents and sister Mary had attended the Rochester women's rights meeting in August 1848, at which Mrs. Stanton had read the Declaration of Sentiments. Like many other female reformers, Anthony was initially more interested in temperance and abolition, yet her curiosity about women's rights had been aroused.

The descendant of a long line of Quakers, Susan Brownell Anthony was not unfamiliar with the tenets of female equality. Her father, Daniel Anthony, a cotton mill owner in Adams, Massachusetts, had married out of meeting but raised his children as Hicksite Quakers. Born February 15, 1820, Susan was the second of eight children. Surviving near bankruptcy following the panic of 1837, the Anthony family resorted to farming in upstate New York. An uncle had taken control of Mrs. Anthony's property to protect it from her husband's creditors. To supplement their income, Susan Anthony became a teacher, earning one-fourth of what male teachers were paid. In 1849 she resigned as head of the female department of the Canajoharie Academy. When her father succeeded in the insurance business, Anthony took over management of the family farm near Rochester and joined several local reform groups.[30] Such experiences prepared her for a career as a feminist advocate, but until she met Stanton, Anthony had had no direction or inspiration.

Stanton saw in Anthony a bright, energetic, available recruit. Unmarried and unattractive, on account of a bad eye, Anthony had fewer domestic duties to keep her from public activity.[31] Stanton promptly enlisted Anthony and began to impose on her.

> Oh, Susan! Susan! Susan! You must manage to spend a week with me before the Rochester [Woman's State Temperance] Convention, for I am afraid I cannot attend it; I have so much care with all these boys on my hands. But I will write a letter. How much I do long to be free from

housekeeping and children, so as to have some time to read and think and write. But it may be well for me to understand all the trials of woman's lot, that I may more eloquently proclaim them when the time comes.[32]

Anthony came, and the alliance was sealed.

The Stanton-Anthony affiliation was mutually beneficial. In the beginning Stanton provided the ideas, rhetoric, and strategy; Anthony delivered the speeches, circulated petitions, and rented the halls. Anthony prodded and Stanton produced. Each woman sustained the other. Assuming the role of older mentor, Stanton advised Anthony on how to improve her public speaking and how to handle hecklers ("be good natured and remain cool.")[33] When Stanton was overwhelmed with public and private demands, Anthony installed herself in Seneca Falls, supervised the children, and "stirred the puddings" while Stanton wrote without interruption at the dining room table. One of the children's earliest recollections was "the tableau of Mother and Susan seated by a large table covered with books and papers, always talking about the Constitution." According to Henry Stanton, Susan stirred the puddings, Elizabeth stirred up Susan, and then Susan "stirs up the world!" Or as Mrs. Stanton put it, "I forged the thunderbolts, she fired them."[34]

Stanton could admit to Anthony her frustration at not being more active. Ironically, it was Anthony's demands for more speeches and tracts that increased the pressure on Stanton to expand her public role, and it was Anthony's freedom to travel that intensified Stanton's discontent with staying at home. Stanton was dependent on Anthony as her primary liaison with women's rights activity; Anthony was dependent on Stanton for ideas and philosophic substance. At the same time, Anthony was an outlet for the discontent she helped to engender in Stanton.

Like many female friends in nineteenth-century America, the two women developed a deep affection for one another. Stanton suffered "the rough angles of disappointment" when Anthony was long absent. "I long to see you Susan," Stanton confessed in 1853. "If I had you with me about once a week to rouse my self esteem it would be most beneficial." The feeling was mutual. When Anthony was depressed by their lack of success or public prejudice or her spinster state, she appealed to Stanton. "How I do long to be with you this very minute—to have one look into your very soul and one sound of your soul-stirring voice." Such florid rhetoric and romantic prose were typical of letters between women in the nineteenth century.[35]

Female friendships were important to Elizabeth Cady Stanton. Raised among sisters who had been close companions but were now separated by physical distance or political difference, Stanton created a sisterhood of friends among female reformers. Her extended group of friends included

Martha Wright; Abby Kelley Foster; Elizabeth Oakes Smith, a minor New York literary figure; and Mary Grove Nichols, author of *Lectures to Ladies on Anatomy and Physiology* (1842), who effused, "I like you vastly."[36] They encouraged each other in the work they had undertaken and exchanged candid, confidential letters. Stanton's most important friends—Elizabeth Smith Miller, Lucretia Mott, and Susan Anthony—became an alternate source of approval and affection for her, eventually replacing Henry in the same way that he had supplanted her father and Edward Bayard. Female friendship in the nineteenth century provided these women with an enhanced sense of self, based on the supportive bonds of sisterhood.

Stanton's best friend was her oldest friend and cousin, Gerrit Smith's only daughter, Elizabeth Smith Miller. The two women still called each other "Julius" (Miller) and "Johnson" (Stanton) in their letters. Despite occasional disagreements between themselves or their male relatives, they confided troubles and shared triumphs. Seven years younger than her Cady cousin, Elizabeth Smith was equally high spirited. She had also been well educated at home, at a manual labor school, and at a Friends' school in Philadelphia. Shortly after her twentieth birthday in 1842, she married Charles Dudley Miller of Utica. Her husband gave up his New York City law practice to manage the Smith family affairs. The couple lived first at Peterboro, in Washington during her father's congressional term, and later in Geneva, New York, where they built a mansion in 1869. The Millers had four children—three sons and a daughter. Best known for her advocacy of dress reform, Elizabeth Smith Miller was an ardent supporter of women's rights. She and her husband signed the call for the 1850 Worcester convention and for sixty years supported the cause financially. Her philanthropy also included black schools and indigent women. In 1875 Mrs. Miller published a cookbook and housekeeping manual, *In the Kitchen*.[37] Stanton gave it as a gift to all new brides, including her daughters. It was to Miller that Stanton turned for advice about servants, children, and bonnets, for financial support of pet projects, and for feminist encouragement.[38] With Miller, Stanton was at her most candid and self-critical.

Stanton's relationship with Lucretia Mott was different from her friendships with Anthony and Miller. With them she was usually the dominant party and never less than equal. She saw them often and confided in them without hesitation. With Mrs. Mott, however, Stanton was deferential. She was the novitiate, Mott the mother superior. Admiration rather than intimacy characterized their relationship. Mott was the acknowledged leader of the new women's movement and regarded among all reformers as an equal to the male leaders of the abolition societies. She was older, wiser, and universally respected. She and Stanton had few opportunities to see each other. Sometimes during Mott's summer pilgrimages to Martha

Wright's home there would be one visit. In 1853 Mrs. Mott went to Seneca Falls to inspect baby Margaret.[39] They corresponded regularly but less often than each wrote to others. Mott more than anyone else might reproach Elizabeth or criticize Henry. Stanton did not always accept Mott's counsel or criticism, but she never disagreed with it in public. Whenever she needed to legitimize an action, she sought the older woman's approval.

Mott remained Stanton's inspiration throughout this period. First, Mott had encouraged Stanton's religious inquiry and feminist independence in London in 1840. Then she had urged Stanton to be more active in reform and had cooperated in the Seneca Falls initiative in 1848. Throughout the 1850s Mott repeated invitations to Stanton to attend and preside at the women's rights conventions. When Stanton could not free herself from domestic bonds, Mott approved the small steps she did undertake and praised her writing on behalf of the cause. In Mott, Stanton found a model for intellectual independence, religious skepticism, tart rhetoric, untraditional childbirths, self-nurture, and female friendship.[40]

The arrival of Susan B. Anthony stirred Mrs. Stanton to increased public activity. Soon after being introduced, they met with Lucy Stone to discuss plans for a progressive women's college.[41] The next year the two attended the Woman's State Temperance Society meeting in Rochester. Having been turned out of a Sons of Temperance meeting earlier in 1852 for attempting to speak, Anthony organized a women's session. Stanton wrote the keynote address, and Anthony persuaded her to deliver it herself. It was her first public speech since 1848. She was four months pregnant with her fifth child and wearing bloomers. She left the children home with Amelia.

Stanton's statement indicated advances in her thinking about marriage. She urged that drunkenness be made grounds for divorce. Her underlying theme was that women must be allowed to control their own lives and bodies. "Let no woman remain in the relation of wife with the confirmed drunkard," she declared. "Let no drunkard be the father of her children." She concluded with an attack on churches, demanding that funds used to educate young male ministers or to convert the heathen or to build "gorgeous temples" be directed to care for the hungry at home and "for young men and women thrown alone upon the world."[42]

Following her 1852 address, the Woman's State Temperance Society elected Elizabeth Cady Stanton president and Susan Anthony secretary. This was the first example of a pattern of officeholding that became standard for them, with Mrs. Stanton at the podium and Miss Anthony in the executive role behind the scenes. It was also Stanton's first leadership position. Because of her attack on domestic and clerical patriarchy, the group was ruthlessly criticized. The Troy Journal, for example, was aghast that the women had dared to convene themselves without a man present.[43]

Stanton transformed the temperance society into a forum for feminism. The two causes were closely linked and would be until after the passage of suffrage and the repeal of prohibition in the twentieth century.[44] The physical abuse and financial insecurity suffered by wives at the hands of drunken husbands were raised as vivid examples of why women needed access to legal protections. Interest in temperance increased in New York after a law strictly licensing liquor outlets was revoked in 1850. Active temperance societies not only preached abstinence, they also lobbied for legislation enforcing prohibition, dry districts, Sunday closings, and individual property rights for wives, so that women could earn and keep incomes separate from wastrel husbands.

Because excessive drinking was at that time a male problem with sobering consequences for women, temperance societies were much more popular than women's rights groups. For several years in the early 1850s Stanton used a temperance journal and a temperance society as vehicles for espousing women's rights. She attended temperance rather than women's rights meetings, because they were convenient to her, advanced her interest in converting advocates from one cause to another, and compatible with Anthony's interests. The connection between Anthony and temperance would reassert itself in the future of the women's movement.

State temperance leaders were not pleased with Mrs. Stanton's belligerence. At the next statewide meeting, in 1853, the men packed the house with conservative women. The majority then amended the society's constitution to allow men to be officers of the female society, to rename it the People's League, and to limit its activities. They defeated Mrs. Stanton's bid for reelection but allowed her to stand for vice-president. She refused, and Miss Anthony resigned as secretary. Because she had more genuine temperance ties than Stanton, Anthony was "plunged in grief." In contrast, Stanton was relieved. "I accomplished at Rochester all I desired by having the divorce question brought up and so eloquently supported. Now, Susan, I do beg of you to let the past be past, and to waste no powder on the Woman's State Temperance Society. We have other and bigger fish to fry."[45]

In the meantime Stanton had reiterated her feminist views in a letter to the Third National Women's Rights Convention, in September 1852. Although the meeting took place in nearby Syracuse, Mrs. Stanton, pregnant again, sent a letter to be read by Anthony. Stanton's statement was vigorous. The author of the Seneca Falls suffrage resolution declared that the franchise was only a first step in an ongoing revolution toward full social equality. She proposed that women property owners refuse to pay taxes as long as they could not vote, that women seek coeducational opportunities for their children and themselves, and that the clergy be recognized as women's "most violent enemies—those most opposed to any change in woman's position." Stanton concluded that women should direct their attention to "the education, elevation and enfranchisement of their own sex."[46]

One month after Anthony delivered Stanton's speech, Stanton delivered her fifth child and first daughter. The baby was born on October 20, 1852. Stanton was jubilant. Triumphantly she flew a white flag. She exulted to Lucretia Mott: "I am at length the happy mother of a daughter. Rejoice with me all Womanhood, for lo! a champion of the cause is born. I have dedicated her to this work from the beginning. May she . . . leave her impress on the world for goodness and truth." To Libby Miller she bragged about the ease of her delivery.

> The fact of my having a daughter you already know but the particulars I must give you. Well, on Tuesday night I walked nearly three miles, shopped and made five calls—then I came home, slept well all night, and on Wednesday morning at six I awoke with a little pain which I well understood. I jumped up, bathed and dressed myself, hurried the breakfast, eating none myself of course, got the house and all things in order working bravely between the pains. I neither sat down nor laid down until half past nine when I gave up all my vocations and avocations secular and domestic and devoted myself wholly to the one matter then brought more especially before my mind. At ten o'clock the whole work was completed, the nurse and Amelia alone officiating. I had no doctor and Henry was in Syracuse. I laid down about fifteen minutes and never had so speedy and easy a time before, although this is the largest child I ever had, weighing 12 pounds clothes on. She is very large and plump and her head is covered with black curly hair and how I do rejoice in her.

She continued:

> When the baby was 24 hours old I got up, bathed and dressed, sponge bath and sitz bath, put on a wet bandage, ate my breakfast, walked on the piazza, and then the day being beautiful I took a ride of three miles on the plank road, then I came home, rested an hour or so and then read the newspapers and wrote a long letter to Mama. . . . The short dress I wore until the last. It is grand for such an occasion and I love it more than ever.[47]

Such descriptions seem typical of Stanton's high level of energy. Indeed, one story repeated in Seneca Falls claimed that the nurse had not arrived before the baby and that Mrs. Stanton met her train the next day. Stanton's abundant energy and her ability to nap at will were as characteristic of her daily life as her self-confidence. A few weeks after the baby's birth, however, the hyperactivity and mood elevation of childbirth had been replaced by postpartum depression. Stanton admitted to being unable to nurse, "rundown and anxious." To Libby Miller she insisted, "This is my last baby."[48] Added work, added care, Henry's absence, Anthony's demands, all contributed to her fatigue and discontent.

Stanton had difficulty selecting a name for her daughter. She was hesitant to name her for some adult friend, who might later become a critic. Each of the boys bore names of people who had found fault with her at one time or another. Nor did she select the name of one of her close female friends—Elizabeth, Susan, or Lucretia. "What shall I call her?" she asked Libby Miller. "What is the most beautiful name ever given to woman?"[49] She finally named her daughter for her mother, Margaret Livingston. Her decision was testimony to the new relationship between mother and daughter as adult women. It was Stanton's first public acknowledgment of the significance of her mother's influence.

Each new child increased Stanton's caretaking tasks. After Margaret's birth, Stanton took inventory. "I have five children, two Irish servant girls, and many public duties." Even with the older boys in school and the help of a full-time housekeeper, Stanton's daily life was spent with small children and chores. After her defeat by the Woman's State Temperance Society in June 1853, she had stopped wearing bloomers and stayed home from the Fourth National Women's Rights Convention in Cleveland. A letter to Libby Miller in September 1853 described the range of Stanton's domestic duties.

> After you left me, if I may go back so far, I plunged at once into preserving, in which dispensation I continued until my little closet and every available bowl and tumbler in the house were filled. . . . The spoons and tables, the knobs of the doors, the children's bibs, the servants' hands, and even your blessed Johnson were all more or less sticky. . . . After this I cleaned house, then fitted up the children and their parents for winter, and it is only now that I am just beginning to breathe freely and to feel like taking a kind of geographical survey of my friends. . . . After going to bed last night, I read *Bleak House* for an hour or two. I laughed so hard over Mr. Chadband's sermons that I awoke Maggie who lay in bed beside me, and that ended my reading.[50]

As Stanton's disaffection with her domestic routine grew, her sense of humor about it would diminish.

Stanton read whatever and whenever she could, unsystematically and voraciously. She continued to write short essays and long letters. She was searching for ways to express her ideas. Rather than initiate activities, she waited to be invited. Outbursts of impatience were rare in the early 1850s, but to Anthony she exclaimed in 1853: "Men and angels, give me patience! I am at the boiling point! If I do not find some day the use of my tongue on this question, I shall die of intellectual repression, a women's rights convulsion! . . . How much I long to be free of housekeeping and children, so as to have time to think and read and write."[51]

Henry's prolonged absences had not yet become annoying. From the time he had moved to Boston ahead of her, much of their married life had been lived apart. Henry was not present for the births of any of his children, nor was he always home for Christmas. Having acquired itinerant habits as an abolition agent during the 1830s, he enjoyed the variety of travel. His retirement from elective politics in 1851 had not guaranteed his return to the domestic circle. His law practice required regular trips to register patents and try cases. He continued to attend political meetings and to campaign for other candidates and causes. Henry was away from home for almost ten months every year during the 1850s.

When he was away, Henry claimed to miss his wife very much. He wrote entertaining, interesting letters, which she seldom answered. From Albany, en route to New York, Henry entreated her: "Do write me, for I want to hear from you very much, and I want to see you and kiss you, not having enjoyed the pleasure of kissing anybody for nearly two months." His letters admonish the older boys to mulch the apple trees, hoe the vegetables, haul the firewood, and mind their mother.[52] He no longer had time to supervise the orchard or his children.

Elizabeth's reaction to Henry's absence was ambivalent. She was used to it, she missed him, she resented him, she wished she could accompany him. She did not like reading his reports of debates and dances she could not attend. Both of them anticipated his homecomings and enjoyed brief interludes of ordinary domesticity. One of the younger children remembered Henry as the man who came home with presents, but once he was home the whole household knew not to interrupt what his wife sarcastically called "his devotions to his God, his evening paper."[53]

When Henry left again, his wife enjoyed having total authority at home. Henry joked that every time he went away, "Elizabeth cuts a door or window." She relished the role of head of household and encouraged similar independence among her neighbors.[54] Managing efficiently was another source of self-confidence and success, reinforcing her independence. On the other hand, Henry's absence made it more difficult for her to travel on her own.

Unable and unwilling to leave her children for long, Stanton invited friends to visit her. Many accepted. Her sisters came for extended visits, as did Henry's relatives, who had followed him from Connecticut to the Rochester area. When Seneca Falls became a stop for lyceum lecturers, she invited them to stay at her home. Son Gerrit Stanton claimed that his father stayed away or at hotels because he found "rooms full of people and no vacant chairs in the dining room" when he did come home.[55] But the expansive Henry extended his share of invitations, too. Both Stantons liked to offer hospitality. Their invitations were accepted because they were engaging and attractive people.

Local friends soon replaced their Boston coterie. "A magnetic circle of reformers" lived in the vicinity of Seneca Falls: William Henry Channing, nephew of the founder of American Unitarianism, and Frederick Douglass, the former slave, in Rochester; the novelist Catherine Sedgwick in Syracuse; United States senator William Seward and Martha Wright in Auburn. In Seneca Falls, Mrs. Stanton became "quite intimate" with Frances Hoskins, the principal of the girls' department at the academy; Mary Crowningshield, who taught piano; and Mary and Ansel Bascom, neighbors and political allies.[56]

These friends were members of the Seneca Falls Conversation Club, which Stanton had founded in late 1848. Modeled on Margaret Fuller's Boston "Conversations," it was less elite and erudite in composition. A disparate group of men and women met every Saturday evening to discuss public issues. After conducting a serious debate, the company adjourned to dancing and social chatter. To cut back on elaborate refreshments and observe temperate standards, only cake and water were served. In the 1850s the group sponsored a public lecture series, including a presentation on female physiology. The Conversation Club was the closest Seneca Falls came to having a salon, and Mrs. Stanton was its savant.[57]

Stanton's actions and comments provoked attention and gossip. Once when she was briefly out of town, Mrs. Bloomer wrote on the back of a letter she was forwarding in her capacity as assistant postmaster, "Shorten your visit as much as possible, for people have nothing to talk about while you are gone." Not everybody in town liked Stanton. One young woman refused to ride with her. "I wouldn't have been seen with her for anything, with those ideas of hers."[58]

Unable to attend national women's rights meetings, Stanton turned her attention to the first meeting of the New York association. Stanton signed a call for a February 1854 meeting in Albany, scheduled to coincide with the state legislative session. The women decided to present their case to the lawmakers directly. It was apparent to the organizers that Mrs. Stanton was their most able advocate, so they urged her to testify. "On all accounts you are the person to do it, at once from your sex, talent, knowledge of the subject, and influence," wrote William H. Channing. "There is not a man of us, who could tell the story of woman's wrongs as strongly, clearly, tersely, eloquently as yourself."[59] Stanton accepted the challenge.

Worried about finding time to prepare adequately, she turned to Anthony for help.

> I can generalize and philosophize easily enough of myself but the details of the particular laws I need. . . . You see, while I am about the house, surrounded by my children, washing dishes, baking, sewing, etc., I can think up many points, but I cannot search books, for my hands as well as my brains would be necessary for that work. . . . Prepare yourself to be

disappointed in its merits, for I seldom have one hour undisturbed in which
to sit down and write. Men who can, when they wish to write a document, shut themselves up for days with their thoughts and their books,
know little of what difficulties a woman must surmount to get off a tol-
erable production.[60]

Anthony hurried to Seneca Falls and Stanton went to Rochester to read
her address to Channing. With additional legal references, the speech was
ready.

Whether Judge Cady provided those references is unclear. In her autobiography and in an unpublished essay Stanton claimed that her father lis-
tened to the speech before it was delivered and improved it with additional
citations. According to these accounts, Stanton stopped in Johnstown en
route to Albany. There she was confronted by her father, who had read a
newspaper announcement of the upcoming event. He demanded to hear
what she planned to say. When she read her speech, Judge Cady was
"magnetized" and "moved to tears" by her eloquence. Stanton claimed that
her father wept that she had ever been exposed to such injustice as women
suffered. She responded that she had learned about women's legal wrongs
in his law office. Then father and daughter stayed up late revising her draft.[61]

Other sources and contemporary evidence contradict her later memory.
These variations repeat the details of the episode—Judge Cady learning about
her speech in the paper and confronting her for an explanation. But in these
versions, rather than offering assistance, Judge Cady first attempted to bribe
and then threatened Stanton: he offered her the deed to some property she
wanted, then he claimed he would disinherit her entirely. This account ends
with father and daughter storming out of the room by separate doors.[62]
Despite the embarrassment Stanton was causing her father, she gave the
speech.

Whether these accounts represent one or two encounters, in 1848, 1854,
or later, they indicate the state of Stanton's mind at two periods. The autobiographical fragments, emphasizing her father's approval, sympathy, and
cooperation, show that the older, public Stanton did not want to admit
that she had been opposed by her family. She wanted to legitimize her feminism by making it seem acceptable to Daniel Cady, the respected jurist
and social conservative. In the same way that she never alluded to Henry's
absence from the 1848 meeting, she obscured her father's disapproval in
1854. These later accounts indicate reluctance on her part to admit that
she was not supported by her male relatives. Her earlier willingness to vent
her frustration to Anthony or Miller shows how angry she was at the time,
too angry and impolitic to dissemble.

When Stanton stood in the Senate chamber before the legislators on February 14, 1854, none of her family was present. Only Anthony was there.

She had had fifty thousand copies of the speech printed. She put one on every legislator's desk and planned to sell the remainder as tracts. Having abandoned bloomers, Mrs. Stanton wore black silk with a white lace collar, secured with a diamond pin. She was thirty-eight years old. It was, she remembered, a "great event" in her life.[63]

In her address Stanton described the legal position of women in American society—as woman, wife, widow, and mother. Women were "persons," Stanton asserted, "native, free-born citizens, property-holders, taxpayers." Yet they were denied the right to vote, to hold office, to be tried by peers, to equal treatment under the criminal code. Women as wives, Stanton continued, asked that the marriage contract be subject to the laws of civil contracts, outlining its obligations and allowing suits to break it; she even wanted to limit the age of the contracting parties. Once married, wives had to be protected from the abuse and insolvency of husbands, so married women must have the right to earn and inherit money; voting would enable women to protect this newly held property. Women as widows needed fair inheritance and tax laws and the right to serve as their husbands' executors. Women as mothers needed to share in the custody of their children, whom fathers could then apprentice or bond or will to other parties without the consent of the mother. Women also needed education to train their children and protection against habitual drunkards.[64] Logically, passionately, relentlessly, Stanton attacked the subordinate status of women. The speech was a tour de force. It was widely praised, and Stanton was celebrated and congratulated. Yet it was her last public address for six years.

Mrs. Stanton had brought with her to Albany the three children then at home and Amelia Willard. They stayed at Delevan House for one dollar per bed per night. When a hostile woman demanded where Stanton's children were while she was making speeches, she could answer smugly. She replied that she had been absent from her children no longer to make the speech than her questioner had been to attend it. In another version she added that unlike "ladies of fashion or politicians" (like Henry), she stayed home with her children or took them with her. Stanton's repetition of this anecdote indicates that in 1854 she was interested in appearing and remaining a conscientious mother, and increasingly resentful of Henry. Although she found such "frivolous objections . . . as exasperating as they were ridiculous,"[65] she always attempted to answer with patience and wit.

In the two years following Stanton's appearance in Albany, pressures on her mounted on all sides. Admirers urged a wider public role; detractors demanded that she retire. Paulina Davis repeated her earlier suggestion that Stanton become a paid lecturer on women's rights. Lucy Stone continued to correspond with her at length about the divorce issue. Mott urged her to attend national meetings. Anthony increased her requests for speeches, tracts, and appearances. Unsure of what direction to take and discouraged by family opposition, Stanton stayed home.

Stanton's father was vehement in his opposition to her plan to increase her public activity. Recently retired from the state Supreme Court, Judge Cady was offended and embarrassed by the notoriety of her public appearances. He criticized her harshly. Following one confrontation with her father in 1855, Stanton reported to Anthony:

> I passed through a terrible scourging when last at my father's. I cannot tell you how deeply the iron entered my soul. I never felt more keenly the degradation of my sex. To think that all in me of which my father would have felt a proper pride had I been a man is deeply mortifying to him because I am a woman. That thought has stung me to a fierce decision— to speak as soon as I can do myself credit. I wish that I were as free as you and I would stump the state in a twinkling. But I am not. . . . The pressure on me just now is too great. Henry sides with my friends who oppose me in all that is dearest to my heart. They are not willing that I would write even on the woman question. But I will both write and speak.[66]

Family legend insists that Judge Cady carried through on his threat to disinherit his daughter if she continued her public activity, as she did, although in a much more circumscribed manner. At the time Stanton told Libby Miller that her father had said, "Your first lecture will be a very expensive one." To which she replied, "I intend that it shall be very profitable." Whether or not Judge Cady changed his will at the time cannot be determined. The will in effect when he died in 1859 did include Elizabeth as an heir.[67]

Henry's opposition to Stanton's proposed absences and public activities is not hard to fathom. Having been pressured by Judge Cady into giving up the nomination for lieutenant governor in order to meet his family and financial obligations, Henry resented his wife's desire to move beyond her domestic sphere and do the kind of reform work he had done. While he appreciated her talents and usually applauded her achievements, he wished she would spend more time with the children and less with her colleagues. From her point of view, his position was unjustified. The children were well cared for. In his absence she acted as both mother and father to them and had come to rely on female friends for adult company. On her rare excursions out of Seneca Falls, she usually took the youngest children with her. He resented her desire for more independence; she resented his independence. She longed for time and space for herself, and she coveted what she perceived as his freedom to do what he wanted.

For the present, Stanton was too uncertain about her future direction and too worn down by domestic cares to do more. Her efforts to combine public affairs and maternity had failed. She could not move beyond her domestic sphere while the children were small and while she was still having babies. As she apologized to Anthony in the mid-1850s, "My whole soul is in the work, but my hands belong to my family."[68]

6

Discontent and Divorce Reform
1856–61

Elizabeth Cady Stanton sacrificed public ambitions to private affections during her last years in Seneca Falls. For a short period in the early 1850s she had successfully combined reform work and domestic duties. From the beginning of her friendship with Anthony until the speech to the New York legislature in 1854, Stanton had slowly increased her involvement with the women's movement. Then, faced with her father's opposition, Henry's resistance, and two more children, Stanton surrendered to the bonds of affection and responsibility that confined her. She chose to stay home, read, write, and mind the children, but she chafed at the delay and resented the restrictions. At the same time, she accepted them and comforted herself with visions of a productive, public period after her children were grown.

Once again Stanton was without a useful role model. No single person was doing what she wanted to do, so she had no one to observe and learn from. Instead she could copy and adopt different specific behaviors from different people. In her public life she had borrowed strategy and rhetoric primarily from the abolitionists. In her private life she had accepted the maternal expectations of mid-nineteenth-century America. She was putting family first, but she applied some untraditional approaches to traditional tasks. Angelina Grimké Weld, Lucy Stone, Antoinette Brown Blackwell, and many other reform women retired into maternity at various times in their careers. In anticipating a period of independence to follow child care, Stanton was following a course set by her mother and Mrs. Mott. Margaret Cady had recovered from her grief over dead sons and returned to an active life in the community in her late middle age. Lucretia Mott managed an extended family and a variety of public works with great efficiency and energy. Further, none of the people important to Stanton disapproved of her decision to stay home with her children—except Anthony, who was outnumbered, and discounted because she was not married.

After 1854 Stanton began to refuse public invitations. She did not even accept social invitations, explaining to Libby Miller, "If you knew how impatient I feel in my domestic bondage and how aggravating a thing an invitation is, so far from ever tempting me to step beyond the garden gate, you would point out all the joys, privileges, advantages and blessings that pertain to the wife, mother, nurse and cook."[1] Throughout this period Stanton channeled more and more of her energy into writing. She seized her pen at every opportunity, writing journal articles, lectures, newspaper columns, and letters.

Since 1849 she had been a regular contributor to the *Lily* and remained one until the Bloomers moved to Ohio in 1853. From then until 1856 Stanton wrote monthly essays for the *Una*, "a paper devoted to the Elevation of Women." The journal was edited and funded by Paulina Wright Davis. One of Stanton's pieces, "I Have All the Rights I Want," was widely reprinted. It was a scathing attack on the women who opposed equal rights and suffrage. Stanton disdained the women "with bare arms and neck" who joined in midnight revels with drunken men and then criticized the "want of delicacy in those who assemble in woman's conventions to talk with sober men . . . on great questions of Human Rights."[2]

When the *Lily* was sold and the *Una* folded for lack of subscribers, Stanton began to send articles to city newspapers, including the *New York Tribune*. Editor Horace Greeley encouraged her and printed her pieces regularly. At first she asked Henry for editorial advice but then rebelled at his revisions. "Husbands are too critical," she declared to Anthony. "I am vexed." Stanton saw in writing a means to sharpen and spread her ideas on women's rights. "If I were a man and not pinned here, how I would hie to New York . . . and become one of the *Tribune* corps of regular writers," she wrote to Anthony.[3]

It was during this period that Stanton recalled an earlier interest in writing a history of the women's movement. Lucretia Mott fostered her plan and advised her on the work's scope. "In thy coming work thou must do thy self justice," wrote Mott. "Remember the first convention originated with thee."[4] But Stanton did not have time for such an undertaking; it would be twenty-five years before she began *The History of Woman Suffrage*.

Approaching her fortieth birthday in 1855, Stanton undoubtedly anticipated the end of her childbearing years. In spite of the objections of her male relatives, she still planned to travel the women's rights circuit as soon as Margaret was weaned and walking. She could joke to Anthony in February of that year, "As soon as you all begin to ask too much of me, I shall have a baby!" She added, "Now be careful; do not provoke me to that step."[5] Or perhaps Stanton was serious and chose to become pregnant again to avoid further family conflict about her assuming a public career.

Childbirth for women over forty was not uncommon in the nineteenth century, and Stanton took no steps to avoid it. Before 1848 Stanton had had no reason to limit the size of her family. Both she and Henry had come from large families, and until 1851 they had no reason to practice birth control. The first three boys were born between 1842 and 1845. Then there were no births and no record of miscarriages until 1851, when a fourth son was born. Stanton was coping well with the demands on her time then, and Henry was happy in elective office. Henry's decision not to run for reelection diminished their income. Her participation in reform increased their expenses and lessened her interest in housework. Yet they had a fifth child in 1852, perhaps in an attempt to fulfill her well-known desire to have a daughter.

Stanton's two late pregnancies appear to have been unplanned and unexpected, although she had made no attempt at prevention. In a diary entry much later in life Stanton implied that she had been too ignorant to use any birth control during the late 1850s, but it is hard to believe her claim.[6] For whatever reason she chose not to prevent these pregnancies. The result was lack of control over her reproductive life, a sense of subordination, renewed outrage at the institution of marriage, increased resentment of Henry, a delay in her public career, and two more children.

Harriot Eaton Stanton was born January 20, 1856. Stanton greeted her sixth child and second daughter with less enthusiasm than earlier offspring. Her mixed feelings were apparent in a letter to Anthony, announcing the birth. "I have got out the sixth edition of my admirable work, another female child is born into the world! . . . I am very happy that the terrible ordeal is past and that the result is another daughter. But I feel disappointed and sad at the same time at this grievous interruption of my plans. I might have been born an orator before spring, you acting as midwife. . . . My whole thought for the present must center on bread and babies."[7] Stanton may have been saying what Anthony wanted to hear, but other evidence confirms her growing discontent and impatience.

It was unusual for Stanton to suffer the "agonizing pain" of childbirth and even more unusual for her to admit it. "Oh how my soul died within me, as I approached that dreadful, never-to-be-forgotten ordeal," she confessed to Libby Miller. "The deed was done and here I am in the land of the living." Stanton was no longer congratulating herself on maternal triumphs. She felt angry and trapped. Within a month of the birth of her second daughter she complained to Anthony: "Imagine me, day in and day out, watching, bathing, nursing and promenading the precious contents of a little crib in the corner of my room. I pace up and down these two chambers like a caged lion, longing to bring nursing and housekeeping cares to a close. I have other work at hand."[8] But whatever feminist occupation she might undertake in the future, Stanton recognized that she would first have to contend with her domestic responsibilities and her family's opposition.

Another undercurrent of discord in the Stanton marriage in the 1850s was Henry's shifting political allegiance. Since 1840 Elizabeth had remained a political abolitionist. Had she been able to vote she would have supported the Liberty, Free Soil, and Barnburner parties. To stop gossip when Henry switched to the Democrats, she claimed to be an "unterrified Democrat" as well.[9] But like his former allies and most of her current friends, she was troubled by evidence of his political opportunism. Having given up elective politics, Henry hoped to get an appointed position. To that end, he shifted his support from one likely winner to another.

Following his attendance at the Democratic National Convention in Baltimore in 1852, Henry had campaigned for the national ticket. The former abolitionist hero supported Franklin Pierce and a platform that endorsed the gag rule in the House of Representatives, the war with Mexico, the Compromise of 1850, and the Fugitive Slave Law. His opportunism shocked his old allies, some of whom considered Henry a political prostitute. "Poor Stanton! How art thou fallen!" chastised a *National Era* editorial. Seemingly unembarrassed by such criticism, Stanton backed the Democratic ticket enthusiastically. He gave major speeches in Albany, Syracuse, and Buffalo and claimed credit when the Democrats carried New York. He expected his loyalty to be rewarded with an appointment in the Pierce administration, "a first rate consulship," the post of solicitor of the treasury, or United States district attorney.[10] But the New York quota was filled without his name on the list. Ironically, his nomination had been opposed by Democrats suspicious of his abolitionist leanings.

Angry at his treatment by the Pierce administration and increasingly sensitive to criticism from former friends, Henry began to disentangle himself from the Democrats. He attended the state party convention in September 1853, but withdrew his name as a candidate for attorney general. Passage of the Kansas-Nebraska Act in 1854 by a Democratic Congress provided Henry with an excuse for bolting the party. The act, which opened Kansas and Nebraska for settlers, repealed the Missouri Compromise, and allowed settlers to determine whether the territories would be slave or free states, infuriated antislavery Whigs and Democrats like Henry. These partisans began to hold "fusion" conventions, out of which came the Republican party.[11]

As Henry explained to Charles Sumner, he hesitated only until the new party became a reality and then joined with a convert's zeal, again.[12] Henry gave his first Republican speech in Rochester, in September 1855. In it he confessed his error in remaining recently silent on the slavery issue. He blamed his lapse on a "constitutional distaste for perpetual controversy," an odd apology from an old abolition agent.[13] In the last week before the legislative elections that fall, Henry gave the same speech once a day in each county in western New York. He helped pull the state party out of "utter chaos," he reported to his old employer and political mentor Thurlow Weed. Henry's return to the principles of his youth pleased his wife. "I am rejoiced to say that Henry is heart and soul in the Republican movement and is faithfully stumping the state once more," she recounted to Anthony.[14]

The summer after Harriot's birth in 1856, Henry Stanton was a delegate to the Republican National Convention in Philadelphia, which nominated John C. Frémont for president. During the campaign for "Frémont and Freedom," Henry was assigned to canvass Pennsylvania. He also made stump speeches from New England to Ohio. His speeches, more radical than any he had made in the 1830s, were better received. "Great questions are at stake. A victory would be glorious, a defeat now most disastrous," Henry reported; "I have got my feelings so enlisted that I cannot stop till we reach the end for good or evil."[15]

When Frémont lost, Henry again lost any chance for a government appointment. He returned to Seneca Falls disappointed and exhausted. As in the past, he found solace in the garden, harvesting ten acres of squash and strawberries.[16] To recover financially, Henry became a temporary lecturer on the lyceum circuit. The irony cannot have been lost on Elizabeth. Henry was doing what she wanted to do and what he had discouraged her from doing. Meanwhile she stayed home, minding the children and making no public appearances.

Stanton was not the only feminist staying home rocking cradles in late 1856. The small circle of leaders of the women's rights movement had been further diminished by marriage and motherhood. In May 1855 Lucy Stone had married Henry Blackwell, a Cincinnati abolitionist and merchant with strong feminist connections.* Stone's decision to keep her own name was

---

*Lucy Stone (1818–93) was born on the family farm near West Brookfield, Mass., to a well-to-do farmer and tanner with *Mayflower* connections. Lucy, who resented her mother's subordinate social and domestic position, became a teacher and continued her education at Mount Holyoke Female Seminary and Oberlin College, graduating with honors in 1847. She became one of Garrison's AASS agents and soon was making women's rights speeches as well. An

newsworthy even among feminists. Stanton congratulated her for the decision, and Mrs. Mott, less convinced of the propriety of such an action, finally approved. "Seeing there are so few to advocate woman's whole cause, it is needful for some of us to be ultra," she explained to a niece; "I have become quite a defender of Lucy Stone's name." [17]

The Stone-Blackwell marriage produced one daughter, Alice Stone Blackwell, born in September 1857, and a son who died in infancy. For the next ten years Lucy Stone limited her public appearances, refusing to be away from her daughter overnight. In January 1856 another Oberlin graduate and the first female minister, Antoinette Brown, married Stone's brother-in-law, Samuel Blackwell. The first of their seven children was born in 1857. Meanwhile Mrs. Stanton was nursing her sixth baby. Miss Anthony, on whom the mothers relied to take up the banner in their absence, was understandably annoyed. "Those of you who have talent to do honor to poor—oh! how poor—womanhood have all given yourselves over to baby-making; and left poor brainless me to do battle alone." Mrs. Stanton counseled Anthony to be patient.

> Let Lucy and Antoinette rest awhile in peace and quietness and think great thoughts for the future. It is not well to be in the excitement of public life all the time; do not keep stirring them up or mourning over their repose. You need rest too, Susan. Let the world alone awhile. We cannot bring about a moral revolution in a day or year. Now that I have two daughters I feel fresh strength to work. It is not in vain that in myself I have experienced all the wearisome cares to which woman in her best estate is subject. [18]

The maternal responsibilities of its leadership were not the only problem plaguing the women's movement in 1857. The momentum of the early 1850s had been dissipated in antebellum politics. One crisis after another propelled the nation toward civil war. Current events consumed the attention of the reformers from whom the women's rights groups drew their support. What time women like Lucy Stone and Antoinette Brown did have was increasingly devoted to antislavery fairs or abolition agitation. Issues like the *Dred Scott* decision, which held that slaves remained chattel even in free states, and the Lecompton Constitution, relating to the extension of slavery into the Kansas Territory, divided their ranks as well. [19] It was hard to focus any attention on women's rights.

Under such circumstances the scattered leadership of the women's move-

organizer of the 1850 Worcester convention, she traveled widely, advocating women's rights and wearing bloomers.

Henry Blackwell's sisters Elizabeth and Emily were pioneer women physicians; his sister-in-law, Antoinette Brown, was the first woman ordained a minister in America.

ment decided not to hold its annual national convention in 1857. Lacking leaders, followers, and money, the early women's movement had reached its nadir. The financial crisis was severe. Previously funded by individual contributions as needs arose, there was no ongoing fund-raising scheme. Gerrit Smith, a major donor in the past, withheld his usual support in 1856. He was displeased that earlier conventions had not pressed for dress reform, which he believed to be the most important aspect of female emancipation. In appealing to her cousin to repeat his past generosity, Elizabeth Stanton summarized the gains women had made so far.

> My noble cousin,—You said you have but little faith in this reform—the Woman's Rights Movement—because the changes we propose are so great, so radical, so comprehensive; whilst they who have commenced the work are so puny, feeble, and undeveloped. The mass of women are developed at least to the point of discontent. . . . In the human soul, the steps between discontent and action are few and short indeed. As to the general cause of women, I see no signs of failure.[20]

Smith was not persuaded. He remained more interested in antislavery and instead underwrote John Brown's bloody raid in Kansas.

Then in 1858 another philanthropist, the wealthy Boston merchant Francis Jackson, made an anonymous gift of five thousand dollars to the women's rights cause.* Wendell Phillips, Lucy Stone, and Susan Anthony were named trustees of a fund to be used to win the ballot for women. The Jackson gift was generously supplemented in 1859 when another Boston entrepreneur, Charles Hovey, endowed a fifty-thousand-dollar trust fund for "the promotion of the antislavery cause and other reforms," including women's rights. The four trustees of the Hovey Fund—Phillips, William Lloyd Garrison, Parker Pillsbury, and Abby Kelley Foster—were required to expend a minimum of eight thousand dollars annually.[21]

After the 1857 hiatus, the stalled women's movement pulled itself together. Finally solvent, the feminists could reflect on the gains they had made. Wisconsin and Nebraska territories were considering local suffrage for women. Ohio and New York had passed model property rights legislation for married women. Iowa allowed women to sue for divorce on grounds other than adultery. Mount Holyoke and Elmira College were advancing women's education, and Oberlin was graduating men and women. In 1857 Dr. Elizabeth Blackwell had opened the New York Infirmary, staffed entirely by women. The leaders organized an eighth national convention in 1858, scheduling the meeting to coincide with an annual meeting of the

---

*Jackson's daughter, Eliza Eddy, had lost her children when her husband seized their two young daughters and took them to Europe without her consent. The episode prompted Jackson to support women's rights. Mrs. Eddy also left a bequest of fifty thousand dollars to be divided between Susan B. Anthony and Lucy Stone.

American Anti-Slavery Society in New York City. Lucretia Mott presided. Unable to avoid the connection between abolition and women's rights, the organizers decided to combine their resources.

Meanwhile Elizabeth Cady Stanton was at home in Seneca Falls, surrounded by children, immured in domesticity. In responding to yet another of Anthony's exhortations, Stanton described her life in 1857.

> How I wish I could respond to your letter in a tone I know you desire. But I dare not promise to undertake any work beyond the imperative duties each day brings forth. In the first place, the weather is enervating. If we ever have another shower, I may recover in a measure my vitality; but at present I am thoroughly dried up. In the next place, my baby is cutting her eye teeth, is restless at night and troublesome by day. Then again, my boys have a four weeks' vacation and so they are on my hands. Furthermore, my friends will all visit me in August and I have no Amelia to share a single care. From the roast beef and jellies down to the dish cloth and soap grease, my eye must penetrate everywhere and my influence be omnipresent. Under such circumstances how could I sit down to think and write? But in two or three years I shall be able to have some hours of each day to myself. My two older boys will then be in college or business and my three younger children will be in school.[22]

With Amelia Willard on vacation, Stanton was so undone that she forgot to count the newest baby in her enumeration.

Stanton comforted herself by anticipating her future. She tried to reassure Anthony, and herself. "Courage, Susan, this is my last baby and she will be two years old in January. Two years more and—time will tell what! You and I have the prospect of a good long life. We shall not be in our prime before fifty, and after that we shall be good for twenty years at least."[23] Stanton had models of serene, independent, active older women, like her mother and Mrs. Mott. She expected to live as long as her other Cady relatives had, and she expected to spend her prime working for women's rights. What she lacked was a model to help her contend with her immediate situation.

Despite her outbursts against the work and constraints imposed by her children, Elizabeth Cady Stanton thrived as a mother. She recognized the power women had both in their homes and over their children. Her children were a source of enormous satisfaction for her. What she perceived as her success as a mother increased her self-confidence. She chose to stay close to her children rather than travel because she felt responsible for them and cared for them. Coming home after a short trip, Stanton reported to Libby Miller: "I have kissed and hugged [the baby] til she went to sleep. The joy a mother feels on seeing her baby after a short absence is a bliss no man's soul can ever know. There we have something that they have not! But we have purchased the ecstasy in deep sorrow and suffering." Although she sometimes regretted her choice, she surrendered to the bonds of affection that tied her to Seneca Falls. As she joked to Wendell Phillips in 1860, when her children ranged in age from one year to eighteen, "I am anchored here, surrounded by small craft, which I am struggling to tug up life's stream."[24]

The voluntary, sometimes involuntary, retirement of Stanton, Stone, and Brown infuriated Anthony. She worried about the responsibilities thrust upon her and nagged her colleagues. She felt superior to their married states and at the same time resented their security. She was tempted by the idea of romance but never found an agreeable partner. She had "very weak moments," she confessed to Stanton. "I sometimes fear that *I too* shall faint by the wayside—and drop out of the ranks of the faithful few [to marry]."[25] But no one ever proposed, and Anthony never surrendered.

Once she enlisted, Anthony committed her life to reform. During the 1850s she was employed as a temperance society organizer and an abolition agent. For the first five months of 1855 she collected petitions favoring extending married women's property rights. Carrying a carpetbag full of tracts written by Mrs. Stanton, Anthony walked through fifty-four New York counties. She supported herself by passing a hat while making speeches and by selling the tracts. After the *Dred Scott* decision, Anthony canvassed western New York for antislavery. Meanwhile she continued to devote most of her energies to women's rights. She was unstinting in the demands she made on herself and others.

In Stanton's case, Anthony was relentless. She refused to let Stanton surrender to domestic bondage. In June 1856, six months after Stanton had given birth to Harriot, Anthony asked the new mother to write a speech for an upcoming state teachers' meeting.

> So for the love of me and for the saving of the reputation of womanhood, I beg you, with one baby on your knee and another at your feet, and four boys whistling, buzzing, hallooing "Ma, Ma," set yourself about the work. It is of but small moment who writes the address but of vast moment that it be done well. . . . Don't say no nor . . . delay it a moment. . . . Now will you load my gun, leaving me to pull the trigger and let fly the powder and ball? . . . Do get all on fire and be as cross as you please. You remember, Mr. Stanton told how cross you always get over a speech.

Stanton replied tersely: "Come here and I will do what I can . . . if you will hold the baby and make the puddings."[26]

The speech advocated coeducation at all levels. It expanded on themes Stanton had first outlined in a lecture on education to the Seneca Falls Village Lyceum in 1855. Controversial as always, she urged that, since both sexes were equal in intelligence, schools, from academies to universities, should provide equally for boys and girls. The speech ended by upbraiding women teachers for not demanding equal wages. It was not well received. One opponent charged that coeducation would undermine feminine delicacy and destroy the sanctity of marriage. The teachers, put on the defensive, rejected the concept of equal pay as unseemly. When Anthony reported the reaction, Stanton was outraged. "What an infernal set of fools these school-marms must be!! Well, if in order to please men they wish to live on air, let them. The sooner the present generation of women die out the better. We have jackasses enough in the world now without such women propagating any more."[27]

Stanton made one more effort for Anthony in 1856. In November she sent her annual letter to the Seventh National Women's Rights Convention in New York City, for Anthony to read. In her letter, Stanton condemned marriage for putting women in a "false position" and defended divorce.[28] The subject of divorce, first raised by Stanton at temperance meetings in the early 1850s, became a tenet of her feminist philosophy.

In thinking about the conditions of an ideal marriage, Stanton undoubtedly reflected on her own situation. She was trapped by tradition. She loved Henry and the children, but she longed to be free of her obligations to them. Having postponed her dreams of a reform career for ten years, since she penned the Declaration of Sentiments, Stanton grew increasingly angry. Her frustrations exploded in a letter to Anthony on the Fourth of July, 1858.

> Oh how I long for a few hours of blessed leisure each day. How rebellious it makes me feel when I see Henry going about where and how he pleases. He can walk at will through the whole wide world or shut himself up alone, if he pleases, within four walls. As I contrast his freedom with my bondage, and feel that, because of the false position of women, I have been compelled to hold all my noblest aspirations in abeyance in order to be a wife, a mother, a nurse, a cook, a household drudge, I am fired anew and long to pour forth from my own experience the whole long story of women's wrongs. I have been alone today as the whole family except Hattie and myself have been out to celebrate our national birthday. What has woman to do with patriotism? Must not someone watch baby, house and garden? And who is so fitting to perform all these duties, which no one else wishes to do, as she who brought sin into the world and all our woe![29]

Worn out by motherhood, Stanton refused to consider it a "noble aspiration" until she was no longer occupied by its demands. Eventually, however, she would claim that motherhood ennobled women. It was in this angry frame of mind that Stanton took two major steps—one planned, the other unexpected. In August she accepted invitations to deliver important speeches in Philadelphia and Boston, and she conceived her seventh child. They were not compatible undertakings.

After a decade of offers, Elizabeth Cady Stanton finally agreed to visit

Mrs. Mott and to attend the yearly meeting of Philadelphia Friends in the fall of 1858. Unfortunately Mrs. Stanton's trunk was lost or stolen en route. Her anxiety about the loss turned her visit into a "short and disastrous" episode, according to Mrs. Mott. Stanton returned to Seneca Falls without making her speech. At the request of Mott's son-in-law, Stanton sent an inventory of the trunk's contents, listing such items as a shawl valued at one hundred dollars. Mrs. Mott was shocked at such extravagance. She sent Stanton a hundred dollars to cover the entire loss, noting sternly that the money was to be used "to supply only the necessities, not the luxuries."[30]

Stanton then used the lost trunk as an excuse to cancel her Boston appearance in November. She had been honored to be the only woman asked to participate in a prestigious lecture series endowed by the Hovey Fund. Her last-minute, tactless withdrawal surprised and disappointed her friends. She claimed that both her speech and her public wardrobe had been lost with the trunk.[31]

Such wholly uncharacteristic behavior can probably be attributed to Stanton's seventh pregnancy. For the first time in her experience, she suffered from daily discomfort and distemper. She felt awful. But having claimed equal abilities for men and women, she refused to admit a gender-related disability. To her, lost luggage was a more acceptable excuse than morning sickness. Indeed, there is some indication that she had decided even before her trip to Philadelphia to back out of the Boston event.[32]

Anthony was almost as upset by the pregnancy as was Stanton. Writing to Antoinette Brown Blackwell before the Philadelphia and Boston incidents, Anthony exclaimed:

> Ah me!!! Alas!! Alas!!!! Mrs. Stanton!! is embarked on the rolling sea— three long months of terrible nausea are behind and what the future has in store, the *deep* [baby] only knows. She will be able to lecture however up to January provided she will only *make* her surroundings bend to such a work. But her husband, you know, does not *help* to make it *easy* for her to engage in such work—and all her friends throw *mountains* in her path. Mr. Stanton will be gone most of the Autumn, full of *Political Air Castles* and so soon as Congress sits, at Washington again. He was gone 7 *months* last winter. The whole burden of home and children, therefore, falls to her, if she leaves the post, *all* is afloat. I only *scold now* that for a *moment's pleasure* to herself or her husband, she should thus increase the *load* of *cares* under which she already groans. But there is no remedy now.[33]

It is significant that Anthony recognized the responsibility of both Stantons in the conception, rather than blaming only Henry's masculine appetites. Mrs. Stanton was frank about her sexuality and objected to the Victorian view that women did not enjoy intercourse. As a phrenologist had noted, she was "capable of enjoying the connubial relation to a high degree."[34] Throughout her life Stanton encouraged discussions of female sexuality and physiology.

Stanton's last child, Robert Livingston Stanton, was born March 13, 1859. Mrs. Stanton was forty-three years old. This last, difficult pregnancy left her exhausted. Although reluctant to admit any weakness, she did confess it to her closest female friends. To Anthony she wrote: "I have a great boy, now three weeks old. He weighed at his birth without a particle of clothing 12 ¼ pounds. I never suffered so much. I was sick all the time before he was born, and I have been very weak ever since. He seemed to take up every particle of my vitality, soul and body. Thank Heaven! I am through the siege once more." No longer leaping from her childbirth bed to go driving, Stanton suffered severe postpartum depression. Another week passed, and she wrote Anthony: "All I had or was has gone with the development of that boy. It is now four weeks since my confinement and I can scarcely walk across the room. You have no idea how weak I am and I have to keep my mind in the most quiet state in order to sleep."[35] The baby was fussy, possibly slightly crippled, and Stanton was worn out. It was a disappointing conclusion to her earlier childbearing triumphs.

Ill and depressed for most of 1859, Stanton made a slow recovery. Her enthusiasm returned briefly in the summer months, but it was quickly exhausted. In June she put a notice "To the Women of the Empire State" in the *Courier,* calling for petition signatures for a revised women's property bill to be brought before the next session of the legislature. Writing to Anthony that same month, she declared: "I am full of fresh thoughts and courage and feel all enthusiasm about our work. I hope to grind out half a dozen good tracts during the summer. The [servant] girls and the children are all well. The house is cleaned. The summer's sewing all done and I see nothing now to trouble me much if all keep well." But she could not maintain her interest in women's rights issues. Six weeks later both serving girls had quit to go into a factory, the older boys were home on vacation, and her household was in disarray. In another epistle to Anthony she explained: "I am in no situation to think or write but the occasion demands that I exert myself to do all I can. When you come I will try to find time to grind out what you say must be done. In the past we have issued all kinds of bulls under all kinds of circumstances, and I think we can still do more . . . even if you must make the puddings and carry the baby while I ply the pen."[36]

To her troubles with a sickly infant, unreliable servants, and Anthony's nagging were added even more serious concerns. Daniel Cady, blind since April and increasingly deaf, died on October 31, 1859, at age eighty-six. His daughter was bereft. There is no record that Stanton and her father had healed the breach that followed her 1854 speech to the New York legislature or that she had resumed her long family visits to Johnstown in the interim. She had lost her father and any future opportunity to win his approval; she was also freed of his disapproval. To compound her grief, John Brown, a hero to abolitionists and liberals like Stanton, was sentenced to hang for his October raid on Harper's Ferry. Gerrit Smith, implicated in the case on account of his financial support of Brown as one of the Secret Six, had himself temporarily committed to an insane asylum.

Childbirth, anxiety about an injured baby, the death of a parent, the execution of a hero, and the institutionalization of her cousin created a period of great stress and depression for Stanton. She was haunted by images of death: her father, Eleazar, tolling bells, worms, hanging, decay. She endured a season of mourning. For the first time since her conversion experience at Emma Willard's, Stanton was incapacitated by despair. She begged Anthony to come and stay with her.[37] With Anthony's common sense, a return to health, the reestablishment of her household routine, and immersion in public duties, Stanton soon worked herself out of her depression. She fell back on her old pattern of activity to cheer herself up. By working and writing she defeated the depression.

In the will in existence in 1859, Stanton shared with her mother and sisters in Judge Cady's considerable estate. The widow Cady was left the bulk of his fortune and use of their house for life. Each daughter received cash and real estate. Tryphena Bayard was named executrix and trustee of the Johnstown mansion. Elizabeth's inheritance, estimated at fifty thousand dollars, gave the Stantons new financial security.[38] Henry's income since 1840 had been at best erratic. When he practiced law, earnings depended on the success of his cases and the solvency of his clients. As his family grew and expenses mounted, Henry had supplemented his income as an author, state senator, newspaper correspondent, and lyceum lecturer. There were always unpaid bills. Now the Stantons had enough cash to settle their debts and invest the remainder.[39]

Judge Cady's death had another result. Stanton renewed her Johnstown visits and restored her relationship with her mother. In return, Mrs. Cady invited the Stanton children to stay with her during school vacations and when their mother traveled. Soon they were installed in the mansion on the square every summer, to be supervised by "the aunts," Tryphena Bayard and Harriet Eaton.

Having survived the disapproval of her father, Stanton chose to ignore Henry's objections to her career. As the new decade opened, Stanton came to depend on female friends for ongoing encouragement and enduring affection. With Lucretia Mott aging and Libby Miller preoccupied with her father's mental health, Stanton relied especially on Susan B. Anthony. At the same time, Stanton was becoming more and more self-sustaining. Writing to an acquaintance in 1860, Stanton acknowledged her need for approval from friends but at the same time revealed her increasing independence of it.

> Every expression of approval from noble women is most grateful to me. I feel so perfectly sure that the . . . blow struck [in the divorce speech] was a good one that I am truly sorry to have any one turn away. My life has been one long struggle to do and say what I know to be right and true. I would not take back one brave word or deed. My only regret is that I have not been braver and truer in uttering the honest conviction of my own soul. I am thankful that I did not know how [an old ally now opposed] felt, for I fear the knowledge of his disapproval might have held me back. The desire to please those we admire and respect often cripples conscience.[40]

Previously Stanton had tried to please her traditional family and her untraditional friends. She was still practicing and comparing different behaviors. She depended on, or at least anticipated, the approval of those important to her. She expected that her actions would be accepted if not applauded. As earlier sources of approval had been exhausted or offended (her father, Edward Bayard, Henry), they were replaced by new sources of encouragement within the wider reform community, principally among Stanton's female friends. Of these Anthony was the most immediate. She shared Stanton's everyday life, visiting frequently and eventually living with her for extended periods. Their friendship and mutual dependence would be cemented by the adversities of the Civil War.

Aided by Anthony, Stanton had endured the depression caused by the events of 1859. She looked forward to the New Year with renewed vigor and excitement. With no more pregnancies to sap her energy, she anticipated approaching her prime after age forty-five and being active twenty years or more. Stanton entered menopause with mixed feelings. Many Victorians assumed it to be an illness that drained female vitality. But compared to the discomforts and disappointments associated with her last two pregnancies, Stanton looked forward to a return to public activity and intellectual creativity.

As she entered the new year, stability and serenity returned. Amelia Willard had long been a household fixture, relieving Stanton of many domestic duties. Baby Bobby was weaned, her next youngest child would be in school with the other five children in another year, and the older boys were almost adults. Stanton's inheritance freed her finally to consider leaving Seneca Falls. She even endorsed Henry's campaign for a political appointment. Yet Henry's fortunes, and those of the abolitionists with whom the couple had been associated for twenty years, depended on the success of the Republican party in 1860.

Unaware of all the changes the decade would bring, Stanton in early 1860 was preoccupied with three speeches Anthony had volunteered her to give. After a pause of six years, she made three major addresses in three months. In March she testified on married women's property rights before the Judiciary Committee of the New York legislature. In May she demanded suffrage for white and black women from the American Anti-Slavery Society in New York City. Two days later she defended divorce before the National Women's Rights Convention. Each speech addressed a major tenet of her as yet uncodified feminist ideology. Each gave her an opportunity to present the conclusions of her Seneca Falls experiences to a wider audience. She traveled by herself or with Anthony and left her children at home or with her mother.

The Married Women's Property Act, passed by the New York legislature in 1848, was the first of its kind in the country. It protected a wife's property from her husband's creditors. The bill had been amended once in 1857, and another bill for enlargement of its scope had been introduced in 1860. The amendments provided that married women had the right to hold real and personal property without the interference of a husband; to carry on any trade or perform any service; to collect and use their own earnings; to buy, sell, and contract with the consent of husbands, unless those husbands were insane, felons, drunkards, or deserters; to sue and be sued; to share joint custody of their children; and to inherit equally with any children on the death of their spouse. The bill, in part a response to petitions initiated by Stanton, Anthony, and their colleagues, gave women the right to act independently.

After spending Christmas 1859 with the Stantons in Seneca Falls, Anthony had camped out in Albany for six weeks. There she lobbied members of the state Senate, which passed the measure enlarging the scope of the Married Women's Property Act in February. Anthony's strategy for the lower house was to focus public attention on the subject and to keep pressure on wavering supporters. She engineered an invitation to Mrs. Stanton to address the Judiciary Committee of the legislature on March 19, 1860. Then she arranged for the testimony to be given in the Assembly chamber, from the speaker's desk, before a huge audience.

In her second appearance before the legislature, Mrs. Stanton compared woman's legal status to that of the slave, demanding that women be treated as citizens rather than as slaves. The ultimate protection for women, their property, and children, Stanton asserted, was the right to vote. Anticipating the usual "separate spheres" objection to women's engaging in the coarseness of public life, Stanton responded:

> But, say you, we would not have women exposed to the grossness and vulgarity of public life, or encounter what she must at the polls. When you talk, gentlemen, of sheltering woman from the rough minds, and revolting scenes of real life, you must be either talking for effect, or be wholly ignorant of what the facts of life are. The man, whatever he is, is known to the woman. She is the companion not only of the statesman, the orator, and the scholar, but the vile, vulgar, brutal man, as his mother, his wife, his sister, his daughter . . . and if man shows out what he is anywhere, it is at his own hearthstone. There are over 40,000 drunkards in this State. All these are bound by the ties of family to some woman. . . . Gentlemen, such scenes as woman has witnessed at her own fireside, where no eyes save Omnipotence could pity, no strong arm could help, can never be realized at the polls.[41]

She called her address "A Slave's Appeal." The Married Women's Property Act passed the New York Assembly the next day.

Emboldened by her reception in Albany, Stanton decided to tackle the divorce issue next. In mid-nineteenth-century America divorce was a scandalous subject. Popular opinion assumed that only adulterers divorced. Many believed that permitting divorce was the same as licensing free love. Divorce threatened the traditional family structure; if allowed, it might rend the fabric of society. Hence the hesitation with which it was treated.

Nonetheless, divorce was the subject of legal debate. In 1859 the Indiana legislature passed a controversial divorce reform bill adding desertion, habitual drunkenness, and cruelty to adultery as grounds for divorce by wives. A similar bill, introduced in the New York legislature in 1860, lost by four votes in the Senate. These developments generated a public discussion of divorce, including a debate in the *New York Tribune* between Robert Dale Owen, author of the Indiana bill, and Horace Greeley, the paper's editor. Despite his generally favorable disposition toward women's rights, Greeley was a principal opponent of the New York bill. It was in this atmosphere that Stanton raised the issue in the spring of 1860.[42]

Stanton notified both Susan Anthony and Lucy Stone that divorce would be the subject of her address to the Tenth National Women's Rights Convention. Ever since their early association in the temperance movement in 1852, the three women had agreed that wives must be able to escape from degrading marriage bonds. In the intervening years Stanton had become more committed, Stone more cautious, while Anthony compromised. Having made her point about habitual drunkenness as grounds for divorce in her presidential address to the Woman's State Temperance Society as early as 1852, Stanton had begun to analyze the question more thoroughly.

Writing to Anthony in 1853, she concluded: "I do not know if the world is quite willing or ready to discuss the question of marriage [but] I feel in my innermost that . . . it is in vain to look for the elevation of woman as long as she is degraded in marriage." Anthony passed the letter on to Stone, who agreed privately with Stanton but considered it "premature" to talk about divorce as a remedy for women's ills as it would scare potential converts away from the women's rights movement. Stone did ask Stanton to write a letter about divorce to the 1856 women's rights convention. She was willing to allow the subject to be raised as long as she was not the lightning rod, so she urged Mrs. Stanton to take the lead.[43]

Stanton's letter to the convention had been straightforward.

> How can she calmly contemplate the barbarous code of laws which govern her civil and political existence? How can she devotedly subscribe to a theology which makes her a conscientious victim of another's will, forever subject to the triple bondage of man, priest, and law? How can she tolerate our social customs, by which womankind is stripped of true virtue, dignity and nobility? How can she endure our present marriage relations by which women's life, health, and happiness are held so cheap that she herself feels that God has given her no charter of rights, no individuality of her own? I answer, she patiently bears all this because in her blindness she sees no way of escape. Her bondage, though it differs from that of the Negro slave, frets and chafes her all the same. She too sighs and groans in her chains and lives but in hope of better things to come. She looks to Heaven, while the more practical slave looks to the North Star, and sets out for Canada. Let it be the object of this convention to show that there is hope for woman this side of Heaven, and that there is work for her to do before she leaves for the Celestial City.[44]

Marriage, Stanton had reiterated, "stripped womankind of true virtue, dignity and nobility." Husbands legally owned wives, body, soul, children, and clothing. Every woman was familiar with stories of sexual abuse in marriage beds. "Man in his lust has regulated this whole question of sexual intercourse long enough," Stanton had written on an earlier occasion. "Let the mothers of mankind [now] set bounds to his indulgence."[45] Revised divorce statutes were necessary to give women a means to protect themselves.

Most of the audience who had heard these remarks in 1856 were shocked. The nature of the response caused Stone to revert to her earlier reservations about not raising the marriage question in the context of women's rights. From then on she insisted that the issue be addressed separately, with "infanticide," abortion, and other sordid topics.[46] When Stanton notified Stone of her plans for the 1860 meeting, Stone declined an invitation to join Stanton on the program.

In the meantime Mrs. Stanton had accepted a last-minute invitation from William Lloyd Garrison to address the opening session of the annual American Anti-Slavery Society meeting in New York, on May 8, 1860. She reminded the abolitionists that women were also slaves in need of emancipation. She urged the society to rise above "custom, creed, conventionalism and constitutions" to liberate women.[47] Her resolutions and the criticism they provoked foreshadowed the fight that would divide and undermine the group before the decade of the 1860s was out.

Many of the same people who had heard her address to the antislavery group were in the hall of the Cooper Institute when the Tenth National Women's Rights Convention was called to order two days later. Mrs. Stanton introduced ten resolutions favoring divorce, such as: "An unfortunate or ill-assorted marriage is ever a calamity, but not ever, perhaps never a crime— and when society or government, by its laws or customs, compels its continuance, always to the grief of one of the parties, and the actual loss and damage of both, it usurps an authority never delegated to man nor exercised by God himself."[48] Having startled her audience to attention, Stanton then spoke for an hour in defense of divorce.

In Stanton's view marriage was a "man-made institution," inherently unjust to wives. With the sanction of church and state, husbands were given absolute authority over wives. She considered the traditional marriage ceremony a "humiliating" symbol of the transfer of a powerless female from "one master to another." While Stanton conceded that "man, too, suffers in the false marriage relation," she was unsympathetic.

> What can his suffering be compared to what every woman experiences, whether happy or unhappy? . . . A man marrying gives up no right, but a woman, every right, even the most sacred of all, the right to her own person. . . . So long as our present false marriage relation continues, which in most cases is nothing more or less than legalized prostitution, women can have no self respect and of course man will have none for her, for the world estimates us according to the value we put upon ourselves. Personal freedom is the first right to be proclaimed, and that does not and cannot now belong to the relation of wife, to the mistress of the isolated home, to the financial dependent.[49]

Women in these and more desperate straits needed the escape hatch of liberalized divorce laws.

Stanton's thesis was that marriage and divorce were private matters that ought not to be regulated by civil or canon law. If the legislatures were to interfere, she urged them to make divorce easier to obtain and marriage more difficult to undertake by establishing age requirements and waiting periods. Marriage should be treated as a simple contract that could be dis-

solved quickly in cases of drunkenness, insanity, desertion, cruel and brutal treatment, adultery, or mere incompatibility. She envisioned divorce
"without delinquencies" or guilty parties.

Stanton cited examples of tragic marriages and asked her audiences if
they believed that those marriages had been made in Heaven. She teased
her friend, Greeley, the chief public opponent of divorce reform.

> I know Horace Greeley has been most eloquent in recent weeks on the
> holy sacrament of ill-assorted marriages; but let us hope that all wisdom
> does not live and shall not die with Horace Greeley. I think if he had been
> married to the *New York Herald* instead of the Republican Party, he would
> have found some scriptural arguments against life-long unions where great
> incompatibility of temper existed between the parties. Horace Greeley in
> his recent discussion with Robert Dale Owen, said that the whole ques-
> tion had been tried in all its varieties and conditions, from indissoluble
> monogamous marriage down to free love. . . . There is one kind of mar-
> riage that has not been tried, and that is a contract made by equal parties
> to lead an equal life, with equal restraints and privileges on either side.
> Thus far, we have had man marriage and nothing more.[50]

When Stanton finished, her friends responded with loud applause while
opponents demanded the floor. Debate raged for an entire session of the
convention. The Reverend Antoinette Brown Blackwell reminded Mrs.
Stanton that the marriage relation was made in heaven and was "as permanent and indissoluble as the relation of parent and child." Lucy Stone
surprised Stanton by joining the negative side. Among recognized feminists, only Ernestine Rose and Anthony supported Stanton. Finally Wendell Phillips, the hero of the 1840 London meeting, moved to table the entire discussion. He sought to remove it from the record, asserting that as
marriage and divorce affected men and women equally, the subject ought
to be out of order at a women's rights convention. William Lloyd Garrison, another opponent, wanted to table the discussion but keep it in the
minutes. Typically Anthony had the last word in defense of Stanton. The
vote was called. The question was tabled and recorded.[51]

Cloture did not end discussion. Public reaction was heated and hostile.
As Stanton recalled later, "Enemies were unsparing in their denunciations
and friends ridiculed the whole proceedings." Although widely censured,
she would not drop the subject. Stanton was becoming accustomed to disapproval. She was characteristically convinced that she alone was right. "My
reason, my experience, my soul proclaim it." Innocently she asserted, "I
began to feel that I had inadvertently taken the underpinning from the social system." That was exactly what she had intended to do. She realized
that any attack on marriage or defense of divorce was indeed a blow at a
patriarchal social system, so she kept hammering away. "This marriage

question," she wrote, "lies at the very foundation of all progress."[52] Divorce reform would continue to attract her support in the decades to come.

But Stanton was also astute enough to realize that divorce was an unacceptable alternative for most women, depriving them of their reputations, homes, children and financial security. Her peripheral involvement in a runaway wife case in 1861 emphasized for her the cruel and unsavory aspect of divorce for the individuals involved.[53] Stanton worked to liberalize and legitimize divorce as one aspect of the larger reform. She believed women must become independent so they could marry and remain married out of choice rather than economic necessity. In order to be free to choose, women had to have equal legal rights, and they had to be able to vote in order to safeguard educational and economic opportunities. Stanton's feminist philosophy encompassed all these issues.

While the debate about divorce continued in the press after the annual women's rights meeting had adjourned, it was soon overshadowed by news of the 1860 Republican National Convention. Delegates swarming into Chicago's Wigwam had to choose a nominee from four candidates: Edward Bates of Missouri, Sen. Salmon P. Chase of Ohio, former congressman Abraham Lincoln of Illinois, and Sen. William Seward of New York. Seward seemed to be the favorite until Chase switched his votes to Lincoln, who was perceived as the most moderate on slavery. One of the delegates was Henry Stanton. Always ready to support a winner, Henry would have jumped on the Lincoln bandwagon had there been one. Unfortunately for Henry's future, he backed Seward, who lost.[54]

Republican opposition to the extension of slavery into the territories won over many abolitionists, including both of the Stantons, but not Anthony. She opposed Lincoln because he favored enforcement of the Fugitive Slave Law and did not endorse Negro citizenship. With the perennial enthusiasm of an old fire dog, Henry joined Lincoln's campaign against Stephen A. Douglas of Illinois, a popular sovereignty Democrat; John C. Breckinridge of Kentucky, a Southern Democrat; and John Bell of Tennessee, representing the Constitutional Union party. Henry secured stump speakers for Lincoln in the Northeast, wrote pamphlets, and then mounted the hustings himself. For only the second time since 1828, Henry supported a winner.[55]

Both Henry and Elizabeth Stanton rejoiced in a Republican victory. They greeted rumors of Southern secession with enthusiasm. Making plans for a family Thanksgiving, Elizabeth wrote her sons at school, "I suppose it is the last time we shall be compelled to insult the Good Father by thanking him that we are a slave holding Republic; I hope and look for dissolution." Eventually the abolitionists would become disenchanted with Lincoln's lack of resolve about ending slavery. Anthony already found him "weak and trembling."[56] But in the flush of victory the Stantons were optimistic. Henry was appointed to a committee to assign New York patronage and began to maneuver for his own promotion.

Elizabeth was swept up in pro-abolition, anti-Southern sentiment. In January 1861 she joined a tour of abolition speakers across upstate New York from Lockport to Albany. Designed to rally antislavery sentiment, pressure Lincoln, and alarm the South, it was Stanton's first public tour. Anthony had organized the troupe, which included Lucretia Mott, Martha Wright, Gerrit Smith, Frederick Douglass, Samuel May, and Stephen Foster. They were met with angry mobs, who feared the possibility of waging war over slavery. The situation was so volatile that mayors along the route viewed the speakers as a threat to public safety. They assigned extra police or refused to open halls to them.[57]

Henry, a veteran of earlier antislavery mobs, was alarmed. "In the present temper of the public mind, it is of no use to try to hold Abolition meetings in large cities," he wrote Elizabeth from Washington. "I think you risk your lives. . . . [The] mobcrats would as soon kill you as not." At Henry's request that she be less reckless, Elizabeth retired from the circuit temporarily, rejoining it in Albany. While there, she and Mrs. Mott testified on behalf of the Ramsey divorce reform bill.[58] In the antislavery meetings she changed her subject from abolition to the abolitionists' right of free speech. Looking back on their experience, Anthony remembered 1861 as "the winter of mobs."[59]

Although Mrs. Stanton had ventured farther afield and been more outspoken on more subjects in 1860 than during the 1850s, she was still tethered to her home and children. In 1861 Wendell Phillips, as trustee of the Hovey Fund, had offered her a three-month European tour to lecture on women's rights. The invitation was his attempt to make amends after the divorce debate. Stanton longed to go, writing to Anthony:

> I would consider it a religious duty to accept this invitation to go abroad as a means of intellectual and spiritual development. It would give me new life and inspiration. I would leave my children with you without the least hesitation. I have more than once doubted the wisdom of sacrificing myself to them as I have done. Oh, what a harvest would three months of travel, reading and society be for me! The thought of it renews every impulse of my soul, but I fear the cup of bliss is not for me. Oh, Susan, how I long to leap into new conditions, but I can only work and wait.[60]

Stanton reluctantly refused. She could not yet shrug off her maternal bonds.

There were many uncertainties in Stanton's life in the spring of 1861. The state of the union was equally unsettled. Seven Southern states had seceded and elected Jefferson Davis provisional president. Lincoln had been inaugurated and war loomed. Stanton's sons were old enough for army service. Two of her nephews had already run away to enlist; one was to die in combat. The Stantons were still living in Seneca Falls. Henry's hopes for an appointment by the Republicans had so far been disappointed. In the interim, as a Washington correspondent for Greeley's *New York Tribune,* Henry had watched Lincoln being sworn in, interviewed Stephen Douglas, and witnessed the arrival of the first army volunteers in the capital city in April. As he wrote Elizabeth, "Me thinks above the general din I hear Old John Brown knocking on the lid of his coffin and shouting, 'let me out, let me out!!' " [61]

Henry's chances for an appointment were tied to Lincoln's cabinet choices. As a delegate who preferred Chase but had voted for Seward, Henry was characteristically caught in the middle. Lincoln brought all his rivals into the cabinet, giving Seward the State Department, Bates the attorney generalship, and Chase the Treasury. Henry coveted the job of solicitor of the treasury, but that plum went to Edward Jordan, an Ohio newspaper editor and attorney who had helped Chase carry the state for Lincoln. Nor was Henry given the deputy solicitor post. After months of finagling, letter writing, meeting, and conniving, Henry was finally given a minor Treasury position, as deputy collector of the Customs House in New York City. The contest over federal jobs in the New York Port Authority had pitted Chase's cronies in the Treasury Department against Seward's closest adviser and Henry's first mentor, Thurlow Weed. Once again Henry was distrusted by both sides. By the time the appointment was announced in August 1861, Henry was fifty-six years old and grateful for any opportunity. [62]

The job required a move to New York City. Eager to leave Seneca Falls, Mrs. Stanton looked forward to the change. Although she would make almost annual pilgrimages to Johnstown, Peterboro, Geneva, and Rochester, she returned to Seneca Falls only once after 1862, when she was paid to speak there.*

For Stanton, Seneca Falls was both a physical and psychological landmark. It was there that Edward Bayard had proposed, that she had broken her engagement to Henry, that she first spoke in public, that she convened the first women's rights convention, first demanded the right to vote, first appeared in print, first donned the bloomers, first met Susan B. Anthony, and first developed and articulated the tenets of her feminist ideology. Yet in Seneca Falls she was unable to resolve the conflicting demands of private and public life. Not until the children were older and she had left Seneca Falls would she be able to fulfill her own expectations of a life devoted to women's rights agitation.

---

*After Stanton's death in 1902 only her family and closest friends commemorated her Seneca Falls connection. In May 1908 the New York Women's Political Union, of which Stanton's daughter Harriot was a leader, unveiled the tablet that today marks the site of the 1848 meeting. Part of the program was led by Elizabeth Smith Miller.

7
War and Scandal
1862–65

Elizabeth Cady Stanton moved to New York City in the spring of 1862. Like Boston, New York was bustling with activity and bursting with energy. Stanton was invigorated by the move and by the war spirit invading the city. As a political abolitionist, she was eager to support a war to end slavery. "The war is music to my ears," she wrote. "It is a simultaneous chorus for freedom."[1] By supporting the Union, Stanton believed feminists would earn the gratitude of both abolitionists and Republicans and be rewarded with suffrage. She did not anticipate any alternate outcome, so she dedicated herself to equal rights for Negroes and women.

Henry had been deputy collector of the Port Authority since August 1861. With Anthony's assistance, Stanton moved first to a house in Brooklyn and then into a brownstone at 75 West 45th Street. Anthony had her own room in each of the Stantons' subsequent households. With her sisters Tryphena Bayard and Harriet Eaton living nearby and many of her reform colleagues in the city on business, Mrs. Stanton established herself easily.

In a city teeming with soldiers, freed blacks, draft resisters, and displaced Southerners, the war seemed more immediate than in sleepy Seneca Falls. Battle news and casualty lists were posted outside the telegraph office, where crowds gathered daily. Even at home the military mood pervaded. Stanton reported to her cousin that the "war's spirit" had a direct influence on her "domestic system." The boys were "drilling every evening in the gymnasium," while the girls skated and played outdoors. All the children took school "in homeopathic doses." "I place the gymnasium above the meeting house," Stanton concluded. "I have great respect for saints with strong bodies."[2]

War dominated the Stanton household. Henry's job at the Customs House was to supervise and secure the port against smugglers and shippers of Southern goods. Neil, the oldest son, had no desire to enroll in the Union Army and eventually joined his father's staff as a clerk. His brother Henry, not yet eighteen, was eager to enlist. Elizabeth tried to arrange a West Point appointment for him from Seward. "The boy has the essential elements of a hero in him, and as all his proclivities are to the army," she wrote to the secretary of state; "I desire that he should have a scientific military education." Before Seward had a chance to reply, young Henry had run away and volunteered. A son in uniform made the war even more personal for Stanton and her family. She proudly counted herself as "one of the mothers of the Republic," willing to sacrifice her son for the cause.[3]

In the summer of 1863 the war came too close to home. Draft rioters burned a black orphanage one block from the Stantons' brownstone, sacked the offices of the *Tribune,* and hanged innocent freedmen. When the mob surged past her house, Stanton sent the servants and children to the fourth floor to escape through the skylight if necessary. She remained at the door, mentally preparing a speech to expel the ruffians. Unexpectedly her oldest and youngest boys were swept up in the crowd on the street. Typically Neil rescued himself by deceit, asking the rowdies to join him in a saloon, "to drink to Jeff Davis." Bobby was later found happily throwing stones at a burning building. Everyone spent the night at Tryphena and Edward Bayard's home and sought refuge the next day in Johnstown. From there Stanton reported the incident to Gerrit and Ann Smith.

> Last Thursday I escaped from the horrors of the most brutal mob I ever witnessed, and brought my children here for safety. The riot raged in our neighborhood through the first two days of the trouble. . . . Greeley was at Bayard's a day and night for safety, and we all stayed there thinking that, as Henry, Susan and I were so identified with reform and reformers, we might at any moment be subjects of vengeance. . . . But a squad of police and two companies of soldiers soon came up and a bloody fray took place near us which quieted the neighborhood.[4]

Like antiabolition mobs, the draft rioters seemed to intensify antislavery commitment, including Stanton's.

Stanton's belligerence galled Anthony, who opposed the war. She thought it was not being fought to free the slaves but to maintain union with slaveholders. Like Mott, Anthony was a pacifist. But her primary objection was that the war would interrupt and reverse the progress being made on behalf of women's rights. Already the New York legislature had gutted the Married Women's Property Act passed in 1860. A newly elected, conservative Assembly had taken away the right of mothers to equal guardianship of their children and eliminated the right of widows to control property left at the death of their husbands. Anthony was outraged. It angered her that few of their former allies even noticed this setback, swept up as they were in the war. Writing to James Mott's sister Lydia, she confessed: "All of our reformers seem suddenly to have grown politic. All alike say, 'Have no conventions at this crisis!' Garrison, Phillips, Mrs. Mott, Mrs. Wright, Mrs. Stanton, etc. say, 'Wait until the war excitement abates.' I am sick at heart, but cannot carry the world against the wish and will of our best friends." To Martha Wright, Anthony complained, "I have not yet seen *one good reason* for the abandonment of all our meetings, and am . . . more and more ashamed and sad . . . that the means must be sacrificed to the end." The practical Martha responded that it was foolish to call a meeting "when the nation's whole heart and soul are engrossed with this momentous crisis and . . . when nobody will listen."[5]

Unlike Anthony, Stanton gave the war priority. She understood that women's rights could not compete for public attention with war and emancipation. While she accepted the facts of Anthony's analysis about war as a setback, Stanton drew another conclusion. She believed that if women aided the war effort wholeheartedly, their good efforts would be rewarded with equal citizenship and suffrage. Indeed, Stanton was so sure that women would soon enter politics that she worried about their lack of preparation. Anthony was unconvinced and pessimistic. She had no confidence in "man's sense of justice" and remained skeptical and critical.[6]

This disagreement over policy was the first major conflict between Stanton and Anthony. Each woman was hurt and angered by the other's recalcitrance. Anthony's refusal to accept Stanton's conclusion and her tenacious counterarguments made Stanton truculent. Her attitude is apparent in her letters to Anthony. "No person is able to understand all the difficulties of another's position, therefore do not read me off your books because I cannot do all that to you seems feasible." In the end Anthony's analysis proved correct and Stanton's wrong. Stanton admitted her error in her autobiography. "When the best of men asked us to be silent on our question during the war, and labor for the emancipation of the slave, we did so, and gave five years to his emancipation and enfranchisement. To this proposition my friend, Susan B. Anthony, never consented, but was compelled to yield because no one stood with her. I was convinced at the time that it was the true policy. I am now equally sure it was a blunder."[7] Women's war work was not rewarded, but neither would Anthony's single-minded strategy have succeeded.

Although they could not agree on feminist tactics, as abolitionists Stanton and Anthony were allied. Both spoke and wrote for the abolition cause. Both believed that the war must end slavery. Both were critical of Lincoln's hesitation to issue the Emancipation Proclamation. As Stanton admitted to Martha Wright, "The administration is too slow and politic to suit my straightforward ideas of justice and vengeance."[8] Both Stanton and Anthony believed that black slaves and freedmen deserved citizenship and suffrage, just as women did.

Although Elizabeth Cady Stanton identified herself as an abolitionist, ending slavery had never been her priority. She was comfortable with the blacks she had known as a child and as an adult. Several of the Cady family servants were black; they had supervised her childhood adventures and protected her from parental discipline. Throughout upstate New York, communities of freed blacks had settled, including those in Peterboro, who were employed and educated by Gerrit Smith. Stanton's memory of meeting a runaway slave in Cousin Gerrit's attic hideaway was vivid. The girl was almost Elizabeth's age and had scars from the lash.[9] In London in 1840 and in Seneca Falls in 1848 black men had supported women's rights. Henry and all his friends were abolitionists, and it was assumed that she shared her husband's commitment.

Stanton was sympathetic to the plight of black slaves. She adapted the metaphor of bondage to women's rights and genuinely believed that a middle-class white wife was as powerless as a Southern field hand. But whenever a choice had to be made, Stanton put women first. Until the war she had never had to make a choice. She had not been as active in anti-slavery as in women's rights. This was partly because she had married a political abolitionist, whose organizational and political allies did not welcome female participation. To join female antislavery societies in Boston or elsewhere would have meant allying herself with Henry's opponents. Her refusal to participate in antislavery fairs or petition drives was the result of a decision to put feminism first. After a conversation with Lucy Stone in the late 1850s, Stanton observed that "Mrs. Stone felt the slaves' wrongs more deeply than her own—my philosophy was more egotistical."[10]

Unlike most nineteenth-century white Americans, Stanton did not believe Negroes or women to be physically or mentally inferior. Her eventual hostility to black men was the result of her assumption that they behaved exactly like white men. She believed that black and white men opposed equal rights for women because it was in their self-interest to keep women subordinate. She later attacked black men on account of gender rather than race.

Stanton and Anthony also agreed on what kind of war work should be undertaken by women. Although they busied themselves with knitting socks and scraping lint for bandages, they did not consider these important tasks. Nor did they volunteer as inspectors for the Sanitary Commission or as nurses for the medical corps. Committed as they were to abolition, the two joined their antislavery friends to push for emancipation in the political arena.

The abolitionists did not hesitate to criticize the administration they were credited with electing. They used the same tactics that had succeeded earlier. In speeches and newspaper articles they castigated Lincoln for not moving fast enough to free the slaves. To prove that emancipation had popular support, they initiated a massive petition drive. After Lincoln's proclamation, issued January 1, 1863, the abolitionists became even more demanding.

Eager to play a visible role in this activity and prompted by Henry Stanton, Stanton and Anthony decided to create a political organization for Northern women. In March 1863 they issued "An Appeal to the Women of the Republic," urging them to band together to "determine the final settlement" of the war. When interested women gathered in New York City in May, Stanton described the group's purpose as education—they would educate themselves and the nation about the "great issues at stake." Stanton proposed that the women "canvass the nation for freedom." The women would serve as a national conscience, reminding the politicians that they were willing to sacrifice their husbands and sons only in a war that would end slavery.[11]

The women decided to collect three million petition signatures in favor of the Thirteenth Amendment to the Constitution, to free the slaves permanently. The connection between slaves and women was reiterated in a typically controversial resolution that was narrowly adopted. "There never can be a true peace in this republic until the civil and political rights of all citizens of African descent and all women are practically established."[12] Persuaded by her own rhetoric Stanton was convinced that they were working both to free slaves and to enfranchise women.

After a two-day meeting the National Woman's Loyal League was established. Elizabeth Cady Stanton was elected president and Susan B. Anthony secretary. Angelina Grimké Weld, Antoinette Brown Blackwell, Lucy Stone, and Ernestine Rose were members. The Loyal League opened offices in the Cooper Union in New York City. A membership badge, showing a slave breaking his own bonds, was designed. Local members met weekly to discuss current political events and military developments and to address and collect petitions. Theodore Stanton, then twelve years old, worked after school counting names and rolling petitions into bundles.[13] By the time it disbanded in August 1864, the Loyal League had collected four hundred thousand signatures. Congressional allies used the petitions as evidence of nationwide support for the Thirteenth Amendment, which was ratified in 1865.

While the National Woman's Loyal League was modeled on the Union

League Club, a bastion of male patriotism, its leadership, membership, and purpose made it suspect to the establishment. The *New York Herald* reported that the Loyal League, "originally designed for the most patriotic and praiseworthy motive, had been distorted into . . . a revolutionary women's rights movement." Its editors hoped that the feminists would "beat a hasty retreat until further notice," since no one had "time for such nonsense and tomfoolery." Ignoring such insults, the Loyal League flourished. Like the Sanitary Commission, it gave women roles and responsibilities, contacts and skills that they would not otherwise have had, and that they applied to other endeavors after the war. As Stanton concluded from the vantage point of old age:

> The leading journals used to vie with each other in praising the patience and prudence, the executive ability, the loyalty, and the patriotism of the women who, when demanding civil and political rights . . . for themselves, had been uniformly denounced as "unwise," "impudent," "fanatical," and "impracticable," . . . and thus it ever is. So long as woman labors to second man's endeavors and exalt his sex above her own, her virtues pass unquestioned; but when she dares to demand rights . . . for herself, her motives, manners, dress, personal appearance, and character are subjects for ridicule and detraction.[14]

Lincoln's procrastination about emancipation, his impunitive reconstruction plan, and the vacillating course of the war caused abolitionists to seek an alternate candidate. Chase, Seward, and Frémont were promoted. Although the Stantons had met Lincoln in Washington, they refused to support him. Elizabeth enjoyed his anecdotes but made fun of his "shriveled appearance" and Mrs. Lincoln's foolish economies.[15] By the end of 1863 Elizabeth Cady Stanton had both political and personal reasons to want Lincoln out of office. She believed that Henry had lost his post on account of enemies in the Lincoln administration.

As deputy collector of the Port Authority of New York, Henry Stanton was in charge of bonds and seizures. According to tariff law and war regulations, all shippers were required to put up bonds to guarantee the legality of their shipments to foreign or domestic ports. The bonds were securities against illicit shipments. If the shipments proved contraband, the government kept the bonds; otherwise they were returned at the end of each voyage. If the bonds were returned to the shippers prematurely, the government had no other immediate remedy. Shippers without bonds had their goods temporarily seized.

Henry did not like his job. He disapproved of the practice of requiring bonds and was eventually removed from seizures by a superior critical of his "hesitation and unwillingness." In a report to Secretary Chase in 1862, the chief collector, Hiram Barney, expressed disappointment in Stanton's performance. He charged that Stanton was neither diligent nor thorough, had failed to systematize the department, and was frequently absent, adding that "his mind is more absent than his body." [16] Stanton apparently had no hint that he was in disfavor. He moved his family to New York City, kept up his antislavery activities, and brought his oldest son into the office as his clerk.

The next report of trouble came when Barney learned from an informer that some bonds had been illegally removed from the office. In effect, no bonds were being held for certain shipments. Eventually it was ascertained that Neil Stanton had taken a bribe and forged his father's signature on several documents. In the spring of 1863 Neil had accepted, recorded, and then removed six or eight bonds from the Customs House. An internal investigation was begun by the Treasury Department. All the evidence implicated Henry Stanton. When confronted in late October 1863, Henry questioned his son. Neil at first denied the charge, then admitted accepting the bribe. The boy was sent home, and Henry was temporarily relieved of his duties.

Then the newspapers got hold of the story. Headlines in the *Times* and the *World* screamed fraud in the Customs House. It was reported that the unnamed deputy collector had been arrested and charged with "conniving with the enemies of his country." The next day, November 1, the *Times* corrected its original report: Henry Stanton had not been arrested and claimed to be ignorant of the theft of the bonds. Rumors spread. The *Albany Atlas* claimed that Henry had allowed munitions to reach enemy lines. The *Tribune,* out of loyalty to its former correspondent and Greeley's friend, ignored the first rumors of scandal. Now it claimed that its competitors' coverage was slanderous. It vouched for Henry's character, noting with unwitting irony, "He is the sort of man who needs office neither to confer distinction nor to secure a livelihood." [17]

In the absence of a Treasury Department report to clear his name, Henry sent an open letter to the *Times* and the *Tribune.* He denied any wrongdoing but admitted that Neil had returned the bonds. As the boy's father and employer, Henry accepted responsibility. As he explained to an old associate in a letter marked "Private":

> My whole case lies in a nutshell. Nobody believes I had anything to do with the [theft] of the bonds. My young son, unfortunately, had. It is this embarrassing feature that cripples me when I try to defend myself. . . . Nothing I did was prohibited by law—though some fools think so—while political enemies raid on me. I have stood up against the rapacities of two officials in the Customs House. They have long tried to drive me out. They seize upon this sad case of my son, to carry out their purpose. . . . Thus one weak boy and two wily scoundrels try to do their worst as boys and scoundrels generally do.[18]

The incident gave the antiadministration press a chance to attack Lincoln through Chase and the Treasury Department. To counter charges of conspiracy, Chase ordered a special inquiry. Henry Stanton was put on leave in October and forced to resign in December 1863. The matter was turned over to a congressional subcommittee. After a three-month investigation the Committee on Public Expenditures presented its report to the House of Representatives. Although no grounds for criminal prosecution could be found, the report was critical of the conduct of Henry Stanton and his son.[19] In some circles Henry's reputation was ruined. His oldest friends, the antislavery radicals, believed he had been the victim of Chase's antipathy. Henry believed that "political necessity and personal malignity were at the bottom of it."[20] Elizabeth believed Henry.

Neither parent blamed Neil. Although Henry's family later claimed that Neil's weak character was the result of his mother's mismanagement, there is no record that Henry felt that way. Neither had ever been able to discipline their firstborn. A letter to his son in 1861 indicates Henry's ineffectiveness.

> My dear son, when I got home I was sorry to learn that you did not go to Geneva till the week after the term commenced. If you knew how bad such things make me feel you would not do them. This delay must have put you behind in your studies all this term. Unless you push on you will never be ready for college. Two years is the usual time allowed to prepare for college, and you are now in the last half of your third year at Reed's. Mr. Keith has brought me his bill. It seems to be pretty much all for "pants for sons." I want you at Geneva to wear your old clothes and not put on your new or best ones every day. . . . Rush on with your Latin, Greek, and Mathematics. Your affectionate father.

Neil never did complete his college preparatory course, and he avoided military service. Before he had taken the Customs House post, his mother had secured him a "good place" in a Livingston relative's commercial firm. Seemingly undaunted by Neil's role in the scandal, Mrs. Stanton asked another relative to give him government post in Washington. He got the job, but the Treasury Department ordered him discharged. There is no further record of his employment until the end of the war, when he joined the Reconstruction regime in Louisiana.[21] First he was a harbor master for New Orleans, then supervisor of elections, and finally a "carpetbag" member of the legislature. When Daniel Cady Stanton finally returned to New York in the 1870s, he was a rich man and still his mother's favorite son.

Both Henry and Elizabeth wrote autobiographies, but neither referred to the Customs House scandal or Henry's tenure there, obviously a source of personal, political, and financial embarrassment. Unemployed from October 1863 until late 1864, Henry joined Greeley's *Tribune* staff as an editorial writer. In 1868 he moved to Charles Dana's *New York Sun,* where he stayed for almost twenty years, until his death in 1887. Henry specialized in state politics, contributed occasional book reviews, and wrote the obituaries of many of his old friends and enemies, including William Lloyd Garrison, Lucretia Mott, Thurlow Weed, William Seward, Salmon Chase, Charles Sumner, and Horace Greeley.[22] When his second son graduated from law school, Henry became an associate in young Henry's practice.

In the aftermath of the Customs House scandal, Elizabeth Cady Stanton felt personally and politically isolated. Old friends avoided the Stantons. She felt compelled to support Henry during this crisis, as she had in the past. She and Henry had been living together without interruption or absences for three years, longer than at any other period in their marriage, but she was more aware of and more critical of his character flaws than she was of Neil's. She wondered if they should move west to start over again. She was also worried about her second son. By February 1865 young Henry was home from the war, suffering from a severe, undefined illness.[23]

Anthony, who had been steadfast during the various investigations, left for an eight-month visit to her brother in Kansas. Her father had died, and she was seeking solace within her own family. Elizabeth felt alone and lonely. A move into a new house at 464 West 34th Street failed to cheer her. It only made her miss Anthony more. As she wrote to her friend:

> I hope in a short time to be comfortably located in a new house where we will have a room ready for you. . . . I long to put my arms about you once more and hear you scold me for all my sins and shortcomings. . . . Oh, Susan, you are very dear to me. I should miss you more than any other living being on this earth. You are entwined with much of my happy and eventful past, and all my future plans are based on you as coadjutor. Yes, our work is one, we are one in aim and sympathy, and should be together. Come home.[24]

The problems with Henry made Stanton value her friendship with Anthony even more. Anthony had never embarrassed or disappointed or deceived her. She had always encouraged Stanton's public ambitions and helped her achieve them. More than any other friend, Anthony had sustained and supported Stanton.

Mrs. Stanton needed an ally. The antislavery movement was torn by political friction, including a dispute over whether to support Abraham Lincoln for reelection. The Stantons preferred Frémont and were critical of old friends who worked for the incumbent after Frémont withdrew. Abolitionists and radical Republicans believed that Lincoln's reelection was a disaster for the nation. When Lincoln was shot, many abolitionists saw it as a "terrible exhibition of God's wrath." As Anthony wrote to Stanton, an angry God who resembled John Brown in appearance had struck the president down, "just at the very hour he was declaring his willingness to consign those five million faithful, brave, loving, loyal [black] people of the South to the tender mercies of the ex-slavelords of the lash." At the time, Mrs. Stanton agreed with Anthony that Lincoln deserved to die for his moderate reconstruction scheme. Later she would regret her harshness.[25]

Unfortunately for Stanton and the women's movement, the reconstruction plans of Lincoln's successors were even less acceptable to women or abolitionists. The politics of postwar reconstruction would compromise the goals of the abolitionists and destroy Stanton's alliance with them. She would be forced to become even more self-reliant.

8
Revolution and Schism
1865–70

For Elizabeth Cady Stanton and advocates of women's rights, Reconstruction would be more divisive and destructive than the Civil War. The fight over postwar reconstruction policy began before Lee had surrendered or Lincoln had been shot. It inflamed the summer of 1865. Its outcome would determine the future of the women's movement in America.

In the five years following the Civil War feminists found themselves pitted against the Republican majority in Congress, against their longtime allies in antislavery, and against the former slaves they had worked to free. The women were defeated in every encounter. By insisting on primacy for women's rights and parity for female suffrage, Stanton and her associates angered everybody. Having failed to promote suffrage in coalition efforts, Stanton and Anthony finally formed a separate organization, the National Woman Suffrage Association. But because of Stanton's radical rhetoric and her wide-ranging demands, conservative feminists formed a rival group, the American Woman Suffrage Association. This division lasted twenty years and diminished the impact of feminists in the Gilded Age.

During the postwar period Elizabeth Cady Stanton was engaged in the public arena. Fifty years old in 1865, she was more active and controversial than at any other time in her life. Even before the end of the war she had traveled independently as an abolitionist speaker, addressed the New York legislature on married women's property rights and divorce, established the National Woman's Loyal League, and organized the largest petition drive to date in support of the Thirteenth Amendment to end slavery. After the war she reconvened the annual women's rights conventions; started four organizations (the American Equal Rights Association, the

Working Women's Association, the Woman Suffrage Association of America, and the National Woman Suffrage Association); campaigned for female suffrage in the District of Columbia, New York, and Kansas; ran for Congress as an independent; edited a newspaper; helped stop a move by the legislature to legalize prostitution in New York; opposed the Fourteenth and Fifteenth amendments; and formulated a plan for ratification of a sixteenth amendment enfranchising women. Stanton reasserted her claim to leadership of the women's rights movement. She had not yet envisioned all that her future would encompass, but she was ready to become the political strategist, philosopher, and propagandist of the new movement. In five years her ambitions would become actualities.

Throughout this period Stanton was at the center of controversy for a more sustained period than she had been or would be again. By 1870 she had few friends among her former reform colleagues. In promoting female suffrage she opposed granting the vote to black males and made many racist and anti-male remarks. William Lloyd Garrison, the dean of antislavery reformers, castigated her as a "female demagogue." He regarded her as "untruthful, unscrupulous and selfishly ambitious."[1]

In the face of widespread disapproval Stanton depended more on the few people who did approve of her tactics. This small group still included Anthony, Libby Miller, and Mrs. Mott, although the older woman had more reservations than the others. Increasingly, Stanton approved herself. She relied on her self-confidence, good humor, optimism, self-protective habits, and resourcefulness to combat the pervasive public criticism of this period.

Stanton was again without role models among the women she knew. No one else had been so singularly outspoken. Unable to identify one model, she sought to combine the strengths of the women she admired, like Mott, with the talents of the men she had known in the antislavery movement, among them William Lloyd Garrison and Henry Stanton. Her failure to secure woman suffrage after the war may reflect the weakness and inappropriateness of her role models as well as the political realities of the era.

In essence, Stanton came to rely on the Garrisonian tactics of propaganda and persuasion. Because she had not been able to muster support for political action, her political efforts failed. So she chose preaching over politics. Stanton became convinced that she could not influence legislatures until she had changed public attitudes. She believed that women must be enfranchised because they had a natural right to vote and needed legal guarantees of equality. But she was unwilling to sacrifice her stands on marriage and divorce or working women, whatever was most immediate, in order to win eventual legislative support for suffrage. She did not compromise; she demanded every right. After this period of intense political activity Stanton would withdraw from the arena and redefine her role.

Personal and political developments enabled Stanton to undertake a more independent role after 1865. Her relationship with Henry was changing. Throughout the Customs House ordeal she had been resolute. For a short period, before the demands of her own life took precedence, she was affectionate, concerned, and optimistic. She envisioned a "new life" for them both, perhaps in a new place. As she wrote to Henry from Kansas in 1867:

> This is the country for us to move to. . . . Ponies are cheap here, so that all our children could ride and breathe, and learn to do big things. I cannot endure the thoughts of living again that contracted eastern existence. Here the boys could rise. . . . You would feel like a new being here. I have not had a stiff knee or rheumatism since I came into the State. You could be a leader here as there is not a man in the State that can make a really good speech.[2]

But the Stantons did not settle in Kansas. By the time she returned from her trip the personal and political disagreements between them had sharpened, making it difficult for them to live together anywhere.

Rather than create a new life for them both, Stanton tried to make one for herself. For the first time in their marriage the decision to move was motivated not by Henry's well-being but by hers. She no longer allowed Henry's employment or lack of it to determine her residence or occupation. In 1868 she purchased a large country house in Tenafly, New Jersey.* After longing to escape Seneca Falls for the city, Mrs. Stanton now wanted to move to the country. The Tenafly house, with its encircling porch and surrounding gardens, was financed by her Cady inheritance. It was within a mile of the commuter train station, so she, Henry, and the older boys could come and go into the city. During the week the Stantons and Susan Anthony stayed in town on Tenth Avenue. Soon Elizabeth was spending more time in Tenafly, while Henry spent less. "He comes home but once in two weeks," she commented to Cousin Gerrit in 1869.[3] Eventually their city-country arrangement evolved into two separate households, a conclusion that suited both her personal and physical needs.

As a couple, the Stantons spent less and less time together. By 1870 they maintained separate households, and they seemed to divide responsibility for the children. Both remained concerned parents, but Elizabeth no longer allowed her domestic roles to confine her. Her independence is reflected in one child's early memory, in which train whistles signaled her mother's arrival.[4] There is little written evidence of the couple's feelings for one another, but many factors may have contributed to the rift.

Mrs. Stanton's refusal to acknowledge Neil's guilt in the Customs House matter may have contributed to the couple's physical and psychological

---

*The house still stands on Highwood Avenue; it is privately owned.

separation. Neil was responsible for the loss of her husband's job and his reputation, yet her firstborn remained her favorite and could do no wrong in her eyes. This attitude may have alienated her older sons as well as her husband.

Sixty years old in 1865, Henry Stanton continued to attend political rallies and reform meetings, including some featuring his wife as speaker. He no longer despised Republicans, but they distrusted him. Among abolitionists, the Customs House scandal had obscured memories of his earlier heroism. He was forced into the background at the same time that his wife rose to prominence among his peers. In addition to writing for newspapers, Henry occasionally practiced law. He could afford less prestigious and less lucrative employment now that the Cady inheritance and his wife's income from writing and lecturing provided for the children and maintained the Tenafly house.

Elizabeth Cady Stanton's relationship with Susan Anthony was also changing. Anthony's freedom to travel in the 1850s had made Stanton dependent on her. As she remarked in 1870, "Through all these years, Miss Anthony was the connecting link between me and the outer world—the reform scout who went to see what was going on in the enemy's camp and returned with maps and observations to plan the mode of attack."[5] Put in the passive role of reacting to Anthony's demands, Stanton responded with speeches, tracts, or organizational activity. Anthony's interest in temperance, abolition, and education took precedence over Stanton's concern for divorce reform, married women's property rights, and suffrage. To compensate, Stanton made every topic she addressed a question of women's rights. Their talents and tactics were complementary, but Stanton's emphasis on agitation and Anthony's preference for organization eventually created a rift between them as well.

It was during the 1860s that the two women first came into conflict. As Mrs. Stanton became more active and more visible, she became more assertive in their partnership. She overrode Anthony's objections and forced her to put aside women's rights questions for the duration of the Civil War. Stanton's regret over that decision and her acknowledgment that she had been wrong subsequently enabled Anthony to regain the upper hand for a short time. During the critical period following the war Stanton preferred to act in unison with Anthony. "I have always found that when we see eye to eye we are sure to be right, and when we pull together we are strong," she admitted to Anthony in 1867. "I take my beloved Susan's judgment against the world."[6]

If they could not agree, Stanton and Anthony argued in private until one of them conceded. During the postwar period Stanton was usually the first to compromise. Having broken with Henry she was unwilling to break with Anthony. She believed that "like husband and wife," she and Anthony must always appear to agree in public. Even with Henry she maintained the appearance of marriage. She really had no model for discord. Her parents' marriage and those of her friends had been cordial relationships, and the diplomatic mode appealed to her own disposition.[7]

By 1865 the Stanton-Anthony friendship had evolved into a partnership of equals. Each admired the other's capacities and accepted any shortcomings. In the aftermath of the Customs House scandal and prelude to the reconstruction fight, Stanton needed the comfort of uncritical friendship and Anthony needed Stanton's intelligence. As Stanton reassured her: "If your life depends on me, I will be your stay and staff to the end. No power in heaven, hell, or earth can separate us, for our hearts are eternally wedded together. Ever yours, and I mean *ever*, Elizabeth Cady Stanton."[8]

Throughout the war Stanton had been a loyal abolitionist. More active than during the antebellum years, she had worked for Lincoln's election after the convention in 1860, joined the antislavery crusade in upstate New York in 1861, postponed her feminist demands, founded the National Woman's Loyal League, amassed petition signatures for the Thirteenth Amendment, supported Frémont over Lincoln in 1864, and backed Wendell Phillips when he challenged William Lloyd Garrison for leadership of the American Anti-Slavery Society. At the society's annual meeting in May 1864 Garrison had moved to disband the organization. He insisted that its work had been completed with the Emancipation Proclamation and the anticipated passage of the Thirteenth Amendment. The slaves had been freed. The majority of the society, including Elizabeth Cady Stanton, disagreed. They supported Phillips's argument that the work was incomplete until the slaves had been made citizens and enfranchised. Garrison's motion to disband was defeated, and he resigned. He suspended publication of the *Liberator*, accepted a gift of thirty thousand dollars from admirers, and went to Paris. Stanton's candidate, Phillips, was elected president of the group. For her loyalty to Phillips and the Anti-Slavery Society, Stanton expected abolitionists to include woman suffrage on their postwar agenda.

Similarly Phillips and the abolitionists expected the Republicans to enact their suggestions. The triumphant congressional majority, eager to punish the South and enroll ex-slaves as Republican voters, adopted many abolitionist measures as their own. By the summer of 1865 language for another amendment was circulated. The draft of the Fourteenth Amendment conferred citizenship on every male born or naturalized in the United States, prohibited states from abridging "equal protection" of citizens, reduced congressional representation for states that denied the ballot to blacks, disbarred ex-Confederates from holding office, and repudiated the Confederate debt. Officially proposed by the Joint Committee on Reconstruction in April 1866, the Fourteenth Amendment had to be ratified by three-fourths of the reunited states. In effect, Southern legislatures would be forced to ratify it.[9]

During the summer of 1865 Congressman Robert Dale Owen of Indiana, an ally of Stanton's on divorce reform, sent her copies of the various drafts of the Fourteenth Amendment.[10] Insertion of the word "male" to define citizens and legal voters jarred Stanton. Previously women had assumed they were citizens. The question of whether or not women might vote had been considered a state matter, similar to property rights or divorce reform. Female property owners had frequently voted before the Revolution, and in New Jersey women had voted in all elections until 1808. More recently widows and other female taxpayers had been allowed to vote in some states on some subjects, such as school board members and bond issues. The proposed Fourteenth Amendment equated citizenship with voting rights and made both dependent on gender. Without the word "male," the language could be interpreted to include women as citizens and voters. With the word "male", it would require another constitutional amendment to enfranchise women.

Having been seduced by her own wartime rhetoric, Stanton still believed that women would be rewarded with the vote for their service to the nation. She was outraged at the infidelity of her antislavery allies. She demanded that Phillips and the abolitionists insist that the Fourteenth Amendment include women. He refused to "mix the movements," because "such mixture would lose for the Negro far more than we should gain for the woman." In order to abolish slavery, Phillips and the abolitionists insisted on recognizing Negro citizenship, "where citizenship supposes the ballot for all men." An angry Stanton shot back: "May I ask in reply to your fallacious letter just one question based on the apparent opposition in which you place the Negro and woman. My question is: Do you believe the African race is composed entirely of males?" With Phillips and "the whole fraternity" favoring Negro rather than universal suffrage, "woman's cause is in deep water," Stanton reported to Anthony in mid-1865. "Come back and help."[11]

Anthony returned from Kansas in August. Together she and Stanton planned several steps, first initiating a petition drive and then convening a women's rights convention. As Stanton recalled, "Miss Anthony and I were the first to see the full significance of the word 'male' in the Fourteenth Amendment, and we at once sounded the alarm." They sent out petitions for a constitutional amendment to "prohibit the states from disenfranchising any of their citizens on the grounds of sex."[12]

After a six-month effort they had collected only ten thousand signatures, less than 3 percent of the number who had favored the Thirteenth Amendment. Few former members of the Loyal League were helpful now. Nor were earlier advocates of women's rights supportive. When Martha Wright admitted wanting to "rest on her oars," Stanton chastised her, promising to persevere alone if necessary.

> [Your] letter . . . would have been a wet blanket to Susan and me were we not sure that we are right. . . . If the petition goes with two names only, ours be the glory, and shame to all the rest. We have had a thousand petitions printed, and when they are filled they will be sent to Democratic members who will present them to the House. But if they come back to us empty, Susan and I will sign every one, so that every Democratic member may have one with which to shame those hypocritical Republicans.[13]

Republican refusal to accept the suffrage petitions contributed to the reluctance of reform women to sign them. Sen. Charles Sumner considered the petitions "most importune"; Rep. Thaddeus Stevens refused to introduce those Mrs. Stanton sent him.[14] The refusal infuriated Stanton and confirmed her worst suspicions about the Republican party. When Stanton and Anthony then turned to Democrats to introduce the petitions, they further angered the Republican majority and undercut any chance they might have had for success.

The argument that black and white women deserved the vote as much as freedmen had few advocates. The insistence of abolitionists and Republicans that black male suffrage take precedence over female suffrage enraged Stanton. In defense she adopted an antiblack, antimale, profemale argument. According to Stanton, it was better and safer to enfranchise educated white women than former slaves or ignorant immigrants. The same women she had previously found small-minded and superstitious were now more intelligent and more noble than most men. "The best interests of the nation demand that we outweigh this incoming pauperism, ignorance, and degradation, with the wealth, education, and refinement of the women of the republic," she declared. Her elitist, racist, nativist appeal appalled even her most stalwart friends. Mrs. Mott was ashamed of Stanton's lack of "sympathy for Sambo" and bluntly asked her to justify herself.[15] Stanton responded by claiming that without votes or influence, her only weapon was to attack those who opposed her.

In their effort to rally the support of women's rights advocates and the reform community, Stanton and Anthony announced the first women's rights convention since the war, "to reconstruct a government on the one enduring basis that has never been tried—Equal Rights to All." But because their opposition to the Fourteenth Amendment was well known, few people re-

Judge Daniel Cady. From an oil painting. *Courtesy of Rhoda Barney Jenkins*.

Margaret Livingston Cady. From an oil painting.
Courtesy of Vassar College Library.

Cady mansion, Johnstown, New York.
Courtesy of Rhoda Barney Jenkins.

Elizabeth Cady, age twenty. *Courtesy of Brigham Young
University Photoarchives.*

Emma Willard, *c.* 1830. *Courtesy
of Emma Willard School,
Troy, New York.*

Gerrit Smith. From an oil painting by Daniel Huntington, 1874.
*Courtesy of the Madison County Historical Society,
Oneida, New-York.*

Henry Brewster Stanton, at age eighty, in 1885. *Courtesy of the New-York Historical Society.*

The Executive Committee of the Philadelphia Anti-Slavery Society, 1851.
BACK ROW: Mary Grew, Edward Davis, Haworth Wetherald, Abbey Kimber,
J. Miller McKim, Sarah Pugh. FRONT ROW: Oliver Johnson, Margaret Jones
Burleigh, Benjamin Bacon, Robert Purvis, Lucretia Mott, James Mott.
Courtesy of the Sophia Smith Collection, Smith College.

Susan B. Anthony, *c.* 1850, about the time she met Elizabeth Cady Stanton.
Courtesy of Vassar College Library.

Elizabeth Cady Stanton with her sons
Henry and Daniel, *c.* 1848.
Courtesy of Rhoda Barney Jenkins.

Elizabeth Cady Stanton with young Henry, *c.* 1855.
Courtesy of Rhoda Barney Jenkins.

Elizabeth Cady Stanton's middle children: Margaret, born 1852, and Theodore, born 1851. *Courtesy of Rhoda Barney Jenkins.*

Elizabeth Cady Stanton with her second daughter, Harriot, age three and a half months, 1858. *Courtesy of Rhoda Barney Jenkins.*

Elizabeth Cady Stanton, shortly after she organized the National Woman Suffrage Association, 1869. *Courtesy of Rhoda Barney Jenkins.*

Elizabeth Cady Stanton and Susan B. Anthony, *c.* 1870. *Courtesy of the Smithsonian Institution, Washington, D.C.*

Stanton's daughters, Margaret and Harriot, in Johnstown with their Cady aunts, Harriet Eaton, Tryphena Bayard, and Catherine Wilkeson, *c.* 1870. *Courtesy of Rhoda Barney Jenkins.*

George Francis Train. *Courtesy of the Library of Congress.*

Victoria Woodhull, *c.* 1872.
*Courtesy of the Sophia
Smith Collection, Smith College.*

Elizabeth Cady Stanton and
Susan B. Anthony, *c.* 1880.
Courtesy of the Library of Congress.

Stanton home in Tenafly, New Jersey. *Courtesy of* The Record, *Hackensack, New Jersey.*

Three generations: Elizabeth Cady Stanton with granddaughter Nora and daughter Harriot Stanton Blatch, 1892. *Courtesy of Rhoda Barney Jenkins.*

The International Council of Women met in Washington, D.C., on March 25, 1888. Mrs. Stanton is seated in the front row, fifth from left. Anthony is third from left, Matilda Joslyn Gage is sixth. In the second row, starting with the second person, are Anna Howard Shaw, Frances Willard, and Lillie Devereux Blake. In the last row, Rachel Foster Avery stands second from left. *Courtesy of the Smithsonian Institution, Washington, D.C.*

Susan B. Anthony and Elizabeth Cady Stanton, 1891, at Anthony's home in Rochester. *Courtesy of the Susan B. Anthony Memorial, Rochester, New York.*

Elizabeth Cady Stanton, *c.* 1895, with her oldest daughter, Margaret Lawrence, and her youngest son, Robert Stanton, with whom she lived in the 1890s.
Courtesy of Rhoda Barney Jenkins.

Elizabeth Smith Miller. *Courtesy of Vassar College Library.*

Elizabeth Cady Stanton, "America's Grand Old Woman," 1895. *Courtesy of the Smithsonian Institution, Washington, D.C.*

Busts of Elizabeth Cady Stanton, Susan B. Anthony, and Lucretia Mott, in the crypt of the United States Capitol. *Courtesy of the Library of Congress.*

The regal self sovereign: Elizabeth Cady Stanton in 1900.
Courtesy of Rhoda Barney Jenkins.

sponded to their call. One who did was Sojourner Truth, the former slave famous for her "Ain't I a Woman?" speech. She attended the Eleventh National Women's Rights Convention and stayed with the Stantons.[16] The majority of reformers agreed that it was "the Negro's hour."

The Eleventh National Women's Rights Convention had been called for May 1866. It was scheduled to coincide with the first meeting of a new organization, the American Equal Rights Association (AERA), the brainchild of Theodore Tilton, the young, long-haired editor of the *Independent*.* He proposed the AERA as a coalition for supporters of black and female suffrage and persuaded the leaders of both groups to merge into one body. Stanton accepted Tilton's proposals so that "the same conventions, appeals, and petitions, might include both classes of disfranchised citizens." At Stanton's urging, Lucretia Mott accepted the AERA presidency. Stanton was elected first vice-president, and Anthony became corresponding secretary. All three women served on the executive committee. Stanton wrote the preamble to the platform. At Anthony's insistence it promised "universal suffrage."[17]

It was soon apparent that the feminists had been naive. The vehicle that Stanton and Anthony had hoped would unite reformers behind their cause ended up being used against them. At the end of May 1866 Wendell Phillips convened the executive committee of the AERA in Boston. In the absence of Mott and Stanton, the committee approved his plan to make black male suffrage paramount. With the support of the AERA and without the opposition of any other organization, the Fourteenth Amendment was ratified in July 1868, excluding women from citizenship and voting rights.

Unable to change the wording of the Fourteenth Amendment, Stanton next tried to reinterpret it. She claimed that nothing in the Constitution forbade women from holding office, whether or not they could vote. In August 1866 she nominated herself as an independent candidate for Congress, the first woman to run for that office. In a letter addressed to "the electors" of New York City's Eighth District, Mrs. Stanton advocated "free speech, free press, free men, and free trade." She chose an independent candidacy, she explained, because the Democrats did not have "a clear vision of personal rights" and because the Republicans lacked "sound . . . principles on trade and commerce." Finally, of course, she endorsed wom-

---

* Theodore Tilton (1835–1907) was hired by Horace Greeley to report for the *Tribune*. He married a Plymouth Church Sunday school teacher in 1855 and became a protégé of the minister Henry Ward Beecher. After publishing Beecher's sermons, Tilton took over the *Independent* and supervised the Sunday school. In the aftermath of the Beecher-Tilton scandal (see chap. 9), Tilton lived in Paris until his death.

en's rights. "I would gladly have a voice and vote in the Fortieth Congress to demand *universal* suffrage, that thus a republican form of government might be secured to every state in the Union."[18]

Stanton found the campaign a "merciless duty." She handed out two-inch square white cards, imprinted "For Representative to Congress, Elizabeth Cady Stanton." In addition to "printing tickets and handbills and . . . holding up her political opponents to the criticism of men and angels," she had other demands on her time, as she reported to Libby Miller. "I must buy butter and meat, hear youngsters spell and multiply, coax parted threads in stocking heels and toes to meet again . . . and smooth down the ruffled feathers of imperious men, of cross chambermaids and cook. Then comes Susan, with the nation on her soul, asking for speeches, resolutions, calls, attendance at conventions." Running against an incumbent Democrat and regular Republican, Mrs. Stanton received only twenty-four votes. Looking back on her defeat, she only regretted that she had not "procure[d] photographs of her two dozen unknown friends."[19]

Stanton suffered one more defeat in 1866. In December a Senate bill to extend the vote to Negroes in the District of Columbia again raised the issue of woman suffrage. Sen. Thomas Cowan, Republican of Pennsylvania, moved to strike the word "male." His motion resulted in the first congressional debate on woman suffrage. It was marked by ridicule, disdain, and contempt. Suffrage advocates in the Senate used arguments provided by Stanton and Mott. They stated that women were citizens with legal rights equal to those of men and therefore deserved to vote. The opposition countered with claims that would be repeated for the next fifty years. Women did not need to vote because they were well represented by husbands, fathers, brothers, or sons. Women lacking protective male relatives were ignored. Further, the opponents argued, women were physically and mentally unfit for "the turmoil and battle of public eye." Indeed, female suffrage would create a sexual "state of war." The Cowan amendment was defeated thirty-seven to nine.[20]

Unable to win suffrage for women at the federal level or in the federal city, Stanton and Anthony spent 1867 trying to assure it at the state level, in New York and in Kansas. The revision of the New York state constitution provided the women with an opportunity to present their case on home ground. Already well known in Albany, Stanton and Anthony used all the tactics that they had perfected in the past. In January, Stanton addressed the Judiciary Committee. She argued that the committee had the power to allow women to vote for and serve as delegates to the constitutional convention. Members objected that few women besides Mrs. Stanton and Miss Anthony seemed to desire the vote. Stanton countered by asking if they had asked urchins if they wanted common schools, drunkards if they wanted temperance, or slaveholders if they wanted emancipation?[21]

Failing to persuade the committee, Stanton asked for and was granted a public hearing at the convention in June. Meanwhile Stanton and Anthony organized a statewide petition drive, collecting the signatures of women who did want to vote. One signer was Margaret Cady of Johnstown, Stanton's mother. They also circulated ten thousand copies of John Stuart Mill's speech to Parliament advocating woman suffrage and tried to raise fifteen hundred dollars for expenses.[22]

In June 1867 Stanton appeared before the suffrage subcommittee of the constitutional convention, which was chaired by Horace Greeley. Greeley interrupted her testimony by asking why women should have the ballot if they could not defend it with a bullet? Stanton retorted, too flippantly, "We are ready to fight, Sir, just as you did in the late war, by sending our substitutes." Insulted once, Greeley was even more offended when Stanton presented the petitions. She read out the full name of the first signer of each petition until she came to Mary Cheney Greeley, whom Stanton identified instead as "Mrs. Horace Greeley."[23]

Afterwards Stanton believed that Greeley had been so annoyed by her trick that he saw to it that her amendment was defeated. The committee report recommended only universal manhood suffrage. "We are satisfied that public sentiment does not demand and would not sustain an innovation so revolutionary and sweeping, so openly at war with a distribution of duties and functions between the sexes, . . . and involving transformations so radical in social and domestic life," concluded his report.[24]

Stanton also believed that Greeley ordered his staff at the *Tribune* to cover her activities as briefly as possible and to refer to her only as "Mrs. Henry B. Stanton." Although there is no recorded connection, it was at this time that Henry moved from the *Tribune* to the editorial pages of the *New York Sun*. In losing "the friendship of Horace Greeley and the support of the *New York Tribune*," Stanton concluded, militant women had lost "our most powerful and faithful allies," as well as suffrage in New York State.[25] But she never apologized or attempted to make amends with her first editor and old friend.

The split between reformers evident in New York was intensified in Kansas. There the legislature had put two propositions on the ballot: one offered to remove the word "male" from the state's voting requirements, thus enfranchising women; the other would add the word "Negro," thus allowing black suffrage. In November 1867 Kansans could express an opinion on both female and Negro suffrage. The case for black suffrage was made by most abolitionists, some Republicans, and three Eastern newspapers with wide Kansas circulations—Greeley's *Tribune,* Tilton's *Independent,* and Phillips's *Anti-Slavery Standard,* financed by the Hovey Fund. None of these supported woman suffrage.[26]

To make the case for women, state senator Samuel Wood and former governor Charles Robinson invited well-known women's rights advocates, including Stanton, Anthony, and Stone, to come to Kansas. Unable to accept Wood's appeal because of the New York constitutional convention, Anthony urged Lucy Stone and her husband, Henry Blackwell, to go ahead without her or Mrs. Stanton. Stone accepted the assignment. Together Anthony and Stone overrode Wendell Phillips's objections and used fifteen hundred dollars from the Jackson Fund to cover the expenses of Stone and Blackwell, who canvassed the state during the spring of 1867. Their letters, full of optimism about the outcome in Kansas, were read at the May meeting of the American Equal Rights Association in New York. They urged Stanton and Anthony to hurry west. The two women finally arrived in September and stayed until the election. According to colleagues and critics alike, they determined the outcome in Kansas.

Kansas was Stanton's first extended outing and her first trip west. Anthony set up headquarters in Leavenworth, near her brother's home. To cover more territory, she and Stanton toured the state separately. Mrs. Stanton, usually escorted by Robinson, spoke two or three times a day and at least once on Sundays. The speakers frequently faced harassment on the hustings. Reactions of the men in the audiences ranged from hostile to humorous, but the women seemed more sympathetic. No longer subsidized by the Jackson Fund, Stanton and Anthony had the added embarrassment of passing the hat to pay their expenses.

Pioneer conditions prevailed. Stanton traveled by buckboard "to the very verge of civilization, wherever two dozen voters could be assembled, . . . We spoke in log cabins, in depots, unfinished school houses, churches, hotels, barns, and in the open air." As she exclaimed to her cousin, "Oh, Julius, the dirt, the food!!"[27] Mrs. Stanton longed for hot baths, clean beds, butter on her biscuits, and cream in her coffee. But she accepted the discomforts with her usual good humor and was widely accepted. Her respectable appearance, her maternal manner, her quick wit, her genuine pleasure in the prairie, and her appreciation for its pioneers endeared her to the public.

Elizabeth Cady Stanton survived Kansas and felt invigorated. "It gave me added self respect," she wrote to her sisters, "to know that I could endure such hardships and fatigue with a great deal of cheerfulness." She came to the conclusion that she was "well born" and "put together with unusual wisdom" by her parents.[28] Initially worried about the outcome, Stanton had survived physical hardship and political adversity. The experience enhanced her self-confidence. She felt capable of taking on any other challenge because she had learned that she could endure harassment and hardship.

Had Stanton and Anthony been more realistic about the political climate of the country in 1867, they might have been able to predict the outcome of the Kansas referendum. Kansas was a Republican state whose Republican machine opposed woman suffrage. The women lost, tallying less than one-third of the votes cast. Despite support from Republican politicians and the press, black suffrage was also defeated. Before woman suffrage was enacted as a constitutional amendment in 1920, there would be fifty-six such state referenda; Kansas was only the first.[29]

Eastern reformers blamed the double defeat in Kansas on George Francis Train,* an eccentric Democrat who seemed to have captivated Stanton and Anthony. Their association with Train, a "copperhead" dandy and speculator, triggered the final split between the two women and their former colleagues. Tall, handsome, wealthy, and eloquent, Train was a flamboyant young man with presidential ambitions. He was in Kansas to test his dramatic appeal and his even more unusual platform. As sincere as a showman could be, Train espoused women's rights, an eight-hour work day, paper currency, and free trade, but he vehemently opposed black suffrage.

The women were dazzled by Train's charm and audacity. On the hustings the three of them were a spectacle: Train in a colored waistcoat, patent leather boots, and lavender gloves, spewing epigrams; Stanton, round and pleasant in dusty black silk and lace, alternating between wit and logic; Anthony, tall and austere, in a severe habit, scolding the audience for its shortsightedness. They did not appear together often in Kansas, but when they did their effect was such that legends arose.

The strange misalliance was based on a shared commitment to women's rights and "educated suffrage," positions on which Stanton agreed with Train. She also wanted to exclude blacks and immigrants from citizenship unless women were enfranchised at the same time. She did not like being put in an inferior legal position when she considered herself a superior person. In fact, she began to think of herself as extraordinary. She modified her basic republican ideology of the natural rights of all citizens. She continued to believe that equal educational opportunity for women, blacks, immigrants, and others would create an equal citizenry, but in the meantime she elevated superior womanhood and derided "Sambo."

---

* George Francis Train (1829–1904) was America's "Champion Crank." A merchant and promoter, he made and lost fortunes in American shipping and British streetcars. An orphan who had worked since he was fourteen, he lived a sensational life marked by scandals and arrests. He was married in 1851 and had four children.

Already embarrassed by Stanton's educated suffrage rhetoric, the reform community was outraged by her condemnation of the Republican party. Her critics claimed that by associating with a Democrat like Train she had alienated the Republicans and lost Kansas. Stanton and Anthony refused to believe that their connection with Train had undercut the effort and in the end lost the campaign. They blamed the defeat on the Republican party for failing to support universal suffrage. Robinson believed that the cause was "indebted to Elizabeth Cady Stanton," but he dismissed "the noise and bluster of a *bombastes furiousi* [Train] or the driving and scolding of any-one [Anthony]."[30] Although woman suffrage would soon be popular in the West it was premature and unsophisticated to expect to win in Kansas.

What made Train even more appealing to Stanton and Anthony than his politics was his money. In the midst of the Kansas campaign he had promised them a newspaper of their own. He arranged for them to publicize it with a sixteen-city lecture tour on their return east and paid all the bills for their trip. Stanton was so caught up with Train that when their tour brought her close to Libby Miller's upstate New York home, she had to apologize for not stopping. She could not alter her itinerary because she was "fastened to the tail of a comet."[31] Other reformers thought she had tied herself to the devil, disguised as George Train.

Lucy Stone was convinced that Stanton had sold her soul. Reading newspaper reports of the unlikely alliance, Stone vehemently denied any connection between Train and the American Equal Rights Association, which had sponsored, but not subsidized, Stanton and Anthony in Kansas. "Mr. Train is a lunatic, wild and ranting," she wrote afterwards. "[His] presence as an advocate of woman suffrage was enough to condemn it in the minds of all persons not already convinced." She condemned Anthony for making a "spectacle" of herself. "It seems to me that she is hardly less crazy than he is." William Lloyd Garrison chastised them directly, writing Anthony:

> In all friendliness, and with the highest regard for the woman's rights movement, I cannot refrain from expressing my regret and astonishment that you and Mrs. Stanton should have taken such leave of good sense as to be traveling companions and associate lecturers with that crack-brained harlequin and semi-lunatic, George Francis Train. . . . You will only subject yourselves to merited ridicule and condemnation, and turn the movement which you aim to promote into unnecessary contempt. . . . The colored people and their advocates have not a more abusive assailant than . . . Train. He is as destitute of principle as he is of sense, and is fast gravitating toward a lunatic asylum. He may be of use in drawing an audience, but so would a kangaroo, a gorilla or a hippopotamus.[32]

Such criticism made Stanton and Anthony more stubborn and less discriminating about Train's flaws. "Mr. Train is a pure, high toned man, without a vice," Stanton wrote to Martha Wright in defense. "He has some extravagances and idiosyncracies, but he is willing to devote energy and money to our cause when no other man is." Soon she would say, regarding Train, "It would be right and wise to accept aid from the devil himself, provided he did not tempt us to lower our standard."[33] Train met Stanton's single standard for loyalty and friendship: he supported woman suffrage. She would not abandon him.

Unlike Republicans or abolitionists, Stanton shared many of Train's opinions. His attention was flattering and his bad boy charm may have reminded her of Neil. But it was his promise of a newspaper that Stanton found most seductive. Having antagonized the editor of the *Anti-Slavery Standard* (Wendell Phillips) and alienated the editor of the *Tribune* (Horace Greeley), Stanton was no longer assured coverage of her activities or publication of her speeches. Since the end of the war she had been trying to find the means to establish her own journal. She had even solicited funds for the project but to no avail. Now, with Train's help, she had her forum.

When Elizabeth Cady Stanton returned from her whirlwind tour, she plunged into publication of the *Revolution*. The paper had been christened by Train in the heat and dust of the Kansas campaign. Its motto was "Men, their rights and nothing more; women, their rights and nothing less." The name suited Stanton's vision of her own newspaper.

> The establishing of woman on her rightful throne is the greatest revolution the world has ever known or will know. To bring it about is no child's play. You and I have not forgotten the conflict of the last 20 years—the unmixed bitterness of our cup. . . . A journal called the *Rosebud* might answer for those who come with kid gloves and perfumes to lay immortal wreaths on the monuments which in sweat and tears others have hewn and built; but for us . . . there is no name like the *Revolution*.[34]

The division of labor in the *Revolution* offices suited the principals. Anthony managed the office, paid the bills, and hired the printers out of funds supplied by Train. Stanton became the senior editor and primary author of every inch of column. They were joined by Parker Pillsbury as coeditor.* Having served as an editor of the *Anti-Slavery Standard,* he was the only participant with any previous editorial experience. They established their first office at the headquarters of the American Equal Rights Association in New York City; the AERA quickly withdrew. After a year the *Revolution* staff moved to rent-free space in the Woman's Bureau, a large townhouse owned by Elizabeth B. Phelps at 49 East 23d Street. Mrs. Phelps's

---

* Parker Pillsbury (1809–98), a Massachusetts reformer, was a farmer and a wagoner before becoming a minister in 1838. Encouraged by his wife, he served as an antislavery agent and newspaper editor.

ambition was to create a gathering place for like-minded women. Unfortunately, to protest the occupancy of the *Revolution,* no other women's group would hold meetings there.[35]

For the staff of the *Revolution,* however, it was a hospitable office. The floor was carpeted, the white walls were hung with photographs of Lucretia Mott and Mary Wollstonecraft, and the bookcase brimmed with tracts and books about women's rights. The large first-floor room was divided by screens into offices. Pillsbury had his own room, and Stanton and Anthony shared the "inner sanctum." There, according to one critic, they laid out a newspaper "charged to the muzzle with literary nitro-glycerine."[36]

The first issue of the *Revolution* was published January 8, 1868. The six-page newspaper resembled a little magazine. Larger type and wider margins made it readable and attractive and filled the space usually sold to advertisers. The first four pages contained editorials and articles written by Stanton. She reported on the status of women tailors, divorce reform, suffrage in Colorado, European feminists, anything to do with women. Pillsbury covered political affairs, such as Johnson's impeachment trial and the 1868 party conventions. Eventually others contributed, among them popular writers like Alice and Phoebe Cary, Mary Clemmer (Ames), Lillie Devereux Blake, and some "European correspondents."

Page 5 was devoted to the views of George Francis Train favoring greenbacks, open immigration, organized labor, the abolition of standing armies, and penny ocean postage. Page 6 was a column of Wall Street rumors written by Train's crony, David Meliss. Critics agreed that the last two pages were even more offensive than the editorial section. The paper was not unbiased. Its thrust was the elevation of women and the defeat of the Fifteenth Amendment. This position generated more opposition than Train's economics and Stanton's editorials combined.

Ten thousand copies of the first issue were distributed under the congressional frank of New York Democrat James Brooks, against whom Stanton had run in 1866. One reviewer considered the *Revolution* "plucky, keen, and wide awake although . . . not altogether to our taste." Another found it "sharp and spicey." But its editorials were condemned as demagogic, sarcastic, and irresponsible.[37] Subscriptions peaked at three thousand, including one for the White House, but there were few renewals.

Circulation in the reform community was low. Stanton's decision to remain in league with a man Garrison branded as a "ranting egotist and . . . blackguard" appalled the abolitionists. They sent one angry letter after another to the editor. With boldness that was becoming characteristic, Stanton reprinted many of these letters and then answered them point by point. To Thomas Wentworth Higginson she responded, "Time will show that Miss Anthony and myself are neither idiots or lunatics." She reminded Gerrit Smith that "Tyranny on a southern plantation is far more easily seen by white men in the North than the wrongs of women in their own house-holds." Privately she tried to make amends for these public attacks. "I admire you more than any living man," she wrote to her cousin, "though you do persist in putting Sambo, Hans, Patrick and Yung Fung above your noblest countrymen." Smith did not relent, and Stanton "never let him know I noticed his coldness."[38] She did not avoid confrontations. If she could not repair a broken relationship she tried to minimize the long-term damage and then ignored the problem.

The Train connection, unpopular editorial stands, and Stanton's strict prohibitions against certain products cut advertising revenue as well as circulation figures. As senior editor, Stanton refused to run ads for patent medicines, the largest newspaper advertisers at that time. Typically skeptical of medicine and physicians, she was convinced that patent medicines were dangerous and that some were thinly disguised abortifacients. Stanton opposed abortion because it was dangerous for women. She found abortion and the related act of infanticide "disgusting and degrading crimes," but she did not blame the women who committed them. Temporarily contradicting her own recognition of female sexuality Stanton believed that women were forced into these desperate measures by the uncontrolled sexual appetites of men.[39] It was a subject she would expand upon in the 1870s.

With few subscriptions or advertisements, Stanton and Anthony became more dependent on Train for financial support. But soon after the first issue of the Revolution appeared, Train left for England. There his outspoken support of Irish rebels resulted in a one-year jail sentence. No longer able or willing to subsidize the paper, Train insisted that the women remove his name from the masthead, but they were reluctant to do so.[40] For a while David Meliss underwrote the paper's growing debt, but soon he too withdrew.

After two and a half years, the Revolution failed. In May 1870, for the consideration of one dollar, it was sold to Laura Curtis Bullard. Ironically, Mrs. Bullard's large fortune had been made from the sale of a quack cure, Dr. Winslow's Soothing Syrup. For eighteen months the newspaper became a literary and society journal, until it was taken over by the New York Christian Enquirer. Paulina Wright Davis, and later Theodore Tilton, replaced Pillsbury as editor. Anthony was saddled with a closing debt of ten thousand dollars and despaired at the loss of her "firstborn." Stanton, in contrast, refused to reflect on their failure or to share responsibility for the debt.[41]

The Revolution had only been in print five months when the American Equal Rights Association convened its annual meeting in May 1868. Outraged reformers seized this opportunity to attack Stanton and Anthony on

account of the Kansas defeat and their editorial demeanor. Henry Blackwell and Stephen Foster accused Anthony of using AERA funds to finance
the Train lecture tour and the *Revolution*. Stunned by this smear, Anthony
accounted for every penny spent in Kansas. Traveling without a subsidy,
Stanton and Anthony had raised their own expenses and had spent them
as they chose. Anthony's financial statement satisfied the majority, but a
residue of resentment and suspicion remained on both sides. The group then
castigated both women for refusing to support the Fourteenth or Fifteenth
amendments in their editorials.

The major battle of the convention was waged over the Fifteenth
Amendment, granting suffrage to black males. Stanton and Anthony stub-
bornly refused to endorse voting rights for black men only. They insisted
that the proposed wording be changed to include black and white women.
Olympia Brown and Lucy Stone demanded an explanation of the male-
only strategy but did not side with Stanton. Frederick Douglass, Stanton's
ally since Seneca Falls, now claimed that black male suffrage was more urgent than female suffrage because women were less vulnerable than blacks.
"The government of this country loves women, but the Negro is loathed,"
exclaimed Douglass. Black male suffrage was a matter of life and death;
only the vote protected "unoffending" blacks from the Ku Klux Klan and
the Regulators. Woman suffrage, Douglass concluded, "meets nothing but
ridicule."[42]

Stanton refused to accept these claims or to acknowledge that her position had no support. Blind to political reality, insensitive to the abolitionist
position, Stanton and Anthony argued for the defeat of the Fifteenth
Amendment altogether. Why should she support voting rights for black men,
demanded Stanton, when she could not trust them to ensure hers? The vehemence and racial invective of Stanton's arguments stunned the AERA
audience. Although Stanton and Douglass were reelected vice-presidents and
Anthony was returned to the executive committee of the AERA, Stanton
recognized that she had very little influence within the Equal Rights Association.

In the summer of 1868 Stanton and Anthony decided upon a three-part
suffrage strategy. They needed to identify supporters of women's rights and
suffrage, to draft a sixteenth amendment that would enfranchise women,
and to organize women who shared their separate platform. Again Stanton
moved from persuasion to political action and back again, keeping up constant pressure for suffrage. With limited resources, she used every means
available to her.

To identify political allies, the women turned to the national party conventions meeting that summer. A written appeal from Stanton and Anthony to the Republican party was ignored. The same appeal to the Dem-

ocrats was met with an invitation to attend their convention. Stanton dispatched Anthony at once. The Democrats applauded Miss Anthony and seated her on the dais but jeered her proposal and relegated suffrage to a subcommittee. With a jibe at her spinster state, Greeley reported the incident. "Miss Susan B. Anthony has our sincere pity. She has been an ardent suitor of democracy, and they rejected her overtures . . . with screams of laughter." The inaction of both national parties confirmed Stanton's independent leanings. She had no lingering loyalties to the Republicans, the party of Henry's enemies and hers. She called for a new party standing for "universal suffrage and anti-monopoly."[43] Stanton and Anthony did identify a core of congressional supporters. They worked with these men to introduce a woman suffrage amendment.

In October 1868 Stanton laid plans for a Washington meeting of the Woman Suffrage Association of America. She formed the new group to counter the American Equal Rights Association. Stanton had discussed her plans at a luncheon in New York City attended by Anthony, Stone, Mott, and Mott's daughter. "Lizzie [Stanton] was like herself—full of spirits and so pleasant," Mrs. Mott reported to her family, but the discussion was so intense that it made Mrs. Mott "ache all over."[44]

With the exception of Stone, the group appointed itself a central committee of correspondence and issued a call for a January 1869 meeting. Increasingly annoyed at Stanton's behavior, Stone returned to Boston. With Julia Ward Howe and Isabella Beecher Hooker, she formed the New England Woman's Suffrage Association. Stone invited Mott to join but did not include Stanton or Anthony. Mrs. Mott refused their offer, finding it "too partisan." Stanton accidentally received an invitation. "As I was invited to the convention by a mistake of yours," she replied, "I might have made a mistake in going, but for your frankness in telling me that the committee did not desire my presence."[45]

Stanton ignored the New England group and concentrated on the newborn Woman Suffrage Association of America. Women representing twenty state suffrage groups attended its first meeting in January 1869 in Washington, D.C.[46] Republican Samuel Pomeroy of Kansas, who had introduced woman suffrage in the Senate a month earlier, presided until the election of Lucretia Mott as president. Recently widowed, Mrs. Mott was as "calm, dignified, clear and forcible as ever," at age seventy-six. Yet Mrs. Stanton was clearly the star of the convention. Novelist Grace Greenwood described her appeal in the *Philadelphia Press*.

> Of all their speakers, she seemed to me to have the most weight. Her speeches are models of composition, clear, compact, elegant and logical. She makes her points with peculiar sharpness and certainty, and there is no denying or dodging her conclusions. . . . [She is] now impassioned,

now playful, now witty, now pathetic. . . . Mrs. Stanton has the best arts
of the politician and the training of the jurist, added to the fiery, unresting
spirit of the reformer. She has a rare talent for affairs, management, and
mastership. Yet she is in an eminent degree womanly, having an almost
regal pride of sex.[47]

At the first evening session Elizabeth Cady Stanton urged the "speedy
adoption" of a sixteenth amendment to enfranchise women. Women must
be made voters because a government based on the principle of "caste and
class" could not stand, and a government without women was subject to
the "male element of destructive force." Stanton's points indicated more
feminist sensitivity than political sense.

When the meeting concluded, the women presented an appeal for woman
suffrage in the District of Columbia to the congressional committee on
District affairs. Two months later, in March 1869, Rep. George W. Julian,
Republican of Indiana, offered a joint resolution in both houses, proclaim-
ing that "The Right of Suffrage" must be guaranteed "equally without any
distinction or discrimination whatever founded on sex."[48]

Immediately following Stanton's first Washington convention, she and
Anthony left on a two-month tour of the Midwest. Their purpose was to
recruit followers among women who had no antislavery ties. Traveling in
the new Pullman cars, they attended state suffrage meetings in Ohio, Illinois, Wisconsin, and Missouri. They made friends with women who had
been active in the Sanitary Commission and were now interested in suffrage.[49] Counting the antislavery crusade of 1861, the Kansas campaign of
1867, and her publicity tour with Train, this was Stanton's fourth public
tour. Halfway through her itinerary, she became ill and returned to New
Jersey.

Stanton recovered quickly enough to be the center of attention again at
the May 1869 meeting of the American Equal Rights Association. In Mrs.
Mott's absence, Stanton, as first vice-president, presided. Stephen Foster
objected. He charged that Mrs. Stanton had "repudiated the principles of
the society" and demanded that "those who prevented harmony within the
group retire from prominence."[50] Stanton coolly ruled the Massachusetts
delegate out of order. Challenged, her ruling was sustained. Henry Blackwell tried to restore peace. He reminded the membership that Train had
withdrawn from the scene and that Stanton and Anthony had long been
pro-Negro. Discussion of the Fifteenth Amendment opened the sore again.
During the debate both Anthony and Stone supported female as well as
black suffrage. Stanton, wielding the gavel, remained neutral. Foster, fed
up, led a walkout of New England delegates.

Although Stanton had played no immediate part in these incidents, they
were decisive for her. She realized that the Equal Rights Association would

never give woman suffrage priority. She was no longer willing to take second place. At the end of the AERA meeting, on May 11, 1869, Stanton invited all the women delegates to a reception at the Woman's Bureau offices of the *Revolution*. Under the guise of a social gathering, she reorganized the rump group into the National Woman Suffrage Association. The group was "distinctively for woman's suffrage" and ratification of a federal amendment. Disgruntled at the dominance of men in AERA meetings, the women agreed to disallow male members. Henry Stanton, who was in attendance, is credited with having suggested the step. Reportedly, he claimed that, "having been drilled for twenty years privately, he was convinced that women could do it better alone."[51] Elizabeth Cady Stanton was elected president, Elizabeth Smith Miller became treasurer, and Anthony led the executive committee of the new organization. Other members included stalwart Stanton friends Lucretia Mott, Martha Wright, Ernestine Rose, Paulina W. Davis, Olympia Brown, Matilda Joslyn Gage, Anna Dickinson, and Mary Greeley. Lucy Stone and her Boston circle were noticeably absent.

In another attempt to organize women for suffrage and equal rights, Stanton and Anthony helped some local New York women form a union. As the impoverished publisher of the *Revolution,* Anthony sought out non-union women printers because they charged the lowest rates. Her association with them prompted her to call a meeting of women typographers at the Woman's Bureau in mid-1868 and to help them organize Working Women's Association No. One. Next Anthony persuaded one hundred women in the sewing trades to form Working Women's Association No. Two. The women printers elected Anthony their delegate to the National Labor Union Congress meeting in September 1868. Stanton appointed herself to be a delegate from the National Woman Suffrage Association. She was refused entry because she was not a union member and because her admission might suggest support of suffrage. Eighteen men threatened to resign over the question of her credentials.[52] They had to admit Anthony because she had been chosen by union women even though she was not a union member.

Anthony seized the opportunity to explain why the ballot was especially important for working women. She convinced the committee on female labor to urge women "to secure the ballot" as well as "to learn the trades, engage in business, join labor unions or form protective unions of their own, . . . and use every other honorable means to persuade or force employers to do justice to women by paying them equal wages for equal work." If both men and women were in the same unions, Anthony continued, employers could not replace men with women working for lower wages. The women delegates also called upon the National Labor Union Congress to aid the organization of women's unions, to demand the eight-hour day for women as well as men, and to ask Congress and state legislatures to pass laws providing equal pay for women in government employ. The phrase, "to secure the ballot," was quickly challenged and had to be deleted.[53]

Neither Anthony nor Stanton joined a union. They continued to urge women workers to form unions at the same time that they had their paper printed in a nonunion shop because it was cheaper. Yet their concern for working women was genuine. Stanton frequently came to the defense of factory women and suggested remedies for their social and economic problems. Her position evolved from Anthony's initiative. In later years she became more outspoken on behalf of women workers and wove threads of socialism into her feminist ideology.[54]

Stanton's refusal to admit men to membership in the National Woman Suffrage Association, the racist tone of her opposition to the Fifteenth Amendment, and her association with working women, union organizers, unwed mothers, murderers, and advocates of free love, shocked the Boston branch of the reform community. To a growing number of reformers Stanton was an embarrassment and a troublemaker. Among conservative women suffrage was more respectable than Elizabeth Cady Stanton. Lucy Stone refused to share any leadership roles with Stanton; nor would she participate in an organization that barred her husband from voting. Stone was joined by Julia Ward Howe, Abby Kelley and Stephen Foster, George W. Curtis, Henry Ward Beecher, T. W. Higginson, and other disenchanted New Englanders. They resolved to establish an alternate association.

On November 24, 1869, the Boston contingent founded the American Woman Suffrage Association. In an effort to counter Stanton's inroads into the Midwest, it met in Cleveland. The American Association was organized on a delegate basis: each member had to represent a local suffrage group. With such credentials, men could participate as well as women. The American, as it came to be called, purposely elected a male president, choosing the famous minister Henry Ward Beecher. Stone headed the executive committee. The group proposed to win suffrage by state-by-state referenda campaigns.[55] The American also decided to publish its own newspaper, the *Woman's Journal,* to challenge the claims made by the *Revolution.* Its first issue appeared in January 1870. Edited by Mary Livermore of Chicago with the assistance of Stone and Blackwell, the *Woman's Journal* was well financed, respectable, and conservative in everything but its advocacy of woman suffrage. The newspaper flourished long after the *Revolution* died and eventually became the official organ of the reunited suffrage movement.

Alarmed by these developments, Mrs. Mott urged Stanton and Anthony to attend the Cleveland convention and work toward some reconciliation. She delivered the same message to Stone in Boston. Stone and Stanton both refused, but Anthony decided to attend the meeting. Uninvited, she claimed to represent the National Association. She was not asked to sit on the platform. She was offended by veiled attacks on Stanton and by repetition of rumors about her mismanagement of AERA funds. The *Revolution* was condemned in comparison to the *Woman's Journal*. Unlike the National, asserted one participant, the new organization "will not mistake rashness for courage, folly for smartness, cunning for sagacity, badinage for wit, unscrupulousness for fidelity, extravagance for devotion, effrontery for heroism, lunacy for genius, or an incongruous melange for a simple palatable dish."[56] Anthony was furious. According to one report, she "stamped her foot" and stunned the group by claiming that Stone and Blackwell had never married and were living in sin.[57] The result was an irreparable breach.

The Stanton-Anthony-Stone triangle had a history of misunderstandings. Previously the three had been able to maintain a facade of friendship. After an earlier clash with Stone, Stanton had written to a mutual friend:

> I fully agree with you as to the wisdom of keeping all our misunderstandings to ourselves. No word or pen of mine shall ever wrong or detract from any woman, especially one who has done so good a work for woman as Lucy Stone. I rest assured that time will vindicate our own position. I accept all things patiently, for I see that human nature is the same inside and outside the reform world. Our Abolitionists are just as sectarian in their association as the Methodists in their church, and divisions are always the most bitter where there is the least to differ about. But in spite of all, the men and women who have been battling for freedom in this country, are as grand and noble as any that have ever walked the earth. So we will forget their faults and love them for their many virtues.[58]

But by 1870 Stanton was less patient with opposition, whether male or female, family or friend. Yet her instinct to keep the fight private was strong. Previous observation and experience had taught her that the appearance of cordiality was more comfortable and more useful. After a few salvos in the *Revolution,* Stanton kept silent on the schism, and on the whole Stone did the same.[59] But Stanton found it harder and harder to hold her tongue. As she gained self-confidence, she was less worried about the repercussions of her outbursts. She maintained a congenial public style because it suited her personality and purpose to be perceived as a popular and appealing radical.

In a signed editorial in the *Revolution,* Stanton described the split as "a division in the ranks of the strongminded." She labeled Stone and her allies "the Boston malcontents." She did not sidestep the issue of discontent with her leadership. She offered to resign the presidency of the National, in essence challenging Stone to find the votes to defeat her. "That the difference is one simply of leadership and personalities is well known to all behind the scenes," she wrote. The "antagonism between the old and the new . . . is well known to every worker in the movement." Until the American could share the National's broad, catholic ground and demand "suffrage for All— *even Negro suffrage, without distinction of sex,*" she did not want to associate with it.[60]

The differences between the National and the American Woman Suffrage associations were personal, political, philosophical, organizational, and even geographic. Lucy Stone distrusted Stanton and Anthony because of their involvement with Train in Kansas and on the *Revolution,* and Stanton and Anthony resented the vituperative tone of Stone's criticism. Stanton's refusal to support the Fifteenth Amendment offended Stone and those Bostonians who had been abolitionists before they were feminists. Stanton's rude and racist rhetoric regarding blacks repelled the Garrisonians. Nor did thy share Stanton's view of men as tyrants. "Society," Stanton had editorialized, "as organized today under the man power, is one grand rape of womanhood." According to Stanton, the situation required extensive social change. As she claimed in the National Association's statement of purpose: "The woman question is more than a demand for suffrage. . . . [It] is a question covering a whole range of woman's needs and demands . . . including her work, her wages, her property, her education, her physical training, her social status, her political equalization, her marriage and her divorce." In a direct reference to Stone's position, Stanton objected to "the Boston attempt to distill our whole question into a single drop." Replied Stone, "Suffrage is not the only object but it is the first to be attained. . . . Suffrage for women gained and all else will speedily follow."[61]

Whether to work for suffrage alone and how to achieve that goal were the two most important points of disagreement. Not only did the American want to narrow the focus of the women's movement, it also believed that issues like divorce reform would damage its chances for success. The leaders of the American were afraid to associate suffrage with any extraneous or radical ideas or individuals. Mrs. Stanton, with her all-encompassing view of women's wrongs and how to right them, was anathema to the Bostonians. In contrast, Stanton believed, as the Garrisonians had in the antebellum period, that reformers must seek solutions wherever and however possible. She also adopted the tactic of the political abolitionists in making her issues political questions requiring political solutions in the legislatures and the courts.

The different political and philosophical positions of the National and the American reflected the personalities of their leaders. For a feminist Lucy Stone was a straitlaced, traditional, happily married Bostonian who had risen from poverty to respectability and disliked flamboyant display. Stanton was more self-confident, intellectually curious, and compassionate. Despite her upper-class upbringing and leanings, she was more aware of and more concerned about the lives of ordinary women, in factories and on farms. She believed they needed more than suffrage.

The difference between Stone and Stanton was apparent in their attitudes toward the West, attitudes that carried over into their organizations and reflected their personalities. Stone hated the frontier. She had convinced her husband to leave his Cincinnati business and move to Boston. Comfortably established there, she was reluctant to leave. Pioneer conditions appalled her; she had hurried home from Kansas in 1867, relieved to be leaving. She was satisfied to stay in Boston, surrounded by other ladies of similar outlook. As a result, most of the membership of the highly structured American Association resided in New England. Stanton, in contrast, was invigorated by the West. She began to travel widely beyond the Mississippi River, testing her endurance, enhancing her self-esteem, recruiting new members for the National, and making allies among men and women who had less traditional attitudes about appropriate sex roles. Although the National, like the American, had its headquarters in an Eastern urban center, New York was much more vital than Boston. In New York and in the West Stanton was continually exposed to new ideas and could test the solutions she proposed. Because the National Association was larger and more geographically diverse in membership, it became a loose affiliation of state groups and individuals.[62]

Stanton was convinced that her goals, her means, and her organization were superior to those of Lucy Stone and the American Association. She agreed with Anthony that "cautious, careful people always casting about to preserve their reputation and social standing, never can bring about a reform. Those who are really in earnest must be willing to be anything or nothing in the world's estimation, and publicly and privately, in season and out, avow their sympathy with despised and persecuted ideas and advocates, and bear the consequences."[63] The consequences for Stanton were considerable.

Publicly unruffled, Stanton chose to ignore the American. In January 1870 she attended the second and last meeting of the Woman Suffrage Association of America. While in Washington she testified before the Senate Judiciary Committee in favor of woman suffrage in the District of Columbia. In May she arranged the first anniversary meeting of the National Association in New York City. The membership of these two groups was almost identical. Beginning in 1871 the National, although headquartered in New York, held its annual meetings in Washington. This action reflected the priority that the National gave to federal action and congressional contacts.[64]

At the May 1870 meeting of the National, Theodore Tilton tried to unite the two rival associations. Working independently, he suggested creating a Union Association, made up of the National and American. Rather than refuse him outright, Stanton agreed to allow the question to be considered. She did not want to appear to be uncompromising. She trusted that Stone would never consent to Tilton's plan. In another unusual move, the National abandoned its antimale policy and elected Tilton its president. Stanton agreed to step down.

After five years of fighting, Stanton had lost every battle and most of her allies. She had lost married women's property rights, divorce reform, and limited suffrage for the New York constitutional convention. She had lost woman suffrage in New York, Kansas, the District of Columbia, and the Constitution. She had lost her newspaper and the presidency of the National Association. Even more significant, she had alienated a host of former allies. Her antagonists in 1870 numbered the members of the American Association plus Garrison, Greeley, Higginson, Douglass, Phillips, Foster, and even Gerrit Smith.[65]

Where Henry Stanton stood is unclear. In his last years he returned to his early commitment to abolition and citizenship for the black man. He was offended by his wife's rhetoric and tactics. But rather than indulge in a public break, he withdrew into the company of his older sons and political cronies in the city. He repeated the pattern of separation that had come to characterize their marriage.

Mrs. Stanton was increasingly isolated. Looking back at the postwar period, she recalled being besieged and then abandoned.

> The few who insisted on the absolute right [to universal suffrage] stood firmly together under a steady fire of ridicule and reproach even from their lifelong friends most loved and honored. . . . With all these . . . friends against them . . . and most of the liberals in the press, the position of the women seemed so untenable to the majority that at times a sense of utter loneliness and desertion made the bravest of them doubt the possibility of maintaining the struggle or making themselves fairly understood. . . . Few were equal to the emergency.[66]

Yet Elizabeth Cady Stanton persisted.

By 1870 she had become emotionally self-sufficient. She lived apart from Henry in her own establishment in Tenafly. She entertained him as a guest and divided care for the children with him but was financially and socially independent of him. Now that her children were older, she was less involved with them. She had a full-time housekeeper and few qualms about leaving those children still at home. She no longer begged Anthony to visit, write, or stir the puddings. She shared more of her life with Anthony than with anyone else, but she was less dependent on her for approval or encouragement than she had been earlier.

Stanton's affectionate circle included Anthony, Mott, Miller, and the children. Her relationship with her mother and sisters had improved as well. Although she cherished this group, she was less careful of their feelings and ignored their criticism. She was willing to risk any outrageous public action or statement with impunity. She expected her female friends to support, understand, forgive, and sustain her, and on the whole they did.

In the public sphere she learned to deflect criticism. She either disdained it or turned it into an opportunity to repeat her point. When the *New York Times* charged that Mrs. Stanton was neglecting her family in order to publish the *Revolution,* she replied: "We know what not one woman in ten thousand does know, how to take care of a child, make good bread, and keep a home clean. . . . Our children . . . are healthy, rosy, happy, and well-fed. . . . Culinary abominations are never found on our table. Now let every man who wants his wife to know how to do likewise take the *Revolution* in which not only the ballot, but bread and babies will be discussed."[67] At the same time that she was moving out of her domestic sphere, Stanton began to use her maternal role to legitimize her public activities. She shrewdly chose to appear matronly, respectable, charming, and genial. Soon she would substitute public admiration for private affections. In the meantime she still cared about her family and friends. But most of all she cared for herself and her cause.

9
Independence
1870–79

For Elizabeth Cady Stanton, 1870 ended in anger and frustration. She had declared her feminist independence in the pages of the *Revolution* and in the organization of the National Woman Suffrage Association. Soon she found herself harassed by conservatives, embarrassed by radicals, and resented by Anthony. Her reaction was to turn her back on her troubles and forge ahead. As she declared to Anthony: "You know when I drop anything I drop it absolutely. You could not believe what a deep gulf lies between me and the past. My life since we left Kansas is to me like a long, sad dream; the experience may have its uses but I feel the chain that bound me to that incubus is broken."[1]

Fed up with infighting and intrigue, Stanton wanted nothing more to do with organizations. The discord of the past five years confirmed her decision to abandon conventions. After a trial tour in 1869, she spent the next decade as a paid lecturer. Her subject was always women's rights. She chose as her role models the abolition agents and evangelical preachers of her youth. Convinced that political action would follow public pressure, she set out to convert the country to her cause.

As much as possible, Stanton cut her ties with the past. After the *Revolution* was sold in May 1870, she refused to contribute articles to its successor. When acting editor Theodore Tilton asked her to be "spicey and brilliant on some pleasant topics," she would not "submit my ideas to the pruning knife of youngsters." More serious, Stanton took no responsibility for the paper's remaining debt of ten thousand dollars. She claimed that neither she nor Parker Pillsbury, the coeditor, had the resources to pay it off because they were married and had dependents. Ironically the obligation was legally Anthony's, who as the unmarried partner had agreed to sign all the contracts. Stanton had the audacity to suggest that Anthony get a job or borrow from her family to meet the obligation.[2] Such unconscionable behavior is difficult to explain. Stanton had the resources to pay her share of the debt, but during this period she was feeling insecure and selfish about what money she did have. It took Anthony six years to pay it off.

Within a year of its organization, the National Woman Suffrage Association had been thwarted by elements eager to merge with the American. The National's name had been changed to the Union Association, and Stanton had stepped aside as president to make way for a man. She found the situation "most humiliating." She did not want reunion, but she did not want to appear to thwart it. She participated in the negotiations because she wanted to embarrass and isolate Lucy Stone. For a while she relished the fight, writing to Martha Wright: "We have had grand times in getting the National and the Equal Rights both merged with the Union movement. Boston is *awful* sore. . . . Unless Boston comes into Union she will stand alone in the cold. . . . Lucy is as hostile as ever [and] cannot be mollified."[3] In the end the merger negotiations only exacerbated the bad feelings on both sides.

The continued existence of the American Association and the influence of the *Woman's Journal* galled Stanton. Further, the weight of conservative women within her own association alarmed her. At the January 1870 meeting of the National, a newcomer named Isabella Beecher Hooker had presented their position. With aggressive self-assertion she had urged alternatives to Stanton's radicalism. Where Stanton desired revolution, Hooker sought respectability. Unfazed by Stanton's opposition, Hooker volunteered to organize and underwrite the 1871 Washington convention. She planned to subordinate all extraneous issues to a decorous discussion of suffrage. Although annoyed, Stanton agreed. "She thinks she could manage the cause more discreetly, more genteely than we do, so let her take hold and try the drudgery," Stanton explained to a colleague. "I am ready to rest."[4]

Stanton found Mrs. Hooker's self-confidence, so like her own, an unbearable Beecher family trait. Isabella Beecher Hooker was the youngest and prettiest daughter of Lyman Beecher. Her father had been head of Lane Seminary when Henry Stanton and Theodore Weld had led the student protest. Henry Ward Beecher, the minister and president of the American Woman Suffrage Association, was her half-brother; Catharine Beecher, the home economics expert and educator, and Harriet Beecher Stowe, the famous author, were her half-sisters. After attending various schools established by members of her family, Isabella married John Hooker, a Hartford attorney, and bore four children. Their home at Nook Farm became the center of a close-knit literary and social colony, which later included Mark Twain and Mrs. Stowe.

Although exposed to the currents of feminism, Mrs. Hooker had resisted them "out of distaste for the notoriety of Elizabeth Cady Stanton and Susan B. Anthony." Yet by the end of the Civil War she had converted to women's rights. She organized the Connecticut Suffrage Association, lobbied for a married women's property bill drafted by her husband, and helped found Stone's New England Woman's Suffrage Association.[5] Why she sided with Stanton and Anthony rather than Stone in the 1869 schism remains an unanswered question. It may be that she preferred to be the only Beecher in the National rather than the youngest of the clan loyal to the American.

Throughout most of 1870 Mrs. Stanton kept her distance from these developments. After closing the offices of the *Revolution,* she spent the summer of 1870 in Tenafly, preparing for an autumn lecture tour. "I am very busy reading and writing my speeches," she reported to Anthony.[6] She visited her mother, gave a commencement address, and watched the merger negotiations from the sidelines. After the Fifth Avenue Conference, the effort to unite the suffrage groups, collapsed in August, Stanton left for a six-week foray into the Midwest, confident that no merger would weaken the National.

Before long, Stanton's equanimity was shaken by Hooker's suggestion that she not attend the upcoming January 1871 meeting. She had not planned to attend, but she was insulted when asked to stay away. Stanton poured out her anger in a letter to Martha Wright.

> I expressed a perfect willingness to leave the whole matter in her hands and contribute, if need be, to the expenses of the convention, but was not prepared for just such a slap in the face. . . . If Anthony wishes to thrust herself everywhere, she may, but she shall not push me, any longer. We have made the thing popular, and now let Mrs. Hooker run the machine if she chooses, but she will not run me. So long as people pay me $75 and $100 every night, to speak on my own hook, there is no need of my talking in conventions where my presence is not desired. I think her letter quite blunt and egotistic and somehow it hurts my self-respect.

To Mrs. Hooker, Stanton coolly responded that she thought the convention would be a success "as all previous ones had been." Three days later she was still angry. "I did not express in *words* the *contempt* I felt at her cool impudence, but somehow *the spirit ran off the end of my pen,*" she declared to Mrs. Wright. "The Beecher conceit surpasses all understanding."[7]

Stanton was offended by Mrs. Hooker and annoyed at herself. A few months earlier Stanton had tried to woo Hooker and win her admiration and loyalty. At Hooker's invitation, Stanton had attended a meeting of New England women in Rhode Island. As Stanton described the occasion:

> Mrs. Hooker wrote each [of us] a letter of instructions re dress, manners, and general display of all the Christian graces. I did my best to obey orders, and appeared in a black velvet dress with real lace, and the most inoffensive speech I could produce; all those passages that would shock the most conservative were ruled out, while pathetic and aesthetic passages were substituted in their place. From what my friends said, I believe I succeeded in charming everyone but myself and Anthony who said it was the weakest speech I ever made. I told her that was what it was intended to be.

The charade had not convinced the conservative women, but it satisfied Mrs. Stanton. She had appeared gracious and genteel. Even Mrs. Hooker was charmed, praising Stanton as "the truest, womanliest woman of us all."[8] But she did not invite Stanton, past president of the National Woman Suffrage Association, to its 1871 meeting.

Stanton wanted Anthony to boycott the meeting, but her friend refused. Instead Anthony insisted that Stanton attend and urged Hooker to invite her. "To my mind there never was such a suicidal letting go as has been yours these last two years," Anthony wrote Stanton. "How you can excuse yourself is more than I can understand." But Stanton would not budge from Tenafly. As she confided to Martha Wright, she felt she was "between two fires all the time. Some are determined to throw me overboard, and [Anthony] is equally determined that I shall stand at the masthead, no matter how pitiless the storm."[9] For the rest of her life, even after she had been returned to the presidency of the National Association, Stanton would attend women's rights conventions only reluctantly.

The 1871 women's rights meeting was Mrs. Hooker's production. She had organized it, paid for it, and in the absence of either Tilton or Stanton, she presided over it. But competition for control appeared from an unexpected quarter. Victoria Woodhull, the "Bewitching Broker of Wall Street" and former tent show charlatan, had launched an effort to take over the suffrage movement. On her own, Mrs. Woodhull had presented a suffrage petition to Congress in December 1870 and had been invited to testify before the House Judiciary Committee in January. Her hearing was scheduled for the opening day of the National Association convention. Mrs. Hooker grudgingly interrupted the proceedings to accompany Miss Anthony to hear Woodhull's presentation. Both women were smitten by Woodhull's beauty and intelligence. They immediately invited her to address their convention and join them on the platform.[10]

Before the committee and the convention Woodhull argued that there was no need for a woman suffrage amendment. She asserted that the Fourteenth Amendment already gave women as citizens the right to vote. She urged suffragists to register, vote, go to court, and go to jail for that right. Woodhull was repeating an argument offered by Mrs. Stanton the year before in her testimony on behalf of female suffrage in the District of Columbia. Stanton and now Woodhull claimed that all citizens of the republic, whether male or female, had equal legal rights. Well delivered and well received, Woodhull's cogent restatement of Stanton's case came to be known among suffragists as the "new departure." In reading the reports of the Washington meeting, Stanton naturally found Woodhull's remarks persuasive and flattering. For the next few years Stanton and the National pursued this tack rather than a federal amendment strategy. "With this view our manner of agitation is radically changed," Stanton concluded in a newspaper article.[11]

Attractive as Woodhull's new departure strategy seemed, Stanton was worried about her unsavory reputation. Still outside the range of Woodhull's magnetism, she could be more objective than Anthony and Hooker. Uncharacteristically cautious, she told Anthony bluntly, "Do not have another Train affair with Mrs. Woodhull."[12] Compared to Woodhull, Train was a saint; Woodhull would be even more dangerous and damaging to their cause.

Victoria Claflin Woodhull came to the women's movement from a sordid past. One of ten children born to an obscure family, she had an itinerant childhood and a meager education. Her family staged a traveling medicine show; the adolescent Victoria took the part of a psychic healer. At fifteen she married Canning Woodhull, a physician and a drunkard. They had two children. The couple separated, and Victoria returned to her flamboyant family. She was especially close to her younger sister Tennessee. Together they specialized in spiritualism and séances. Allegations of fraud, blackmail, prostitution, and manslaughter chased the Claflins from town to town in the Midwest. After the war Victoria divorced Dr. Woodhull to marry her lover, Col. James Blood, but she kept her first husband's name.

Following a vision Woodhull moved her entire extended family to New York City in 1868. With admirable enterprise the Claflin sisters called upon Cornelius Vanderbilt, the railroad magnate and a recent widower. Enamored of Tennessee, he established the sisters as financial speculators and stockbrokers. Vanderbilt leaked them information, and Woodhull, Claflin and Company was soon successful. In 1870 the sisters moved their firm to Wall Street and their ménage into a mansion on Murray Hill.

Another male mentor encouraged Woodhull to enter politics. In April 1870 she declared herself a candidate for president of the United States. Soon after, she and Tennessee published *Woodhull and Claflin's Weekly* to expound her political platform. More strident and eccentric than the

Revolution, but better financed, the *Weekly* combined gossip, muckraking, and politics. The paper favored free love, short skirts, and legalized prostitution, and it printed the first translation of the Communist Manifesto in America.[13]

Having succeeded in all these outlandish enterprises, Victoria Woodhull next seized upon women's rights. Her speech to the Judiciary Committee in January 1871 was the first major public address of her career. It was rumored to have been written by Rep. Benjamin Butler of Massachusetts, another admirer. Having charmed her way into Congress, Woodhull proceeded to disarm Mrs. Hooker's convention. Despite Stanton's warning, Anthony was ready to defend Woodhull. Anthony sympathized with any woman attacked for radical views or unconventional behavior, and now she was enchanted by the lovely looking Mrs. Woodhull.

Because Anthony had sided with Woodhull, so did Stanton. Even before she met "the Woodhull," Stanton had defended her before hostile lyceum audiences. The two finally did meet at the May 1871 meeting of the National. The New York press had been full of negative publicity about Woodhull and her unusual living arrangements; both Colonel Blood and Dr. Woodhull now shared her home. Anthony was growing increasingly wary and had begun to distance herself from Woodhull. But Stanton, acting on Anthony's earlier endorsement, was cordial. She seated Woodhull between Lucretia Mott and herself on the platform. By now an accomplished orator, Woodhull delivered an electrifying speech. "We mean treason, we mean secession," Woodhull declared. "We are plotting revolution; we will overthrow this bogus republic and plant a government of righteousness in its stead." Thrilled by such rhetoric, Mrs. Stanton became Woodhull's staunchest defender. "Victoria C. Woodhull stands before us today a grand, brave woman, radical alike in political, religious, and social principles," she proclaimed, in praise similar to that she had lavished on Train.[14]

Woodhull soon became another source of discord between Stanton and Anthony, festering like the *Revolution* debt and Stanton's absenteeism. The tension between them had been apparent as early as 1870. When the *New York Sun,* referring to the *Revolution,* reported that they had dissolved their partnership, Stanton asked Anthony if she wanted a divorce. "Have you been getting a *divorce* out in Chicago without notifying me? I should like to know my status. I shall not allow any such proceedings. I consider our relation for life so make the best of it." Although Stanton assured Anthony that her love was "unchanged, undimmed by time and friction," the situation deteriorated. They disagreed more often and less gently. To restore their earlier intimacy, the two old friends decided to take a trip together. Both of them looked forward to it. Wrote Stanton, "As I go dragging around in these despicable hotels, I think of you and often wish we had at least the little comfort of enduring it together." [15]

The itinerary included speaking engagements in the Far West and a vacation in California. Stanton and Anthony left as soon as the May meeting adjourned. Leland Stanford, governor of California and president of the Central Pacific Railroad, sent them free passes. Stanton reported on their adventures in letters to her family. They moved at a leisurely pace and stayed with prominent citizens. They shared the lecture platform, speaking twice in each city. In Salt Lake City they were invited to address Mormon women in the Tabernacle. Convinced that they would never be allowed to return, they talked about marriage and women's rights, birth control and divorce, in a marathon five-hour session. Stanton was sympathetic toward Mormon women. She approved their practice of abstinence from intercourse during pregnancy and lactation and always supported their effort to win suffrage in the Utah Territory. [16]

According to Anthony, she and Stanton enjoyed hours of conversation. "We have a drawing-room all to ourselves, and here we are just as cozy and happy as lovers." But their bliss was marred by disagreements. Anthony badgered Stanton, and Stanton annoyed Anthony. Stanton was peeved when Anthony scolded her for continual snacking and progressive weight gain. Anthony could not persuade Stanton to challenge Mrs. Hooker for the presidency of the National. More serious, she was jealous of Stanton's public appeal. A dynamic speaker, Stanton attracted immense audiences, standing ovations, gifts of fruit and flowers, and invitations to dine. As Anthony confessed to her family, she resented that she was not also called upon, "instead of merely sitting a lay figure and listening to the brilliant scintillations as they emanante from her never exhausted magazine. There is no alternative—whoever goes into a parlor or before an audience with that woman does it at the cost of a fearful overshadowing, a price which I have paid for the last ten years." [17]

The crisis came to a head when the pair reached San Francisco in late 1871. The town was caught up in the trial of a prostitute, Laura Fair, for the murder of Alexander Crittenden, an attorney who had hired her services. Stanton and Anthony defended the crime, visited the woman in jail, and called a public meeting to discuss the case. Before an audience of twelve hundred women Stanton laid the blame on the uncontrolled sexual drive of men, which made both wives and whores its victims. Anthony followed with identical arguments, but she was booed. Although both women had made the same point, Anthony's intensity was unrelieved by the humor that marked Stanton's presentation. The California press attacked only Anthony; the Eastern papers scorned Stanton. [18]

Bearing the brunt of the local criticism, Anthony expected Stanton to come to her defense, but Stanton remained silent. "Never in all my hard experience have I been under such fire," Anthony confided to her diary. Anthony was hurt and angry, but there is no record of a private apology or a public defense by Stanton. Once again she selfishly, thoughtlessly ignored the needs of her best friend. Nonetheless, they continued on their journey as planned, going to Yosemite for a vacation. They spent days riding horseback on "men's saddles" in "linen bloomers." Stanton's weight had become such a hindrance that she wore out two mares and had to be conveyed by buckboard.[19]

After two unhappy weeks, the women returned to San Francisco. Anthony refused to lecture or attend meetings. At the end of August, Stanton learned that her mother was ill and cut short her trip. After Stanton returned east, Anthony spoke throughout the Northwest for several months more. "I miss Mrs. Stanton," she wrote her family. "Still I can not but enjoy the feeling that the people call on *me*."[20]

Hurrying across the country to her mother's deathbed, Stanton found Margaret Cady "impatient to see me." A week later Mrs. Cady died in her sleep at age eighty-six. Stanton asked Theodore Tilton to notice the death in his newspaper, the *Independent*. She wanted her mother to be remembered as a "grand brave woman" who had hoped to vote before she died.[21] Stanton was eager to tie her mother to suffrage and to publicize her mother's approval of her own actions and career.

After the funeral Stanton returned to Tenafly rather than rejoin Anthony. There she was "busy, busy, busy getting the four [youngest children] ready for school" and nursing two of the older ones through a long illness. As she eventually apologized to Anthony, "I have had no time or thought of speeches or to write letters even to you."[22] They would not travel together again for more than a decade, and never again for an extended period.

In an effort to assuage Anthony, Stanton did attend the National's January 1872 convention. Mrs. Hooker presided; Stanton, Anthony, and Woodhull sat behind her on the dias. This time only Anthony and Stanton met with the Senate Judiciary Committee to present the new departure arguments. Anthony managed to confine Woodhull to a single speech on spiritualism. In her own speech, Anthony defended Woodhull's right to speak but tried to dissociate the National from Woodhull's platform of bizarre causes.[23] She feared that the suffragists had not only further alienated the conservatives but had also made themselves vulnerable to a Woodhull takeover. She was right to worry.

In the spring of 1872, while Anthony was in Kansas, Woodhull published a call for the creation of an independent third party to advance her presidential aspirations. With Stanton's approval, she planned to turn the May meeting of the National into a nominating convention for the so-called People's party. The third-party scheme did not alarm Stanton, who went so far as to write the call and to sign the names of the National's leadership, including Anthony's.[24] Then Stanton returned to the lecture circuit, leaving the field open for Woodhull. Anthony was indignant. When her protests went unanswered and she was unable to arouse either Stanton or Hooker, Anthony rushed to New York.

The showdown came in May 1872. The night before the National meeting convened, Anthony and Stanton had a heated argument about Woodhull. They did not resolve their differences, and neither relented. The next day Anthony refused to share Steinway Hall with the People's party. As the lessee, Anthony could insist that they meet elsewhere. Annoyed at Anthony's seeming pettiness, Stanton refused to preside; Anthony was elected both president pro tem and for the following year. Over Anthony's objections, Stanton called in her keynote speech for women to vote under the Fourteenth Amendment as members of the new third party. Anthony had more success in controlling the other speakers and refused to recognize Mrs. Woodhull.

Tension mounted throughout the day. At the close of the evening session Woodhull moved that the meeting adjourn to Apollo Hall to nominate candidates for the People's party. The motion was seconded, but Anthony refused to call the question. An appeal was made to overrule the chair. Woodhull stood and demanded an immediate vote; her motion passed. Anthony declared the vote out of order and then adjourned the meeting until the next morning. But Woodhull seized the podium and kept talking. She would not leave. Finally, a furious Anthony, in her capacity as tenant, ordered the janitor to turn off the lights.[25]

Without the official backing of the suffragists, Woodhull overnight turned the People's party into the Equal Rights party. It nominated her for president and Frederick Douglass for vice-president. Douglass declined and chose rather to support Ulysses S. Grant for reelection. Convinced that the Woodhull connection would condemn them all, Anthony was relieved at their narrow escape. She was still angry with Stanton. "There never was such a foolish muddle—all come of Mrs. S. [Stanton] consulting and conceding to Woodhull," Anthony recorded in her diary. "I never was so hurt by the folly of Stanton." Stanton never publicly referred to the incident again, but in private correspondence she discounted any damage Woodhull may have caused. According to Lucretia Mott, "Elizabeth . . . is disposed to be very cautious how she identifies herself in any way with [Woodhull] now."[26] Woodhull reacted to the censure and contempt of her former admirers by attacking them in *Woodhull and Claflin's Weekly*.

Stanton spent the summer of 1872 in Tenafly, enjoying a respite from politics. With her housekeeper away on vacation and all of her children "flocking home," she was busy with household demands. As she reported to Libby Miller, "I have everything running like clockwork, splendidly." The increasingly plump Mrs. Stanton added that she planned to "try hard work for the summer and see if I could take down my robust proportion." Now that her children were "intelligent companions," ranging in age from thirteen to thirty, Stanton found them "a real pleasure." She rejoiced at having survived "the tearing, the tumbling, the feeding . . . [the] pap spoons and diapers." But by the Fourth of July, Stanton was so tired she could hardly see the fireworks. She begged her housekeeper to hurry back. Other summers during the 1870s were spent entirely in research and rehearsal for the circuit.[27] In reports of any summer's activities, there are few references to her husband.

Both Henry Stanton and Susan Anthony spent the summer of 1872 engaged in presidential politics. Henry joined forces with Liberal Republicans and supported his former employer and Elizabeth's enemy, Horace Greeley. Henry believed Greeley would complete reconstruction with less sectional hostility and less violence against the Negro than Grant and the regular Republicans.[28] Needless to say, Greeley did not favor female suffrage. His defeat was assured when he was endorsed by the Democrats.

Unable to support Greeley and eager to separate herself and the suffragists from Woodhull, Anthony appealed to the regular Republicans. Meeting in Philadelphia, the Republicans did not endorse suffrage, but they did include the first reference to women in a major party platform: "The Republican Party is mindful of its obligations to the loyal women of America for their noble devotion to the cause of freedom; their admission to wider fields of usefulness is received with satisfaction, and the honest demands of any class of citizens for equal rights should be treated with respectful consideration." Stanton referred to the Republican plank as the "Philadelphia splinter," which the party soon whittled to a "toothpick." She agreed to accept it as "our choice lay between that and nothing." In appreciation of the Republican acknowledgment, Anthony and Matilda Joslyn Gage, an officer of the National from upstate New York, issued an endorsement of Grant. In return the Republicans appropriated funds to circulate the women's appeal and organize women to campaign for Grant. Mrs. Stanton eventually joined in supporting Grant, declaring that she would rather "see Beelzebub president than Greeley." When Greeley dropped dead three weeks after the election, Stanton regretted their past animosity. But by then she had more to occupy her than an old enemy.[29]

Although they had disavowed Woodhull, both Stanton and Anthony accepted the logic of the new departure strategy. On her own, Anthony decided to test their conviction that women already had the right to vote under the Fourteenth Amendment. Nationally, between 1871 and 1872, nearly one hundred fifty women tried to vote. Anthony's case was the most famous. Joined by three of her sisters and twelve other Rochester matrons, all of them Quakers, Susan B. Anthony cast a ballot in the 1872 election. The poll officials were unprepared for such flagrant lawbreaking and did not know what to do, so the ladies walked home unmolested. "I have gone and done it!!" Anthony crowed to an unenthusiastic Stanton.[30] As Anthony had hoped, she was singled out for prosecution. She was charged with "knowingly, wrongfully, and unlawfully voting," a federal offense.

Confronted by Miss Anthony's widely publicized act of defiance, the Republican establishment sought to avoid a Supreme Court decision on her case. Having retained superior legal advice even before she had voted, Anthony had her defense ready. Speaking in every county surrounding Rochester before the trial, she claimed that she had voted in good faith since she considered herself legally entitled to do so; therefore, she should not be found guilty of criminal action or intent. The trial was set for June 17, 1873, in the local district court. The prosecution obtained a change of venue and moved the trial to the next district.

Unorthodox procedure marked this unusual case. It was the first trial of a recently appointed judge, Ward Hunt, a protégé of Republican boss Roscoe Conkling. When Anthony's attorney called on her to testify, the judge sustained the claim that she was incompetent, as a woman, to speak for herself. Yet her testimony, given during a pretrial hearing, was allowed. Finally Judge Hunt directed the jury to find the defendant guilty, because "under the Fourteenth Amendment . . . Miss Anthony . . . was not protected in a right to vote." Pleas for a jury poll, a new trial, and an appeal were denied.

Asked if she had anything to say, Anthony denounced the judge, jury, court, and trial in blistering terms. When Hunt was finally able to silence her, he sentenced her to a hundred dollar fine. Anthony retorted that she would never pay even one dollar. Rather than order Anthony jailed until she paid the fine, Hunt once again ignored accepted procedures. If she had been jailed, her attorney could have appealed the case directly to the Supreme Court on a writ of *habeas corpus*. Out of jail, Anthony could take her case no further. She never paid the fine, and she was never arrested. Eventually the Grant administration quietly pardoned all sixteen women and the election inspectors who had allowed them to vote.[31]

Anthony was understandably indignant at the outcome of her trial and dismayed that she could not rouse Stanton's sympathy. While Anthony was preparing her case, Stanton was away lecturing. She passed near Rochester to visit her family in Peterboro and Johnstown but did not stop to see her friend or attend the trial. Nor did Anthony visit Tenafly. As Stanton observed in a letter, "If our friendship were not cemented with long years of faith and trust, it could not stand the rough handling we give it."[32]

After the verdict was rendered Stanton went so far as to defend the judge. "Perhaps I do not comprehend your point of indignation," she remarked rudely in midsummer, and then retreated. "It is difficult to be indignant with the thermometer at ninety degrees." But she was not indifferent. She was, she explained, always in a "chronic state of rebellion."

> The insult of being tried by men—judges, jurors, lawyers, all men—for violating the laws and constitution of men, made for the subjugation of my whole sex; to be publicly impaled by the unwavering finger of scorn, by party, press and pulpit, so far transcends a petty verdict of butchers, cab-drivers and ploughboys, in a given case, that my continuous wrath against the whole dynasty of tyrants in our political, religious, and social life has not left one stagnant drop of blood in my veins to rouse for any single act of insult.[33]

Again and again Stanton expressed her anger in anti-male, nativist, racist terms. She had no model for this kind of behavior among the reformers who did not condone blatantly racist rhetoric, although they shared many of her xenophobic prejudices. Her rhetoric seemed better suited to the Know-Nothings, the anti-immigrant, anti-Catholic political party. More important, disapproval of her language by friends or enemies did not outweigh her own convictions. She had moved beyond the bounds imposed by previous political models and continued to rant. She justified her attacks by claiming that it was the votes of immigrant males that defeated suffrage referenda.

With her past legal training, Stanton followed another voting rights case, *Minor* v. *Happersett,* with keen interest. Virginia Minor, president of the Missouri Woman Suffrage Association, and her husband Francis, a St. Louis attorney, sued the registrar, Renée Happersett, for refusing to allow Mrs. Minor to vote in the election of 1872. The Minors based their suit on the new departure theory, a concept they had originated in 1869. Stanton had published their idea in the *Revolution* and used the idea as the basis of her 1870 speech, upon which Woodhull had expanded in 1871. The Minors claimed that a state could not deny woman suffrage, a national right guaranteed by the Fourteenth Amendment.

After losing in the lower courts, the couple appealed to the Supreme Court. In a unanimous decision handed down in October 1874, the Court upheld the lower court. *Minor* v. *Happersett* held that the Constitution did not automatically confer the right to vote on those who were citizens: suffrage was not "co-extensive" with citizenship. States could withhold suffrage from women, the court continued, just as they could deny it to children or crim-inals.[34] While Stanton watched these developments in the *Anthony* and *Minor* cases, she kept her distance in Tenafly or on the lecture circuit. She was still annoyed at Anthony's handling of the Woodhull incident. Now the problem arose again. Throughout the period of Anthony's trial, Wood-hull involved them both in a scandal that intrigued the nation for three years.

Soon after the May 1872 meeting, Victoria Woodhull had been arrested for passing obscene material through the mails. The charge referred to a *Weekly* article in which Woodhull had defended her unusual domestic ar-rangements. Scandalmongers cried bigamy, and Woodhull returned their fire, charging hypocrisy in high places. She was evicted from her home, jailed for six months, and forced to suspend publication of her paper, but she did not give up. In a September speech in Boston, Woodhull accused Henry Ward Beecher of having an affair with one of his parishioners. The woman in question was Elizabeth Tilton, a Sunday school teacher at Beecher's Plymouth Church in Brooklyn and the wife of his protégé, the editor Theo-dore Tilton. Woodhull demanded a public confession of adultery by Beecher. Her invective "poured out like a stream of flame," but the newspapers re-fused to print the story.[35]

Undaunted and out of jail, Woodhull resumed publication of the *Weekly* in order to publish the Beecher story herself. Her melodramatic prose de-tailed the story of Mrs. Tilton's seduction by the sensual minister. Demand for the November 1872 issue of the *Weekly* was so great that it sold for forty dollars a copy. Whether in an effort to legitimize her story or to dis-credit her former ally, Woodhull named Elizabeth Cady Stanton as her source.

Returning from her autumn tour, Stanton found "half a bushel of letters asking me about Mrs. Woodhull" and "stuck them all in the fire."[36] Stan-ton was not the only person who knew about Beecher's affair with Mrs. Tilton. She and Laura Bullard had heard the story from the wronged hus-band, who had also told Victoria Woodhull, with whom he was infa-tuated. Elizabeth Tilton had told her mother, who gossiped, and Anthony, who did not. The rumor spread among reformers and journalists but was silenced out of deference to the popular, powerful preacher. The irony of the situation did not escape the feminists, among them Isabella Beecher Hooker, who believed that her half-brother was guilty. For all her faults, Woodhull was being jailed and tormented for the same kind of behavior in which Beecher indulged without shame and without rebuke. It was a classic example of the double standard of Victorian morality.

Although Stanton claimed to have been misquoted, she never denied

Woodhull's story. Her animosity toward the Beecher family was such that Stanton may have been pleased to have the scandal aired.[37] Anthony was not pleased and blamed it all on Stanton's indiscretion. In self-defense, Stanton wrote Anthony: "I had supposed you knew enough of papers to trust a friend of twenty years' knowledge before them. . . . You do not monopolize, dear Susan, all the honor there is among womankind. I shall not run before I am sent, but when the time comes, I shall prove myself as true as you. No, I do not propose to shelter a man when a woman's liberty is at stake."[38] Anthony's rigid self-righteousness galled Stanton.

Henry Ward Beecher was a formidable opponent for Woodhull. Equally egotistic and powerfully connected, he destroyed her. Through three years of investigations and trials, he maintained a dignified demeanor and denied all charges. He dismissed the Claflin sisters as "two prostitutes." Woodhull was vilified by Beecher's friends in the press and taunted in public. Next Beecher eliminated Tilton. He had him removed from the editorship of a paper Beecher subsidized, encouraged him to write a flattering biography of Mrs. Woodhull, and then charged that Tilton had been compromised by his subject. Elizabeth Tilton was pressured by Beecher into denying the two-year affair entirely and then later instructed to claim that she had forced her affections on the minister.

Throughout these maneuvers Beecher found the cold silence of the suffragists damaging to his defense, so he set out to discredit them, too. Beecher attacked his more conservative half-sister, Mrs. Hooker, on grounds of instability verging on insanity. Worried that Stanton and Anthony both knew too much and might be called to testify against him, Beecher and his friends launched a campaign against them in the press. The women were identified as allies of Woodhull and advocates of free love. Libby Miller was prompted to ask Stanton what her position was. She replied:

> You ask if I believe in "free love." If by "free love" you mean promiscuity, I do not. I believe in monogamic marriage, and for men as well as women. Everything short of this makes a mongrel, sensual, discordant progeny. . . . I do not believe in man having a wife for breeding purposes and an affinity [mistress] for spiritual and intellectual intercourse. Soul-union should precede and exalt physical union. Without sentiment, affection, imagination, what better would we be in procreation than the beasts? If by "free love" you mean woman's right to give her body to the man she loves and no other, to become a mother or not as her desire, judgment and conscience may dictate, to be the absolute sovereign of herself, then I do believe in freedom of love. The next step of civilization will bring woman to this freedom.[39]

Henry Ward Beecher was tried twice. First a church board that he had appointed investigated the charges, and pronounced Beecher innocent. Then a civil court heard a suit brought by Tilton in 1875. The civil trial dragged on for 112 days, each heralded by sensational headlines. Elizabeth Tilton was not allowed to testify. The jury was unable to reach a verdict, and the case was dismissed. Most of the public believed Beecher innocent, and his popularity as a preacher soared. Woodhull also survived the scandal. Eager to sever their connection, Commodore Vanderbilt established her in England, where she married a wealthy landowner. Theodore Tilton, financially ruined by legal fees, spent the rest of his life in Paris. His wife died in obscurity and poverty.[40]

Stanton and the women's movement also survived, but they were not unscathed. Throughout the trials reporters hounded Stanton and Anthony. Anthony refused to make any comment, but Stanton was unable to endure Beecher's hypocrisy. She believed that both Victoria Woodhull and Elizabeth Tilton had been sacrificed to save his reputation. She was disgusted by Beecher's triumph and incensed by the slanderous attacks on the suffragists aroused by the case. When a reporter from the *Brooklyn Argus* camped on her Tenafly doorstep, she invited him in. She was eager to tell all she knew, including some indiscreet references to what Anthony knew. When Anthony saw the story in print, she was once again outraged. Stanton apologized immediately, but did not back down.

> Offended Susan—Come right down and pull my ears. I shall not attempt a defense. Of course I admit that I made an awful blunder in not keeping silent so far as you were concerned on this terrible Beecher-Tilton scandal. The whole odium of this *scandalum magnatum* has . . . been rolled on our suffrage movement as unjustly as cunningly; hence I feel obliged just now to make extra efforts to keep our ship off the rocks. . . . We must not let the cause of woman go down in the smash. It is innocent.[41]

After Beecher was pronounced innocent by the church committee, Stanton published her own account of the case. Her article was reprinted by the *Chicago Tribune* and received wide circulation. In it she moved from the specifics of the Beecher-Tilton case to an analysis of the social problem it raised and on to a defense of divorce.[42] Stanton was the only public figure bold enough to criticize the two verdicts.

The tensions created by the *Revolution* debt, the question of Stanton's convention attendance, the California trip, the Woodhull relationship, the Beecher-Tilton scandal, and their rivalry on the hustings and within the National scarred the Stanton-Anthony friendship. Anthony tied herself more closely to the National, took over its development in Stanton's absence, and became more critical of her friend. She found that Stanton's salvos on every subject hurt the group and its goal of suffrage. Anthony resented Stanton's popularity and her unwillingness to accept any responsibility for the day-to-day jobs. In their newly competitive relationship Stanton had her grievances, too. She thought that Anthony had been "pushing" her too much and failed to appreciate the value of her agitation. In the aftermath of the Beecher-Tilton affair, the two old friends saw less of each other, corresponded irregularly, and kept their distance until tempers cooled.

The Beecher-Tilton scandal also marked the end of Stanton's involvement with notorious trials. Although she still used current events to illustrate her lectures on women's rights, she became more circumspect. Throughout this period she had been at the center of several major trials: the Hester Vaughan trial for infanticide in 1869, the McFarland-Richardson case of 1870, the Laura Fair incident in San Francisco in 1871, and the Beecher-Tilton trials in 1872–75. In each instance, Stanton rushed to the defense of the women involved, whether defendant, plaintiff, or victim.

Hester Vaughan was a twenty-year-old woman, deserted by her husband, who had become a servant in a Philadelphia household. She had been seduced, become pregnant, and was dismissed. Destitute, she delivered the baby alone in an unheated garret and collapsed. Twenty-four hours later mother and child were discovered. The baby was dead, and Vaughan was charged with infanticide. Tried without counsel, forbidden to testify, she was found guilty and sentenced to hang. Week after week Stanton wrote about the case in the *Revolution*. She and Anthony held a public protest meeting attended by one thousand women. They demanded a pardon for Vaughan, an end to the double standard of morality, the right of women to serve as jurors, and the admission of women to law schools. Elizabeth Smith Miller led a delegation of women to call on the governor of Pennsylvania, and eventually Vaughan was pardoned. According to Stanton, Vaughan's trial by a jury of men, the prohibition on her taking the stand in her own defense, and the assumption of her guilt illustrated the indignity and injustice of women's legal status.[43]

The McFarland-Richardson case combined murder and divorce. In 1869 a brutal and dissolute character named Daniel McFarland had been divorced by his wife, Abby Sage, an actress and writer. When his ex-wife was courted by a well-known newspaperman, Albert Richardson, McFarland shot the suitor in the offices of the *Tribune*. On his deathbed Richardson married Mrs. McFarland, with Henry Ward Beecher officiating and Horace Greeley acting as witness. Despite the facts of the case, the press condemned the divorced woman. McFarland was acquitted of the murder on a plea of temporary insanity and subsequently awarded custody of the couple's young son. Again Stanton editorialized and Anthony organized. Three thousand people heard Stanton defend divorce and condemn artificial morality. She shocked her audience by declaring:

> I rejoice over every slave that escapes from a discordant marriage. With the education and elevation of woman we shall have a mighty sundering

of unholy ties that hold men and women together who loathe and despise each other. Such marriages are a crime against both the individual and the state, the source of discord, disease, death, of weakness, imbecility, deformity and depravity. . . . This wholesale shooting of wives' paramours should be stopped. . . . Suppose women should decide to shoot their husbands' mistresses, what a wholesale slaughter of innocents we should have![44]

Stanton advocated divorce reform and criticized the double sexual standard again during the murder trial of the prostitute Laura Fair in 1871. Finding that "women respond to this divorce speech as they never did to suffrage," Stanton expanded on it as a lyceum lecture, addressing it only to audiences of women.[45]

The publicity of three murder trials, added to the notoriety of the Beecher-Tilton affair, linked Stanton and suffrage with scandal. Although she claimed not to be bothered by this libel, she became more careful in her friendships and associations. As a captive of her lyceum schedule she had less opportunity to make trouble. She welcomed the chance to escape from infighting and ill-humor.

As a result of the Vaughan and Fair trials Stanton reaffirmed her interest in the "social purity" crusade, as the effort to end prostitution was called. Although most of her sexual attitudes seem modern compared to the Victorian standard, she did believe that the undisciplined sexual appetite of men forced a double standard on society and that sexual energy was not renewable and should not be squandered. She credited women with a healthy sexual interest and praised Walt Whitman for addressing female sensuality in his poetry. She believed that men and women, preferably husbands and wives, could enjoy intercourse for procreation and pleasure. But women, in or out of marriage, needed to be protected from coarse, drunk, brutal men. In 1853 she sponsored a female physiology lecture in Seneca Falls and urged that drunkenness be made grounds for divorce. In 1860 she warned against the sexual abuse of wives. In 1867 she and Anthony blocked a move to legalize prostitution in New York because the bill benefited only the clients. In 1873 she advised her son Theodore, then at Cornell, to "dwell on the importance of keeping the sensuous nature ever under control of the spiritual. The ordinary young girls are not worth your thought or attention. Better exercise with dumb-bells than visit them."[46] As always Stanton relied on education for elevation.

In the course of the 1870s Stanton's life developed a pattern. Every January, usually before the annual January meeting of the National, she left for a five-month lecture tour. She returned to Tenafly for the summer, when the children gathered. After revising her lectures and sending the youngest offspring back to school in the fall, she returned to the circuit for three more months, until Christmas. She was away from home eight months a year for ten years.

Stanton's lyceum experience epitomized her own independence. After years of staying at home, she now traveled widely. She had become a public person, a professional reformer, a newspaper editor, an organization president, a paid lecturer, and a minor celebrity. For her the lyceum was a great adventure, and she enjoyed it. She was acting out the role of the reformers she had observed from 1830 until the Civil War. Whether consciously or not, she was engaging in an activity similar to that of her father as a circuit judge and Henry as an abolition agent.

The postwar lyceum phenomenon was the inspiration of James Redpath, a former war correspondent and abolitionist who established the first commercially successful lecture bureau. The lyceum brought entertainment and education to small communities throughout the country but mostly in the West, where libraries and theaters were scarce. The lyceum followed the railroad and became enormously popular. Among the orators engaged by Redpath were Julia Ward Howe, Henry Beecher, and various generals, journalists, authors, and politicians. The bureaus engaged the speakers, arranged their itineraries, and promoted the tours. The speakers were paid between one and two hundred dollars per appearance, from which they had to deduct their expenses and a 10 percent commission for the organizers. Mrs. Stanton joined the New York Bureau in November 1869. In the first three months of her new career, she bragged to Gerrit Smith that she had earned "$2000 above all expenses . . . besides stirring up women generally to rebellion."[47] The remark reflected Stanton's double motivation in joining the lyceum—income and influence.

Stanton always claimed that she needed the income earned by her lectures to provide for her family and, specifically, to pay for the college educations of her children. Her financial status in 1870 is uncertain. Some of her inheritance from her father had been lost through Henry's poor investment strategy, and some of it had paid for the Tenafly house. Henry's income had diminished after 1864, and the couple's expenses increased. Maintaining two households and educating six children may have strained their joint resources.

The six youngest children all attended college, but Stanton's earnings paid for only two tuitions, those of Theodore and Bob at Cornell. Henry and Gerrit had completed their training before Stanton began lecturing, and her sister Harriet Eaton paid for Margaret and Harriot to attend Vassar. Mrs. Stanton would have preferred them to attend Swarthmore, a coeducational Quaker college, but she accepted the gift. The fact that she retired from the lyceum about the time Bob finished college might support her claim that she paid the younger sons' tuitions. Her frequent references to the need for economy and her refusal to help Anthony with the *Revolution* debt indicate that she may indeed have had limited resources or felt insecure even with those she had.[48] But she had inherited property from her mother in 1871 and was a popular, well-paid lecturer. Throughout this period she engaged a housekeeper and other servants and dressed stylishly. Rather than admit her desire to be free of family responsibility, she offered economic need as the rationale for her separations from her adolescent children. In reality, she had learned to put herself first.

Stanton had long believed that "radical reform must start in our homes, in our nurseries, in ourselves," rather than in conventions. She used the same rationale to go lecturing that she had used to stay home. Now Stanton wanted to take women's rights into the homes and lives of the American people. She thrived in her self-made role as agitator and propagandist. As she had declared in the final issue of the *Revolution,* she intended to spend her future "teaching woman her duties to herself."[49] She began by enhancing her own independence, by becoming physically and financially independent.

A typical lyceum tour might take Stanton to three dozen cities and small towns in six weeks, then back to Chicago or St. Louis or New York to start again. She crossed the Mississippi several times each season. She usually spoke once a day and twice on Sundays. When she had an afternoon free, she liked to meet alone with the women of a community. Speaking at night, she traveled by day or through the night. In a letter written to her daughter Margaret in 1872, Stanton described her routine.

> Imagine me today sitting in a small, comfortable room in the railroad hotel about a half mile from this little Minnesota town where I do not know a soul. But as everybody is polite and attentive, I suppose they all know me. I spoke last evening [in Iowa] and in order to reach here . . . I was obliged to leave at midnight. So after my lecture I had an oyster supper, packed up my finery, and all ready to start, took a short nap on the sofa. I was called at two, but as the horses were sick and I was the only guest going . . . westward, I was toted, I and my baggage, in a little cart drawn by a mule through a fearful snow storm, the wind cutting like particles of glass. Having arrived safely at the depot, a good natured overgrown boy deposited me and mine beside a redhot stove. Learning . . . that the train was two hours behind, I rolled my cloak up for a pillow, lay down on the bench, and went to sleep. . . . In due time I was awakened . . . tickets bought, valise checked and I transferred to a sleeping car, where . . . I at once "flopped" asleep again, without even taking my bonnet off. At eight, I was roused . . . for this place, where, it being Sunday, the train lies over. So I ordered a fire, washed my face, ate breakfast, undressed regularly, went to bed and slept soundly until one, when I arose, took a sponge bath, had dinner, read all the papers I could procure and now sit down

to answer your letter. . . . You ask if it is not lonely traveling as I do. It is indeed . . . but you see, dearest, [having Hattie with me] would double my expenses, and as I am so desirous of making money for the household, I must practice economy in some direction. And above all considerations of loneliness and fatigue, I feel that I am doing an immense amount of good in rousing women to thought and inspiring them with new hope and self-respect, that I am making the path smoother for you and Hattie and all the other dear girls.[50]

The lyceum was a vigorous undertaking for a woman in her late fifties. Travel through the West was still undependable, sometimes arduous, occasionally fraught with hardship. One winter when heavy snows closed the railroads, Mrs. Stanton hired a sleigh. Bundled in furs, she traveled forty to fifty miles a day in subzero cold to keep her engagements. On another occasion, when her Mississippi ferry was stranded on ice for hours, she entertained the passengers with selections from her speeches. When the trains were running, she often traveled all night. She had to put up with foul weather, unreliable transportation, irregular meals, uncomfortable hotels, and a demanding itinerary. Wherever she was on the lyceum circuit, she cultivated her knack for falling asleep anywhere.[51]

In compensation for these hardships, Mrs. Stanton had the satisfaction of being self-supporting and self-reliant—and admired. She was doing what she wanted to do and was proud of herself for doing it well. She considered herself a "pine knot . . . no standard for ordinary women." Furthermore, she had become a celebrity. "You would laugh to see how everywhere the girls flock around me for a kiss, a curl, an autograph," she wrote to her daughter.[52]

Mrs. Stanton was skilled at pleasing crowds. Her platform style was engaging, her voice was low and soothing, her manner was gracious and feminine. One observer recalled that she was a "powerful, uplifting" speaker, whose natural wit made her audiences laugh. Despite the gravity of her subject matter, the San Francisco *Chronicle* found Mrs. Stanton simply "jolly." Another onlooker described her as "plump as a partridge." With her rosy complexion, "unstuffy" white hair, and generous figure, "she would anywhere be taken for the mother of a governor or a president," wrote one male admirer. Stanton's appearance began to be compared to that of Queen Victoria or George Washington's mother. She was perceived as maternal, dignified, and eminently respectable.[53]

Stanton was what she appeared to be. She was a gracious, good-humored, charming mother of seven. She was also a radical feminist. She shrewdly exploited her maternal identification to legitimize and camouflage her revolutionary vocation. On trains she offered to help with crying infants and dispensed advice on baby care and hygiene in any setting.[54]

Her most popular lectures were those on marriage and children, in which she advanced from advice on household management and baby care to a discussion of divorce reform, property rights, or birth control.

Mrs. Stanton constantly revised and updated her repertoire of lectures. In addition to her basic suffrage speech she was prepared to speak on a dozen subjects: "The Subjection of Women," "Home Life," "The True Republic," "Coeducation," "Marriage and Divorce," "Marriage and Maternity," "Our Girls," "Our Boys," "Prison Life," "Thurlow Weed, William Seward, and Horace Greeley," and for Sundays, "Famous Women in the Bible" and "The Bible and Women's Rights." Every time Mrs. Stanton gave her address on "Marriage and Divorce," she came away "a reservoir of sorrows." Her audience would "flock" to her to tell her about their unhappy marriages. "Slavery is nothing to those unclean marriages," Stanton sighed, as she continued to expand on the theme that had held her attention since the 1850s.[55]

Stanton felt a special empathy for Western women. "The isolation of the lives out here strikes me most," she wrote to Libby Miller. "Living month after month and year after year on a boundless prairie, miles from any living soul! The women suffer most." Whenever possible, she praised the contribution of women pioneers. Attending a railroad dedication in Nebraska, she insisted that the speakers include women settlers in their praise. "Man's trials, his fears and losses, all fell on woman with double force; yet history is silent concerning the part women performed in the frontier life of the early settlers."[56]

Stanton's most vehement statement of women's rights, "The Antagonism of Sex," was a speech she saved for special occasions, when she was feeling particularly outraged. She sought to contradict the "twaddle about the essential oneness of man and woman—a oneness that makes a woman a slave." In her view it was nearly impossible for woman to evolve into a higher, more independent being when she was confined from "cradle to grave" by "dwarfing, crippling influences," such as man-made customs and the "spiritual bondage" of the church. "And then some men are astonished," she concluded, "that there is a 'shrieking sisterhood' [of feminists]." As Stanton confessed to Martha Wright, sometimes her anger at men was

> enough to rouse one's blood to the white heat of rebellion against every "white male" on the continent. When I think of all the wrongs that have been heaped upon womankind, I am ashamed that I am not forever in a condition of chronic wrath, stark mad, skin and bone, my eyes a fountain of tears, my lips overflowing with curses, and my hand against every man and his brother. Oh! How I do repent me of the male faces I have washed, the mittens I have knit, the pants mended, the cut fingers and broken toes

I have bound up, and then to multiply my labors for these white male
popinjays by 10,000 more, and then to think of these lords and lackeys
strutting. . . . oh! dear oh! dear it is too much![57]

Usually Mrs. Stanton held her anger in check.

Stanton's most famous address was "Our Girls." In it she urged the next
generation of women to prepare themselves for independence and self-
fulfillment. "You may never be wives, mothers, or housekeepers, but you
will be women," she advised her audience. "Therefore labor for the gran-
der and more universal fact of your existence," meaning their individual
identity. But she also warned them, "When men see a woman with brains
and two hands in practical life, capable of standing alone, earning her own
bread and thinking her own thoughts, conscious of the true dignity and
glory of womanhood, they call her unsexed." So popular was "Our Girls"
that Stanton's daughter claimed that her mother had earned thirty thousand dollars from that speech alone.[58] Stanton worked hard to improve its
companion piece, "Our Boys," but it never had the same impact.

Elizabeth Cady Stanton was the women's movement's major thinker
during this period. Yet other than *The Woman's Bible,* published in 1895,
she left no treatise summarizing her ideology. Only in her political speeches,
lyceum lectures, newspaper editorials, and random articles did she articulate, reiterate, and expand on her theme of female autonomy. Because of
the haste with which she wrote and the number of speeches she gave, they
are full of repetitions and contradictions. But she always insisted that women
must stand on their own before they could choose whether or not they
wished to be allied with men. "In all the essential relations of life," Stanton repeated again and again, women were alone and should learn to take
care of themselves. As Stanton had challenged herself to undertake the rigors
of the lyceum circuit, so must other women challenge themselves to reach
their limits and achieve self-reliance.

Only occasionally did Elizabeth Cady Stanton interrupt her lecture
schedule to appear at conventions of the National Association. Of the fifteen meetings held during the period 1870 to 1879, she presided at four
and attended one other. Otherwise her involvement was negligible. That
left Anthony in control of the National. Since the eventful Woodhull takeover meeting, Anthony had served as president. With Woodhull in retreat,
Hooker in retirement, and Stanton out of town, Anthony became dominant. She thrived on the organizational details and earned the loyalty of
the younger members.

Stanton had come away from her last Washington convention in 1872
"nauseated" by meetings. As she exploded to Martha Wright:

Two days full of speaking and resolving and dreading lest some one should make fools of us all, rehearsing the same old arguments in the same old way, must this be endured to the end of our heresy? I endured untold crucifixion at Washington. I suppose as I sat there I looked patient and submissive, but I could have boxed that Mary Walker's ears with a vengeance. Now this is for your ears only, don't read it to [your husband] or write it to [Lucretia], for as I usually preserve the exterior of a saint there is no use of everybody knowing how like a fallen angel I often feel.[59]

Her frustration at such conventions confirmed her decision to abandon them.

In the aftermath of the Beecher-Tilton scandal, Anthony had decided that the suffragists needed to improve their reputation. She believed that the nation's Centennial in 1876 provided an opportunity to present women's rights in a patriotic setting. What was needed was a new Declaration of Women's Rights. To prepare one Anthony needed Stanton's cooperation. In order to assure it, Anthony dispatched Matilda Joslyn Gage, vice-president of the National and an author, to woo Stanton to Philadelphia.[60] Acting as Anthony's emissary, Gage entreated Stanton to come.

Stanton was not enthusiastic about Anthony's plan. Although still robust at age sixty-one, she offered her health and age as excuses, urging that younger women take over. Stanton may well have recognized that none of the others had the ability to produce the needed document, or Anthony would not have asked her. The opportunity to share such a historic occasion with Lucretia Mott finally moved her to accept, but she delayed her arrival in Philadelphia until late June. By then, Anthony admitted to her diary, she was "glad enough to see her and feel [her] strength come in." Six weeks earlier Anthony had paid off "the last dollar" of the *Revolution* debt.[61]

The highlight of the Centennial was an international exhibit in Philadelphia's Fairmount Park. It was opened in May by a beleaguered President Grant, with an ode, a march, a prayer, and a hymn commissioned for the occasion. At the conclusion of the ceremonies, the president pulled a switch to activate an enormous Corliss steam engine, the sole source of power for the eight thousand machines in the main exhibit. Almost everything made in the United States was on display, from safety pins to caskets to false teeth, from the unfinished Statue of Liberty to the newly invented telephone.

Legions of women organized by Mrs. E. D. Gillespie formed the Women's Centennial Committee. By selling stock at local bazaars and concerts, the women had raised the money to pay for the exhibition. In return for their efforts, they were promised a display area in the Main Building. But shortly before the opening they were told there was no room for them. To everyone's amazement, the women then raised enough additional cash to erect a separate, ornate Women's Building. It featured its own steam engine, driving machines operated by skilled women. One of the machines printed a women's rights newspaper.[62]

The Centennial headquarters of the National Woman Suffrage Association was outside the Centennial Park, on Chestnut Street. Every day Mrs. Mott rode in from the country with a picnic lunch to be eaten while the women assembled to lay their plans. Earlier in the summer the National had sent memorials to the Democratic and Republican conventions, urging them to grant woman suffrage during the centennial year. Working with Mrs. Gage, Stanton produced the new declaration. Perhaps because it was a joint effort or because Stanton lacked interest, the document was not up to her standard for either ideas or rhetoric.[63]

Nonetheless, Anthony intended to interrupt the Fourth of July ceremonies to present it. When her request for a part in the program and fifty seats on the platform was turned down, she decided to crash the event anyway. Armed with five press passes from her brother's Kansas newspaper, Anthony and four other women marched into Independence Hall as the band played. The women advanced on the startled chairman and presented him with a parchment copy of their Declaration. Then they filed rapidly out of the hall, distributing copies as they went. Once outside, Anthony mounted a bandstand and read the Declaration to unsuspecting onlookers. She was shielded from the hot sun by Mrs. Gage's open umbrella. Then the five women hurried back to report to a meeting organized by Mott and Stanton at the First Unitarian Church. Stanton claimed to have been so angry at the rebuff of the women by the officials of the Centennial that she refused to participate in Anthony's gesture of protest. Stanton's inability to move fast in hot weather and her pique at Anthony may also have been considerations. It was unlike Stanton to avoid the limelight.

Although the press was full of the escapade, Stanton was not satisfied that the strategy had been successful. The women had attracted ridicule as well as attention. They had reminded the nation of its historic commitment to equal rights, but they had accomplished nothing tangible for women's rights. Stanton returned to Tenafly to recover from these activities and to think about what should be done. She refused to attend another meeting to commemorate another anniversary of Seneca Falls. Sending a letter in her place, a discouraged Stanton concluded, "As I sum up the indignities toward women, as illustrated by recent judicial decisions—denied the right to vote, denied the right to practice in the Supreme Court, denied jury trial— I feel the degradation of sex more bitterly than I did on that July 19, 1848."[64] Spurred by discontent, Stanton decided to attend the next convention and run again for president of the National.

With the loss of Anthony's voting rights case and the Supreme Court decision in *Minor* v. *Happersett,* Stanton recognized that the suffragists must abandon their new departure strategy. Congressional inaction and court rulings had undercut any possibility of interpreting the Fourteenth Amendment as a means of granting women the vote. The suffragists were forced to fall back on a federal amendment strategy. Because there was so little support for woman suffrage in the Congress, the women were doomed to a long-term, time-consuming, costly, difficult, frustrating task, and almost five more decades of defeat.

With the return of her usual optimism, Stanton regarded the primary focus on a federal suffrage amendment as opening a new era in the movement. She and Anthony attended the 1877 meeting of the National together. The association resolved to collect petition signatures favoring a federal amendment and turned the task over to Anthony. When they had gathered ten thousand signatures from twenty-six states, she presented them to the Senate. That body found them uproariously funny; one newspaper reported that "the entire Senate presented the appearance of a laughing school practicing sidesplitting."[65] The petitions were rescued from obscurity by the courtesy of Sen. Aaron Sargeant of California, whom Stanton and Anthony had first met in California in 1871. He subsequently introduced a woman suffrage amendment.

In order for Stanton to return to a leadership position in the National Association, Anthony had to agree to step down from the presidency. They exchanged offices: Stanton became president and Anthony took over the executive committee. Anthony remained the power behind the scenes; Stanton became the figurehead. Stanton did not challenge Anthony's actual authority within the organization. She realized that Anthony had the allegiance and affection of the majority of members, who had voted for Stanton at Anthony's direction. Stanton wanted the podium back as a pulpit. Anthony, recognizing Stanton's superior gift for oratory and inspiration, agreed. The situation satisfied both women. Their cooperation marked the beginning of a partial restoration of their friendship.

As the new president of the National, Stanton took on the planning of the 1878 Washington convention. For the first time since the organization of the National, Anthony was absent. Stanton's agenda emphasized federal action. Stanton persuaded Aaron Sargeant, the California Republican, to introduce in the Senate a new version of a proposed sixteenth amendment: "The right of citizens of the United States to vote shall not be denied or abridged by the United States or any state on account of sex." Following the National meeting Sargeant arranged for Stanton to testify before the Senate Committee on Privileges and Elections. The senators were not attentive to her remarks on "National Protections for National Citizens." While the white-haired Stanton stood before them, they lounged and smoked and talked. She was offended by their rudeness but pleased that they agreed to two of her lesser demands. The women were granted the use of a meeting room in the Capitol, and the suffrage amendment was assigned to a new Committee on Woman Suffrage.[66]

Eight days later Stanton left for another five-month tour of the West. After a summer of family festivities and a trip to Rochester to mark another anniversary of Seneca Falls with Lucretia Mott, she was back on the circuit. In November 1878 she told Anthony that she could not attend the upcoming National convention. "You must not ask me to give up a single possible engagement for women," she explained. "With . . . my usual heavy family expenses during the summer, it will take all I can make to come out even by the first of June."[67]

At age sixty-three, Stanton was ready to retire from the lyceum circuit. Her exhaustion and exasperation are apparent in a letter to Libby Miller written from Missouri in March 1879.

> Dear Julius: I have been wandering, wandering ever since we parted; up early and late, sleepy and disgusted with my profession, as there is no rest from the time the season begins until it ends. Two months more containing 61 days still stretch their long length before me. I must pack and unpack my trunk 61 times, pull out the black silk train and don it, curl my hair, and pin on the illusion puffing around my spacious throat, 61 more times, rehearse "Our Boys," "Our Girls," or "Home Life" 61 times, eat 183 more miserable meals, sleep on cotton sheets with these detestable things called "comforters" (tormentors would be a more fitting name) over me 61 more nights, shake hands with 61 more committees, smile, look intelligent and interested in everyone who approaches me, while I feel like a squeezed sponge, affect a little spring and briskness in my gait on landing in each new town to avoid making an impression that I am 70, when in reality I feel more like crawling than walking. With her best foot forward, Johnson.

The tour was interrupted when an omnibus in which she was riding overturned. Once rescued, Mrs. Stanton was able to walk but she suffered from lameness and a sore back for several more weeks. Before resuming her schedule, she recuperated at her son Gerrit's home in Iowa. She begged Anthony to substitute for her at a suffrage meeting in St. Louis: "I feel as if one more ounce of responsibility would kill me," she complained. "I am sick, tired, [and] jaded beyond description."[68] In the end Stanton attended the meeting and completed her tour. But when she contracted pneumonia, in the fall of 1879, she decided to retire from the lyceum and undertake a more sedentary occupation. After ten years of practicing independent behavior, she looked forward to maintaining that status in her old age.

IO
Writing and Widowhood
1880–88

Elizabeth Cady Stanton did not retire when she resigned from the lyceum circuit. Reminded of her mortality by the omnibus accident and her bout of pneumonia, she was spurred to greater productivity. Always energetic, she no longer squandered her resources. She insisted that her remaining energy be spent in ways she found either profitable or pleasant. She approached projects with a now-or-never zest, giving priority in the new decade to completion of the *History of Woman Suffrage,* a massive compendium on women's rights in America. She devoted more time to her family, came to terms with Henry, restored her friendship with Anthony, made two long trips to Europe, began writing regularly for newspaper and magazine publication, used the National Association to test new tenets of her ideology, began to investigate women and theology, and still found time for reading, music, games, and naps.

Stanton entered old age combative, keen witted, self centered, and uninhibited. She had always looked forward to her "prime," when she was past fifty. The women she had identified as "queens" earlier in her life— her mother, Emma Willard, and Lucretia Mott—had all been older women. She had observed and admired them. Whether married or widowed, they ruled their own worlds. They were independent and influential. Now Stanton was ready to become an imperial old lady.

On the lyceum circuit Stanton had escaped her domestic bondage, enhanced her self-esteem, and established her physical and financial independence. Now she sought independence at home. With her children grown and Henry living separately, she could practice self-reliance and self-indulgence in comfort. As she wrote privately in late 1880:

I have fully made up my mind not to budge this autumn one inch outside my premises. I am so happy at the thought of staying at home that nothing that [anyone] could offer would be so charming as to cause me to change my mind. I do not believe there ever was a woman who esteemed it such a privilege to stay at home. It is often said that if women are given a taste of public life, they will never be satisfied with home, but I think experience shows that all men and women who have been much in the outside world are only too glad to retire.[1]

Stanton at sixty-five may have viewed her resignation from the lyceum as a retirement, but the pace of her activities did not diminish.

As soon as Anthony heard that Stanton had recovered her strength, she began to pester her for speeches. "Since [Mrs. Stanton] has been to the dinner table," wrote Anthony, "I infer she is well enough to work up the thunder and lightning [for the national conventions]." Anthony had called for members of the National Woman Suffrage Association to converge on the sites of the Democratic and Republican presidential conventions to demand suffrage. Stanton agreed to work on the necessary statements, but she was not sanguine about the outcome. She despaired of the Democrats and thought "we had sat on a limb of the Republican tree singing 'suffrage if you please' like so many insignificant humming-birds quite long enough."[2]

Nor was Stanton interested in remaining president of the National. "Do not let my name come up for consideration," she directed Anthony prior to the 1881 meeting, "as I positively decline. My work in conventions is at an end, they are distasteful to me." But she admitted to another colleague that "when [Susan] is at hand, she always dragoons me into what she considers my duty, so I never venture to say what I will or will not do."[3] Stanton preferred to devote all her vitality to writing, and she tried to convince Anthony to join her.

Mrs. Stanton did arouse herself enough to try to vote in November 1880. She and Anthony, who had come to Tenafly to work on the History, presented themselves at the local polling place. Stanton explained to the inspectors why she should be allowed to vote: she was three times the legal voting age, she had been a resident of Tenafly for twelve years, she had paid the real estate and poll taxes, she was a property owner, she could read and write, and her legal representative (Henry) was absent. Unmoved by her litany, the men would not let her put her ballot in the box, so she hurled it at them. "The whole town was agape with my act," she bragged, well satisfied with herself.[4]

That November Mrs. Stanton marked her birthday by starting a diary. Her first entry began with a quotation from Robert Browning and a description of herself. "Grow old along with me; The best is yet to be. Today I am sixty-five years old, am perfectly well, am a moderate eater, sleep well, and am generally happy. My philosophy is to live one day at a time; neither to waste my forces in apprehension of evils to come, nor regrets for the blunders of the past." Stanton's remarks about her eating habits indicate that the diary presented only her view of reality rather than a factual account. Although she kept the diary locked, it was clear from the outset that Stanton intended it to be read by her children. Writing to Hattie and Theodore she explained, "When I have passed away, you children [will] have a better knowledge of some of the things I have thought and done during the final years of my life."[5]

It was important to Elizabeth Cady Stanton that she convince her children of the significance of her work. She wanted them to understand why a mother would sacrifice time with her children to pursue women's rights. Although she had been absent from their lives for almost a decade and had chafed against her maternal bonds when they were younger, she sought their approval of herself and her work. She wanted to reassure them of her devotion and affection. Stanton believed that parents had a duty to give their children intelligence, health, sound values, money, and enough education "to render life something more than one ceaseless struggle for necessaries."[6] Stanton reassured herself that she had done all she could and that the children were well launched.*

Although all the children were over twenty-one in 1880, several of them still lived at home, whether in Tenafly with their mother or in New York with their father. Rarely were they all together. Stanton described one atypical gathering to Anthony; only Gat was missing from her family portait. "At the present writing Maggie and Bob are playing delightfully on piano and violin; Theodore is out taking his evening walk; Hattie is reading Hallam's *Middle Ages,* and Kit, Grote's *History of Greece;* the "Governor" [Henry] and Neil are smoking and talking on the piazza; Amelia and Nanny [the housekeeper and maid] sewing in the basement; Julian is munching oats in the barn; and Bruno barking at some passerby."[7] Stanton enjoyed the lively company of her adult children.

Her firstborn and favorite son, Daniel Cady Stanton (Neil), was thirty-eight years old in 1880. The completion of reconstruction and the withdrawal of federal troops from Louisiana had ended his career as a "carpetbag" politician. He returned north in the late 1870s and supported himself on the cash he brought with him. There is no other record of Neil's employment. For a while he lived at Tenafly, where, according to his mother, "he likes to have the house to himself and me. If he can have me there to read to him in the evenings he asks nothing more." At some point he moved to Iowa, married, and had a daughter; he divorced his wife before 1887.

* A genealogical sketch of Stanton's children appears in app. B.

He died in 1891, at age forty-eight, the only Stanton child to predecease his mother. Elizabeth was heartbroken. For months afterward she dreamed of seeing him walking on the piazza.[8] He left his entire estate to his mother rather than to his former wife or daughter.[9]

Henry B. Stanton, Jr., practiced law with his father in New York. They lived and worked together in a townhouse on Tenth Avenue. After his father died, young Henry lived in a hotel until 1892, when he married a widow named Mary O'Shea. He was forty-eight; they had no children. In 1873 he had applied to be a territorial judge but had been turned down, despite, or perhaps on account of, a letter from his mother to the attorney general. He finally made a fortune as an attorney for the Northern Pacific Railroad. A veteran of the Civil War and a graduate of Columbia Law School, he belonged to the Union League Club, the Saint Nicholas Society, the Sons of the Mayflower, and a yacht club. He died a year after his mother, in 1903.[10]

Stanton's third son, Gerrit Smith Stanton, received his law degree from Columbia the same year as his older brother. Although he claimed in his alumni record to have volunteered in the Civil War, his service had consisted of guarding his parents and Horace Greeley during the 1863 draft riots. After the war he had moved to a farm near Beaman, Iowa, where he and his wife, Augusta Hazelton, adopted a daughter. Over their sofa, facing each other, hung portraits of his mother and Susan B. Anthony. After serving as mayor of Woodbine, Iowa, Gerrit returned east in the 1890s. He became a successful real estate speculator on Long Island and died in 1927.[11]

Also trained as a lawyer, Theodore Weld Stanton turned to journalism and reform. It pleased his mother that he was "heart and soul . . . interested in my work." Too young to serve in the war, Theodore had attended the City College of New York, graduated from Cornell, attended the Sorbonne, and earned an M.A. from Cornell in 1876. After a brief engagement to the daughter of Cornell president and United States ambassador to Germany Andrew Dickinson White, he married a Frenchwoman, Marguerite Berry, in 1881. Stanton was pleased that her athletic, attractive daughter-in-law had "strong bones and sound teeth."[12] The couple presented Stanton with her first grandchild, Elizabeth Cady Stanton II, called Lizette, in 1882. Theodore and his wife had two other children who survived infancy, Robert and Helene.

After publishing The Woman Question in Europe (1883), Theodore became the Paris correspondent for Harper's, Appleton's, the Associated Press, and the New York Tribune. His mother tried to promote his career by bringing him to the attention of Joseph Pulitzer.[13] Theo was a member of the International Jury of the Paris Exhibition in 1889. Returning to the

United States in the 1890s to be near his mother, he became a lecturer in French history and politics at Hobart College in Geneva, New York. After his mother's death he returned to Paris, where he served as a volunteer in the American Ambulance Hospital during World War I. He came home to America for the last time to work with his sister Harriot on publication of two volumes of his mother's letters, diary, and autobiography. When he died in 1925, he was at Rutgers University preparing to open a library as a memorial to his mother.[14]

Stanton's first daughter, Margaret Livingston Stanton Lawrence, became a professor of physical education at Columbia Teachers College. A large baby at birth, Maggie was a natural athlete whose skills were encouraged by her mother. After graduating from Vassar in 1876, Margaret planned to marry. To prepare her, Stanton put her in charge of the Tenafly household, advising her to:

> Devote the month of May to reading the cook book and getting all the practical knowledge of the kitchen that you can. It will be a pleasant change from books. Learn a few simple things, such as how to make bread, tea, coffee, cake, and how to cook vegetables. See how washing, starching, ironing and everything of that kind is done. Master the sewing machine. Then you will know how to direct every sort of household work. Every man and woman should have these acquirements.

As a wedding gift, Stanton gave her daughter an inscribed copy of Libby Miller's cookbook.[15] Margaret married Frank E. Lawrence of Omaha, Nebraska, on October 2, 1878, under the "old familiar oaks" at Tenafly. The couple settled first in Council Bluffs, Iowa, and later moved to California.

Margaret had no children. She described herself as a "bright young woman," with "no remarkable genius" but "some practical talent in the ordinary affairs of life." She added that she had "sufficient aesthetic taste to dress well, decorate my house with fall leaves and golden rod, and supply my table with appetizing food." After her husband died in 1890, Maggie moved to New York City and lived with her Aunt Tryphena while she studied "gyms." On completion of her training she taught at Teachers College and lived with her mother and brother Bob. Although she considered herself "a lukewarm suffrage saint," she organized an Elizabeth Cady Stanton Birthday Centennial in November 1915 in Seneca Falls and worked for suffrage in New York State.[16]

It was Stanton's second daughter, Harriot Eaton Stanton Blatch, who inherited "the real spirit of the reformer," according to her mother. Harriot became an active suffragist in both England and the United States and was an officer of the Women's Political Union and the National Woman's party. Even as a youngster she had shown feminist tendencies. When her father ordered her to come down from a high tree limb, Hattie remembered replying, "Tell Bob—he's three years younger and one branch higher!"[17] After being educated in private preparatory schools, she graduated with honors from Vassar in 1878 and spent another year at the Boston School of Oratory.

Until her marriage in 1882 to an English businessman, William Henry Blatch, Harriot traveled in Europe, attended a French university, and worked with her mother. She returned to the United States after a twenty-year residence in England to enroll her daughter Nora at Cornell. After her husband went bankrupt and died in an automobile accident, Harriot stayed in America. She lobbied for suffrage and women's rights in Washington and Albany. During World War I she headed the Food Administration Speakers Bureau and wrote a book, *Mobilizing Woman Power.* In 1926 she was a candidate for the United States Senate. Unable to get along with Carrie Chapman Catt, one of her mother's successors as president of the National American Woman Suffrage Association, Blatch joined the rival National Woman's party. She took on the role of defender of her mother's reputation, creating archives and preserving her memory. Five feet, five inches tall, with a crown of white hair, she resembled her mother and remained an active feminist until she died at age eighty-four in 1940.[18]

Stanton's last child and youngest son, Robert Livingston Stanton, remained a bachelor and lived with his mother most of his life. Slightly crippled as a youngster, he nonetheless followed his older brothers to Cornell and Columbia Law School. The family skeptic, he never married, joking that experience had taught him that marriage was "an immoral custom." He became assistant corporation counsel for the City of New York. At the time of his death from pneumonia in February 1920, his friends had been trying to get him appointed to his grandfather's seat on the New York Supreme Court. Bob played the violin, chess, and whist; collected stamps; and shared his mother's zest for games.[19]

The second entry in Elizabeth Cady Stanton's diary in November 1880 recorded the death of Lucretia Mott. Unable to attend the Quaker memorial in Philadelphia, Stanton spent the day thinking, reading, and writing about her mentor. "I have vowed again," she wrote in her diary, "as I have so many times, that I shall in the future try to imitate her noble example."[20] Mott had provided Stanton with an example of a reformer, a feminist, an orator, an independent thinker, a wife, a mother, a matriarch, and a public figure. Mott's mask of Quaker serenity and modesty, disguising a quick temper and tart tongue, taught Stanton to develop an attractive public manner. Mott's enormous energy and concomitant instinct for self-preservation and pampering encouraged Stanton to follow a parallel pattern. Mott was an efficient housewife and a devoted mother; Stanton also aspired to be both. Mott was courageous, outspoken, and independent; so was Stanton. As a result of modeling herself on her older mentor and of her own mature disposition, Stanton shared many of these characteristics, although she lacked Mott's humility and pacific tendencies. Unable to match Mott in everything, Stanton in her old age became more tolerant of her own shortcomings and more self-confident in her own identity.

In order to honor Lucretia Mott, Stanton attended the next convention of the National Association in January 1881. A memorial to Mrs. Mott, the meeting was attended by the First Lady, Lucy Webb Hayes (known as "Lemonade Lucy" for her stand on temperance), members of the Supreme Court, and congressmen. A choir of ex-slaves provided the hymns. Stanton gave the eulogy. She recalled the impact that Mrs. Mott had had on her life. To her, Mott had been "like an added sun in the heavens, . . . a woman who had sufficient confidence in herself to frame and hold an opinion in the face of opposition, a woman who understood the deep significance of life, to whom I could talk freely," remembered Stanton. "My longings were answered at last."[21] Stanton would never forget that Mott had led her to religious integrity and feminist independence.

When she was alive, Mrs. Mott had frequently urged that Stanton write a history of the women's movement. Stanton undertook the work in earnest two weeks after Mott died. She had first conceived the project following the 1848 meeting and had returned to it in her frustration in the 1850s. Finally the events of the nation's Centennial convinced Stanton that someone must document the accomplishments of American women. In 1876 Stanton signed partnership papers with Anthony and Matilda Joslyn Gage "for the purpose of preparing and editing a history of the woman suffrage movement." Stanton and Gage agreed to "write, collect, select and arrange material" and Anthony agreed to "secure publication." All three names would appear on the title page; all three women would share the copyright and divide the profits.[22]

Like Stanton and Anthony, Matilda Joslyn Gage was from upstate New York.* She was the well-educated daughter of a Cicero physician, the wife of a wealthy Fayetteville merchant, the fashionably dressed mother of four children. Active in women's rights since the 1852 Syracuse meeting, she had been a charter member of the National Association and a contributor to the *Revolution*. Too soft-spoken to be an effective speaker, she was a skilled organizer and writer. She had tried to vote in 1872, served as pres-

---

* Matilda Joslyn Gage (1826–98) became more radical in her old age and agreed with ECS on many points, enunciating her views in *Woman, Church and State* (1892). In 1890 she broke with the National and formed a more progressive organization, the Woman's National Liberal Union. She was its only president until her death in 1898. Had Gage not been plagued by ill health and a weak voice, she might have been even more prominent.

ident of the National in 1875, edited the *National Citizen and Ballot Box*, and headed the New York Association. Her work on the *History* was cut short by her husband's death in 1884.[23]

In November 1880 the three women gathered in Tenafly to begin work. Mrs. Stanton had given up the lyceum and was delighted not to be "wandering on those western prairies."[24] Anthony's mother had died the previous spring, so she was free to leave Rochester and move into her own room in Stanton's house. Mrs. Gage still had family obligations but came for a month at a time when she could.

They began by collecting documents. They gathered personal reminiscences, biographical sketches, photographs, state reports, copies of speeches and resolutions, excerpts from the *Congressional Record*, newspaper clippings, and miscellany. They solicited source material from individuals and state organizations. Stanton and Anthony also combed their own files. At her father's suggestion Anthony had kept clippings about the women's movement since 1855, but they were scattered throughout her family's Rochester home. In contrast to her well-ordered image, Miss Anthony, according to Stanton, "could never keep her papers in order. In search of any particular document, she roots out every drawer and pigeon hole."[25] Unlike Anthony, Stanton had saved few items other than copies of speeches. Every time she had moved, she had thrown things out. Now she had to rely on her memory, which all agreed was inaccurate.

Stanton was in her element and enjoyed the work immensely. Anthony, assigned to the drudgery of details and anxious about publication prospects, hated it. "I am just sick to death of it," she complained to a younger friend within a month of starting. "I had rather wash or whitewash or do any possible hard work than sit here and go digging into dusty records of the past—that is, rather *make* history than write it." Stanton's children began to resent the *History,* too. As daughter Margaret admitted, "We all feel towards these volumes as a family of children would to some favorite adopted child, that filled their places in a mother's heart."[26]

With Mrs. Gage needed at home, Stanton and Anthony did most of the work. Much of it was the manual labor of making copies; they chose not to employ a stenographer. Margaret provided a picture of the two of them at work.

As our house faces the south the sunshine streams in all day. In the center of a large room, 20 by 22, with an immense bay window, hard wood floor and open fire, beside a substantial office desk with innumerable drawers and doors, filled with documents,—there *vis-a-vis* sit our historians, surrounded with manuscripts and letters. . . . In the center of their desk are two ink stands and two bottles of mucilage, to say nothing of diverse pens, pencils, scissors, knives, etc., etc. As these famous women

grow intense in working up some thrilling quotation, . . . I have seen them
again and again dip their pens in the mucilage and their brushes in the
ink. . . . It is as good as a comedy to watch these souls from day to day.
They start off pretty well in the morning, fresh and amiable. They write
page after page with alacrity, they laugh and talk, poke the fire by turn,
and admire the flowers on their desk. . . . Everything is harmonious for
a season, but after straining their eyes over the most illegible, disorderly
manuscripts, . . . suddenly the whole sky is overspread with dark and
threatening clouds, and from the adjoining room I hear a hot dispute about
something. The dictionary, the encyclopedia, *The Woman's Journal, Our
Herald, The National Citizen, The Revolution, The Woman's Tribune,* . . .
are overhauled, tossed about in an emphatic manner for some date, fact,
or some point of law or constitution. Susan is punctilious on dates, mother
on philosophy, but each contends as stoutly in the other's domain as if
equally strong on all points. Sometimes these disputes run so high that
down go the pens, one sails out of one door and one out the other, walking in opposite directions around the estate, and just as I have made up
my mind that this beautiful friendship of forty years has at last termi-
nated, I see them walking down the hill, arm in arm. . . . When they
return they go straight to work where they left off, as if nothing had ever
happened. . . . The one that was unquestionably right assumes it, and
the other silently concedes the fact. They never explain, nor apologize,
nor shed tears, nor make up, as other people do.[27]

One dispute they could not resolve concerned Stanton's claim that state
legislatures were the final authority on suffrage. She believed as the Supreme Court had held in the *Minor* case that states had the power to enfranchise women. Anthony challenged her claim, reminding Stanton of the
overriding authority of the Constitution. The argument was important as
it related to political strategy for the National: would it pursue a state-by-
state referendum strategy or fight only for congressional action on a federal amendment. Unable to agree, they continued the battle in letters. "You
have not made me take your position," wrote Stanton, "I repudiate it from
the bottom of my soul." She charged that Anthony was being autocratic.
"Beware, Susan, lest as you become respectable, you become conservative." They never did resolve their differences.[28]

The first volume of the *History* was completed within six months and
appeared in May 1881. In 878 pages, it brought them up to 1860. Stanton
wrote all the material except three chapters by Mrs. Gage. Anthony searched
for documents and illustrations, copied the manuscript, and proofread their
product. To critics who charged that a history of woman suffrage could
not be written before it had been accomplished, Stanton defended their approach: "The United States has not completed its grand experiment of
equality . . . and yet [George] Bancroft has been writing our history for
forty years."[29]

After being turned down several times, Anthony had finally found a publisher. She had to assume part of the costs, but was repaid by a thousand-dollar gift from a New York feminist. Stanton's housekeeper, Amelia Willard, donated another three thousand dollars toward publication. Volume I sold for three dollars a copy. In order to assure circulation, Anthony wrote to wealthy friends asking them to purchase copies for the libraries and schools in their area. Such gifts were not always welcome. When Vassar College returned the copies that she had donated for its library, Stanton was furious.[30]

Congratulating themselves on the completion of the first volume, Stanton and Anthony quit work for the summer. Anthony had her boxes of papers hauled to the barn and headed for New England to recruit National members in American territory. Stanton delayed long enough to refurbish the guest rooms for Theo and his French bride and then joined Anthony in Boston. Soon Stanton was eager to return to Tenafly and writing, but Anthony procrastinated. Now it was Stanton's turn to nag, urging Anthony to "leave these state conventions alone . . . at least until we can finish the History."[31]

By the end of July 1881 Stanton's diary records that she was "in the toils of another one thousand page volume." She and Anthony fell into their old routine, "laughing, talking, squabbling, day in and day out." They worked in the mornings and took a walk at noon, after which Stanton napped; then they dined at two and returned to their desks. Progress on volume 2 was cut short when Stanton had a "tedious and alarming" attack of malaria in August. Her family blamed her ill health on the History, but Anthony disagreed, declaring to another friend: "It is so easy to charge every ill to her labors for suffrage, while she knows and I know that it is her work for women which has kept her young and fresh and happy all these years. Mrs. Stanton has written me that during her illness she suffered more from her fear that she never would finish the History than from the thought of parting with all her friends." By October, Stanton had recovered, Mrs. Gage was in residence, and Anthony joined them reluctantly. She dreaded the task, describing it as "a wilderness of work, a swamp of letters and papers almost hopeless."[32]

Anthony's anxiety about publishing volume 2 was relieved in January 1882. She was surprised and delighted to learn that she had inherited more than twenty-five thousand dollars from Eliza Jackson Eddy, the daughter of Francis Jackson, Boston reformer and earlier benefactor. Eddy's attorney, Wendell Phillips, informed Anthony that she and Lucy Stone were to divide the estate. The only stipulation was that the money be used "for the advancement of the woman's cause."[33] Because of delays in probate, Anthony did not receive the legacy until 1885, but the gift assured publication of the History. Anthony used the money to buy out the partnership shares of Stanton and Gage and to publish and distribute subsequent volumes. Instead of selling them, Anthony sent free copies to libraries, schools, and individuals, including every member of Congress. With Ida Husted Harper, an Indiana journalist and her biographer, Anthony published volume 4. After Anthony's death in 1906, Harper completed the record up to ratification with volumes 5 and 6.

With publication guaranteed, Stanton and Anthony hurried to complete volume 2, covering 1861 to 1876. In February 1882 Stanton's younger daughter Harriot returned from Europe and announced plans to take her mother abroad that summer. To speed the book along, Hattie read proofs and did research. Noting the absence of any mention of Lucy Stone or the American Association, she insisted that a chapter be written on the rival organization and that photographs of Stone and Julia Ward Howe be included. Stanton finally agreed to let Harriot write that section. Then Stone refused to cooperate. In response to a request for information, Stone had sent a three-sentence biography and signed her note, "Yours with ceaseless regret that any 'wing' of suffragists should attempt to write the history of the other." Without the aid of the Boston group, Hattie relied on the *Woman's Journal* and the *Agitator* for source material. She did not refer to the 1869 schism. Her authorship of 106 pages—chapter 26 in volume 2—was acknowledged only in a footnote.[34]

Harriot also convinced her mother to return to Europe with her. "As the children were scattered to the four points of the compass and my husband spent the winter in the city," Stanton recalled, she rented the Tenafly house and spent a hurried month in New York finishing the *History*.[35] Mother and daughter and Anthony stayed at the Bayards' rather than with Henry. Volume 2 was finished in May 1882, and the two Stanton women departed for France.

Stanton and her daughter shared a stateroom with "innumerable pieces of baggage, a baby carriage, rocking chair, a box of *The History of Woman Suffrage* for foreign libraries, besides the usual number of trunks and satchels, and one hamper, in which were many things that we were undecided whether to take or leave," including a loaded pistol that went off accidentally. Stanton's narrow berth had been widened by one foot to accomodate her bulk, but she was uncomfortable at sea. Unlike earlier crossings, she dreaded the voyage and found it a "twelve day imprisonment."[36]

The women delivered the baby equipment to Stanton's new grandchild, Lizette, and spent a month with the infant's parents near Jacournassy, where Stanton helped Theodore edit *The Woman Question in Europe*. Then they traveled to Toulouse, where Hattie enrolled in the university to earn a master's degree in mathematics. Barred from graduate education in the United States, many American women sought advanced degrees abroad.

Stanton accompanied Hattie to classes, taking naps in the back row. Mother and daughter boarded in a Catholic convent, where Stanton appreciated the benefits of "associative living" but missed American home cooking. "I would give five francs for a good meal of Amelia's cooking. I bemoan the absence of butter . . . and I long for muffins and oatmeal and cream. We eat our strawberries with a fork. There is no powdered sugar. . . . If I grow thin on this diet, I shall feel fully compensated for my many culinary deprivations."[37]

In September Harriot abandoned mathematics for French; in October she abandoned French for marriage. She became engaged to another student, William Henry Blatch, an Englishman whom she had met on her February ocean crossing. With Mrs. Stanton chaperoning, the couple traveled via Paris to London. They were married on Stanton's sixty-seventh birthday by the American Unitarian minister and Stanton's old friend, William Henry Channing. When the newlyweds took up residence on a Blatch family estate in Basingstoke, west of London, Mrs. Stanton stayed on in the city. "I am fixed . . . for the winter," she reported to Libby Miller. "I have made many pleasant acquaintances among liberal people and am out nearly every day to tea, dinner, breakfast or lunch."[38]

It had been over forty years since Stanton's first trip to England and the Continent. She relished the recognition she now received as a celebrated reformer and suffrage leader. She traveled to Glasgow to give her first European speech, on municipal suffrage for women, and visited old friends in Edinburgh. In London she was invited to a reception honoring William Dean Howells, whose female characters she thought showed "a lamentable want of common sense."[39] She preached on "Women and the Bible"; endorsed the "bifurcated skirt," a variation of bloomers; and advised British suffragists to demand the vote for all women rather than only unmarried women. By accident she ran into Victoria Woodhull, noting that she was now "the legal wife of an Englishman of wealth and position."[40] London's winter fog made Mrs. Stanton cough, so she moved to Basingstoke. Hattie installed a central furnace, and Stanton filled her days with reading, napping, writing and driving. She awaited two important arrivals: Hattie's first child and Susan B. Anthony.

Anthony made her first trip to Europe in March 1883, accompanied by Rachel Foster, a young friend of the Mott family and one of Anthony's "nieces." Writing Anthony that she was "on the tiptoe of expectation to meet you," Stanton returned to London and settled into a boardinghouse with her friends.[41] The three of them met with British suffragists, visited Parliament, made speeches, and hosted receptions. That summer Anthony and Foster toured Europe, and Stanton returned to Basingstoke.

Stanton's second grandchild, Nora Stanton Blatch, was born on September 30, 1883. Stanton stayed at Basingstoke until Nora was a month old, lavishing attention on the baby and new mother. As she confided in her diary, "As I sit here beside Hattie with the baby in my arms, and realize that three generations of us are together, I appreciate more than ever what each generation can do for the next one, by making the most of itself." She frequently said that having daughters and granddaughters gave her incentive to keep working for women's rights for future generations. No longer responsible for diapers and pap spoons, she could dote on her grandchildren. On November 12, her sixty-eighth birthday, she parted from Hattie, "without a tear," but her "legs trembled so that I could scarcely walk to the carriage."[42] After a week of farewell calls in London, she and Anthony sailed for home. Stanton had been in Europe eighteen months.

During this period of writing in Tenafly and touring in Europe, Stanton and Anthony had quietly refurbished their friendship. From November 1880 to the fall of 1886 they lived and worked together almost every day. They shared more of their lives than they had since the war years. After the friction and dissatisfaction of the 1870s, their initial efforts at reconciliation had been tentative. Mrs. Gage was brought into the *History* project as much as a buffer as a coauthor. Stanton fell back on her family to shield herself from Anthony, and Anthony surrounded herself with "nieces," young women drawn from the ranks of the National Association. Both of them had alternative sources of affection and approval, but each still expected support from the other. A foundation of enduring affection sustained their political alliance. After all, wrote Stanton, they were "fastened, heart to heart, with hooks of steel in a friendship that years of confidence and affection have steadily strengthened."[43]

As the two women grew older, more opinionated, and more secure, their relationship became more contentious. But they always came back together. As Stanton wrote to Anthony: "We have jogged along pretty well for forty years or more. Perhaps mid the wreck of thrones and the undoing of so many friendships, sects, parties and families, you and I deserve some credit for sticking together through all adverse winds with so few ripples on the surface." No matter how cruel or careless one was, she expected to be forgiven by the other. "We have said worse things to each other face to face than we have ever said about each other," Stanton admitted. "Nothing Susan could say or do could break my friendship with her and I know nothing could uproot her affection for me."[44]

Stanton and Anthony addressed the subject of their friendship in the *History*. Stanton referred to them as "two sticks of a drum . . . keeping up . . . the rub-a-dub of agitation."

> In thought and sympathy we were one, and in the division of labor we
> exactly complemented each other. In writing we did better work together
> than either could alone. While she is slow and analytical in composition,

> I am rapid and synthetic. I am the better writer, she the better critic. She
> supplied the facts and statistics, I the philosophy and rhetoric, and to-
> gether we have made arguments that have stood unshaken by the storms
> of thirty long years. . . . Our speeches may be considered the united
> product of two brains.

Refusing to acknowledge the fights and hurt feelings between them, Stanton continued:

> So entirely one are we that in all our associations, ever side by side on the
> same platform, not one feeling of jealousy or envy has ever shadowed our
> lives. We have indulged freely in criticism of each other when alone, and
> hotly contended whenever we differed. . . . There has never been a break
> of one hour. To the world we always seem to agree and uniformly reflect
> each other.

The only accurate statement is that they always tried to agree in public. A
slightly more objective source, presumably Theodore Tilton, noted: "Op-
posites though they be, each does not so much supplement the other's de-
ficiences as augment the other's eccentricities. Thus they often stimulate each
other's aggressiveness and at the same time diminish each other's discre-
tion."[45]

The steadfast loyalty of Stanton and Anthony to each other became part
of their mutual public image. People thought of them as a team long after
they had ceased to cooperate closely. For most of their lives the friendship
was genuine. But the assumption of automatic agreement between them by
the public, the press, and their peers added stress to periods of disagreement and made their final years more difficult.

Rather than return from England with Rachel Foster earlier in 1883,
Anthony had waited to travel with Mrs. Stanton. Anthony was aware of
how hard it was for her friend to part from Hattie and Nora, and how
Stanton no longer enjoyed sea travel. Although Stanton was not seasick,
she found the confinement of their November voyage across the North Atlantic "beyond all endurance." Sailing into New York harbor, she was
"unspeakably happy to set foot on native shores once more."[46]

Upon landing, Anthony headed for Rochester, and Stanton undertook a
series of visits to friends and relatives. Rather than stay in New York with
Henry, she spent six weeks in Geneva with Libby Miller, accompanied by
her daughter Margaret. Because the Tenafly house was still rented, Stanton
opened the "family homestead" in Johnstown. She started work on volume 3 of the *History* and wrote articles for newspaper and magazine publication. She was full of energy and interest in suffrage work and even looked
forward to the next National convention scheduled for February. As she
declared to Anthony: "A year shut up in a community of snails has developed in me an amount of enthusiasm that is a surprise to myself. They say

people always revive just before they go out altogether; so if immediately after this performance I have symptoms of softening of the brain, you need not be surprised." But as the date of the meeting approached, Stanton was forced to renege. "I have never wanted to be at a convention so much in my life, but I cannot." She admitted to shortness of breath and heart trouble. "Don't tell anybody all this; just say I have a cold."[47]

Anthony was actually relieved. She had been afraid that her iconoclastic colleague would make public her letter congratulating Frederick Douglass on his marriage to a white woman. "I do hope you won't put your foot into the question of intermarriage of the races," Anthony entreated Stanton. "You very well know that if you plunge in . . . your endorsement will be charged upon me and the whole association."[48] Anthony's loyalty to suffrage was paramount. She would no longer allow any other ideas or individuals to share her platform, not even Elizabeth Cady Stanton.

In March 1884 Anthony traveled to Johnstown through six feet of snow to write volume 3 of the *History of Woman Suffrage*. Rather than live with Stanton, she established headquarters in a boardinghouse. Together they tried to rouse "sleepy old Johnstown." In May Stanton gave her "Our Boys" speech in the Presbyterian church. In August they organized a women's convention in the old courthouse where Judge Cady had once presided. Lillie Devereux Blake, the attractive novelist and president of the New York Suffrage Association, was the featured speaker. The women urged the election of a woman for school trustee. New York was one of seventeen states in which women could vote in local school campaigns. According to a local newspaper report, both Stanton and Anthony voted in the Johnstown school election in November 1884 without incident. They were accompanied by Henry Stanton.[49]

Still president of the National Woman Suffrage Association, Elizabeth Cady Stanton attended the 1885 meeting in Washington. She presided over all the sessions and delivered the principal address, "The Limitations of Sex." Her argument emphasized that men and women could not be segregated into separate spheres on account of ability or biology.

> There would be more sense in insisting on man's limitations because he cannot be a mother, than on a woman's because she can be. Surely maternity is an added power and development of some of the most tender sentiments of the human heart and not a "limitation," . . . "But it unfits her for much of the world's work." Yes, and it fits her for much of [it]; a large share of human legislation would be better done by her because of this deep experience. . . . If one-half the effort had been expended to exalt the feminine element that has been made to degrade it, we should have reached the natural equilibrium long ago. Either sex, in isolation, is robbed of one-half its power for the accomplishment of any given work.[50]

Although Stanton's speech was applauded, she soon fell into disfavor by supporting a controversial resolution condemning all religious creeds teaching that "woman was an afterthought in the creation, her sex a misfortune, marriage a condition of subordination, and maternity a curse." It had been introduced by Clara Bewick Colby* and was defended by Stanton. She had met Colby, the first female valedictorian of the University of Wisconsin and a journalist, while lecturing in Nebraska.[51] Typically, Stanton was outspoken in her approval of the resolution. In her first public dispute with Stanton since the Woodhull incident, Anthony opposed Colby's resolution as irrelevant and unprofitable. At Anthony's signal the resolution was tabled by the membership.

Anthony's opposition was practical rather than philosophical. When the two old friends attended a sermon on "Women and Skepticism" the next week, Stanton reported that Anthony was just as offended as she was. The preacher, the president of Howard University, concluded that "freedom for women meant infidelity and unchastity." Stanton found his conclusion "abominable." Anthony was so angry that she stood up in her pew and announced that the minister ought to be spanked. For once horrified by her own behavior, Anthony was not comforted by cartoons of the pair portraying them as "a spanking team."[52]

Stanton, accompanied to Washington by Henry's niece, enjoyed a busy social schedule and visited many old friends. Altogether she had a "grand time." At the end of February she "returned home to Johnstown quite satisfied with myself bodily and mentally, having been on the go for over a month." She was pleased with herself, her work and her life. For the next several months of 1885 Stanton was busy "both as regards hands and brains." She continued to collect state reports for inclusion in volume 3 of the *History* and closed the Johnstown house again. She spent April and May preparing to reopen the Tenafly house. Anthony came in midsummer, and together they settled down to complete the often interrupted *History*. Volume 3 brought the women's movement up to 1885 and was published the following year.[53]

By that time Mrs. Stanton was more interested in other writing assignments. She had returned from Europe rested and refreshed, full of new thoughts based on wider reading and quiet reflection, stimulated by her contact with English Fabians and socialists.[54] She made one attempt at fiction, a short story called "Our Romance," which was never published. Then

---

* Clara Bewick Colby (1846–1916) had been born in England and raised in the Midwest. She married another student and moved to Nebraska, where her husband served in the state Senate. The childless couple adopted two children, one a Sioux Indian baby found after the battle of Wounded Knee. Mrs. Colby was very active in the National and the National American and cooperated with Stanton on the Bible project.

she began writing essays on current events for newspapers and magazines. In 1885 the *North American Review* carried her article on divorce reform and one entitled, "Has Christianity Benefited Women?" The *Boston Index* printed "The Christian Church and Women." "Our Boys on Sunday" in the *Forum* (April 1886) argued against closing parks and museums on Sunday, the only day working people could relax and improve themselves.[55] Stanton began to envision a longer work that would challenge the theological assumptions and conclusions of male ministers about woman's place.

Stanton was not the only family member busy writing. In March 1885 Henry Stanton published *Random Recollections,* an abbreviated autobiography. It was an anecdotal account of his career as a journalist, preacher, reformer, lawyer, and politician. Its prose captured much of his casual charm and quick wit. The book had three printings. In the first and second editions Henry's only reference to Elizabeth noted that he had married the daughter of the famous jurist, Daniel Cady, but the daughter was not named. In the third edition Henry mentioned his wife once, identifying her as the reformer Elizabeth Cady Stanton, who worked with Susan B. Anthony for woman suffrage.[56]

Henry's eightieth birthday, in June 1885, was marked by an "informal reception" at the New York Press Club. "As no ladies were invited," his wife recalled tartly, "I can only judge from the reports in the daily press and what I can glean from the honored guest himself, that it was a very interesting occasion." The octogenarian was described as a tall, trim figure with a gray beard and alert, piercing eyes. A few years earlier Stanton had written Theodore Weld that "Henry is well, looks about fifty, scarcely any gray hairs in his head."[57] He was still a handsome man, still practicing law in New York, and still writing for the *Sun.*

Although Henry retained his townhouse and his law practice in the city, he became more visible in his wife's life in the 1880s, perhaps because she was at home more. They were brought together again by the graduations and marriages of their children. He appears in accounts of local political meetings in Johnstown and in descriptions of family life in Tenafly—sitting on the piazza, reading in the parlor, driving with his wife. After 1884 Henry spent more and more time at Tenafly, revising his *Recollections.* Mrs. Stanton had the veranda screened with mosquito netting, "so the paterfamilias, with his pipe, could muse and gaze at the stars unmolested."[58]

By 1885 the Stantons had been married forty-five years and seemed to have come to terms with each other. Stanton was no longer romantically devoted to her husband, but she still cared about him. "Henry is so old now," she wrote to Libby Miller that year, "that I feel my first duty is to make a home for him." By March 1886 he reported to a friend that he was "tormented with acute rheumatism."[59] His health continued to fail. During that summer Hattie and Theo brought their families to visit. It was Henry's first and last encounter with his grandchildren. The other children gathered as well, thinking it was their father's last season, but in the fall Henry rallied and returned to the city.

The attention paid to Henry Stanton's birthday prompted suffragists to honor Mrs. Stanton with a similar but larger event. On her seventieth birthday in November 1885 simultaneous memorial meetings were held throughout the North and West. Sponsored by the National Woman Suffrage Association, they were organized by May Wright Sewall, head of the executive committee and founder of the Indianapolis Girls' Classical School, and by Elizabeth Boynton Harbert, editor of the New Era. The instigators advised that the events should be simple, inexpensive, proper, and "as Mrs. Stanton is herself pre-eminently social, the element of sociability should be provided for in the programme."[60]

Stanton attended the New York City party at the home of Dr. Clemence Lozier, one of the first generation of female gynecologists.* She and Stanton had worked together in 1863 to persuade the New York legislature to charter the New York Medical College and Hospital for Women, five years before Elizabeth Blackwell opened her infirmary. At her party Stanton read an essay on "The Pleasures of Old Age," in which she concluded that over fifty is the "heyday" of a woman's life. "Then the forces hitherto finding an outlet in flirtations, courtship, conjugal and maternal love, are garnered in the brain to find expression in intellectual achievements, in spiritual friendships and beautiful thoughts, in music, poetry and art." Presents, flowers, letters, and cables poured in. Mrs. Harbert devoted the November issue of her magazine to tributes to Elizabeth Cady Stanton. "If I were not kept humble by the continual cuffing of the opposition," wrote Stanton in appreciation, "I am really afraid this number of the Era might fill me with conceit."[61]

As it was, Stanton was well pleased with herself. Her life was in order. Her house was redecorated and functioning smoothly, her children were prospering, and Henry was recovering. She had reestablished her friendship with Anthony and her ties to the National Association. She was invigorated by plans for a new theological study and proud of her work on the History.

To reward herself, Stanton decided to return to Europe. In late October

---

* Clemence Harned Lozier Baker (1813–88) was an orphan who opened a school to support herself, taught physiology, and read her brother's medical books. She completed her training at Syracuse Medical College at age forty. Reports of Stanton's speech on divorce inspired Lozier to divorce her second husband. She had a large practice, specialized in the removal of tumors, and attained distinction in obstetrics and general surgery.

1886 she sailed for England with Hattie, Nora, and a nanny. Installed once more at Basingstoke, Stanton resumed a comfortable pattern. She played games with Nora, read constantly, wrote regularly, napped often, and ate well, only occasionally sallying forth to confer with English suffragists or other reformers. Her routine was broken on January 14, 1887, by news of Henry's death.

Henry Stanton had died of pneumonia at age eighty-one with his sons Bob and Henry at his side. He had caught cold standing in the rain on election night to watch the posting of the returns. He had not been considered seriously ill, and his wife had not gone home to nurse him. Nor did she return to bury him. As she recorded in her diary:

> This morning while I was taking breakfast in my room, Hattie entered with a cablegram from New York, announcing the death of her father. Death! We all think we are prepared to hear of the passing away of the aged. But when the news comes, the heart and pulses all seem to stand still. . . . The startling news comes upon you without preparation, it is a terrible shock to every nerve and feeling, to body and mind alike. Then well up regrets for every unkind, ungracious word spoken, for every act of coldness and neglect. Ah! If we could only remember in life to be gentle and forbearing with each other, and to strive to serve nobly instead of exacting service, our memories of the past would be more pleasant[62]

Compared to entries noting the passing of more distant relatives, Stanton's tone was cool, reserved, almost impersonal. She does not mention Henry's name or his relationship to her or recall fond memories of their life together. Since the diary was intended as a record for her children, perhaps she felt no need to amend or change the impression her adult children already had of their parents' marriage.

Family history insists that Henry and Elizabeth Stanton were estranged when he died and that the children were divided in placing the blame. The older boys except Neil sided with Henry, the younger children with their mother. There is no evidence to confirm that Henry's return to New York and Elizabeth's return to England augured a permanent or even an ongoing separation. Nor is there any evidence that Henry had had any affairs, although he always had an eye for the ladies.[63] The couple had spent more time together since 1883 than they had in the previous fifteen years. Whether their cohabitation was the result of Stanton's greater tolerance, Henry's increasing infirmity, convenience, or a charade for the children cannot be determined. Stanton still cared for Henry, but she no longer loved him. She regretted that they did not share "the joy of a deep soul-love." "No depth of friendship can compensate for it," she wrote to Libby Miller. "The older I grow the deeper my sorrow that I have no son of Adam to reverence and worship as a god."[64] She had loved no other man more than Henry, and she mourned him more than she expected.

For all her radicalism, or because of it, Stanton was a romantic. As a bride she had been intellectually and physically attracted to her husband, but her expectations of marriage as a partnership of equals had been disappointed early. Her resentment of Henry's male freedom raged during her years of domestic drudgery. Her respect for him as a principled and heroic reform agent diminished. Yet she stayed married. For someone who condemned "ill-assorted unions," surely Stanton would have divorced Henry had he been guilty of drunkenness, brutality, or an illicit affair. Without grounds, with remnants of their earlier affection, they separated informally and unofficially, an arrangement that satisfied both of them. After 1868 the marriage placed no burdens on her; there were no reasons not to remain nominally married to Henry.

The unexpected shock, grief, and regret that characterized Stanton's reaction to Henry's death subsided in subsequent months. After spending the winter in Basingstoke in bed, she roused herself to visit Theodore in Paris in the spring. There she sat for a bust by Paul Bartlett and a portrait by Anna Klumpke, the protégé of Rosa Bonheur. Stanton was "quite pleased with the result," she reported to her son Bob. "I sit in a large ruby-colored chair, dressed in black satin and black lace around the throat and hands. Nothing white in the picture but my head and hands. My right hand rests in my lap, my left on the arm of the chair holding my gold spectacles. A little table on my left contains one volume of the Woman Suffrage history and two pamphlets." Theodore hosted weekly Wednesday afternoon receptions for his mother and guided her through the city's museums and gardens. Stanton exhibited her usual curiosity and humor. She was impressed by the easy companionship of French men and women, who "mixed freely in business and amusements."[65]

In October, Stanton returned to England. She resumed her routine of reading and writing, admitting in her diary, "This is the first time in my life that I have had uninterrupted leisure for reading, free from all care of home, servants, and children." She read works by John Stuart Mill, John Ruskin, J. P. F. Richter, Auguste Comte, George Eliot, and Leo Tolstoy. Of *Anna Karenina* she remarked, "I do not like it much as all the women are disappointed and unhappy; and well they may be, as they look to men, and not to themselves, for their chief joy."[66] The first anniversary of Henry's death passed without comment. Stanton was ready to think about returning to the United States and the suffrage crusade.

Widowhood legitimized Stanton's long-sought independence from marriage, husband, and family. She had lived separately and supported herself financially prior to his death, but few people knew it and fewer would have approved of her behavior. As a widow, her independence was considered admirable. Her reputation as a reformer, unrelated to Henry, was enhanced by the public respect due to widows. Widowhood for her meant status without responsibilities. For many women less self-reliant then Stanton, widowhood was the only time in their lives that they were legally free from the domination of fathers or husbands; for many it was a painful and difficult transition. But Stanton, in her quest for individual independence, had unconsciously prepared herself for widowhood. For her, widowhood was characterized by personal satisfaction, public accomplishment, and undiminished militance.

II

Self Sovereign
1889–1902

Elizabeth Cady Stanton was a defiant old lady. The beginning of the 1890s coincided with the onset of Stanton's old age. One could date her maturity from her sixty-fifth birthday or her retirement from the lyceum in 1880; from the marriage of her youngest child, in this case Harriot, in 1882; or from her widowhood in 1887. During the 1880s and 1890s Stanton had to contend with the symptoms of aging: physical ailments, retirement, financial insecurity, death of friends, family estrangement, and generational conflict.[1] But these factors did not define or dominate her old age. Soon to be immobilized by obesity and blindness, she was restrained only by physical infirmity. She had survived her husband, outlived most of her enemies, and exhausted her allies. Her mind remained alert, her mood optimistic, and her manner combative.

In a period of anticipated and actual dependence for most older people, Stanton became increasingly independent. Personally, she had established the kind of "associative household" she had long advocated and enjoyed her "matriarchy." Professionally, she supported herself by writing, completing her autobiography and The Woman's Bible in addition to numerous speeches, articles, and newspaper columns. Politically, she remained aloof from the merger of the rival factions in the suffrage movement, finally breaking with the younger leaders over their timid tactics. Philosophically, she synthesized her feminist ideology in "The Solitude of Self" speech and culminated her attack on patriarchal institutions by condemning traditional Biblical scholarship. Psychologically, she shed the last vestiges of dependence. She moved beyond her last confidante, Susan B. Anthony, and came to rely wholly on her own judgment and values.

As an old woman, Stanton came into her own. She was honored as a feminist foremother and as a grandmother. She was self-supporting and self-sustaining. Physically crippled, she was otherwise unfettered. Throughout her life Stanton had admired and identified "queenly" women; now she had become the kind of woman she had defined as her ideal: a self sovereign, a queen.[2]

While Stanton had been in Europe following Henry's death, she had missed the first Senate vote on the proposed federal woman suffrage amendment, in January 1887. In a lengthy floor debate one senator declared that females were not physically strong enough to be citizens; another announced the opposition of two hundred preachers and the president of Harvard. Frances Willard, head of the Woman's Christian Temperance Union (WCTU), joined with the suffragists and presented two hundred thousand signatures of women who had petitioned for the vote. The final tally was 16 yeas (all Republicans), 34 nays (24 Democrats, 10 Republicans), and 26 abstentions. From abroad Stanton concluded, "Of one thing men may be assured . . . that the next generation will not argue the question of woman's rights with the infinite patience we have displayed for half a century." By the winter of 1888 Stanton was eager to rejoin the fray, writing Anthony that she was "thoroughly rested now and full of fight and fire, ready to travel and speak from Maine to Florida."[3] She promised to return in time for the international meeting planned for March, but, faced with another ocean crossing, Stanton lost her nerve and tried to back out on her promise.

Anthony was so angry that she delayed before replying. The theme of the pending meeting was the fortieth anniversary of Seneca Falls. Anthony had contacted all the signers of the Declaration she could locate, urging them to come, and now the principal organizer threatened to back out. "I wrote the most terrific letter to Mrs. Stanton," Anthony recorded in her diary. "It will start every white hair on her head." Anthony urged Libby Miller to write Stanton as well. "*Very evil fates will persecute* her if she dares to be absent," Anthony warned. "She will never be forgiven by me or any of our Association, if she fails to come." Chastened, Mrs. Stanton cabled curtly, "I am coming," but then delayed her departure.[4]

Stanton arrived in the middle of the Great Blizzard of '88. When she finally reached Washington, Anthony was alarmed to learn that she had no speech prepared for the occasion. According to an often repeated suffrage anecdote, Anthony handed Stanton pen and paper, locked her in her room at the Riggs House, kept a guard at the door, and allowed no visitors. Mrs. Stanton emerged three days later, "ready with her usual magnificent address."[5]

Stanton and Anthony had conceived the idea of an international meeting during their European junket in 1883. They hoped to create a "universal sisterhood" of women's rights advocates. Anthony convinced the National Association to organize and finance an International Council of Women, and an estimated twelve thousand dollars was raised to pay the expenses of all the delegates. Anthony shrewdly used the council to accomplish several of her own ends. She wanted to take advantage of her new European contacts to enlarge and legitimize the scope of women's rights; she wanted to honor Mrs. Stanton by commemorating Seneca Falls; and she wanted to create a coalition with other women's groups around an uncontroversial subject.

In planning the meeting Anthony called on the American Woman Suffrage Association and the Woman's Christian Temperance Union, the two powerful and prestigious rivals of the National, to participate in the preparation and the program. Fifty-three other national organizations represented "every department of woman's work." Literary clubs; art leagues; temperance, missionary, peace, and social purity societies; labor unions; charitable, professional, educational, and industrial groups all joined the suffrage associations in a massive show of unity. In addition, delegates from England, France, Norway, Finland, Denmark, India, and Canada attended.

Anthony presided with an autocratic parliamentary will over half of the sixteen sessions. Tactfully, she made sure that the other leaders had equally prominent roles. It was the first time in twenty years that Anthony and Lucy Stone had appeared on the same platform or that members of the organized suffrage movement had cooperated or met together. When Anthony joined Julia Ward Howe and Frances Willard in crediting Stone with her own conversion to women's rights, Stanton was speechless. But throughout the week-long meeting she remained publicly gracious and serene.[6]

The program of the International Council of Women was elaborate. It opened and ended with religious services conducted by five female ministers. Mrs. Stanton was greeted with a standing ovation. Her opening speech, on Monday, March 25, emphasized the similarities among women of different classes and different countries: "Through suffering," women had the key to understanding each other. Women shared the bondage of their sex, whether they were "housed in golden cages with every want supplied, or wandering in the dreary deserts of life, friendless and forsaken."[7]

Stanton also presided at the "pioneers" meeting of eight men and thirty-six women who had attended the 1848 convention and signed the Declaration of Sentiments. Other sessions were devoted to discussions of philanthropy, temperance, industry, the professions, women's organizations, political and legal conditions, and social purity, each led by a female expert in the field. Stanton most enjoyed the part of the program in which the common claim that a woman's brain was inferior in size and quality was refuted. She had always believed that her own brain was large and superior.[8]

Following the International Council sessions, Stanton addressed a Senate hearing on suffrage. She made a plea for legal recognition of human equality. Frances Willard of the WCTU, Julia Ward Howe of the American Association, and six foreign women also testified. Stanton was pleased that the emphasis on lobbying for a sixteenth amendment had not been neglected in the midst of the International Council. She believed that legislative hearings educated the public and modified the prejudices of lawmakers. Many of the committee members met "strongminded women" for the first time, and did not find them "such a bad lot after all," as one Congressman had remarked to her.[9] She also appreciated the significance of suffragists being feted at the White House and honored with receptions and dinners.

Stanton was satisfied that the International Council had been a success, but she was alarmed by signs of Anthony's alignment with conservative women. Anthony was convinced that suffrage had to have more support among larger groups of middle-class women. To win that support, suffrage must appear as respectable a cause as temperance or benevolence. Anthony, influenced by the younger suffragists within the National, now sought to narrow the Association's agenda in order to enlarge its constituency.

Anthony had already forged an alliance with Frances Willard and the Woman's Christian Temperance Union, the largest organization of women in the country. In return, suffragists quietly supported prohibition and Sunday closing laws, used "righteousness" as a rationale for voting, and earned the opposition of the liquor lobby. Similarly, Anthony had made overtures to the American Woman Suffrage Association. Settlement of the Eddy estate had reopened her correspondence with Wendell Phillips and other Bostonians, and the International Council brought them together in a joint enterprise. Next Anthony and others created a National Council of Women as an umbrella organization under which the rival factions might meet. Now that the National Woman Suffrage Association had become respectable and conciliatory, in effect reversing the stand taken in 1869, there was no reason not to close ranks with the American.

A suffrage-first, conservative strategy and a religious alliance were anathema to Stanton. She believed that the vote was only one of many reforms required for female independence. "Miss Anthony has one idea and she has no patience with anyone who has two," Stanton later complained to Clara Colby. "I cannot . . . sing suffrage evermore; I am deeply interested in all the questions of the day." In her diary she declared, "I get more radical as I get older, while [Anthony] seems to grow more conservative."[10] Stanton disapproved of Anthony's strategy and tactics. But rather than directly challenge Anthony, who had the support of more than the majority of National members, Stanton removed herself from the merger negotiations. Unable to win, she chose not to fight that battle; but she did not surrender.

Stanton spent the eighteen months between her return from Europe in March 1888 and the National-American merger in February 1890 visiting her family. She needed a place to stay, and she wanted to restore her relationship with her children and siblings. After Henry died she had sold the Tenafly house. For the next five years she had had no permanent residence and traveled from relative to relative. After two months at the Riggs House in Washington for the International Council, Stanton spent June in New York City. There she saw her sons Henry and Bob and her sisters Tryphena Bayard and Harriet Eaton. Stanton spent the summer in upstate New York with Libby Miller and then went west. She visited suffrage colleagues in Ohio and moved on to Iowa to see her son Gerrit and her sister Margaret McMartin. From there she went to Omaha to spend the winter with her daughter Margaret Lawrence. In the spring of 1889, when Margaret had to take her husband to San Diego for his health, Neil escorted his mother back to New York. She spent the summer on Long Island with Gerrit, who had moved east as well. Her son Henry had given her a phaeton, "as low and easy as a cradle," for her daily drives. Anthony came to visit, and the two reformers went to Coney Island to preach women's rights to two hundred women at one of the big summer hotels. That fall Margaret Lawrence came east to consider graduate school, and Harriot Blatch arrived from England to spend the winter earning a master's degree from Vassar. Stanton visited friends in the city and then went to Geneva for several more months with Libby Miller.[11]

Stanton had undertaken this eighteen-month odyssey in an effort to renew her ties with her children. Despite her well-known charm and wit, her reconciliation efforts were sometimes awkward. "As we had not met in several years, it took us a long time, in the network of life, to pick up all the stitches that had dropped since we parted," she recalled, referring to her visit with Gerrit. "I amused myself darning stockings and drawing plans for an addition to his house." Soon she could report that she had been "receptioned and photographed" as well.[12]

Stanton made the effort because she thought she might die soon, loved her children and adored her grandchildren, and relished the role of matriarch. Being the head of her geographically extended family appealed to her sense of dominion. It was her granddaughter Nora Blatch who first referred to Stanton as the "Queen Mother," both because of her rotund resemblance to Queen Victoria and because of her regal self-regard. For Stanton, the adjective "queenly" had always been the highest accolade, applied only to admirable women like her mother and Lucretia Mott. She accepted the title.

Always dressed in black silk, her tight white curls under a lace cap, blue eyes twinkling, Stanton was the picture of the wise and witty American grandmother. Newspapers hailed her as the "Grand Old Woman of America." It was an image she exploited to legitimize her reform career and camouflage her radical theology. Grace Greenwood, the popular author and reporter, saw through Stanton's disguise. "Stately Mrs. Stanton has secured much immunity by a comfortable look of motherliness and a sly benignancy in her smiling eyes, even though her arguments have been bayonet thrusts and her words gun shots." [13] Stanton's radical rhetoric abounded with maternal metaphors: women seeking equal rights were "the mothers of the race."

The "cult of motherhood" in nineteenth-century America was "nearly as sacred as democracy." Motherhood gave women an unassailable claim to "authority and prestige" as well as an occupation from which one did not retire. [14] As mothers became grandmothers, respect increased and responsibility decreased. Furthermore, theories of motherhood were used by Stanton and others to justify conventionally unmaternal pursuits, like suffrage. For Stanton, the cult of motherhood enhanced her matriarchal role: it provided personal satisfaction, public esteem, political utility, and independence in her old age.

Mrs. Stanton spent the last few weeks of 1889 in the Dansville Sanitorium in upstate New York. "I decided to go . . . and see what Doctors James and Kate Jackson could do for me," to reduce her weight and increase her energy. After six weeks of "rubbings, pinchings, steamings, Swedish movements, dieting, massage, [and] electricity," she had lost only five pounds. [15] Stanton's obesity was becoming a serious problem. Photographs over a forty-year span record the growth of her girth from petite to plump to overweight to obese. After 1870 Stanton looked fat. Seven childbirths, a big appetite, and her refusal to wear corsets contributed to the problem. In 1860 she admitted weighing 175 pounds but did not seem embarrassed by her size. By the 1870s her bulk had become a handicap. Though she could no longer ride horseback, she remained agile. Her interest in food is evident in her letters from the lyceum circuit. Although she had once been a nutrition-conscious Grahamite, in her maturity she craved cream, sugar, butter, and biscuits. She liked to eat and she ate a lot, despite her claims of moderation. As her occupations became more sedentary in the

1880s, her weight spread. Writing from Iowa in 1888 she confessed to Libby Miller that she had to be weighed on a hay scale: "I have one melancholy fact to state which I do with sorrow and humiliation. I was weighed yesterday and brought the scales down at 240, just the speed of a trotting horse, and yet I cannot trot 100 feet without puffing. As soon as I reach Omaha, I intend to commence dieting. Yet I am well; danced the Virginia reel with Bob. But alas! I am 240! Pray for your lumbering Julius."[16] In the 1890s Stanton's enormous bulk resulted in lameness, heart disease, and immobility.

During her travels in the 1880s Stanton had paid little attention to the organizational details of suffrage politics. Whenever Anthony asked for a speech or a convention call, Stanton complied, but Anthony asked less often. Anthony enjoyed the freedom of operation permitted by Stanton's absence. Concerned that Mrs. Stanton, the nominal president of the National, had not even kept up her membership, Anthony used four hundred dollars from lecture fees to buy life memberships for herself, Mrs. Stanton, and two of her real nieces.[17]

Anthony preferred to keep Stanton out of the negotiations that were under way to merge the National and the American Suffrage associations. While Stanton disapproved of the conservative attitudes of most of the participants, she was willing to accept reunion. Antagonism had been "distracting," she explained to a colleague. "In union [there is] added strength as well as an immense saving in money and forces."[18] She chose to believe that it was the American Association that wanted to join forces with the National, so she assented to the merger. She did nothing to disrupt the negotiations.

Following collaboration for the International Council and the formation of the National Council of Women, plans for the merger had developed rapidly. In October 1888 the American Association directed Lucy Stone to confer with Susan Anthony. Stone insisted that Anthony come to Boston to meet her. The two former adversaries agreed to appoint a joint committee "to confer."[19] The chief negotiators were Lucy Stone's daughter, Alice Stone Blackwell, and Anthony's "niece," Rachel Foster Avery. Each woman was secretary of her Association; each represented the interests of the younger suffragists.

The two major impediments to the merger were allotment of blame for the 1869 split and the selection of a president for the reunited association. Although not present, Stanton figured prominently in these discussions. Finally the negotiators decided not to refer to the schism and to elect someone other than the three troublemakers. All three of the senior women agreed but no alternative candidate was proposed. Meanwhile Mrs. Stanton objected to a section of the proposed constitution allowing men to hold office. The woman who had voted against a female president for the 1848 Rochester meeting now declared:

> I would never vote for a man to any office in our societies, not, however, because I am "down on" men *per se*. Think of an association of black men officered by slave holders! Having men pray or preside for us at our meetings has always seemed to me a tacit admission that we haven't the brains to do these things ourselves. . . . On the whole I find the suggested constitution very wordy and obscure. It is a very mannish document. It makes my head whirl to read it.[20]

The committee did not change its position on male officers and merger plans advanced on schedule.

In February 1890 the National and American Woman Suffrage associations met in Washington, D.C., to merge into the National American Woman Suffrage Association. Lucy Stone claimed to be too ill to attend, but her husband and daughter were present. Mrs. Stanton's presence had been guaranteed by scheduling a tribute to Anthony and by inviting her to make a congressional address. Both of Stanton's daughters came for the three events.[21]

Stanton began the month by testifying before the Senate Select Committee on Woman Suffrage. She tried to counter the argument that women were unsuited for public life by dismissing the "separate spheres" theory of male and female behavior. Stanton believed that both sexes were mentally equal and therefore should have equal legal rights. She discounted biological and physical differences, asserting that lawmakers did not need to interfere with God's handiwork: if a woman was capable of doing something, then God must have intended that she should. Finally she raised the difficulty of artificially defining male or female spheres. "I find men in many avocations—washing, cooking, selling needles and tape over a counter—which might be considered the work of women. The consideration of questions of legislation, finance, free trade, etc., certainly would not degrade woman, nor is her refinement so evanescent a virtue that it could be swept away by some work which she might do with her hands."[22] Stanton repeated her testimony before the House Judiciary Committee, which issued its first majority report favoring a federal amendment to enfranchise women.

The next big event—the celebration of Anthony's seventieth birthday—occurred a few days later, on February 15, 1890. Designed to be both a personal tribute and a political maneuver, the celebration was the first public evidence that the younger suffragists would accept Anthony's leadership over that of Stanton or Stone. It was a festive, emotional occasion. After a lavish banquet for two hundred at the Riggs House, Mrs. Stanton rose to give the main address, on "The Friendship of Women." With good humor and genuine feeling, she honored her friend as "the most charitable, self-reliant, magnanimous human being that I ever knew. . . . Miss Anthony's grand life is a lesson to all unmarried women, showing that the love-element need not be wholly lost if it is not centered on husband and children. To live for a principle, for the triumph of some reform by which all mankind are to be lifted up—to be wedded to an idea—may be, after all, the holiest and happiest of marriages"[23] Anthony replied in kind, but within days the two old friends were challenging each other for leadership of the new association.

The delicate question of the presidency of the National American Woman Suffrage Association had not been resolved when the two groups convened on February 17, 1890. Lucy Stone had forbidden the use of her name. Stanton and Anthony also claimed to be willing to withdraw. Rumors reported that Anthony had made a deal with former American members, offering herself as a compromise candidate, less controversial and more acceptable than Stanton. When both women were nominated for the office, neither declined. Stanton's supporters wanted to recognize her seniority and superior talents. Opponents claimed that she was too old and too often in Europe. Anthony defended Stanton's nomination.

> I will say to every woman who is a National and who has any love for the old Association, or for Susan B. Anthony, that I hope you will not vote for her for President. . . . Don't vote for any human being but Mrs. Stanton. . . . When the division [between the National and the American] was made twenty-two years ago it was because our platform was too broad, because Mrs. Stanton was too radical. . . . If Mrs. Stanton shall be deposed . . . you virtually degrade her. . . . I want our platform to be kept broad enough for the infidel, the atheist.

But Anthony did not withdraw her name. The vote was 131 for Stanton, 90 for Anthony. Anthony was elected vice-president-at-large with 213 votes, and Lucy Stone became head of the executive committee on a unanimous motion.[24]

Aware of the complaints about her absenteeism, Stanton opened her inaugural remarks by declaring, "I consider it a greater honor to go to England as President of this Association than would be the case if I were sent as Minister Plenipotentiary to any court in Europe." Then she reviewed the history of the women's rights movement and graciously mentioned her old antagonist Lucy Stone before tackling the narrow-mindedness of the new organization. Rather than limit their platform, Stanton wanted to extend it: "Whenever a woman is wronged, her voice should be heard on our platform." She wanted NAWSA to be inclusive rather than exclusive, to encompass all "types and classes, races and creeds," including "Mormon, Indian, and black women."[25] Although the organization may have become more conservative, Stanton saw no reason to mute her appeals to its formerly liberal leanings.

When Stanton arose the next day to say farewell, her audience waved their handkerchiefs and cheered. Many of them were relieved that she was returning to England and that Anthony would replace her as acting president. Stanton was just as glad to get away. She was filled with misgivings about the merger. She distrusted the infiltration of temperance women, recognizing that the possibility of prohibition imposed by female voters would generate antisuffrage sentiment among male voters. As she complained to Clara Colby, "Frances Willard needs watching. She is a politician." Nor did Stanton like the singing and praying that had been added to meeting programs at the insistence of their pious new allies, and she opposed their crusade for Sunday closing laws. But her major concern was the intolerance of the conservative majority. In her view, it had been a "mistake" to take them in as equal partners. As she confided to Mrs. Colby, once they had "absolute control," they would "kill" her and "whoever else dares to differ."[26] The policies of the new organization and the attitudes of the younger suffragists effectively shut Stanton out, so she voluntarily removed herself.

Stanton enjoyed her return trip to England but could not resist commenting that an intelligent woman graduate could design better ships. She was accompanied by Harriot Blatch, eighteen pieces of baggage, and the phaeton, broken down and packed in six crates. She visited her friends among English suffragists, made several speeches, entertained visitors, drafted articles, and "talked on all manner of topics, radical and otherwise." She attended the theater in London, observing that she saw few other people "on the shady side of seventy drinking in these worldly joys at the midnight hour." Most of all, she enjoyed family pleasures.

> I find Hattie's home truly delightful. Nora plays and laughs and romps all day as happy as a lark. Hattie and I drive every day from eleven to half past one [and] after dinner I take a nap. Nora goes to school and Hattie [pregnant] is taking life easy. I am trying to teach her the beauty of repose, rest, the recumbent posture. People in general term it so praiseworthy to keep their eyelids forever stretched open to their full capacity, standing on tip-toe on the watch tower of mortal anxiety about some trifle. But my gospel is to preserve the horizontal as opportunity offers and cultivate laziness as a virtue when you are unable to work.[27]

Even as a whirlwind of energy as a young mother and reformer, Stanton had always been able to sleep easily. When her children were infants, Stanton would not allow her husband or father to awaken them to show them off. Nor did she awaken her older children in the morning until they were ready to rise. "Early risers are always uncomfortable people," she declared. She buttressed her opinion with examples of statesmen who napped. "This is very common among great men who use their brains." Her father was one of those. Judge Cady, after covering his face with a handkerchief, had been able to sleep on any occasion. Throughout her life Stanton followed his example. "I pass many luxurious hours in the horizontal position," she wrote in 1890. "In fact, I pass but few in the perpendicular."[28]

Despite her reluctance to move, Stanton fell and hurt her knees in the winter of 1892. The following summer Theo brought his family to England, and Stanton took care of all of her grandchildren, dressing dolls for Nora and Lizette and minding the infants. But sadness impinged on her idyll. Hattie lost her second child, and Stanton learned of the deaths of her son Daniel and her sister Tryphena Bayard. In contrast to her reaction to Henry's death, she decided to return to the United States for "the remainder of her days." When she sailed in August 1891, she had been gone another eighteen months. No longer able to travel unassisted, she was accompanied by a private stewardess.[29]

The returning Stanton was homeless. She had so far spent her widowhood as a houseguest in Europe and the United States. Now she had to make a decision about how and where she would spend her old age. She had several alternatives. She could live by herself, with her married or unmarried children, with Libby Miller, or with Anthony. Anthony urged her to live in Rochester, so that the two of them could continue to collaborate.

> I could help you carry out the dream of my life—which is that you should take all your speeches and articles, carefully dissect them, and put your best utterances on each point into one essay—and then publish [them] in a nice volume. . . . This is the first time since 1850 that I have anchored myself to any particular spot, and in doing it my constant thought was that you would come here, where are the documents necessary to our work, and stay for as long, at least, as we must be together to put your writings into systematic shape to go down to posterity. . . . Then, too, I have never ceased to hope that we would finish the *History of Woman Suffrage* at least to the end of the dear old National.

The idea of spending her last years being goaded and scolded by Anthony—"the thorn in my side for forty years"—did not appeal to Stanton.[30] Her children also objected. They resented "Aunt Susan's" dominant role in their early childhoods, blamed her in part for their parents' estrangement, and wanted their mother to rest rather than work. Stanton had no intention of either retiring or keeping still, but she used their opposition as an excuse to remain independent of Anthony. She decided to share an eight-room penthouse apartment at 26 West 61st Street in New York City with her son Bob and recently widowed daughter Margaret Lawrence. Later the trio moved to the Stewart Apartments on the southwest corner of Broadway and West 94th Street.

Stanton's solution to her housing problem was a form of "associative living." In her apartment meals could be catered and maids were provided. Although Stanton appreciated the convenience of elevators and central heating, her initial adjustment to high-rise living had been difficult. "Having always lived in a large house in the country, the quarters seemed rather contracted at first," she recalled, "but I soon realized the immense saving in labor and expense in having no more room than absolutely necessary, and all on one floor."[31]

The plan appealed to Stanton for several reasons. She had long advocated "associative households," an idea that Charlotte Perkins Gilman and other experts on domestic economy would later develop.[32] Her previous impressions of community living had been positive: her visit to Brook Farm in the 1840s; her association with the utopian community at New Harmony, Indiana, through Robert Dale Owen; her stay in a French convent; and her pleasure in Theodore's Paris apartment. In England, Stanton's daughter Harriot, an advocate of Fabian reforms, had started a cooperative neighborhood laundry in Basingstoke. Stanton was convinced that cooperative arrangements would benefit women. The care of nuclear families in isolated homes trapped women in domestic bondage. In association with other households, women could share child care, cooking, and cleaning; they would have more leisure and less loneliness.

After making her decision about where to live, Stanton had made month-long visits to Anthony and Miller in the fall of 1891. In Rochester she and Anthony sat for a sculpture by Adelaide Johnson. In the finished piece, first exhibited at the Columbia Exposition in 1893 and now in the crypt of the United States Capitol, the heads of Stanton, Anthony, and Lucretia Mott rise from a five-foot high, unfinished marble block. Stanton and Anthony also joined forces to urge that the University of Rochester admit women. They presented their case to the school's trustees. On the morning of their meeting with the board the wife of the university's president gave birth to twins, a son and a daughter, prompting Stanton to remark, "If the Creator could risk placing the sexes in such near relations, they might with safety walk on the same campus and pursue the same curriculum." The president agreed, but the trustees did not.[33]

Although Stanton and Anthony had not worked together on any substantive project since the completion of volume 3 of the History, the habit of cooperation was hard to break. They continued to correspond and to collaborate occasionally. While Stanton was in England, Anthony had sent her reports of the activities of the new National American Association. In one twenty-two page epistle, Anthony described the 1891 annual meeting and explained that Stanton could not retire from the presidency until it was "quite certain" that Anthony rather than Lucy Stone would be elected to take her place. On her own initiative Stanton sent speeches for Anthony to read at the meetings she missed. For the 1891 convention she prepared "The Degradation of Disfranchisement" and for a February meeting of the National Council of Women, "The Matriarchate." In that speech she claimed that civilization was indebted to women for the intelligence, morality, and material progress of the race. Now that Stanton was back in America, Anthony urged her to attend the 1892 convention. When Stanton, referring to her children, responded that "all the influences about me urge me to rest rather than action," Anthony went to New York to escort her to Washington.[34]

Stanton used the 1892 occasion to deliver a definitive statement of her feminist ideology, "The Solitude of Self." It was a demand for woman's absolute self-reliance—physical, emotional, financial, political, intellectual, and legal independence. Stanton argued that women must be free to take responsibility for their own lives. In life's great crises, she said, women, like men, have only themselves to rely upon, and yet they are not trained to fend for themselves. The speech combined Stanton's natural rights philosophy, her republican bias, her feminist ferocity, and a tragic sense of loneliness.

> No matter how much women prefer to lean, to be protected and supported, nor how much men prefer to have them do so, they must make the voyage of life alone, and for safety in an emergency they must know something of the laws of navigation. . . . The talk of sheltering women from the fierce storms of life is sheerest mockery, for they beat on her from every point of the compass, just as they do on man, and with more fatal results, for he has been trained to protect himself, to resist, to conquer. . . . Whatever the theories may be of woman's dependence on man, in the supreme moments of her life he cannot bear her burdens. . . . [In] the tragedies and triumphs of human experience each mortal stands alone. The strongest reason why we ask for woman a voice in the government under which she lives; in the religion she is asked to believe; equality in social life, where she is the chief factor; a place in the trades and professions, where she may earn her bread, is because of her birthright to self-sovereignty; because, as an individual, she must rely on herself.[35]

Stanton was presenting the standard of self-reliance to which she herself aspired. Throughout her life she had become increasingly confident, capable, and independent. By the time she died she would be a self sovereign, a queen in her own right.

The speech was delivered three times during a three-day period. It was presented first, in written form, to the House Committee on the Judiciary on the morning of January 18, 1892. That afternoon Stanton delivered it as her valedictory address to the National American Association and received a standing ovation. Two days later she repeated the speech at a hearing of the Senate Committee on Woman Suffrage. "The Solitude of Self" was reprinted in the *Woman's Journal* and in the *Congressional Record*. Ten thousand copies were made and franked for her to distribute. The speech marked Stanton's last appearance before the Congress and before the National American Association; she was seventy-six years old.

With the exception of Anthony, Stanton's admirers agreed that "The Solitude of Self" was her finest effort, and she concurred. It was extraordinary in style and content.[36] Instead of inspiring her audience with optimism, Stanton spoke in sober tones about the essential isolation of each individual. Women were more vulnerable than men because they were not expected or prepared to fend for themselves, but both sexes, according to Stanton, shared the same existential fate. No matter what laws were passed, no matter what reforms were enacted, individuals would still be responsible for themselves, unique, and alone. "The point I wish plainly to bring before you . . . is the individuality of each human soul." For an hour she enumerated the "awful solitude" that all individuals, but especially women, endured—in childhood, marriage, childbirth, widowhood, old age, poverty, catastrophe, and death.

Stanton used the political implications of self-sovereignty to negate the claim that men, as voters or lawmakers, could act on behalf of women. No one could represent anyone else. Nor could individuals depend on legal remedies to improve their condition; they would still have to confront their trials alone.

> But when all artificial trammels are removed and women are recognized as individuals responsible for their own environments, thoroughly educated for all positions in life they may be called to fill; with all the resources in themselves that liberal thought and broad culture can give; guided by their own conscience and judgment, trained to self-protection, by a healthy development of their muscular system, and skill in the use of weapons of defense; and stimulated to self-support by a knowledge of the business world and the pleasure that pecuniary independence must ever give; when women are trained in this way, they will in a measure be fitted for those hours of solitude that come alike to all, whether prepared or otherwise.

The speech was Stanton's masterpiece. Her tone was tragic; her argument, existential; her case, powerful.

During the convention Stanton had refused election for another term as president. Stone was too ill for a contest, so Anthony assumed the office. Anna Howard Shaw of the American became vice-president; both Stanton and Stone were named honorary presidents. Stanton did not resist retirement. "I am a leader of thought rather than numbers," she had explained earlier to Olympia Brown. "The . . . Association has been growing conservative for some time. Lucy and Susan alike see suffrage only. They do not see woman's religious and social bondage, neither do the young women. . . . They have one mind and one purpose. I would rather be a free-lance article, to say my say as opportunity offers as an individual, than to speak as president of an Association."[37]

Stanton was relieved to be in a position to find fault with her successors. She criticized the decision to move the national convention out of Washington to different cities and to close the Washington office. She believed that skilled lobbying, accurate vote tallies, a presence in the capital, and public pressure on Congress were necessary for a suffrage victory. In 1900 she noted with amusement and alarm "the presence before Congress for the first time of the antisuffragists, who begged to be left in their chains."[38]

The old radical was contemptuous of the timidity of the new recruits. The ascendance of a younger, conservative membership resulted in a new suffrage strategy. The emphasis shifted from congressional action for a federal amendment to state referenda campaigns. The rationale shifted from Stanton's natural rights argument that men and women were equal and therefore citizens with identical rights, to a claim for suffrage on account of female righteousness. Woman deserved the vote because they were not the same as men, because they were virtuous, maternal, devout, sober, and respectable.[39] In the past Stanton had used some of these same arguments, asserting that women were morally superior to men. Indeed she had used whatever argument seemed practical and advantageous at the time. On accasion she was equally critical of both sexes, claiming that men were destructive brutes and women were small-minded ninnies. But her arguments for suffrage and legal equality were primarily based on the similarities rather than the differences between the sexes.

Stanton was not the only dissident; she gave her blessing to Matilda Joslyn Gage, Olympia Brown, and Isabella Beecher Hooker, who founded alternative organizations and espoused broader platforms than the National American Woman Suffrage Association. "At present our association has so narrowed its platform for reasons of policy and propriety," Stanton complained, "that our conventions have ceased to point the way."[40]

To remind NAWSA members, Stanton sent unwelcome letters to every meeting from 1893 to 1902. Anthony insisted they be read, even on such controversial subjects as "Educated Suffrage." In that speech Stanton urged that suffrage be limited to the educated classes, whether male or female. Delivered in Atlanta, the speech led to charges of racism and xenophobia. Stanton's genuine belief in the benefits of education was both democratic and elitist. She saw education as a social equalizer and safeguard against the prejudices of immigrants and nativists alike; she expected education to improve and elevate the lower classes. In order to achieve that end, she endorsed a five-day work week, free adult education classes on weekends, and free admission to concerts and museums. But it is also true that America's foremost feminist held paternalistic views about blacks, immigrants, workers, and Cubans.[41]

Retirement from NAWSA was one more step toward independence for Stanton. After 1892 she was free to do as she chose. Ironically, she was limited only by her enormous physical bulk. Her legs could no longer support her weight; any activity was difficult. "I cannot clamber up and down platforms, mount long staircases into halls and hotels, be squeezed in the crush at receptions, and do all the other things public life involves," she wrote in her diary.[42] The trouble was compounded by a second fall in late 1894. After that she required two canes, an elevator, an extrawide bed, and eventually a maid to help her bathe and dress.

Immobility determined Stanton's daily routine. Unable to walk very far, she sat in a specially designed low chair. Her amusements were sedentary. Her days included reading and writing, playing the piano, receiving callers, doing occasional mending, and gambling with Bob, "all this interspersed with delicious little naps." She amused reporters by making her famous orange cake while sitting at the dining room table. She was honored at luncheons and dinners. She remained an engaging conversationalist and even attracted young male admirers. Despite the "hard work of getting in and out of vehicles," she took daily drives in Central Park.[43]

Stanton seldom traveled beyond her family circle. She spent most of the year in the city and divided the summers between Geneva or Peterboro with Libby Miller and Long Island with her children, "sitting on the piazza drinking lemonade and beer."[44] After 1897 she was confined to her apartment. Four of her children lived nearby; the two Europeans came for extended stays and eventually returned to be near her in her old age. From 1898 to 1902 her granddaughter Nora Blatch lived with her during vacations from Cornell.

Despite physical infirmities, Stanton's mind remained acute. As Anthony confided to Stanton's cousin, "It is too cruel that such mental powers must be hampered by such a *clumsy body*." Nor did Anthony let Stanton rest. Stanton joked that Anthony must have "got wind" of her mending Bob's socks, for she came to ask for yet another speech. She wrote for Anthony for every occasion: letters, speeches, convention calls, resolutions, and eulogies. In the summer of 1892 she wrote Anthony's remarks to the national party conventions. For the Columbia Exposition of 1893 she wrote five speeches for Anthony to deliver, plus one to be read on her own behalf at a reunion of Emma Willard alumnae visiting Chicago. Stanton's authorship of these speeches was either directly acknowledged or widely assumed. Anthony once remarked that she would never be able to publish a collection of her own speeches, because they had all been written by Stanton.[45]

Stanton seldom delivered her own speeches any more. In June 1892 she attended a reunion at Emma Willard and dedicated the Gurley Memorial Building, the gift of Mrs. Russell Sage. She also spoke at informal "parlor meetings." But although Theodore and Margaret went to the Chicago Exposition, Stanton did not think she could withstand the heat and crowds. Yet in 1897 she addressed a picnic gathering of one thousand for an hour and a half. Though her legs and eyes were weak, "my voice seems to hold its own," she observed in her diary.[46]

Most of Stanton's energy was spent thinking and writing. Ever since 1848 writing about women's rights had been both a career and a crusade for her. She did not abandon either in old age. Indeed, age had made her an expert on many subjects in addition to American feminism. What advice was not solicited by reporters she volunteered. Her articles appeared in the *Arena*, the *Critic*, *Forum*, the *Nation*, *North American Review*, and the *Westminster Review*, among others. The *Omaha Republican* syndicated her column on women, one of the first in the country. Clara Colby's *Woman's Tribune* serialized her reminiscences, which she expanded into an autobiography, *Eighty Years and More*, in 1898.

Published after the uproar caused by *The Woman's Bible*, Stanton's autobiography was her apologia. Although she claimed to be writing only the private history of a public woman whose reform career had been documented in *The History of Woman Suffrage*, her autobiography had a political purpose. Stanton was self-consciously reinforcing the image she had created of herself as benign, nurturing, good humored, smart, respectable, and self-reliant. She did not depict incidents in which she might appear to be radical, arrogant, heretical, demanding, self-centered, or difficult to live with. For a supposedly intimate account, the book seldom mentions her mother, husband, or children. It downplays personal and political conflicts. Both Judge Cady and Henry Stanton are portrayed as sympathetic and supportive; the schism of 1869 and the censure of 1896 are omitted.

Although most of the principals were already dead, Stanton chose to present her life as a series of minor challenges, easily overcome by her enterprise and intelligence. The book lacked the introspection of her best speeches and the candor of her correspondence. She refused to admit the obstacles she struggled to overcome to become an independent women, a self-defined self sovereign. Perhaps she chose to appear more commonplace in an effort to have more in common with her readers, to convert them by

an ordinary example rather than to inspire them with extraordinary accomplishments. As she asserted in the preface, she was just a "wife, . . .
an enthusiastic housekeeper . . . and the mother of seven children."

Every subject interested Stanton, from the Spanish-American War to
Sunday closing laws and bicycle riding. She espoused coeducation; the admission of women to graduate schools; sensible clothing for women; clean
streets; more parks and playgrounds for the children of the poor; free concerts, lectures, dance halls, billiard rooms, and bowling alleys for young
people; free reading and smoking rooms for adults; an end to capital punishment; rehabilitation programs in prisons; better cooking; more scientific
care of babies and children; free kindergartens; better housing for the poor;
and broader participation by women in every aspect of society. She was a
prolific and popular writer.

Stanton wrote for propaganda and profit. Her income from writing enabled her to be financially independent of her children. Economy had been
one of the factors in her decision to share an apartment with Bob and
Margaret. She had a comfortable income from lifetime trust funds established by her son and her sister as well as the profit from the sale of the
Tenafly house. These she supplemented with writing fees. As she got older,
her children provided more and more support. Bob and Henry assumed
the cost of publishing her longer works and paid for the added staff needed
for her care.[47] Unlike Anthony, Stanton had not been provided with an
annuity by the National American Association.

Anthony found it increasingly difficult to dictate Stanton's subject matter. Rather than issue a collection of her old speeches, as Anthony had suggested, Stanton preferred to tackle new and controversial topics. She did
join Anthony in 1894 to lobby another constitutional convention for statewide suffrage in New York. They used tactics similar to those they had
employed in 1867. Stanton wrote letters and speeches, Anthony spoke in
sixty counties, and Carrie Chapman Catt and Lillie Devereux Blake campaigned intensely in the cities. The suffragists collected half a million petition signatures, but the outlook was bleak. "What a set of jackasses we
have at Albany this winter," exclaimed Mrs. Stanton. "I have written several of them, they simply bray in return." The question of woman suffrage
lost by a two-to-one margin. "I feel sad and disappointed at such contemptuous treatment by so ordinary a body of men," wrote Stanton in her
diary. She blamed the defeat directly on the opposition of the liquor lobby
and indirectly on the influence of the Woman's Christian Temperance Union.
But she was not long discouraged. "I never forget that we are sowing winter wheat, which the coming spring will see sprout, and other hands than
ours will reap and enjoy."[48]

In 1895 Stanton and Anthony both celebrated milestones: Stanton turned eighty and Anthony seventy-five. In an era that honored its elders with public receptions, gifts, and testimonials, both women were elaborately feted. In February the National Council of Women sponsored a birthday banquet for Anthony. Her "girls" presented an annuity of eight hundred dollars, and Stanton sent a speech. In return Anthony wanted to recognize Mrs. Stanton, but she had difficulty finding an organizational sponsor. The National American Association had been characteristically reluctant to salute its first president, provoking yet another blast from the feisty old lady. Anthony and Theodore Stanton finally planned a November event under the aegis of the National Council.

In a lavish display the Metropolitan Opera House was rented and festooned with flowers. Carnations spelled out Stanton's name, and roses banked her chair. Spectators crowded the hall and the sidewalks. More flowers, gifts, and messages flooded her apartment. A letter from a well-known editor was typical of the tributes she received. "Every woman who seeks the legal custody of her children; who finds the door of a college or university open to her; who administers a post-office or a public library; who enters upon a career of medicine, law or theology; who teaches school or tills a farm or keeps a shop or rides a bicycle—every such woman owes her liberty largely to yourself and to your earliest and bravest co-workers." Propped up by canes, Stanton could not stand long enough to deliver her speech. With unfamiliar modesty, she attributed the public demonstrations "to the great idea I represent—the enfranchisement of women." Her address was read for her. It stirred up trouble by criticizing the religious traditions and superstitions that subordinated women. Anthony was annoyed "that she did not rest her case after describing the wonderful advances made in state, church, society and home, instead of going on to single out the church and declare it to be especially slow in accepting the doctrine of equality of women."[49]

Stanton was touched by the birthday tribute. Henry's nephew, another Robert Stanton, described her behavior the next day in her apartment, filled with "hundreds of roses." "Aunt Lib came in. . . . Seating herself at the piano [she] began to play and sing, one after another of the . . . old, old songs of her youth, in a voice and manner so beautiful, so sad and to me, knowing her history as I did, so pathetic, that I was spell bound. Not a word was spoken. She seemed to be far away from us and the throngs that greeted her with so much enthusiasm the night before, and was living over again the days of her youth, seeing life as it was to her sixty or seventy years ago. She finally stopped singing, not from exhaustion but as if she were overcome with emotion and the memories of her youth and turning on her seat, with an expression of sadness on her face, and moistened eyes, said, 'Bob, life is a great mystery.' That was all."[50] Stanton may have been sobered as much by future prospects as by memories of the past. In one final act of defiance, she was about to risk all the respect and admiration she had been shown on her birthday.

Two weeks later Elizabeth Cady Stanton published *The Woman's Bible*. It was her most audacious and outrageous act of independence. In the guise of Biblical scholarship and interpretation she attacked the use of Scripture to condemn women to a secondary status. She had long believed that "the chief obstacle in the way of woman's elevation today is the degrading position assigned her in the religion of all countries—an afterthought in creation, the origin of sin, cursed by God, marriage for her a condition of servitude, maternity a degradation, unfit to minister at the altar and in some churches even to sing in the choir. Such is her position in the Bible and religion."[51] For Stanton, as a member of the supposedly inferior female caste, to dare to criticize church authority was considered at best disrespectful, at worst, heretical.

Stanton's interest in the subject was lifelong. Ever since her adolescent rebellion against Presbyterian gloom and evangelical revival she had pursued religious questions and perused religious texts. Encouraged by Edward Bayard, Lucretia Mott, and Theordore Parker, Stanton gained confidence in her own rational interpretation of the Scriptures. After her marriage she stopped going to church regularly, except to enjoy the music, but she regularly studied religious subjects. She believed in an androgynous Creator, who combined the best character traits of men and women. She even addressed her mealtime grace to "Mother and Father God." Her moral code was strict, but she adhered to few other religious tenets. She was "reconciled to rest with many debatable questions relegated to the unknown."[52]

Stanton's antipathy to traditional church teachings is understandable. Throughout her career as a reformer most churches had been hostile to the causes she championed. The Bible had been interpreted to favor intemperance, slavery, capital punishment, and the subjection of women. Whenever women attempted to move beyond their "divinely ordained sphere" of domesticity, churchmen charged them with blasphemy and cited the Bible as justification. Whenever women tried to argue the case for equality, they were reminded of St. Paul's admonition that they remain silent. Whatever advances women tried to make—in education or employment or political rights—were held to contradict the will and the word of God as revealed in the Scriptures and interpreted by ministers.

Stanton's interest in disputing these claims in a formal way began in the 1870s. After publication of the New Revised Bible in 1881 made Biblical scholarship an accepted undertaking, she turned to the task in earnest, trying to establish a committee of academic and church women to share the work. Few accepted her invitation. Clara Colby, who endorsed Stanton's views, published samples of her commentaries in the *Woman's Tribune* in 1888 and urged others to cooperate with the project. News of Stanton's plans resulted in bids from publishers and blandishments from suffragists. Few feminists shared her interest, and many objected. Anthony tried to dissuade and delay her. Personal and political changes postponed the project until the mid-1890s. Anthony was still alarmed by the prospect; her young assistant, Carrie Chapmen Catt,* warned that NAWSA would suffer "great harm" if Stanton persevered. In 1895 Anthony brought Catt to lunch with Stanton to discuss their complaints, but Stanton refused to back down. Catt came away thinking that she was a selfish, foolish old woman.[53]

Stanton proceeded undaunted. Although five other women were identified as coauthors of *The Woman's Bible,* most of the work was Stanton's.[54] Even without much assistance Stanton completed the first volume, covering the Pentateuch, in a year. Published in two parts, the work dealt only with those sections of the Old and New Testaments that mentioned women or that Stanton felt ought to have included them. The Biblical texts were printed at the top of each page with Stanton's commentaries below. For example, Stanton printed both versions of the creation of man from the Book of Genesis. She pointed out that in the one most frequently quoted, Eve was an outgrowth of Adam's rib. In the less well known passage, man and woman were created at the same instant in the image of God. Stanton used that example to argue the existence of an androgynous God and to illustrate how male ministers employed the Bible for their own advantage—to support the socially conservative position favoring subordinate womanhood—rather than an interpretation indicating equality of the sexes.

Stanton was skeptical of Biblical authority and contemptuous of conservative piety, but she did not condemn the Bible completely. She claimed that the position of women in the Bible reflected the bias of male authors in a patriarchal culture rather than sacred writ. Her antiliteral assumptions were not very different from those of most Unitarians or most nineteenth-century Biblical scholars, but her tone was sarcastic, marked by an ani-

---

* Carrie Lane Chapman Catt (1859–1947) grew up in Iowa. She put herself through Iowa State College and became a public school principal. She married Leo Chapman, a newspaper editor, in 1885. Widowed within a year, she became a lecturer and joined the Iowa Woman Suffrage Association. Before her second marriage in 1890 to George Catt, she signed a marriage contract allowing her four months a year for suffrage work. She advanced rapidly in the national organization. An energetic organizer and magnetic speaker, she served as president of NAWSA (1900–04, 1915–20). With her "Winning Plan," she led NAWSA to final passage of the suffrage amendment. The vote assured , she called for the establishment of the League of Women Voters.

mosity for clerical pretension and traditional churches. Her commentaries are interesting, her prose readable, and her thesis valid, but *The Woman's Bible* was never accepted as a major work of Biblical scholarship. Her accomplishment seems less impressive today, now that many of her conclusions about Biblical sources and interpretation are widely accepted. *The Woman's Bible* was most important as another declaration of Stanton's independence, representing her intellectual freedom from religious authority and the culmination of her personal theology.

Public reaction was sensational. *The Woman's Bible* was a best seller; it went through seven printings in six months and was translated into several languages. As Stanton explained to Antoinette Brown Blackwell, she had planned to create a commotion. "We have had hearings before Congress for 18 years steadily, good reports, good votes, but no action. I am dismayed and disgusted, and feel like making an attack on some new quarter of the enemies' domain. Our politicians are calm and complacent under our fire but the clergy jump round . . . like parched peas on a hot shovel."[55] As a result of her tone and her thesis, Stanton was branded as a heretic by a stunned public. Her friends were embarrassed and her enemies jubilant over the scandal. Because they belived that *The Woman's Bible* injured their chances for success, the younger suffragists were furious. In order to dissociate the National American from *The Woman's Bible,* they planned to condemn both the book and its author at their January 1896 meeting.

Although she did not attend the annual convention in Washington, Stanton had prepared for the fight. Before the meeting she asked Clara Colby for her help: "Make the speech of your life in favor of religious freedom."[56] Stanton's children later suggested that she had also written a defense for Anthony to deliver. Stanton's critics among the younger women, led by the influential Carrie Chapman Catt, could not be stopped. First they added a paragraph of renunciation to Catt's annual report as corresponding secretary. In the chair when the offending report was read, Anthony remained silent. Clara Colby quickly moved that the report be tabled or accepted without the paragraph critical of Stanton. After lengthy debate the section was stricken.

Next the committee on resolutions offered a critical motion: "This association is non-sectarian, being composed of persons of all shades of religious opinions, and has no official connection with the so-called *Woman's Bible,* or any theological publication." Debate raged for another hour until Anthony finally stepped down from the chair and joined the fray. Her impassioned remarks defended both the author and her right of free speech.

> Who can tell now whether these commentaries may not prove a great help to woman's emancipation from old superstitions which have barred the way? Lucretia Mott at first thought Mrs. Stanton had injured the cause

of all women's other rights by insisting upon the demand for suffrage, but she had sense enough not to bring in a resolution against it. In 1860 when Mrs. Stanton made a speech before the New York legislature in favor of a bill making drunkenness a ground for divorce, there was a general cry among the friends that she had killed the woman's cause. I shall be pained beyond expression if the delegates are so narrow and illiberal as to adopt this resolution. You would better not begin resolving against individual action or you will find no limit. This year it is Mrs. Stanton; next year it may be I or one of yourselves who may be the victim.[57]

Despite such eloquence, the censure resolution passed, fifty-three to forty-one. Approved by Carrie Chapman Catt, Anna Howard Shaw, Henry Blackwell, Alice Stone Blackwell, and Rachel Foster Avery, the vote was as much a rebuke of Anthony as of Stanton.

Anthony hurried to New York to report to an indignant Mrs. Stanton. According to Anthony, "weeks of agony of soul" followed. Stanton wanted them both to resign. Anthony refused to leave "her half-fledged chickens without a mother"; Stanton preferred to wring their necks. Anthony convinced her to "try to reverse this miserable, narrow action" at the next convention; Stanton agreed, but the action was never reversed. Anthony reprimanded Catt and Avery for their part, but they did not repent. In the press Anthony made clear that she had had nothing to do with either *The Woman's Bible* or its condemnation. She defended women's right to "interpret and twist the Bible to their own advantage as men have always [done] to theirs."[58]

Stanton was angry at Anthony and contemptuous of "her girls." First she resolved to keep her distance, until she realized that her isolation was just what NAWSA wanted. To get back at her critics, she appended the censure resolution to the next edition of *The Woman's Bible*. To annoy them further, she refused to resign and continued to harass them. Whenever possible, she reminded them and the public of her role as founder and former president of the National American Association. She was disappointed at what she believed was Anthony's disloyalty to her, but she did not refer to it again. Two years later, ignoring Anthony's objections, she published the second volume of her Bible. Despite the scandal, or perhaps because of it, the revising committee of coauthors had been enlarged to thirty members.

Political disputes, philosophical disagreements, and physical distance weakened the Stanton-Anthony bond but did not sever it. Like her relationship with Henry in its last years, Stanton's friendship with Anthony changed course. The alliance lost its intensity. Neither any longer felt "incomplete" without the other. After 1895 they alternated between affection, annoyance, and animosity. Only a year before, when Anthony had collapsed while speaking in California, Stanton had admitted, "I never realized how desolate the world would be to me without you until I heard of your sudden illness."[59] But in the aftermath of the Bible controversy Stanton's tone changed. She was no longer inhibited by Anthony's caution or her regard. Stanton was finally free of the need for her friend's sanction. She had internalized her own standard of independence and needed only her own approval.

Each woman pursued a separate course. Anthony, surrounded by surrogate "nieces," remained at the forefront of the suffrage struggle. Stanton, cushioned in her apartment, preferred to spend her time reflecting on larger questions. In the years before Stanton's death in 1902, the two old friends saw each other less often, corresponded sporadically, cooperated less frequently, and even opposed each other in public. Nonetheless Stanton dedicated her autobiography to "Susan B. Anthony, my steadfast friend for half a century." As she explained to Anthony, "the current of our lives has run in the same channel so long it cannot be separated." Anthony continued to ask Stanton for speeches and documents, entreating her, for example, to send four different addresses for the 1898 meeting. "The summing up of the achievements of women in the past fifty years is a big job, one you alone are equal to," Anthony wrote; "Now, my dear, this is positively the last time I am ever going to put you on the rack and torture you to make *the* speech or speeches of your life." The aging author reluctantly complied but complained, "One would think I was a machine, that all I had to do was to turn a crank and thoughts on any theme would bubble up like water."[60] She pointedly suggested to Anthony that some of their younger coadjutors do the bubbling.

When Anthony went to London in 1899 as head of the American delegation to the International Council of Women, she stayed with Harriot Blatch in Basingstoke. But when Stanton suggested a trip to Rochester, Anthony answered that her guest chamber was occupied and asked Stanton to stay with Libby Miller instead, so that she would not have to waste time "visiting and catering." Confident that she would refuse, Anthony invited Stanton to attend each annual NAWSA convention. "I replied I thought she and I had earned the right to sit in our rocking chairs and think and write," recorded Stanton. "But it occurred to me later that that would be purgatory for Susan!" Stanton believed that next to Theodore Roosevelt, Anthony was the "nearest example of perpetual motion" she knew.[61]

In 1898 Anthony announced that she would resign the NAWSA presidency on her eightieth birthday in 1900 and tapped Carrie Chapman Catt to be her successor. Angry over the nomination of her critic, Stanton urged Lillie Devereux Blake to challenge Catt. As head of the New York Suffrage

Association, Blake had won suffrage for women in local school elections.*
She had also succeeded in getting matrons in police stations and women
doctors in mental institutions. From Stanton's perspective, Blake's broad
interests made her an appealing and well-qualified candidate, but Anthony
disapproved of her fashion-plate image and her residual Southern accent.
Stanton blamed Catt for the censure vote and threatened to resign if she
were elected. Through an intermediary, Anthony responded that such behavior would be "very immature, . . . despotic, [and] undemocratic."[62]
At the last moment Blake withdrew her name for lack of support, and Catt
was elected in a landslide.

Rather than resign from NAWSA, Stanton removed herself even further
from Anthony and the suffragists. As she confided to Blake, she was full
of resentment at her "young coadjutors."

> They refused to read my letters and resolutions to the conventions; they
> have denounced the *Woman's Bible* unsparingly; not one of them has ever
> reviewed or expressed the least appreciation of *Eighty Years and More*.
> . . . For all this I make no public protest, I propose no revenge. Because
> of this hostile feeling I renounced the presidency and quietly accept the
> situation, and publish what I have to say in the liberal papers. . . . I have
> outgrown the suffrage association, as the ultimative *[sic]* of human en-
> deavor, and no longer belong in its fold with its limitations.[63]

Stanton directed her antagonism toward the younger women rather than
at her old friend. Her hurt feelings were apparent in a letter written in 1901:
"They have given Susan thousands of dollars, jewels, laces, silks and satins
and me, criticisms and denunciations for my radical ideas."[64] Stanton never
acknowledged in the records remaining that it was Anthony who had recruited, nurtured, and trained "her girls," using them to develop a power
base separate from Stanton and to achieve the ultimate end of woman suffrage. The younger suffragists gave Anthony the votes necessary to escape
from Stanton's shadow, and they gave her lasting status in women's history. Anthony put suffrage ahead of Stanton; Stanton put feminism ahead
of friendship.

Despite the tensions caused by her strained relations with Anthony and
the younger suffragists, Stanton enjoyed her seniority. She had long argued
that the greatest benefit of old age was that it allowed time for reflection.
As she had written to Clara Colby in 1895: "Now I want to give my time
to general reading and thinking. . . . I cannot work in the old ruts any

---

* Lillie Devereux Blake (1833–1913) was born in North Carolina and raised in New Haven,
Conn., where she was tutored by Yale students. Bored following her first marriage in 1855,
she began to write fiction. After her husband's death she supported herself and two children
until her second marriage in 1866. She joined the women's movement in 1869. She was president of the New York Woman Suffrage Association (1879–90) and of the New York City
League (1886–1900). After her loss to Catt, she founded the National Legislative League.

longer. . . . There is such a thing as being too active, living too outward a life. Most reformers fail at this point. . . . In order to develop our real selves, we need time to be alone for thought. To be always giving out and never pumping in, the well runs dry too soon." Stanton was proud of her self-sufficiency. She enjoyed what she was doing—reading, writing, and taking naps. "I am fond of all games," she reported, "of music and novels, hence the days fly swiftly by; I am never lonely, life is ever very sweet to me and full of interest."[65] She was content.

Stanton had completed two volumes of *The Woman's Bible* and in 1898 published her autobiography, *Eighty Years and More*. In 1901 she began to compile her speeches and other papers. Always quick witted and quotable, Mrs. Stanton remained popular with the public. She noted in her diary that she was "constantly asked by reporters to talk and write on every imaginable subject."[66] Newspapers and magazines carried articles by and about her. Her last essay, on divorce reform, was syndicated by the Hearst chain just two weeks before her death.

Finally at leisure, Stanton filled her days with reading. She had always read voraciously. Among the books she devoured now were Andrew White's *A History of the Warfare of Science with Theology;* James Boswell's *Life of Johnson;* Matthew Arnold's *Essays in Criticism;* Herbert Spencer's *Education;* biographies of George Eliot, William Lloyd Garrison, Alfred Tennyson, and George Washington; Thomas Hughes's *Tom Brown at Oxford;* and novels by Charlotte Brontë, William Thackeray, and Leo Tolstoy, noting, "we are sandwiching between these various books a good deal of Mark Twain, whose fun is only equaled by his morals."[67]

Because reading and writing were Stanton's primary occupations, failing eyesight became a more serious physical handicap than her immobility. Like her father, she began to go blind in her old age. Although she never lost her sight entirely, after 1896 the condition deteriorated rapidly. As she confided in her diary in 1897: "Oh what a privation! I say nothing to my children of this great grief, but it is a sore trial, with prospective total blindness! I will than be able to do nothing but think. However, I can still write without spectacles, though I cannot read my own writing. But my hearing is as good as ever, and I am perfectly well otherwise." Not to be hampered, she hired a typist and a reader.[68]

Such optimism and resourcefulness were characteristic. Stanton accepted the reality of her circumstances and emphasized the positive elements. "I never encourage sad moods," she told Harriot. Like Mrs. Mott, whenever she felt depressed, she worked at "physical labor or practical thought . . . cheat[ing] myself into the thought that all is well, grand, glorious, [and] triumphant." About her blindness, she concluded, "As my eyes grow dimmer from day to day, my intellectual vision grows clearer."[69]

On Stanton's eighty-fifth birthday in November 1900 she received "so many congratulatory letters and telegrams and gifts that the reproaches and ridicule of half a century ago are quite forgotten." She spent the day at the dentist with a toothache. "I asked . . . if he could patch me up for five years longer as I wished to live as long as my maternal grandmother did, and thus maintain the family reputation for longevity."[70] Anthony, herself eighty, sent Mrs. Stanton a birthday greeting. Although no longer president of NAWSA, Anthony remained the senior member of its executive committee. Centered over her Rochester desk hung a photograph of Mrs. Stanton. On Stanton's desk sat a plaster cast of their two right hands, clasped together.

In the spring of 1902 Anthony visited Stanton in New York several times. After all they had been through, conversation was somewhat strained. "We have grown a little apart since not so closely associated as of old," Anthony admitted to her diary. Absence had made her even more aware of Stanton's physical deterioration. The summer of 1902 passed without incident; Anthony planned to return in the fall for Stanton's eighty-seventh birthday. In October the *New York American* published Stanton's essay on divorce. Ten days later she dictated an open letter to President Theodore Roosevelt, asking him to endorse the federal woman suffrage amendment in his next congressional message, and sent a similar appeal to Mrs. Roosevelt.[71] They were her last letters. On Sunday, October 26, 1902, Elizabeth Cady Stanton died.

Her daughter Harriot described Stanton's last day and death in a letter to a friend.

> None of us knew mother was so near her end 'til Sunday really (the day she died). She had been suffering from shortness of breath lately, from time to time, and from that cause felt under the mark. On Saturday she said to the doctor, very emphatically, "Now if you can't cure this difficulty of breathing, and if I am not to feel brighter and more like work again, I want you to give me something to send me pack-horse speed to heaven." . . . Two hours before her death (on Sunday) she said she wished to stand up. She was sitting in her arm chair in the drawing room, not dressed but in her dressing gown, and with her hair arranged all as usual. She had told her maid earlier in the day to dress her hair, and when it was finished she said, "Now, I'll be dressed." But I dissuaded her, seeing she was weary. The trained nurse (who had only been summoned an hour earlier) and the doctor, when she asked to stand, helped her to rise and stood on either side of her. I placed a table for her to rest her hands on. She drew herself up very erect (the doctor said the muscular strength was extraordinary) and there she stood seven or eight minutes, steadily looking out proudly before her. I think she was mentally making an address. When we urged her to sit down she fell asleep. Two hours later, the doctor thinking her position constrained in her chair, we lifted her to her bed, and she slipped away peacefully in a few minutes.[72]

All six of Stanton's surviving children were present when she died.

The medical report gave heart failure as the cause of death. Stanton's granddaughter Nora, a recent graduate of Cornell, told her son John Barney much later that Stanton had asked the family physician, a woman, "to be put to death if she were losing her faculties." She might have been referring to the same incident Harriot Blatch described in her letter, when Stanton asked the doctor to speed her death if she were not going to recover. Family history also claimed that Stanton had instructed her children that there should be no autopsy and no investigation. It would not have been out of character for Stanton to ask for a drug overdose to shorten her life. Stanton had said she liked living but hoped to die "as quickly as possible . . . when the time comes."[73] Hers was not an unusual or necessarily suicidal sentiment.

The death of Elizabeth Cady Stanton was front page news. Every major newspaper and most magazines published editorials, eulogies, and announcements of memorial services. Hundreds of letters of condolence poured in and were acknowledged with engraved cards from "the sons and daughters of Elizabeth Cady Stanton." Mrs. Catt scheduled a memorial service for the January 1903 NAWSA convention in New Orleans, but Harriot Blatch refused to attend.[74]

Anthony was stunned by the news. "I am too crushed to say much," she told reporters. En route to the funeral, she wrote Ida Harper, "Well, it is an awful hush—it seems impossible—that the voice is hushed that I longed to hear for fifty years—longed to get her opinion of things—before I knew exactly where I stood." Six months later she was still mourning the death of her friend. "How lonesome I do feel. . . . It was a great going out of my life when she went."[75]

On the occasion of Libby Miller's husband's death, Stanton had told her daughter Margaret how she wanted her funeral conducted. "I should like to be in my ordinary dress, no crepe or black, no fripperies or fandangoes of any sort, and some common sense women to conduct the services." In keeping with her wishes, a private service was held in her New York City apartment. It was conducted by Stanton's friend Moncure Conway. He was assisted by Lucy Stone's sister-in-law, the Reverend Antoinette Brown Blackwell, who gave one of the tributes. The table on which the Declaration of Sentiments had been written in Seneca Falls stood at the head of her casket, bearing *The History of Woman Suffrage*.[76] The Reverend Phebe Hanaford, a coauthor of *The Woman's Bible*, led the graveside service at Woodlawn Cemetery. Elizabeth Cady Stanton had doubted the existence of an afterlife. She died as she had lived, impatient and independent.

METHODOLOGICAL NOTE
Stanton in Psychological Perspective

As the repetition of phrases like "role model" and "behavior" may have signaled, this biography of Elizabeth Cady Stanton is based on a psychological theory. To explain and illuminate Stanton's motivation and behavior, I have employed social learning theory, a tool I found well suited to biography. In terms of social learning theory, Stanton defined and developed a model of independent behavior, and then achieved it. Her sense of self-sovereignty provided her with an ideal role on which to pattern her life.

In the same way that historians attempt to explain events, biographers try to elucidate motivation. In the past this has been done by a straightforward statement of the facts of a life, as the biographer had determined them. Readers were left to draw their own conclusions. Yet biographers from Plutarch to Parson Weems have relied at least implicitly on some assumptions about personality and behavior to account for the actions of their subjects. They drew from their own experience or "common sense" or from the prevailing explanatory modes of their times—mythological, religious, economic, whatever. Such early approaches lacked the discipline of a sustained framework.

Although the craft of biography became more sophisticated at the turn of the century, under the pen of Lytton Strachey, and the available tools improved, most biographies remain assertive and impressionistic. The principal personality theory used in biography in the twentieth century, when any theory is employed, is psychoanalytic, based on the theories of Sigmund Freud.[1] Rapid advances in knowledge about human behavior have created competition among theories and confusion among amateurs. Concepts that were startling sixty years ago have become widely accepted as "common sense" interpretations today and incorporated into child-raising practices, educational theory, management systems, art history, and politics. Terms like "identity crisis," "Oedipal complex," and "egocentric" have become part of our everyday vocabulary. Nonetheless many biographers are hesitant to use them.

There are valid reasons for reservations about psychological methodology. First, few biographers hold dual degrees in history and psychology, and fewer are medical doctors with a specialty in psychiatry. Biographers lack the training and experience to deal with psychological models. Second, social scientists often present their arguments and evidence in an unfamiliar format or unfathomable jargon. Further, historians are skeptical about the nature and validity of the evidence on which some theories of personality are based. For example, Freudian theory regards early childhood experiences as formative, if not determinative. But for many biographers data from this period are inaccessible or inadmissible as evidence.

Freudian theory also postulates the strong influence on individual behavior of the unconscious mind, which cannot be directly observed or documented.

The problem of evidence is compounded by the concern of historians about the applicability of contemporary theory to historical subjects: can seventeenth-century thoughts and deeds be penetrated by twentieth-century social science? That some behavioral theories of human personality resulted from research on animals also disconcerts many historians. Moreover, some theories of behavior contradict the biographer's faith in the uniqueness of individuals, or, if they do allow for individuality, they apply to deviant rather than normal activity. Most behavioral theories of personality do not account for those nuances that make one person malevolent and another mischievous, that take into account the brilliant as well as the average. Finally, because few attempts at "psycho-biography" have been convincing and most are damned by professionals in both fields, biographers may have become gun-shy. They worry that such methodology will distort their subjects, divert their emphasis, and discourage their readers.

Despite these drawbacks, the tools of social science must be employed by the modern biographer. With such methods, historians can make "common sense" explanations more precise and causal statements more penetrating. Because the task of biography is to illuminate its subject, the insights of personality theory must be applied. In order to tell a life story, one must be able to unmask the subject, to unveil "the personal myth," to reveal a person's "self-concept," as Henry James's biographer Leon Edel describes the biographical process.[2] Fortunately some theories of human behavior are both appropriate and available to biography. They allow for individual idiosyncracy and utilize data likely to be credible and obtainable.

This biography of Elizabeth Cady Stanton employs one such psychological model, social learning theory. As defined over the past decade by Stanford University psychologist Albert Bandura and others, social learning theory is a sophisticated form of behaviorism. Individual actions are an amalgam of responses to environment and circumstance and a person's genetic inheritance. A person is motivated by a need for approval and fear of disapproval. Bandura's refinement of basic behaviorism credits the individual with initiative and intelligence. Social learning theory takes into account the human ability to learn from observation, to make comparisons, and to anticipate the outcome of one's actions. Behavior depends on "the continuous reciprocal interaction of cognitive, behavioral and environmental determinants." Within the ongoing process of reciprocal interactions lies the opportunity for people in part to direct their destiny, as well as to set the limits of such self direction.[3]

Put simply, social learning theory claims that individuals "learn" social or antisocial behavior. People have the ability to make thoughtful choices about what course of action they will undertake, based on information they have acquired or "learned" by experience or observation about the probable outcomes of the various options open to them. They can acquire such information either directly or vicariously. Individuals take into account their own ability to undertake such a course, the probability of their success, and their expectations about how others will react to their actions before they actually do anything. How much the individuals value the opinion of various observers is another factor in their decision-making process. Each of these elements influences and is influenced by the others, thus the concept of "continuous reciprocal determinism."

As Bandura explains, "learning" is an ongoing, continuous process with three stages—acquisition, performance, maintenance—but no conclusion. First an individual acquires a behavior by observing others ("models") perform it. One can learn from ideas and books as well as from individuals and experience. If the behavior is attractive, if it is rewarded, if the models are perceived to be powerful or nurturing or both, the incentive to duplicate the behavior is increased. The converse is also true. Individuals can then "perform" the behavior by observing it more closely, by imagining themselves doing it, by actually practicing it, or by some combination of these. Whether or not an individual will advance to this second learning stage—performance—depends on two other factors: whether he has the physical capability to undertake the behavior and what he expects the consequences to be.

Next, the newly learned behavior normally will be "maintained" if it is "reinforced," either externally or internally. If it proves to be successful, if it is positively reinforced by people who are important to the individual, or if it enhances his prospects or status, the individual will continue the newly learned behavior. If reaction to one's behavior is negative, if one is "punished," the behavior will not be repeated. Unrewarded behavior may persist if it contributes to the individual's self-esteem. It might result from satisfaction in a previously acceptable form of behavior, from ongoing admiration for those who initially modeled it, or from having become one's own model. What biographers of an earlier generation might have labeled courage or obstinance, Bandura calls "self-reinforcement" or "internalizing" the approval standard.

As an individual masters a behavior or copes with a situation, survives a crisis or endures punishment, he gains confidence in his ability to do so again and is encouraged to persist. This cycle of competence/confidence/competence Bandura calls "self-efficacy."[4] Finally, because "learning" is continuous and dependent upon reciprocal interactions, any behavior can be adapted or abandoned at any time, as the individual continues to interact and think about his social, physical, and psychological environment. Bandura's individual is not passive. He has the capacity for constant reevaluation of his environment and ongoing reassessment of his performance and competence. He always functions in the context of feedback.

Social learning theory and "common sense" history share an interest in the importance of role models for individuals. Unlike some other aspects of psychological methodologies, historians are accustomed to and comfortable with explanations of behavior based on emulation. The importance attached to the character of parents and teachers among traditional biographers indicates a recognition that children pattern themselves on certain adults, or "role models." As defined by the social scientist, a "role model" is someone whose "role is modeled," whose behavior is copied, or whose actions and attitudes can influence one's own. Bandura's theory cannot predict who will be a role model. His research does indicate that individuals tend to copy the behavior of those who are powerful or successful or nurturing, which could explain why Stanton chose the well-known Lucretia Mott rather than the retiring Angelina Grimké Weld as her mentor in 1840. Both women were abolitionists and feminists, but only Mott had successfully combined her career with marriage. According to Bandura, the concept of role models is essential to the social learning process. Certainly role models were central to the development of Elizabeth Cady Stanton as a feminist.

Social learning theory is a congenial tool for biographers. It uses as data experiences or events or ideas that can be documented by evidence; it credits individuals with the ability to think about actions, alternatives, and results; and it accepts the uniqueness of individuals and events. It is appropriate because it uses as evidence actual human behavior—the experience, examples, and expectations of individuals that can be recovered by historians in the primary sources. It is readily accessible to historians in a series of books and articles by Bandura and his colleagues. Finally it allows for autonomy of individual action and independence of individual thought. Like biography, Bandura's theory puts the person front and center. It illuminates iconoclasts as well as conformists. It credits the individual with the ability to think about decisions—to observe, absorb, symbolize, remember, recall, anticipate, imagine, consider, debate, evaluate, and decide, and then to reconsider.

Three problems remain. The first is the matter of style and syntax. To avoid the intrusion of psychological jargon in the narrative, there have been few direct references to Bandura or social learning theory. Rather, readers should be alert to such key phrases as "role model," "pattern," "developing," "encouraged," and "copying." Second, the question of the relevance of present theory to the past cannot be answered until more attempts to apply it have been made. This biography tests social learning theory in a historical context.

Third, social learning theory cannot directly explain why the same events or role models do not provoke the same reactions. Why was Elizabeth the only one of the five Cady daughters to become a feminist leader? Rather than answer the question, the theory suggests that differences in inherent intelligence, perceptions, interests, abilities, and emotional responses to experience, plus age and birth order, account for diverse, even diametrical behavior among siblings or others of similar background. Bandura again allows for individual differences among siblings and within peer groups, but he does not provide for rigorous explanation of these differences. As Stanton, sounding like a behaviorist herself, explained on the opening page of her autobiography:

> The psychical growth of a child is not influenced by days and years but by the impressions passing events make on its mind. What may prove a sudden awakening to one, giving an impulse in a certain direction that may last for years, may make no impression on another. People wonder why the children of the same family differ so widely, though they have had the same domestic discipline, the same school and church teaching, and have grown up under the same influences and with the same environments. As well wonder why lilies and lilacs in the same latitude are not all alike in color and equally fragrant. Children differ as widely as these in the primal elements of their physical and psychical life[5]

Bandura would agree with the "common sense" convictions of earlier biographers that some people were simply "born that way."

With the exception of these reservations, social learning theory seems well suited to a study of Elizabeth Cady Stanton. Her life can be viewed as a progression of behavior patterns based on successive role models. Throughout her life most of her behavior was approved by only a few people, but those individuals were so important to her that she could persevere despite the criticism of the majority. Eventually, having "internalized" the standard of total female "self-sovereignty," Stanton no longer needed any reinforcement other than her own. One could divide this biography into three parts. In chapters 1–3, Stanton "learned" roles; in chapters 4–8, she "practiced" them; in the last three chapters, she "maintained" the roles she had chosen for herself.

For example, during the period in her childhood when she was trying to win her father's approval, Stanton observed that he admired and praised his son, so she tried to behave like her older brother. She pursued the same activites he did—riding horses, studying Greek, practicing logic. She undertook these activites because she had observed that they were approved by her father, whose approval she sought. She was able to undertake them because she had the physical and mental ability to perform them, and she performed very well. While her father was never enthusiastic about her mastery of these skills, neither was he disapproving; others in her family circle were more positive. By the time Judge Cady realized that such athletic and academic rigors were unusual and inappropriate in his adolescent and unmarried daughter, she had already internalized his earlier standard of achievement. Furthermore, having been challenged by academics, athletics, legal riddles, and theological debates, she became competent in these areas; indeed she became expert. Her early competence was one source of the self-confidence that characterized her behavior throughout her life. Learning that she was capable, she became increasingly capable.

As she matured, Stanton's sense of self-worth was reinforced by a succession of individuals who were important to her. Each of them approved of increasingly untraditional behavior on her part, and each was supplanted by a more radical model. Her father was replaced by her brother-in-law Edward Bayard and her cousin Gerrit Smith, who were in turn replaced by her husband Henry Stanton. Eventually women displaced men as her most important models and mentors. Elizabeth Smith Miller, Lucretia Mott, and Susan B. Anthony shared influence over Stanton's behavior. Finally, Stanton had so internalized her own standard of female autonomy that she became her own authority. In her old age she acted without the approval, and frequently despite the disapproval, of her former allies.[6]

Psychological methodology enables the biographer to identify those behaviors Elizabeth Cady Stanton copied from others and combined into her ideal vision. Her discipline, her academic habits, her logical approach to arguments, skill in debate, wide reading, easy sleeping habits, and her republican attitudes about money and education were patterned after her father. Her horseback riding, executive ability, housekeeping skill, self-indulgence, fashion-consciousness, upper-class tastes, pleasure in her rocking chair, diplomatic manner, and vivacity were behaviors found in her mother. Her matriarchal household, religious skepticism, carpet mending, and gracious bearing were inspired by Lucretia Mott. Her dramatic speaking style, political tactics, and risk taking she adapted from reformers and revivalists; her ideology derived from her wide reading and tolerance for new ideas. None of these models accounts, however, for her humor, curiosity, energy, habitual cheerfulness, sexual attitudes, childbearing practices, or her appetite for food and controversy.

All of Stanton's primary mentors were models of independence of one kind or another. Daniel Cady was a self-made man, a Whig in the Jacksonian era, an agricultural innovator, a wealthy republican. Margaret Cady was a woman who tactfully but effectively imposed her will on her household and community. As one contemporary observed, Stanton had "imbibed . . . from her mother that dauntless independence of thought and speech which, for want of a better name, is called the courage of one's convictions."[7] Similarly Lucretia Mott had been in the forefront of abolition, women's rights, and Quaker reform; she had survived the attacks of established religious and political authorities and yet was widely admired. Significantly, both Stanton's mother and Mott provided examples of active, independent old age and widowhood. Such examples prompted Stanton's admiration and emulation.

Both Stanton's principal and secondary models duplicated and reinforced many of the same behaviors. For example, Edward Bayard, Charles G. Finney, Gerrit Smith, and Theodore Parker all encouraged her religious inquiry. Bayard, Henry Stanton, and the Welds approved of her skepticism of medical authorities. Her mother and Mrs. Mott applauded her habits of self-indulgence, in terms of taking care of herself, although Mott disapproved of unnecessary extravagance.

From the behaviors Stanton exhibited that seem modeled on other people, it is clear that her parents and Mrs. Mott played the most prominent roles. Social learning theory does not explain why those three were more influential than others—Henry Stanton, Susan B. Anthony, or such secondary figures as her sisters, deceased brother, Bayard, Hosack, Emma Willard, Finney, Gerrit Smith, or Libby Miller. It does suggest that Stanton perceived her parents and Mrs. Mott as being more powerful and nurturing than any others.

That Stanton did not model her behavior on that of her husband or her closest ally is apparent from her actions. Henry Stanton and Susan B. Anthony played similar roles in her life: each was at one time a source of approval and affection for her; each provided emotional sustenance, was imposed upon, and resented. With each of them Stanton was publicly paired. With each of them Stanton tried to maintain a public facade of agreement, but with each of them the appearance of a bond outlasted the reality of their relationship. Henry Stanton had encouraged her initial reform interest, and Anthony had provided ongoing incentive. Stanton's husband became less enthusiastic, but her colleague continued to approve of her public behavior. Eventually Anthony supplanted Henry in Elizabeth's affections. Both Henry and Susan moved in and out of her life and her household, but overall, Stanton probably spent more hours and days with Anthony than any other adult. While Stanton admired certain qualities in each of them—Henry's oratory, Anthony's organizational skills—she also disapproved of some of their traits. Her husband's political opportunism and Anthony's cold self-righteousness made them less appealing than the models Stanton did select.

Social learning theory can reveal much about a subject, but its application requires knowing a substantial amount to begin with, both about the subject and its models. Because of the roles played by the Cadys and Mrs. Mott, it would be helpful to know more about them and their habits. The lack of information about Margaret Cady is especially frustrating. Genealogical records, the recollections of relatives, and two photographs hardly provide the kind of information that would be useful to social scientists or biographers.

Social learning theory results in many insights into character development and motivation, but there are some aspects of personality it does not explain. One is curious to know more about Stanton's sexual attitudes and her pervasive interest in religion. Control over decisions affecting pregnancy and the frequency of intercourse were essential aspects of Stanton's definition of female independence, but the record does not reveal much about how she dealt with these issues. Similarly, freedom from traditional church teachings about woman's place was another step toward self-sovereignty. Achieving independence in both of these areas represented for Stanton steps toward her idealized self-definition.

Nor does social learning theory provide an explanation for periods of depression in Stanton's life, although her manner of dealing with them—by cleaning house or taking action—was a learned response. Stanton's depressions follow deaths, childbirths, separation, and conversion, and do not seem abnormal. Nor does the theory answer other questions: why Stanton treated Anthony so shabbily in the 1870s; why she cared about remaining paired with Henry and Susan; why she took risks over Train or the Fifteenth Amendment or The Woman's Bible; why she got so fat.

But the overall conclusions gleaned from social learning theory fit Stanton's life neatly and are reinforced by the findings of other theories. For example, an application of Erik Erikson's developmental approach might locate the source of Stanton's self-confidence and lack of status anxiety in her secure childhood. Studies on the "psychology of commitment," suggesting that having to endure criticism for one's beliefs for a long period of time serves to reinforce one's allegiance, would confirm Stanton's perseverance. New studies of the motivations of modern women repeat the importance of the parental and female role models found in Stanton's life.

The application of other theories can only increase our understanding of this multidimensional woman. For example, although the records are scanty, Freudians might be able to probe questions about Stanton's relationship with her parents, her bonding with Henry and Anthony, her identification with male mentors, sexual attitudes, and obesity. Indeed, the tension Stanton personally experienced in trying to balance public and private roles, or male and female spheres, foreshadows the difficulty of contemporary women in balancing their needs for "affiliation and achievement."[8]

Elizabeth Cady Stanton would have been intrigued by this psychological approach. She recognized the significance of individual psychology on development. She understood that women suffered mental as well as physical bondage. One reason she makes such an appealing subject of biography is that many of the issues she addressed and the opinions she expressed have contemporary vitality. In an era of unusual orthodoxies, she was open to new ideas. She believed in family traits and prenatal influences. She thought she had inherited her father's intelligence and ability to nap, and she attributed her political instincts and her fear of cats to events her mother had experienced while pregnant.[9] She also endorsed phrenology, the nineteenth-century "science of the mind."

Even before psychology developed as a discipline in the late nineteenth century, there had been interest in how the mind influenced behavior. As early as the 1840s America was enamored with the theories of Johann Kaspar Spurzheim,* a German immigrant who introduced phrenology and became a teacher of brain anatomy at Harvard Medical School. According to Spurzheim, the faculties of the mind had specific locations in the folds and fissures of the brain and could be measured on the outside by "bump-reading." A corollary of Spurzheim's theory was especially attractive to Jacksonian-era Americans: if one could have his faculties identified, one might then become what one wanted to be by "depressing" some that were too prominent or "elevating" others.[10] According to phrenology, mental discipline and physical exercise produced mental health.

Although her father considered Spurzheim and his disciples "arrant humbugs," Elizabeth Cady Stanton had her bumps read in 1853, when she was thirty-seven.† The examiner found her "social faculties" and "combativeness" large and her appetite "strong." The report concluded that she was "adapted to the business and subjects of conversation peculiar to men . . . capable of enjoying the connubial relation in a high degree. . . . liable to act from the impulse of the moment and exhibit a boldness and energy of character. . . . afraid of nothing . . . and have more individuality and positiveness than females generally." Stanton believed that her "phrenological character hits the nail on the head—I really did not mean to make a phrenological comparison." It confirmed her proclivity for "idiosyncracies" and independent action.[11]

So does social learning theory.

* At Harvard, Johann Spurzheim (1776–1832) taught with George Combe (1788–1858), who gave up a law career to found the Phrenological Society and the *Phrenological Journal*. Combe's brother, Scottish philosopher Andrew Combe, was another of ECS's intellectual influences.

† See Appendix C for "Phrenological Character of Mrs. Elizabeth C. Stanton."

APPENDIX A
The Livingston-Cady Family

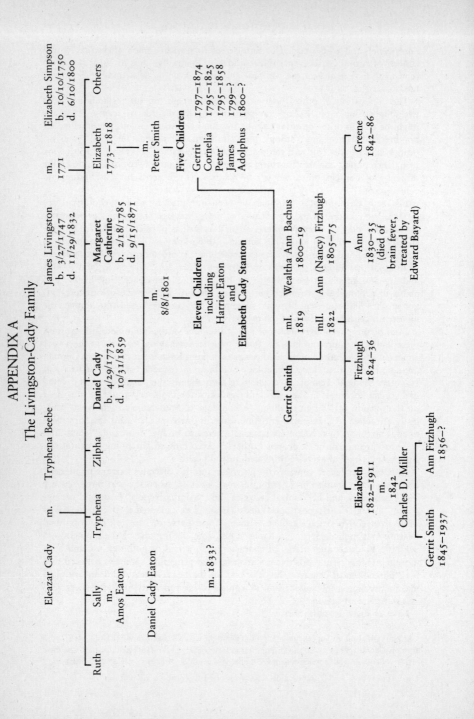

Children of Daniel Cady and Margaret Livingston

1. Harriot
   11/9/1802–1810

2. Tryphena
   9/11/1804–5/1/1891   m. 1826   Edward Bayard 1806–89   no children

3. Daniel
   5/26/1806–1814

4. Eleazar
   5/26/1806–1826

5. James
   10/14/1808–1809

6. Harriet Eliza
   10/5/1810–?   m. 1833?   Daniel Cady Eaton
   1. Harriet
      m. George Brown
   2. Daniel Cady
      1837–1907
      m. Alice Young

7. Daniel
   6/24/1814–10/27/1814

8. Elizabeth
   11/12/1815–10/26/1902   m. 1840   Henry Brewster Stanton 6/27/1805–1/14/1887
   1. Daniel Cady   5. Margaret Livingston
   2. Henry Brewster   6. Harriet Eaton
   3. Gerrit Smith   7. Robert Livingston
   4. Theodore Weld

9. Margaret Chinn
   12/9/1817–1912   m.   Duncan McMartin 2/24/1817–7/6/94
   1. Flora   4. Daniel Cady
   2. Elizabeth   5. Anna
   3. Archibald

10. Catherine Henry
    1/7/1819–?   m.   Samuel Wilkeson d. 1889
    1. Bayard   4. ?
    2. ?   5. Frank
    3. Margaret

11. Eleazar Livingston
    1/28/1827–1828

APPENDIX B
The Cady-Stanton Family
Children of Henry and Elizabeth Cady Stanton

1. **Daniel Cady Stanton**
   b. 3/2/1842, Johnstown, N.Y.
   d. 1/18/1891, Logan, Iowa
   m./div. Fredericka L.
   1 child: Florence L., b. 1885

2. **Henry Brewster Stanton, Jr.**
   b. 3/1844, Albany, N.Y.   Columbia Law School, 1865
   d. 12/5/1903, New York, N.Y.
   m. 1892, Mary O'Shea
   no children

3. **Gerrit Smith Stanton**
   b. 9/18/1845, Boston, Mass.   Columbia Law School, 1865
   d. 4/24/1927, Long Island, N.Y.
   m. Augusta Hazelton
   adopted daughter: Hazel, d. 1929

4. **Theodore Weld Stanton**
   b. 2/10/1851, Seneca Falls, N.Y.   Cornell University, 1872,
   d. 3/1/1925, New Brunswick, N.J.   M.A. 1876
   m. 1881, Marguerite Berry
   4 children:
     Elizabeth Cady Stanton II, b. 1882
     baby, d.
     Robert Livingston Stanton, b. 1885
     Helene, b. 1886

5. **Margaret Livingston Stanton Lawrence**
   b. 10/20/1852, Seneca Falls, N.Y.   Vassar College, 1876,
   d. 1938?   Columbia University, 1891
   m. 10/2/1878, Frank E. Lawrence, d. 1890
   no children

6. **Harriot Eaton Stanton Blatch**
   b. 1/20/1856, Seneca Falls, N.Y.　　　Vassar College, 1878, M.A. 1891
   d. 11/20/1940, Greenwich, Conn.
   m. 11/12/1882, William Henry Blatch,
   　d. 1915
   2 children:
   　Nora, b. 9/30/1883
   　Helen, b. 1892, died

7. **Robert Livingston Stanton**
   b. 3/14/1859, Seneca Falls, N.Y.　　Cornell University, 1880
   d. 2/23/1920, New York, N.Y.　　　Columbia Law School, 1881
   unmarried

Elizabeth Cady Stanton's seven children produced only six surviving grandchildren. Daniel's daughter Florence could not be located as early as 1891, when her Uncle Henry tried to find her in Chicago after Daniel died. There are no further records for Gerrit's adopted daughter or for the daughters of Theodore Stanton, who may have remained in France. Theodore's son Robert was a Cornell graduate and an army officer. One source indicates that he stayed in France, near Mazamet, married a Frenchwoman, and had a son named François, who subsequently married a widow with two children.

Harriot Blatch's daughter Nora returned to the United States to attend Cornell. She graduated magna cum laude in 1905, the first woman there to earn a degree in civil engineering. She was married for one year, 1908–09, to Dr. Lee deForest, a prominent pioneer in radio electronics. They had a daughter Harriet. Harriet produced a daughter, Catherine Clarke Allaben, born in 1936. Harriet deForest is still alive, living in Londonderry, Vermont.

In 1918 Nora Blatch deForest married Morgan Barney. The couple had two children, Rhoda, born in 1920, and John, born in 1922. Rhoda married Frederick Jenkins. Rhoda Barney Jenkins and John Barney live together in Greenwich, Connecticut.

A *Book of Origins for Barney-Blatch Family,* by Katherine Beecher Stetson Chamberlin (Pasadena, Calif., 1951), in the possession of Rhoda Barney Jenkins, provided the essential information for these genealogical charts.

APPENDIX C

Phrenological Character of Mrs Elizabeth C. Stanton, Given at Seneca Falls by E. S. Stark, January 10, 1853 *

Mrs. Elizabeth Stanton

You have a predominance of the vital and mental temperaments with a full degree of the motive but the last is not sustaining in its influence, the vital having the ascendancy and not being abused. Your life principle is ample and health perfect; few persons have a better organization for longevity. You derive the tone of your mind and constitution from your mother hence partake of the nature of the Livingston family rather than that of your father. You have a plump round form fair complexion and amiable expression.

Your brain is above the common size, large at the base, occipital and frontal regions. Some faculties are quite large, while others are inferior in strength and influence.

All the social faculties are large with large combativeness, destructiveness, alimentiveness, firmness, Benev[olent] Construc[tiveness]; and several of the intellectual organs. You are characterized for the following traits.

First, are warm hearted, capable of enjoying the society of your friends much are greatly attached to your kin and find it especially difficult to give up those whom you have once loved, enjoy the society of the gentlemen, are not cold hearted toward them and under favorable circumstances are ready to respond to the expressions of sympathy and affection from them, are better adapted to the business and subjects of conversation peculiar to men than those of women, are capable of enjoying the connubial relation in a high degree, are very fond of children, well qualified to sympathize with them in their helplessness. Attachment to place is also strong. You are fond of home and its associations, still would enjoy traveling by way of gratifying the other faculties.

You lack continuity of mind and close application to some things, find it difficult to attend to details either in business or in thought; prefer to have your mind occupied with things that are extensive and comprehensive in their nature. Your

* Holograph copy, ECS-VC. Considering that ECS was not yet widely known, this description quite accurately predicts her mature personality and political style.

thoughts and feelings are more intense and vivid than prolonged and connected. Love of life is strong. You have great desire to live and enjoy the pleasures of life. Your large Combat[iveness] and Destruc[tiveness] joined with your vital temperament give an unusual degree of force, energy and executiveness of mind. You never stop at trifles, are much more inclined to labor where there are severe difficulties to overcome than to walk in the smoother paths of life, are full of resolution and have a daring spirit and when provoked are capable of being decidedly indignant. Your feelings are not of the tame, quiet class. You are capable of being very sarcastic, vigorous in your style of conversation or writing and at times are not sufficiently gentle and easy in your manners. Appetite is strong and digestion good, none better. Your desire for gain is comparatively good, but owing to the combination of your faculties you are not naturally qualified to attend to the details of business or to make it a special matter of effort to economize, but you prefer to live as you go along and have what you like.

Secret[iveness] and Caut[iousness] are rather wanting, hence with so much propelling and executive power are liable to act from the impulse of the moment and exhibit a boldness and energy of character, that the occasion does not warrant. You are afraid of nothing, are not restrained from acting or speaking through fear of consequences. You show your character just as it is, hence have more individuality and positiveness than females generally. You are no hypocrite, tho' you may not always express in words the depths of your feelings. You detest nothing so much as underhanded means and do not as many do take advantage of circumstances to show off and would not be likely to exhibit those captivating qualities of love or make that display in the manifestation of agreeable qualities necessary to attract attention. Approbativeness is rather prominent but its function joined with self esteem in your case is rather to give sense of character, independence of thought and moral courage than love of show and display or desire for attention and flattery. You are not naturally dignified, have not the feeling of self love, are not devoted to yourself, care more to exert a moral and intellectual influence on society than to put yourself forward as an object of attraction.

Your energy of character might so manifest itself that you would get the credit of being proud and haughty but in reality you are not so, indeed are at times wanting in true pride and self-love. You have remarkable Firmness and perseverance when you have once laid out your plans and taken your position. You are not to be driven from your purposes or prevented from consummating your designs. Your moral brain is unevenly developed. Conscien[tiousness] as connected with Firmness is fully developed and its manifestations are particularly seen with reference to the "Higher Law."

It should [illegible] have a distinct influence in your character, while that portion joining Cautiousness is defective. Hence your regard for human law and the consequences of conduct is less active which may sometimes manifest itself in want of circumspection as seen by others. No law is law to you unless sanctioned by the intellect and in harmony with moral obligation.

Hope is full and has a sustaining influence on your mind, tho' you are not particularly elated by enthusiasm and extravagant expectations of success, still are not easily discouraged and have a disposition to regard things in a favorable more than a discouraging light. Veneration and Marvellousness are also average and their influence would be comparatively small and guided mostly by other faculties. Veneration as manifested toward intellect and superior merit has a fair influence over your character and conduct but as giving deference for mere opinions forms and customs as such is not distinct. Whatever others value as superior is no criterion to you. Faith is weak when compared with your reason. You are governed by what you can understand and comprehend, more than by faith. Benevolence is large, you are naturally kind, humane, generous in your feelings, anxious for the good of society, delight in rendering service and promoting the happiness of others. This is the strongest and most influential impulse in your moral nature. Your mechanical capacity is good, particularly in contriving ways and means to secure ends, also your sense of the beautiful, poetical and love of the sublime in nature and oratory.

You have uncommon power to [isolate?] and conform. You are not noted for your power to apply thoughts and make it tangible and practical. Larger Comparison would give more power of analysis and ability to apply principles to every day life, you would then more readily see the affinities between principles and the wants of mankind. You have a good degree of suavity of manner and youthfulness of mind and prefer younger society rather than older. But the organ of Intuition is not particularly large, still owing to the strength and vigor of your intellect you may readily see the motives of others but this state of mind is not the result of intuition. Language is fully developed but you are more energetic and forcible than copious, can write better than speak, are decidedly fond of music, appreciate good [tones?] have good memory of time and events, excellent memory of places are ["not" scratched out] naturally systematic, fond of order quite inclined to arrange and systematize your thoughts, are very much annoyed at a want of system and method in business. Capacity in figures is good, you might excel in mathematics and the study of Languages, have a good mechanical eye, are a good judge of proportions forms and outlines but are not as ready in seeing adaptations of things, are more given to thought and investigation than to observation. Reported phrenologically by E. S. Stark

ABBREVIATIONS

AASS   American Anti-Slavery Society

AERA   American Equal Rights Association

AES   Arthur and Elizabeth Schlesinger Library, Radcliffe College

AL   Alma Lutz

BPL   Boston Public Library

CE   *Created Equal,* Alma Lutz's biography of Elizabeth Cady Stanton

CU   Columbia University

CY   *Challenging Years,* autobiography of Harriot Stanton Blatch, Elizabeth Cady Stanton's daughter

DL   Mabel Smith Douglass Library, Douglass College, Rutgers University

80Y   *Eighty Years and More,* Elizabeth Cady Stanton's autobiography

ECS   Elizabeth Cady Stanton

ESM   Elizabeth Smith Miller

FHS   Friends Historical Society, Swarthmore College

GS   Gerrit Smith

GSM   Gerrit Smith Miller

HBS   Henry Brewster Stanton

HEHL   Henry E. Huntington Library

HH   Houghton Library, Harvard University

HWS   *The History of Woman Suffrage*

JPL   Johnstown Public Library

LC   Library of Congress

LM   Lucretia Mott

LS   Lucy Stone

MW	Martha Wright
NAW	*Notable American Women*
NAWSA	National American Woman Suffrage Association
NYHS	New-York Historical Society
NYPL	New York Public Library
SBA	Susan B. Anthony
SFHS	Seneca Falls Historical Society
SSC	Sophia Smith Collection, Smith College
SU	Syracuse University
TS	Theodore Stanton
VC	Vassar College
WCTU	Woman's Christian Temperance Union
WLG	William Lloyd Garrison

NOTES

INTRODUCTION

1. Elizabeth Cady Stanton (hereafter ECS), *Eighty Years and More: Reminiscences, 1815–1897*, introd. Gail Parker (New York: T. Fisher Unwin, 1898; reprint, New York: Schocken Books, 1971), 458–68 (hereafter *80Y*). Further descriptive material is ECS diary, 13 Nov. 1895, *Elizabeth Cady Stanton as Revealed in Her Letters, Diary and Reminiscences*, ed. Theodore Stanton and Harriot Stanton Blatch (New York: Harper & Bros., 1922), 2:314–15 (vol. 2 hereafter *Letters*). Quotation from Alma Lutz (hereafter AL), *Created Equal: A Biography of Elizabeth Cady Stanton, 1815–1902* (New York: John Day, 1940), 292 (hereafter *CE*).

2. Suitable roles for nineteenth-century women were referred to by ministers and ladies' magazines as their "appropriate sphere" or the "cult of true womanhood." They confined women to the domestic circle. See Barbara Welter, "The Cult of True Womanhood, 1820–1860," *American Quarterly* 18 (1966):151–74; Gerda Lerner, "The Lady and the Mill Girl: Changes in the Status of Women in the Age of Jackson," *Mid-Continent American Studies Journal* 10 (1969):5–15; Nancy F. Cott, *The Bonds of Womanhood: "Woman's Sphere" in New England, 1780–1835* (New Haven: Yale Univ. Press, 1977).

3. ECS to Clara Colby, [1896?], *CE*, 296.

4. In the heat of the suffrage battle, the "antis" frequently quoted ECS's more radical comments on marriage, motherhood, and domesticity. See "The Case against Woman Suffrage" (Massachusetts, 1916), National American Woman Suffrage Association MSS (hereafter NAWSA), box 42, Manuscript Division, Library of Congress, Washington, D.C. (hereafter LC).

5. Program and other souvenirs of this event, ECS MSS, LC. See also Alice Stone Blackwell, "Woman's 75 Year Fight," *Nation* (18 July 1923), 53–54.

6. Anecdote recorded by Harriot Stanton Blatch on handwritten copy of ECS speech to the New York Senate Judiciary Committee, May 1867, ECS-LC. About keeping her papers for posterity, ECS wrote in her diary, 1 Oct. 1896, *Letters*, 321:

"Since I got back to town, my chief occupation has been looking over my papers, destroying many, and putting the rest in order. As from day to day I have worked alone at this monotonous task, I have felt that perhaps this is the last time I shall ever handle them, and that I should make the work of destruction easier for my children. How we dislike to burn what we once deemed valuable, and yet what a nuisance to those who come after us are bushels of old papers. Well, I have thinned mine out and may try it again should I remain on this planet half a dozen years longer." See also Susan B. Anthony (hereafter SBA) to Elizabeth Smith Miller (hereafter ESM), 2 March 1897, Smith Family MSS, New York Public Library, New York, N.Y. (hereafter NYPL).

7. Rhoda Barney Jenkins (ECS great-granddaughter), interview with author, Greenwich, Conn., 18 Oct. 1976.

8. CE; Harriot Stanton Blatch and AL, *Challenging Years: The Memoirs of Harriot Stanton Blatch* (New York: G. P. Putnam's Sons, 1940) (hereafter CY). See AL MSS, Arthur and Elizabeth Schlesinger Library, Radcliffe College, Cambridge, Mass. (hereafter AES).

9. Ellen C. DuBois, *Elizabeth Cady Stanton, Susan B. Anthony: Correspondence, Writings, Speeches* (New York: Schocken Books, 1981), is the most carefully annotated collection to date. My research method was to locate and compare as many versions of each letter as I could. If there was no holograph copy extant, I usually trusted copies by Ida Husted Harper or Theodore Stanton before any others. The material quoted by AL and Harper in their books I accepted as reliable. That appearing only in *Letters* is more questionable.

10. See content analysis by Anne Grant, "Elizabeth Cady Stanton's Quarrel with God" (typescript, n.d.), 53—54. Theodore Stanton and Harriot Blatch also drastically reduced ECS's references to her friend SBA. They added a tribute to her childhood Greek tutor, Rev. Simon Hosack.

11. *80Y*, xxii.

12. *The History of Woman Suffrage*, ed. Elizabeth Cady Stanton, Susan B. Anthony, Matilda Joslyn Gage et al., 6 vols. (New York: Fowler & Wells, 1881—86; reprint, New York: Source Book Press, 1970) (hereafter HWS). The original editions of HWS were personally distributed by Anthony to libraries, politicians, and associates. Of those remaining, most are too fragile to circulate. In addition to the hardbound reprint edition, there is *The Concise History of Woman Suffrage*, ed. Mari Jo Buhle and Paul Buhle (Urbana: Univ. of Illinois Press, 1978).

13. Theodore Tilton to ECS, 17 March 1897, in Margaret Stanton Lawrence, "Elizabeth Cady Stanton, 1815–1902: A Sketch of Her Life by Her Elder Daughter" (typescript, 1915), 23, ECS MSS, Vassar College Library, Poughkeepsie, N.Y. (hereafter VC).

14. The best examples of recent Stanton scholarship are Lois W. Banner, *Elizabeth Cady Stanton: A Radical for Woman's Rights* (Boston: Little, Brown, 1980), also typescript with footnotes, AES; and Ellen C. DuBois, *Feminism and Suffrage: the Emergence of an Independent Women's Movement in America, 1848–1869* (Ithaca: Cornell Univ. Press, 1978). Banner uses some Eriksonian theory; DuBois traces the political and intellectual sources of Stanton's ideas.

15. ECS, "The Solitude of Self" (address to U.S. Congressional Committee on the Judiciary, 18 Jan. 1892, holograph copy), ECS-LC, also HWS, 4:189–91.

16. Ida Husted Harper, "Elizabeth Cady Stanton," *American Monthly Review of Reviews* (Dec. 1902), 715–19, ECS-LC.

17. Barbara W. Tuchman, "Biography as a Prism of History," in *Telling Lives:*

The Biographer's Art, ed. Marc Pachter (Washington, D.C.: New Republic Books and National Portrait Gallery, 1979), 133–47. The model for this generation is Kathryn Kish Sklar, *Catharine Beecher: A Study in American Domesticity* (New Haven: Yale Univ. Press, 1973).

18. As part of the interest expressed in the 1890s in earlier generations of women leaders, ECS suggested that NAWSA sponsor an annual "Foremothers Day" shortly after Thanksgiving. *Letters,* 290–91.

19. *80Y,* 418–19.

20. ECS to Rebecca Eyster, 1 May 1847, *Letters,* 15–16. This letter is a good example of different versions of the same item. The undated copy of this letter found in the Theodore Stanton MSS (hereafter TS), Mabel Smith Douglass Library, Rutgers University, New Brunswick, N.J. (hereafter DL), is longer and more detailed: "Soon after my marriage Theodore Weld said to me: Do not allow any of your correspondents to insult you by addressing your letters Mrs. Henry B. Stanton. I have followed his advice. . . . Furthermore, I have talked this matter over with my husband and he says it would be quite *outré* for us to appear in the papers with either titles or men's names."

21. ECS, "Noted Suffragist Reviews Her Life" (clipping, n.d.), ECS-LC.

1. PLACE AND PRIVILEGE, 1815–26

1. Catherine Bryant Rowles, *Tomahawks to Hatpins: A History of Johnstown, New York* (Lakemont, N.Y.: North Country Books, 1975).

2. ECS's birthplace faced on Green Street but sat on the same lot as the house that replaced it. That property later became part of the Davis-McIntyre glove factory. The brick Cady mansion was sold in 1888, torn down and replaced by a bank that bears a historical marker noting the ECS connection. Johnstown (N.Y.) Public Library files (hereafter JPL). Description of the Cady mansion in Sallie Holley to C. L. Holley, 4 Feb. 1854, *Letters,* 56–57.

3. *80Y,* 5–6, 9, 29.

4. Margaret Stanton Lawrence MSS, ECS-VC; CY, 8, 16, 18–20, 26.

5. Sallie Holley to C. L. Holley, 4 Feb. 1854, *Letters,* 56–57; CY, 20.

6. For Daniel Cady, see *Dictionary of American Biography,* 1966 ed., article by H. W. Howard Knott; Henry B. Stanton, "Obituary: Daniel Cady," *New York Daily Times,* [Nov. 1859], JPL.

7. Sallie Holley to C. L. Holley, 4 Feb. 1854, *Letters,* 56–57; Daniel Cady to Peter Smith, 23 Oct. 1818, ECS-LC.

8. Daniel Cady to Peter Smith, 2 Dec. 1814, ECS-LC; will of Daniel Cady, on file at Fulton County Courthouse, Johnstown, N.Y.

9. *Letters,* 275; CY, 7, 16, 20. Some of Tryphena Cady Bayard's letters are included in the Gerrit Smith Miller MSS (hereafter GSM), George Arents Research Library, Syracuse Univ., Syracuse, N.Y. (hereafter SU).

10. CY, 10, 11, 13, 16, 36; *80Y,* 108; Yale Univ. Archives, New Haven, Conn.

11. *80Y,* 4, 11, 48–49, 111; CE, 11–12, 69, 203; letter to author from Kenneth L. Brock, Archivist, Emma Willard School, Troy, N.Y., 19 July 1978; *Emma Willard and Her Pupils, 1822–1872* (Published by Mrs. Russell Sage, 1898), 147–49; letter to author from Barbara Wood McMartin, Beaman, Iowa, 27 May 1980. Attendance at women's meetings cited in SBA to ECS, 12 Dec. 1860, and 20 Feb. 1861, ECS-LC.

12. ECS to John Greenleaf Whittier, 11 July 1840. *Letters,* 5–6; Theodore Til-

ton, "Mrs. Elizabeth Cady Stanton," *Eminent Women of the Age,* ed. Tilton (Hartford, Conn.: S. M. Betts, 1868), 336.

13. *80Y*, 26–28; letter to author from Hanns Kuttner, Young People's Committee for Historic Seneca Falls, 27 Nov. 1979.

14. *80Y*, 24; Banner, *Stanton,* 3–4, 11–12.

15. *80Y*, 20–21.

16. Ibid.

17. Tilton, "Stanton," 343; *80Y*, 20–21.

18. ECS to SBA, 10 Sept. 1855, TS-DL, also *Letters,* 59–60.

19. ECS, "Reminiscences of Elizabeth Cady Stanton," 2, Political Equality Club of Minneapolis MSS, Minnesota Historical Society, St. Paul, Minn.

20. Ibid.; ECS, "Speech on Common Schools" (7 March 1855, Seneca Falls, N.Y.), ECS-LC.

21. *80Y*, 3.

22. Ibid., 2.

23. Ibid., 31–32; ECS, "Reminiscences," 3.

24. Tilton, "Stanton," 334; Henry B. Stanton, "Tribute to Daniel Cady," *New York Tribune,* 1 Jan. 1855, JPL, written upon Judge Cady's retirement from the New York Supreme Court.

25. *80Y*, 10, 14–15; ECS interview, *Philadelphia Sun Press,* 8 Dec. 1901, ECS-LC.

26. *80Y*, 15.

27. For discussion of female spheres and friendship, see Carroll Smith-Rosenberg, "The Female World of Love and Ritual: Relations between Women in Nineteenth-Century America," *Signs* 1 (Autumn 1975):1–29.

2. REVIVAL, REFORM, AND ROMANCE, 1827–39

1. Classic and revisionist works on Jacksonian America include Lee Benson, *The Concept of Jacksonian Democracy: New York as a Test Case* (Princeton: Princeton Univ. Press, 1961); Marvin Meyers, *The Jacksonian Persuasion: Politics and Belief* (Stanford: Stanford Univ. Press, 1957); and Edward Pessen, *Jacksonian America: Society, Personality, and Politics* (Homewood, Ill.: Dorsey, 1969). A more recent study of the same phenomenon in a smaller area is Paul E. Johnson, *A Shopkeeper's Millennium: Society and Revivals in Rochester, New York, 1815–1837* (New York: Hill & Wang, 1978).

2. Lerner, "Lady and Mill Girl," 5–15.

3. Whitney Cross, *The Burned-Over District: The Social and Intellectual History of Enthusiastic Religion in Western New York, 1800–1850* (Ithaca: Cornell Univ. Press, 1950).

4. ECS, "Reminiscences," 2; *80Y*, 26–28, 31, 46.

5. *80Y*, 33.

6. Ibid., 34, 46.

7. Ibid., 34; ECS, "Reminiscences," 5. For a discussion of the equal education movement, see Eleanor Flexner, *A Century of Struggle: The Woman's Rights Movement in the United States* (Cambridge: Harvard Univ. Press, Belknap Press, 1959; paperback, New York: Atheneum, 1972), chaps. 2, 8.

8. *80Y*, 35; letter to author from Kenneth L. Brock, 19 July 1978.

9. Letter to author from Brock.

10. *New York American Journal,* 27 April 1902, ECS-LC; *80Y,* 441–47, 36.

11. For Willard, see *Notable American Women* article by Frederick Rudolph (hereafter *NAW*); AL, *Emma Willard: Daughter of Democracy* (Boston: Houghton Mifflin, 1929); Ann Firor Scott, "What, Then, Is the American: The New Woman," *Journal of American History* 65 (Dec. 1978):679–703.

12. Emma Willard, *An Address to the Public, Particularly to Members of the Legislature of New York, Proposing a Plan for Improving Female Education,* 2d ed. (Middlebury, Vt.: J. W. Copeland, 1819). Willard's tactics are discussed by Ann Douglas, *The Feminization of American Culture* (New York: Alfred A. Knopf, 1977), p. 59; Keith Melder, "The Mask of Oppression: The Female Seminary Movement in the United States," *New York History* 55 (July 1954):261–79.

13. Cott, *Bonds of Womanhood,* 119–25.

14. *80Y,* 41.

15. Quoted in Perry Miller, *The Life of the Mind in America: From the Revolution to the Civil War* (New York: Harcourt, Brace & World, 1965), 9. See also James F. Johnson, "The Life of Charles Grandison Finney" (Ph.D. diss., Syracuse Univ., 1959).

16. That "romantic reform in America traced its origins to a religious impulse which was both politically and socially conservative" is the thesis of John L. Thomas, "Romantic Reform in America, 1815–1865," *American Quarterly* 17 (Winter 1965):656–81. See also Gerald Sorin, *Abolitionism: A New Perspective* (New York: Praeger, 1972).

17. Clifford S. Griffin, *Their Brothers' Keepers: Moral Stewardship in the United States, 1800–1865* (New Brunswick: Rutgers Univ. Press, 1960).

18. *80Y,* 42; Henry B. Stanton (hereafter HBS), *Random Recollections,* 3d ed. (New York: Harper & Bros., 1887), 22–23.

19. Quoted in Miller, *Life of the Mind,* 33.

20. *80Y,* 43.

21. Ibid., 47–48, 44.

22. Keith Melder, "Ladies Bountiful: Organized Women's Benevolence in Early Nineteenth Century America," *New York History* 68 (July 1967):243; Cott, *Bonds of Womanhood,* 159.

23. ECS's daughter Margaret recalled her telling this anecdote during a lecture in Chicago, c. 1877. Lawrence, "Sketch," 11–12.

24. Entry dated Johnstown, N.Y., 23 Aug. 1837, ECS commonplace book, Boston Public Library, Boston, Mass. (hereafter BPL); Margaret Stanton Lawrence, "Who Was Elizabeth Cady Stanton? My Mother" (typescript, n.d.), 9–11, ECS-VC.

25. Most sources do not address female adolescence. See Joseph Kett, *Rites of Passage: Adolescence in America, 1790 to the Present* (New York: Basic Books, 1977), 14, 29, 36; Nancy Cott, "Young Women in the Second Great Awakening," *Feminist Studies* 3 (Fall 1975):15–29; Carroll Smith-Rosenberg, "Beauty, the Beast, and the Militant Woman: A Case Study of Sex Roles and Social Stress in Jacksonian America," *American Quarterly* 23 (Oct. 1971):562–84; Carroll Smith-Rosenberg, "Puberty to Menopause: The Cycle of Femininity in Nineteenth-Century America," in *Clio's Consciousness Raised: New Perspectives on the History of Women,* ed. Mary Hartman and Lois W. Banner (New York: Harper Torch Books, 1974), 23–37.

26. ECS to Ida Husted Harper [1897?], Harper MSS, Henry E. Huntington Library, San Marino, Calif. (hereafter HEHL); ECS to Amelia Bloomer, 25 May 1855, ECS-LC.

27. *CE,* 16–17, 21–23; ECS to Harriot Stanton Blatch, 1 Oct. 1889, and photograph, ECS-LC.

28. Charles A. Hammond, *Gerrit Smith: The Story of a Noble Man's Life* (Geneva, N.Y.: W. F. Humphrey, 1900); Ralph V. Harlow, *Gerrit Smith: Philanthropist and Reformer* (New York: Holt Rinehart & Winston, 1939; reprint, New York: Russell & Russell, 1972); Sorin, *Abolitionism,* 26–38. Gerrit Smith hereafter GS.

29. Lucretia Mott (hereafter LM) to ECS, 25 Oct. 1849, William Lloyd Garrison MSS (hereafter WLG), Sophia Smith Collection, Smith College, Northampton, Mass. (hereafter SSC). Mrs. Mott believed that Ann Smith was responsible for all of her husband's reform activity.

30. For GS's involvement with John Brown, see Stephen Oates, *To Purge This Land with Blood: A Biography of John Brown* (New York: Harper & Row, 1970); Otto J. Scott, *The Secret Six: John Brown and the Abolitionist Movement,* (New York: New York Times Books, 1979). The other five were Samuel G. Howe, Theodore W. Higginson, Theodore Parker, Franklin Sanborn, and George Stearns.

31. Benjamin P. Thomas, *Theodore Weld: Crusader for Freedom* (New Brunswick: Rutgers Univ. Press, 1950), 162. After the Civil War, GS and Horace Greeley paid the bond for Jefferson Davis.

32. *CE,* 14–15.

33. ECS to "Uncle" (Peter Smith, GS's brother), n.d., GSM-SU; *80Y,* 59.

34. *80Y,* 54–55.

35. Ibid., 60.

36. See HBS, *Recollections;* biographical file in Robert Brewster Stanton (nephew) MSS, NYPL; Arthur H. Rice, "Henry B. Stanton as a Political Abolitionist" (Ed.D. diss., Teachers College, Columbia Univ., 1967); Rosalie Margolin, "Henry B. Stanton, A Forgotten Abolitionist" (M.A. thesis, Columbia Univ., 1962).

37. "When the hot evening came, to my surprise everybody arranged themselves in the affirmative part of the room except myself. [It] afterward came to pass that this was the beginning of my life-work, and lent color to my whole future existence." HBS, *Recollections,* 3d ed., 24.

38. W. R. Keagy, "The Lane Seminary Rebellion," *Bulletin of the Historical & Philosophical Society of Ohio* 9 (April 1951):153–54.

39. Theodore Weld described Stanton's role as executive secretary to Angelina Grimké, 16 Oct. 1837, *The Letters of Theodore Dwight Weld, Angelina Grimké Weld and Sarah Grimké, 1822–1844,* ed. Gilbert H. Barnes and Dwight L. Dumond, 2 vols. (New York: D. Appleton-Century, 1934; reprint, New York: DaCapo Press, 1970), 1:463–64.

40. HBS to GS, 27 Feb. 1840, GSM-SU.

41. *80Y,* 59.

3. MARRIAGE AND MRS. MOTT, 1840–47

1. *80Y,* 60–61.

2. GS to Ann Smith, 11 Dec. 1839, GSM-SU; *80Y,* 60–61; Daniel Cady to Peter Smith, 2 Dec. 1814, ECS-LC.

3. *80Y,* 32–33, 216, 220–25.

4. Ibid., 71.

5. Ibid., 71, 61; ECS to Ann Smith, 4 March 1840, ECS-LC.

6. Caroline Weston to Anne Weston, n.d., BPL; HBS to GS, 27 Feb. 1840, GSM-SU.

7. Aileen S. Kraditor, *Means and Ends in American Abolitionism: Garrison and His Critics on Strategy and Tactics, 1834–1850* (New York: Random House, Pantheon Books, 1967); James B. Stewart, *Holy Warriors: The Abolitionists and American Slavery* (New York: Hill & Wang, 1976).

8. HBS to Amos Phelps, 17 April 1840, BPL.

9. HBS to ECS, 1 Jan. 1840, *Letters*, 4–5; Theodore Weld to Louis Tappan, 10 April 1840, *Weld Letters*, 2:828; HBS to John Greenleaf Whittier, 18 April 1840, Houghton Library, Harvard University, Cambridge, Mass. (hereafter HH).

10. There has been confusion in primary sources about the wedding date. ECS gave 11 May in her autobiography, leading to speculation that she did not wish to remember it or that the printer erred. *80Y*, 71. Henry gave the correct date in his autobiography, although not until the third edition did he mention his bride's name. Initially he identified her only as "the daughter of Daniel Cady." HBS, *Recollections*, 1st ed., 37. Judging from their letters and other internal evidence, 1 May is the correct date.

11. *80Y*, 71–72.

12. HBS to GS, 17 April 1840, GSM-SU.

13. Thomas, *Weld*; Katharine Lumpkin, *The Emancipation of Angelina Grimké* (Chapel Hill: Univ. of North Carolina Press, 1974); Gerda Lerner, *The Grimké Sisters from South Carolina: Pioneers for Woman's Rights and Abolition* (Boston: Houghton Mifflin, 1967).

14. Stephen W. Nissenbaum, "Careful Love: Sylvester Graham and the Emergence of Victorian Sexual Theory in America, 1830–1840" (Ph.D. diss., Univ. of Wisconsin, 1968).

15. Lumpkin, *Grimké*, 167; ECS to Angelina Weld, 25 June 1840, and Angelina Weld to Gerrit and Ann Smith, 18 June 1840, *Weld Letters*, 2:845–49, 842; HBS to GS, 10 May 1840, GSM-SU.

16. *80Y*, 73; ECS to Angelina Weld, 25 June 1840, *Weld Letters*, 2:845–49.

17. HBS to Whittier, 15 Feb. 1840, enclosing an announcement of the meeting, HH.

18. Rice, "Henry Stanton," 206–8; HBS, *Recollections*, 3d ed., 31.

19. Mary Grew, diary describing the World Anti-Slavery Convention, London, 1840, transcribed by Alma Lutz, AL-AES; LM, *Slavery and "The Woman Question": Lucretia Mott's Diary of Her Visit to Great Britain to Attend the World's Anti-Slavery Convention of 1840*, ed. Frederick B. Tolles, suppl. 23 to *Journal of the Friends Historical Society* (Haverford, Pa.: Friends Historical Assn., 1952).

20. Rice, "Henry Stanton," 141, 144, 207.

21. *80Y*, 80–81.

22. WLG to Helen Garrison, 27 June 1840, *The Letters of William Lloyd Garrison*, ed. Louis Ruchames, 4 vols. (Cambridge: Harvard Univ. Press, Belknap Press, 1971–75), 2:655; LM, *Diary*, 41.

23. ECS to Angelina Weld and Sarah Grimké, 25 June 1840, *Weld Letters*, 2:845–49; ECS to Edward Davis (LM's son-in-law), 25 Dec. 1881 (condolence note), LM MSS, Friends Historical Society, Swarthmore College, Haverford, Pa. (hereafter FHS).

24. Quoted in Otelia Cromwell, *Lucretia Mott*, 2d ed. (New York: Russell & Russell, 1971), 125.

25. Margaret Hope Bacon, *Valiant Friend: The Life of Lucretia Mott* (New York: Walker, 1980), is an excellent biography of Stanton's mentor.

26. *HWS*, 1:419–21.

27. *80Y*, 82.

28. ECS to Edward Davis, 5 Dec. 1881, FHS; *80Y*, 103. HBS's travel notes ran as "Glances at Men and Things" in the *New York American, 1840—41*. Those that were published in the *National Era* became *Sketches of Reforms and Reformers of Great Britain and Ireland* (New York: J. Wiley, 1849; reprint, Miami, Fla.: Mnemosyne, 1969).

29. ECS to GS, 3 Aug. 1840, GSM-SU; Richard Webb quoted in Sarah Pugh to ECS, 24 March 1841, ECS-LC; Webb to Elizabeth Pease, 4 Nov. 1840, BPL.

30. *80Y*, 100—101, 107. ECS had written frequently to her family during her trip, trying to promote a reconciliation. ECS to Daniel Eaton, 18 Aug. 1840, TS-DL.

31. HBS to GS, 8 Jan. 1841, GSM-SU; ECS to Elizabeth Neall, 25 Jan. 1841, Sydney Howard Gay MSS, Columbia University, New York, N.Y. (hereafter CU).

32. James Birney to Lewis Tappan, 5 Feb. 1841, *Letters of James Gillespie Birney, 1831—18517*, ed. Dwight L. Dumond, 2 vols. (New York: D. Appleton-Century, 1938; reprint, Gloucester, Mass.: Peter Smith, 1966), 2:623; ECS to Elizabeth Smith, [1841?], AL MSS, VC; *80Y*, 111.

33. HBS to ECS, [June 1943?], ECS-LC; ECS to Elizabeth Smith, [1841?], AL-VC; HBS to GS, 9 Sept. 1841, GSM-SU; Rice, "Henry Stanton," 243—44. HBS studied under Judge Cady from 23 Feb. 1841 to 23 May 1842.

34. *80Y*, 111—12; ECS to Elizabeth Neall, 26 Nov. [1842?], Gay MSS, CU.

35. ECS to Elizabeth Neall, 26 Nov. [1842?], Gay MSS, CU; ECS to Elizabeth Pease, 12 Feb. 1842, BPL.

36. ECS to Elizabeth Neall, 26 Nov. [1842?], Gay MSS, CU.

37. ECS to LM, [1841?], *CE*, 35; ECS to Rebecca Eyster, 1 May 1847, *Letters*, 15—16. See also introduction.

38. *80Y*, 120.

39. Elizabeth Neall to Abby Kimber, 11 Dec. 1841, Gay MSS, CU; Rice, "Henry Stanton," 245—47.

40. HBS to Birney, 19 April 1843, *Birney Letters*, 2:734—46.

41. Norma Basch, "Her Separate Estate: Married Women's Property Rights Legislation in New York State, 1848—1862" (Ph.D. diss., New York Univ., 1977); Peggy A. Rabkin, *Fathers to Daughters: The Legal Foundations of Female Emancipation* (Westport, Conn.: Greenwood, 1980), also traces the enactment of the New York law. For Rose and Davis, see *NAW* articles by Alice Felt Tyler.

42. HBS to ECS, 30 March [1844?], [Oct. 1842?], and [Oct. 1842?], ECS-LC; Elizabeth Neall to Abby Kimber, 11 Dec. 1841, Gay MSS, CU; Sarah Grimké to ECS, 31 Dec. 1842, TS-DL.

43. *80Y*, 136.

44. Ibid., 138—39.

45. ECS to Elizabeth Neall Gay, 3 Feb. [1846?], Gay MSS, CU; *80Y*, 127, 132; ECS to Margaret L. Cady, 17 July 1845, *Letters*, 13—14.

46. Gerda Lerner, "The Political Activities of Antislavery Women," *The Majority Finds Its Past: Placing Women in History* (New York: Oxford Univ. Press, 1979), 126.

47. *CE*, 42; ECS also discussed the idea with Frederick Douglass, ECS diary, 30 Nov. 1885, *Letters*, 228—29.

48. *Letters*, 11; ECS to Elizabeth Neall Gay, 3 Feb. [1846?], Gay MSS, CU.

49. HBS to GS, 23 Dec. 1844, GSM-SU.

4. SENECA FALLS SENTIMENTS, 1848

1. Henry Stowell, *A History of Seneca Falls, New York, 1779–1862* (reprint, Seneca Falls Historical Society, 1975), 7. Seneca Falls Historical Society hereafter SFHS.

2. HBS to GS, 6 July 1844, GSM-SU.

3. Daniel Cady to HBS, 15 Sept. 185[2], ECS-LC; HBS, *Recollections*, 3d ed., 170–71; Rice, "Henry Stanton," 340–42.

4. Letters to author from Fulton County clerk, 1 Aug. 1977, and from Hanns Kuttner, 27 Nov. 1979.

5. *80Y*, 143–44.

6. Harriot Stanton Blatch, address to National Woman's party, 19 July 1923, Seneca Falls, ECS-LC.

7. ECS to ESM, [winter 1847?], AL-VC.

8. *80Y*, 145–47.

9. Ibid., 147–48.

10. Ibid.

11. *HWS*, 1:68.

12. For Wright see Bacon, *Valiant Friend;* Cromwell, *Mott.*

13. John E. Becker, *A History of the Village of Waterloo, New York* (Waterloo: Waterloo Library and Historical Society, 1949). Additional information compiled by Hanns Kuttner. See also Judith Wellman, "The Signers of the Declaration of Sentiments, Seneca Falls, 1848" (paper presented at the Berkshire Conference of Women Historians, Bryn Mawr College, Bryn Mawr, Pa., June 1976).

14. A. Day Bradley, "Progressive Friends in Michigan and New York," *Quaker History* 52 (Autumn 1963):95–103.

15. *Seneca County Courier*, 14 July 1848 (reprint, SFHS).

16. *HWS*, 1:68–69.

17. "Declaration of Sentiments," *HWS*, 1:70–71. All subsequent quotations refer to this copy.

18. DuBois, *Feminism and Suffrage*, traces the intellectual history of Stanton's feminism.

19. Bacon, *Valiant Friend*, 128.

20. Recalled Margaret Stanton Lawrence, who was not born until 1852, "Dad, who also spoke and worked for the cause of woman . . . was so amazed at her daring when . . . she would not follow his advice, that he left town." "Seventy-two Years Ago: Mrs. Stanton and the First Women's Rights' Convention" (typed copy of letter to the editor of the *Indianapolis Star*, 12 Nov. 1920), SFHS; *CE*, 46.

21. ECS first repeated the story about her father to Theodore Tilton, "Stanton," 347. It also appears in Janet Cowing, "Mrs. Stanton, Our Pioneer Suffragist," *State Service* 3 (May 1919):14; and Elizabeth G. Delavan, "Elizabeth Cady Stanton" (typescript, 1938), 8, SFHS, an essay written for the Comment Club of Des Moines, Iowa. Both Cowing and Delavan conducted interviews of older Seneca Falls residents.

22. Lawrence, "Sketch," 18.

23. LM to ECS, 16 July 1848, ECS-LC; Wellman, "Signers of the Declaration," 4; *HWS*, 1:69.

24. *Proceedings of the Seneca Falls Women's Rights Convention* (reprint, SFHS); *HWS*, 1:69–74. Subsequent quotations refer to the *Proceedings.*

25. "Her voice . . . was weak and timid, and did not reach the remote parts of

the house." Amelia Bloomer, "Early Recollections of Mrs. Stanton," *New Era:* 1 (Nov. 1885):339, ECS–LC. Mrs. Bloomer did not sign the Declaration, and there is some doubt that she actually attended the meeting.

26. *HWS,* 1:809–10.
27. *Seneca County Courier,* 21 July 1848 (reprint, SFHS).
28. Ibid.; *HWS,* 1:804–5.
29. *HWS,* 1:74; *CE,* 53–54.
30. ECS to George Cooper, 14 Sept. 1848, and ECS to LM, 30 Sept. 1848, *Letters,* 18–22.
31. ECS to Cooper, 14 Sept. 1848, ibid., 18–20.
32. *HWS,* 1:75–80; ECS to Amy Post, 24 Sept. [1848], Harper MSS, HEHL.
33. ECS to Amy Post, 24 Sept. [1848], Harper MSS, HEHL.
34. LM to ECS, 3 Oct. 1848, ECS-LC.
35. *80Y,* 157; Lawrence, "Seventy-two Years Ago."
36. ECS speech, 2 Aug. 1848, Cott, *Bonds of Womanhood,* 195.

5. BONDS OF AFFECTION, 1849–55

1. LM to ECS, 3 Oct. 1848, and 11 Sept. 1851, ECS-LC; ECS to LM, 26 Sept. 1849, WLG-SSC.
2. Blanche Glassman Hersh, *The Slavery of Sex: Feminist-Abolitionists in America* (Urbana: Univ. of Illinois Press, 1978), discusses the marital arrangements of fifty-one women active in this era, including ECS.
3. *80Y,* 151–52.
4. Amelia Bloomer, *The Life and Writings of Amelia Bloomer,* ed. Dexter C. Bloomer (Boston: Arena, 1895; reprint, New York: Schocken Books, 1974).
5. HBS to GS, 2 May 1849, GSM-SU; ECS to ESM, 30 April 1850, AL-VC.
6. *Seneca County Courier,* 21 July 1848.
7. ECS to ESM, 20 April 1850, *Letters,* 24; *HWS,* 1:810.
8. *HWS,* 1:242; Paulina W. Davis to ECS, July 1850, ECS-LC.
9. ECS to HBS, 2 Sept. 1851, *Letters,* 35; ECS to Amy Post, 4 Dec. 1850, *Letters,* 24–25. Reports of the national women's rights conventions were published annually; a complete set can be found at HH.
10. Mrs. Sillias Mynderse to ECS, [Feb. 1851], ECS-LC; Delavan, "Stanton," 6; ECS to ESM, [Feb. 1851], ECS-LC; ECS to HBS, 13 Feb. 1851, *Letters,* 26.
11. HBS to ECS, [Feb.], 15 Feb., and 6 March 1851, ECS-LC.
12. HBS, *Recollections,* 3d ed., 167–68.
13. ECS to ESM, 4 June 1851, *Letters,* 28–31; Rice, "Henry Stanton," 338.
14. HBS, *Recollections,* 3d ed., 170; HBS to Charles Sumner, 13 May 1851, Sumner MSS, HH; Daniel Cady to HBS, 15 Sept. 1851, ECS-LC. Judge Cady had been away from home when Eleazar died and may have been sensitive on questions concerning sons.
15. *HWS,* 1:457–58; *80Y,* 163–64.
16. Cowing, "Pioneer Suffragist," 15; [A.E. Hemon (piano teacher)], "Elizabeth Cady Stanton: Some Reminiscences of Her Family Life at Seneca Falls, New York" (typescript, n.d.), SFHS; Robert Brewster Stanton, "Reminiscences" (n.d.), NYPL; Daniel Cady to Daniel C. Stanton, 3 July 1850, ECS-LC.
17. Thomas, *Weld,* 227–31; ECS and HBS to Theodore Weld, 22 Sept. 1848, Weld-Grimké MSS, Clements Library, University of Michigan, Ann Arbor, Mich.; ECS to SBA, 1 Dec. 1858, Harper MSS, HEHL.

18. ECS to Daniel C. Stanton, 2 May 1852, *Letters*, 42; HBS to "Sons," 22 Feb. 1854, ECS-LC.

19. Andrew Combe, *A Treatise on the Physiological and Moral Management of Infancy*, 4th ed. (New York: W. H. Colyer, 1846); ECS to ESM, 2 July 1851, AL-VC.

20. Delavan, "Stanton"; ECS to Mrs. James Birney, 24 May 1849, TS-DL.

21. ECS to HBS, 16 March 1842 and 9 Dec. 1850, *Letters*, 8, 25–26.

22. Hemon, "Stanton," 1; ECS to ESM, 20 June 1853, *Letters*, 52–53.

23. G[errit] Smith Stanton, "How Aged Housekeeper Gave Her All to Cause of Woman's Suffrage" *Indianapolis Star*, Dec. 1920, SFHS; Theodore Stanton annotation on ECS to ESM, 5 Aug. 1851, TS-DL; *80Y*, 204; ECS to Daniel C. Stanton, 2 May 1852, *Letters*, 42. Little else is known about Amelia Willard (1835–1920).

24. ECS to Daniel C. Stanton, 10 Dec. [1851], ECS-LC, reports staying one month and "having a very gay time." HBS to "Dear Sons," 22 Feb. 1852, ECS-LC, reports Theo very ill and that ECS had taken him to Peterboro, then Johnstown, leaving the Seneca Falls house shut up. Henry had to stay in a hotel.

25. ECS to ESM, 1 May 1853, *Letters*, 49–50.

26. ECS to GS, 5 Jan. [1852], ECS-LC; ECS to ESM, 4 June 1857 and 18 Oct. 1851, *Letters*, 31, 37; ECS to SBA, 1 March [1853], TS-DL.

27. ECS to ESM, 6 June and 18 Oct. 1851, *Letters*, 31, 37; HBS to ECS, 15 Feb. 1851, ECS-LC. See also ECS to Daniel C. Stanton, 14 Oct. 1851, *Letters*, 35–36.

28. ECS to ESM, 5 Aug. 1851, TS-DL, also *Letters*, 34; ECS to ESM, 4 June 1851, *Letters*, 29; ECS to SBA, 19 Feb. 1854, ECS-LC; *HWS*, 1:470–71.

29. *80Y*, 162–63. The earliest piece of Stanton-Anthony correspondence extant is dated 2 April 1852. *80Y*, 162–63, puts their meeting after 1850; *HWS*, 1:456, dates it May 1851.

30. Biographical sources for SBA include Ida Husted Harper, *The Life and Work of Susan B. Anthony*, 2 vols. (Indianapolis: Bowen-Merrill, 1899; reprint, Hollenbeck, 1908); Katharine Anthony, *Susan B. Anthony: Her Personal History and Her Era* (Garden City, N.Y.: Doubleday, 1954); AL, *Susan B. Anthony: Rebel, Crusader, Humanitarian* (Boston: Beacon, 1959).

31. Lee Chambers-Schiller, "The Single Woman: Family and Occupation among Nineteenth-Century Reformers," in *Woman's Being, Woman's Place: Female Identity and Vocation in American History*, ed. Mary Kelley (Boston: G. K. Hall, 1979), 334–50, contradicts the assumption that single women had fewer family responsibilities than married women.

32. ECS to SBA, 2 April 1852, *Letters*, 41–42.

33. Ibid. Stanton, inexperienced herself in mob control, must have been passing on advice from Henry or Mrs. Mott, both of whom were experts.

34. *80Y*, 193; ECS quoted remark by HBS to SBA, 20 Aug. 1857, *Letters*, 70–71; *80Y*, 165.

35. ECS to SBA, 23 Dec. 1859, *Letters*, 74; ECS to SBA, [1853], "Early Letters of Elizabeth Cady Stanton," ed. Ida Husted Harper, *Independent* (21 May 1903), 1191, ECS-LC; SBA to ECS, 29 Sept. 1857, ECS-LC. Smith-Rosenberg, "Female World of Love and Ritual," points out that sexual language and marital metaphors abound in correspondence between women in this era without indicating a lesbian relationship.

36. Mary Grove Nichols to ECS, 21 Aug. 1852, *Letters*, 44.

37. For ESM see *NAW* article by Elizabeth Warbasse; *80Y*, 54–55, 418–19, 455; ESM papers in GSM-SU and NYPL.

38. ECS to ESM, 30 June 1853, TS-DL. "I do wish you would invent something for me to wear on my head. . . . You know I despise a bonnet, it is so uncomfortable and useless."

39. Bacon, *Valiant Friend,* 147.

40. LM had "an instinct for self-nurturing." Ibid., 200. See also letter to author from Margaret Hope Bacon, 19 March 1982.

41. Banner, "Stanton" (typescript), 81.

42. *HWS,* 1:481–83.

43. *CE,* 78.

44. Ross Evans Paulson, *Women's Suffrage and Prohibition: A Comparative Study of Equality and Social Control* (Glenview, Ill.: Scott, Foresman, 1973).

45. ECS to SBA [Spring 1853], *CE,* 84.

46. *HWS,* 1:517–20.

47. ECS to LM, 22 Oct. 1852, *Letters,* 44; ECS to ESM, 22 Oct. 1852, ECS-LC, also AL-VC, and *CE,* 81.

48. Delavan, "Stanton," 11; ECS to ESM, [Nov. 1852], ECS-LC.

49. ECS to ESM, 22 Oct. 1852, ECS-LC.

50. ECS to ESM, 21 Nov. 1852 and 30 Sept. 1853, *Letters,* 45, 53–54.

51. ECS to SBA, 2 April 1853, *Letters,* 41–42.

52. HBS to ECS, 5 Jan. 1854, 19 Oct. 1856, and 18 Jan. 1857, ECS-LC.

53. HBS to ECS, 28 Jan. 1859, and Oliver Johnson to ECS, [spring 1856?], ECS-LC; Margaret Stanton Lawrence, "As a Mother," *New Era* 1 (Nov. 1885):323, ECS-LC; ECS reference in the *Lily,* Sept. 1851, complete file at New-York Historical Society, New York, N.Y. (hereafter NYHS).

54. *80Y,* 209, 105.

55. G. S. Stanton, "Aged Housekeeper"; ECS to HBS, 2 Sept. 1851, ECS-LC.

56. *HWS,* 1:465; *80Y,* 153.

57. *80Y,* 152–53.

58. Amelia Bloomer to ECS, on envelope, [April 1851], *Letters,* 27; Delavan, "Stanton," 12.

59. SBA to ECS, 13 Nov. 1853, and William H. Channing to ECS, 18 Dec. 1853, ECS-LC.

60. ECS to SBA, 1 Dec. 1853, *Letters,* 54–55; also "Early Letters," 1189.

61. *80Y,* 187–89. ECS, "Reminiscences," 6–7, confuses details of 1848 and 1854 and describes Judge Cady's offering her a house if she would not speak. In both of these accounts she convinces him and he helps her.

62. Cowing, "Pioneer Suffragist," 14, repeats the bribe story. Harriot Stanton Blatch, *A Sketch of the Life of Elizabeth Cady Stanton* (n.p., 1915), ECS-LC, concludes, "From the time Mrs. Stanton first began her public work she had one long serious battle with her father." The evidence indicating a break with her father comes from two letters written the next year. ECS to ESM, 20 Sept. 1855, *Letters,* 61: "I lie . . . heavily on his soul"; and ECS to SBA, 10 Sept. 1855, *Letters,* 59–60, also TS-DL, quoted subsequently.

63. *80Y,* 187.

64. *HWS,* 1:595–605.

65. *80Y,* 192; Lawrence, "Who Was . . . My Mother," 11–12.

66. ECS to SBA, 10 Sept. 1855, TS-DL, also *Letters,* 59–60. ECS concluded, "I wish you to consider this letter strictly confidential. Sometimes Susan, I struggle in deep waters. . . . I read and write a good deal, as you see. But there are grievous interruptions. However, a good time is coming and my future is always bright and beautiful. As ever your friend, sincerely and steadfast."

67. ECS to ESM, 20 Sept. 1855, *Letters*, 61. The will of Daniel Cady filed with Fulton County Courthouse, Johnstown, N.Y., after his death in 1859 included Elizabeth. Because each legacy is mentioned specifically by lot and location, it is difficult to determine if her share was equal to her sisters'.

68. ECS to SBA, n.d., "Early Letters," 1189.

6. DISCONTENT AND DIVORCE REFORM, 1856–61

1. ECS to ESM, 4 June 1854, *Letters*, 5.

2. ECS, "I Have All the Rights I Want," *Una*, n.d., ECS-LC.

3. ECS to SBA, 15 Feb. 1855, *Letters*, 59; ECS to SBA, 2 Nov. 1857, TS-DL.

4. LM to ECS, 16 March 1855, ECS-LC.

5. ECS to SBA, 15 Feb. 1855, *Letters*, 59.

6. ECS diary, *Letters*, 177.

7. ECS to SBA, 24 Jan. 1856, ECS-LC. Stanton's friend Oliver Johnson, a Boston attorney and abolitionist, responded to a similarly phrased letter: "I suppose you *meant* to say that you had issued the sixth *volume*, not edition, of your great work. . . . I am curious to learn how many more volumes the world may expect to issue from your press!?" Oliver Johnson to ECS, 4 April 1856, ELS-LC.

8. ECS to ESM, 24 Jan. 1856, AL-VC; ECS to SBA, 10 Feb. 1856, ECS-LC.

9. ECS to ESM, 4 June 1851, *Letters*, 28–31.

10. *National Era*, 17 June 1852, p. 99, Rice, "Henry Stanton," 343; HBS to Charles L. Woodbury, 23 Dec. 1852, 10 Jan. and 21 Feb. 1853, ECS-LC.

11. Rice, "Henry Stanton," 353; Allan Nevins, *Ordeal of the Union*, 2 vols. (New York: Charles Scribner's Sons, 1947), 2:320–27.

12. HBS to Charles Sumner, 31 May 1855, Sumner MSS, HH.

13. "I am tired of slavery agitation. I love peace and my profession, home and my books. But slavery will give us no peace." *Albany Evening Journal*, 2 Oct. 1855, p. 2, Rice, "Henry Stanton," 358.

14. HBS to Thurlow Weed, 15 Oct. 1855, HBS MSS, NYHS; ECS to SBA, 4 Nov. 1855, *Letters*, 62.

15. HBS to ECS, 25 Oct. 1856, ECS-LC. See also HBS to ECS, 19 Oct. 1856, ECS-LC; Rice, "Henry Stanton," 361.

16. ECS to GS, 28 Nov. 1856, "Elizabeth Cady Stanton and Gerrit Smith: Excerpts from Their Correspondence between 1856 and 1875, Pertaining to Abolition and Women's Rights," ed. W. Freeman Galpin, *New York History* 16 (1935):323.

17. *CE*, 101; Bacon, *Valiant Friend*, 156. For Lucy Stone (hereafter LS), see Alice Stone Blackwell, *Lucy Stone, Pioneer of Woman's Rights* (Boston: Little, Brown, 1930; reprint, Detroit: Grand River Books, 1971); Elinor Rice Hays, *Morning Star: Biography of Lucy Stone, 1818–1893* (New York: Harcourt, Brace, 1961).

18. SBA to ECS, 5 June 1856, and ECS to SBA, 10 June 1856, ECS-LC.

19. ECS to SBA, Dec. 1857, *Letters*, 71–72: "How do you stand on the Lecompton question? You Garrisonians are such a crotchety set that generally, when all other men see cause for rejoicing, you howl the more grievously."

20. ECS to GS, 3 Jan. 1856, *Letters*, 63; GS to ECS, 6 Jan. 1856, ECS-LC; AL, *Anthony*, 54–57.

21. AL, *Anthony*, 76, 52, 77.

22. ECS to SBA, 30 July 1857, TS-DL.

23. ECS to SBA, 20 Aug. 1857, *Letters*, 70–71.

24. ECS to ESM, 20 Sept. 1855, and ECS to Wendell Phillips, 18 Aug. 1860, ibid., 59–60, 84.

25. SBA to ECS, 29 Sept. 1857, ECS-LC.

26. SBA to ECS, 5 June 1856, ECS-LC, also *Letters,* 64–65, and *CE,* 102–3; ECS to SBA, [June 1856?], ECS-LC. SBA never exhibited any pride of authorship. It was well known in feminist circles that ECS wrote SBA's speeches. SBA's dependence on ECS's skills was an important factor in their long friendship.

27. ECS, coeducation speech, *American Reveille,* 10 March 1855, ECS-LC; AL, *Anthony,* 69; *CE,* 104; ECS to SBA, 20 Aug. [1857], AL-VC.

28. ECS to LS, 24 Nov. 1856, TS-DL.

29. ECS to SBA, 4 July 1858, TS-DL.

30. LM to Martha Wright (hereafter MW), 3 and 28 Nov. 1858, LM-FHS.

31. Charles W. Slack to ECS, 2 Sept. and 9 Nov. 1858, and ECS to ESM, 1 Dec. 1858, ECS-LC; ECS to George W. Curtis, 25 Sept. 1858, Curtis MSS, HH.

32. Caroline Severance to ECS, 24 Oct. 1858, ECS-LC, asks if Henry's remark to Boston friends that she planned to renege on the invitation were true.

33. SBA to Antoinette Brown Blackwell, 4 Sept. 1858, Blackwell MSS, AES.

34. "Phrenological Character of Mrs. Elizabeth C. Stanton," ECS-VC. See also app. C.

35. ECS to SBA, 2 April 1859, *CE,* 106; ECS to SBA, 10 April 1859, AL-VC.

36. *Seneca County Courier,* 25 June 1859, and ECS to SBA, [June 1859], ECS-LC; ECS to SBA, 15 July 1859, AL-VC, also *Letters,* 74. ECS to ESM, 1 Sept. 1859, ECS-LC: "I am in great need of some reliable help."

37. ECS to SBA, [18] Dec. 1859, ECS-LC, also *Letters,* 75. These images are repeated again and again by ECS in her autobiography when she talks about death. *80Y,* 7–8, 18, 22, 24, 25.

38. G. S. Stanton, "Aged Housekeeper," gives the $50,000 figure. Daniel Cady's will, on file at Fulton County Courthouse, Johnstown, N.Y., lists specific properties in addition to cash gifts but provides no actual total value to ECS's legacy.

39. HBS to GS, 7 May 1861, GSM-SU, asks for advice on how to invest his wife's money.

40. ECS to Amy Post, 1 June 1860, *Letters,* 179.

41. *HWS,* 1:679.

42. *80Y,* 215–16.

43. ECS to SBA, 24 April 1860, *Letters,* 76; ECS to SBA, 1 March [1853], TS-DL; LS to ECS, 14 Aug. 1853, ECS-LC; LS to ECS, 22 Oct. 1856, *Letters,* 67–68; LS to ECS, 17 Sept. 1856, ECS-LC.

44. ECS to LS, 24 Nov. 1856, TS-DL.

45. ECS to SBA, 1 March [1853], ECS-LC.

46. LS to ECS, 16 April 1860, *Letters,* 77.

47. *Letters,* 78.

48. *HWS,* 1:716–22.

49. *80Y,* 245; ECS to SBA, 20 July 1857, *Letters,* 69–70.

50. *HWS,* 1:716–22.

51. Ibid., 725.

52. *80Y,* 225; ECS to SBA, 14 June 1860, and 1 March 1853, *Letters,* 82–83, 48–49.

53. *80Y,* 213–14, 225–26; AL, *Anthony,* 29–41; *HWS,* 1:469.

54. Rice, "Henry Stanton," 368–70.

55. AL, *Anthony,* 86; Rice, "Henry Stanton," 371.

56. ECS to "Dear Boys," 27 Nov. 1860, ECS-LC; SBA to ECS, 26 Nov. 1860, *Letters*, 86.

57. *80Y*, 210.

58. HBS to ECS, 12 Jan. 1861, ECS-LC; "Address of Elizabeth Cady Stanton on the Divorce Bill before the Judiciary Committee of the New York Senate in the Assembly Chamber" (3 Feb. 1861), and *Seneca County Courier*, n.d., ECS-LC, describe the event.

59. AL, *Anthony*, 88.

60. ECS to SBA, [early 1861], "Early Letters," 1190.

61. HBS to ECS, [April 1861], ECS-LC, also HBS, *Recollections*, 3d ed., 71; HBS to ECS, 18 April 1860, ECS-LC.

62. HBS outlined his efforts to get an appointment in letters throughout 1861 to Thomas B. Carroll, HBS-NYHS. See also Rice, "Henry Stanton," 377–83.

7. WAR AND SCANDAL, 1862–65

1. ECS to William H. Seward, 19 Sept. 1861, *Letters*, 88.

2. ECS to ESM, 11 Sept. 1861, ibid., 90.

3. ECS to Seward, 19 Sept. 1861, ibid., 88; ECS, "At Parting," 7 June 1861, poem quoted in Cowing, "Pioneer Suffragist," 16.

4. ECS to Gerrit and Ann Smith, 20 July [1863], *Letters*, 44.

5. SBA to Lydia Mott, [April 1862], AL, *Anthony*, 95; SBA to MW, 23 May 1861, and MW to SBA, 31 May 1861, WLG-SSC.

6. ECS to MW, 20 Aug. 1862, TS-DL; SBA to Lydia Mott, n.d., AL, *Anthony*, 95.

7. ECS to SBA, n.d., ECS-LC; *80Y*, 254.

8. ECS to MW, 10 Aug. 1862, TS-DL.

9. *80Y*, 62–64.

10. *HWS*, 1:681.

11. Harper, *Anthony*, 1:226; *HWS*, 2:50–78.

12. *80Y*, 236–39.

13. *Proceedings of the Meeting of the Loyal Women of the Republic, 14 May 1863* (New York: Phair, 1863), ECS-LC; ECS to Fanny and Frank Garrison, 25 May 1865, WLG MSS, BPL.

14. *New York Herald,* Mary Elizabeth Massey, *Bonnet Brigades: American Women and the Civil War* (New York: Alfred A. Knopf, 1966), 164–65; *80Y*, 240–41.

15. ECS to GS, 6 May 1863, GSM-SU.

16. Hiram Barney to Salmon P. Chase, 17 April 1862, Rice, "Henry Stanton," 425–27.

17. *New York Times,* 31 Oct. 1863, p. 5, and 1 Nov. 1863, p. 3; HBS to Thomas B. Carroll, Nov. 1863, HBS-NYHS; *New York Tribune,* 3 Nov. 1863, p. 1.

18. HBS to Carroll, Nov. 1863, HBS-NYHS.

19. The investigation lasted from 11 Jan. to 20 April 1864. Rice, "Henry Stanton," 425. The Stantons' sources had led them to expect that it would not be so damaging, so they were stunned. ECS to GS, 3 July 1864, GSM-SU.

20. HBS to GS, 27 July 1864, GSM-SU.

21. HBS to Daniel Stanton, 7 Feb. 1861, ECS-LC; ECS to GS, 2 June [1861], GSM-SU; R. B. Stanton, "Reminiscences," 9, 94–96. Henry's nephew claimed that

HBS secured his son's Louisiana appointment by promising Gov. Henry Clay War-
mouth that the *New York Sun* would stop attacking his administration.

22. Rice, "Henry Stanton," 469.

23. SBA to ECS, [Feb. 1865?], *CE*, 131; SBA to ECS, 14 Feb. 1865, ECS-LC.

24. ECS to SBA, [Aug. 1865], Harper, *Anthony*, 1:244, also *CE*, 133.

25. SBA to ECS, 19 April 1865, ECS-LC; ECS diary, 12 Feb. 1901, *Letters*, 355:
"I see now the wisdom of this course, leading public opinion slowly but surely up
to the final blow for freedom. . . . My conscience pricks me now when I recall
how I worked and prayed in 1864 for [his] defeat."

8. REVOLUTION AND SCHISM, 1865–70

1. WLG to Theodore Tilton, 5 April 1870, WLG-BPL.

2. ECS to HBS, 9 Oct. 1867, ECS-LC.

3. ECS to GS, 29 Jan. [1869], GSM-SU. The Stantons sold the house at 464
West 34th Street, which they had purchased in 1865.

4. *CY*, 3.

5. ECS's remarks made on SBA's birthday, 15 Feb. 1870, Harper, *Anthony*, 2:972.

6. *80Y*, 254; see also Harper, *Anthony*, 1:293.

7. Banner, *Stanton*, believes that Stanton had an inherent distaste for private
controversy. There is ample evidence to support the opposite view. Stanton was
not only capable of confrontation politics, whether in private or in public, but also
thrived on making trouble. She considered herself diplomatic but often acted bel-
ligerently.

8. ECS to SBA, [1870?], *Letters*, 124–25.

9. Patrick W. Riddleberger, *1866: The Critical Year Revisited* (Carbondale:
Southern Illinois Univ. Press, 1979); James M. McPherson, "Abolitionists, Woman
Suffrage, and the Negro, 1865–1869," *Mid-America* 47 (Jan. 1965):40–46.

10. *HWS*, 2:91.

11. Wendell Phillips to ECS, 10 May 1865, ECS to Phillips, 25 May 1865, and
ECS to SBA, 11 Aug. 1865, *Letters*, 104–6.

12. *80Y*, 242.

13. ECS to MW, 6 Jan. 1866, *Letters*, 111–12.

14. AL, *Anthony*, 115.

15. *HWS*, 2:181; Bacon, *Valiant Friend*, 201.

16. *HWS*, 2:152. Harriot Stanton Blatch remembered that during the 1866
meeting Sojourner Truth stayed at the Stantons' house. As a little girl of ten, she
read the morning papers to the former slave, who could not read. Said Sojourner
Truth: "I can't read little things like letters. I read big things like men." *CY*, 17.

17. *HWS*, 2:152–53.

18. Ibid., 180–81.

19. ECS to ESM, 22 Oct. 1866, *Letters*, 115; Tilton, "Stanton," 354.

20. *HWS*, 2:103; Flexner, *Century of Struggle*, 148–49.

21. ECS, Speech to Judiciary Committee, Jan. 1867, ECS-LC; *HWS*, 2:271.

22. ECS to ESM, 24 June 1867, AL-VC.

23. *HWS*, 2:284–87; ECS to MW, 27 June 1867, *Letters*, 116.

24. *HWS*, 2:285. Greeley's committee also ruled against lowering the voting age
to eighteen as "a total overthrow of parental authority."

25. ECS to Emily Howland, 1 Sept. 1867, *Letters*, 116–17; *HWS*, 2:269. Stanton's early friendship with Greeley had begun to cool after she teased him in public

in 1860 on the divorce question. Since he had not rebuked her then, perhaps she thought she would get away with her public poke at him in 1867.

26. *CE*, 143.

27. *80Y*, 246–47; ECS to ESM, 14 Dec. 1867, *Letters*, 118–19.

28. ECS to "Sisters 1, 2, 3" (Tryphena Bayard, Harriet Eaton, Catherine Wilkeson), 21 April 1872, *Letters*, 138–39.

29. Flexner, *Century of Struggle*, 147, 173, 174–75.

30. Charles Robinson to ECS, 20 Nov. 1867, ECS-LC.

31. ECS to ESM, 28 Dec. 1867, *Letters*, 118, also *CE*, 154.

32. Hays, *Morning Star*, 197; McPherson, "Abolitionists," 43; WLG to SBA, 4 Jan. 1868, *Revolution*, 29 Jan. 1868.

33. ECS to MW, 18 Jan. 1868, *Letters*, 119–20; *Revolution*, 29 Jan. 1868.

34. ECS to SBA, 28 Dec. 1869, *Letters*, 123–24. Note the references to thrones and queens.

35. *CE*, 164.

36. Ibid., 159.

37. AL, *Anthony*, 142–43.

38. WLG to Theodore Tilton, 5 April 1870, WLG-BPL; ECS to Thomas Wentworth Higginson, 13 Jan. 1868, TS-DL; *HWS*, 2:317; ECS to GS, [1868?], *CE*, 167; ECS to MW, 2 March 1868, WLG-SSC.

39. According to Julia Ward Howe, who "sparred with Mrs. Stanton" on the subject, ECS "excused infanticide, on the ground that women did not want to bring moral monsters into the world, and said that these acts were regulated by natural laws." Journal, 16 Oct. 1873, Howe MSS, HH, courtesy of Mary Grant.

40. Exchange of letters between ECS and Train in *CE*, 164.

41. *80Y*, 182.

42. *HWS*, 2:310–11.

43. AL, *Anthony*, 147; *Revolution*, 6 Aug. 1868.

44. LM to MW, 15 Nov. 1868, WLG-SSC.

45. Bacon, *Valiant Friend*, 201; ECS to Stephen Foster, 4 Nov. 1868, TS-DL.

46. Description of and quotations from convention that follow from *HWS*, 2:345–55.

47. Ibid., 360–62.

48. Flexner, *Century of Struggle*, 149.

49. *HWS*, 2:367.

50. Ibid., 381.

51. *Letters*, 59.

52. AL, *Anthony*, 149–50.

53. Ibid., 151.

54. DuBois, *Feminism and Suffrage*, develops the theme of socialism in ECS's ideology.

55. *HWS*, 2:406; Flexner, *Century of Struggle*, 152–54.

56. Bacon, *Valiant Friend*, 203; WLG to the American Woman Suffrage Association, Nov. 1869, *CE*, 183.

57. Bacon, *Valiant Friend*, 205; Blackwell, *Stone*, 219–20. Odd as Anthony's behavior appears, she was very angry and hurt by the repeated attacks, especially those impugning her honesty.

58. ECS to Higginson, [1868?], *CE*, 171.

59. *Woman's Journal*, 9 April 1870, contains a four-part explanation of the schism. The subject was not raised again until 1899, when Henry Blackwell gave

his version of the facts to contradict those given in Harper's biography of SBA. By that time most of the participants wanted to forget the acrimony. Mary Livermore to Harriot S. Blatch, 10 April 1905, ECS-LC.

60. *Revolution*, [28 Dec. 1869?], *CE*, 179–81.

61. Robert S. Riegel, "The Split of the Feminist Movement in 1869," *Mississippi Valley Historical Review* 49 (Dec. 1962):485–96; *Revolution*, 14 Jan. and 24 Nov. 1869; *Woman's Journal*, 3 Dec. 1870.

62. The geographic bias of Stanton and Stone and its implications are suggested by Suzanne Desan, "The 1869 Split in the Woman's Movement" (typescript, Princeton Univ., 1978).

63. ECS to SBA, [Dec. 1869?], Harper, *Anthony*, 1:198.

64. *HWS*, 2:427.

65. Ibid., 264.

66. Ibid., 320–22.

67. *Revolution*, 22 Jan. 1868.

9. INDEPENDENCE, 1870–79

1. ECS to SBA, 30 May 1870, TS-DL.

2. Ibid.; ECS to MW, 27 Dec. 1879, ECS-LC; SBA diary, 27 Jan. 1874, SBA MSS, LC.

3. ECS to Sarah Pugh, 25 Aug. 1870, *Letters*, 129; ECS to MW, [1870?], WLG-SSC.

4. ECS to Josephine Griffing, 1 Dec. 1870, ECS-LC.

5. For Hooker see *NAW* article by Alice Felt Tyler.

6. ECS to SBA, 30 May 1879, TS-DL; see also ECS to Paulina W. Davis, 9 July 1870, AL-VC.

7. ECS to MW, 27 and 30 Dec. 1870, WLG-SSC.

8. ECS to [MW?], 29 Oct. 1870, and Isabella Beecher Hooker to Caroline Severance, [Oct. 1870], *CE*, 182–83.

9. SBA to ECS, [Jan. 1871?], and ECS to MW, [Jan. 1871], ibid., 207–8.

10. *HWS*, 2:441–43.

11. Ibid., 443–61; ECS, "Women's Suffrage Organizations," *Golden Age*, Dec. 1871, SBA-LC.

12. ECS to SBA, 31 Jan. 1871, TS-DL.

13. For Woodhull see *NAW* article by Geoffrey Blodgett. Most treatments of Woodhull are more scandalmongering than scholarly. Satisfactory are Johanna Johnston, *Mrs. Satan: The Incredible Saga of Victoria C. Woodhull* (New York: G. P. Putnam, 1967), and Emanie Sachs, *"The Terrible Siren," Victoria Woodhull* (1928; reprint, New York: Arno Press, 1972).

14. Victoria C. Woodhull, *Secession Speech* (N.p., 1871); ECS, "Women's Suffrage Organizations."

15. ECS to SBA, [spring 1870], and Feb. 1871, TS-DL; ECS to SBA, [June 1870], *CE*, 204.

16. ECS to MW, [1871], WLG-SSC; ECS to ESM, 12 June 1871, *Letters*, 132–33.

17. SBA to family, [summer 1871], *CE*, 204; SBA to family, [summer 1871], Harper, *Anthony*, 1:396.

18. The meeting was to have been closed to men, but male reporters disguised

themselves and then printed an account of the session. *San Francisco Chronicle*, 14 June 1871, Banner, "Stanton" (typescript), 167–68. The geographically different press treatment may reflect Greeley's influence in the East and greater animosity toward ECS.

19. SBA diary, 20 June 1871, SBA-LC; AL, *Anthony*, 188–89; *80Y*, 290–93.

20. SBA to family, [Sept. 1871], Harper, *Anthony*, 1:396.

21. ECS to ESM, 18 Sept. 1871, TS-DL; ECS to Theodore Tilton, 18 Sept. 1871, Tilton MSS, in J. F. Gluck MSS, Buffalo and Erie County Public Library, Buffalo, N.Y.

22. ECS to MW, [fall 1871?], and ECS to SBA, [fall 1871], TS-DL.

23. *HWS*, 2:493; AL, *Anthony*, 192–93.

24. *CE*, 218.

25. Ibid., 219–20.

26. SBA diary, AL, *Anthony*, 195; ECS to Henry Blackwell, 9 Nov. 1872, NAWSA-LC; Mary Ormsbee Whitton, "At Home with Lucretia Mott," *American Scholar* 20 (Spring 1951):182.

27. ECS to ESM, 16 June 1872, TS-DL; ECS to MW, 19 June 1872, WLG-SSC; ECS to Amelia Willard, July 1872, and ECS to ESM, 16 Aug. 1877, TS-DL.

28. Rice, "Henry Stanton," 419.

29. Platform of the Republican party, 1872, Rebecca Leet, *Republican Women Are Wonderful: A History of Women at Republican National Conventions* (Washington, D.C.: National Women's Political Caucus, 1980); ECS to LM, 16 July 1872, *Letters*, 139; ECS to SBA, 30 June 1873, TS-DL; ECS to SBA, 11 July 1872, ECS-LC; ECS to SBA, 5 Nov. 1872, TS-DL.

30. SBA to ECS, 5 Nov. 1872, AL, *Anthony*, 199.

31. Flexner, *Century of Struggle*, 165–67.

32. ECS to SBA, 19 Feb. 1873, TS-DL; see also ECS to GS, 29 Dec. 1872, GS-SU.

33. ECS to SBA and Matilda Joslyn G. Gage, 25 June 1873, TS-DL.

34. Flexner, *Century of Struggle*, 169–70.

35. *CE*, 221.

36. ECS to ESM, 26 Dec. 1872, TS-DL.

37. Both ECS and Woodhull had been caricatured in Harriet Beecher Stowe's latest book, *My Wife and I; or, Harry Henderson's History* (New York: J. B. Ford, 1871). ECS still disliked Mrs. Hooker and found Catharine Beecher a "narrow, bigoted, arrogant woman" who might have become more humane had she ever "loved with sufficient devotion, passion and abandon any of Adam's sons to have forgotten herself, her God, her *family*, and her propriety, and endured for a brief space of time the world's coldness, ridicule or scorn." ECS to Paulina W. Davis, 1 April 1872, AL-VC.

38. ECS to SBA, [March 1874], *CE*, 222.

39. ECS to ESM, 11 Aug. [1875?], TS-DL.

40. ECS never mentioned the Woodhull scandal in *80Y*; see also *CE*, 221–23.

41. ECS to SBA, 30 July 1874, *Letters*, 145–46.

42. *CE*, 226–27.

43. Ibid., 162.

44. *Revolution*, 23 Dec. 1869; *CE*, 190.

45. ECS to Josephine Griffing, 1 Dec. 1879, ECS-LC.

46. ECS to Theodore Stanton, [1873], TS-DL.

47. Carl Bode, *The American Lyceum* (New York: Oxford Univ. Press, 1956; reprint, Carbondale: Southern Illinois Univ. Press, 1968); ECS to GS, 25 Jan. 1879, GSM-SU.

48. ECS to ESM, 10 Aug. 1879, *Letters,* 128–29; *CY,* 36; ECS to Margaret Stanton, 1 Dec. 1872, AL-VC; ECS to ESM, 16 Aug. 1877, TS-DL.

49. *Lily,* Nov. 1851; *Revolution,* 27 May 1870.

50. ECS to Margaret Stanton, 1 Dec. 1872, AL-VC. Margaret traveled with her mother during 1877–78.

51. ECS, "Lyceum Experiences" (clipping), ECS-LC.

52. ECS to SBA, [1879?], TS-DL; ECS to Margaret Stanton, 1 Dec. 1872, AL-VC.

53. Alexandra Gripenberg, *A Half-Year in the New World* (1888), ed. and trans. Ernest J. Moyne (Newark, Del.: Univ. of Delaware Press, 1954), 15; *San Francisco Chronicle,* July 1871, Banner, "Stanton" (typescript), 175; Mary Clemmer Ames, *A Memorial of Alice and Phoebe Cary* (New York: Hurd & Houghton, 1874), 67.

54. ECS to Louise Chandler Moulton, 30 Aug. 1875, ECS-LC.

55. ECS to Josephine Griffing, 1 Dec. 1870, TS-DL.

56. ECS to ESM, 1 Dec. 1872, ibid.; *CE,* 198.

57. ECS to Isabella Beecher Hooker, 12 April 1871, TS-DL, also *Letters,* 131–32; ECS to MW, 21 March 1871, ECS-LC.

58. ECS, "Our Girls" (handwritten copy), ECS-LC; Lawrence, "Sketch," 65.

59. ECS to MW, 8 March 1873, WLG-SSC.

60. SBA to Matilda Joslyn Gage, 19 Jan. 1876, SBA-LC.

61. SBA, diary, [Spring 1876], Harper, *Anthony,* 1:473.

62. *80Y,* 309–11.

63. *HWS,* 3:31–34.

64. *CE,* 238–39.

65. Ibid., 149; Mary Clemmer, unidentified newspaper article, Harper, *Anthony,* 1:485–86.

66. ECS, "National Protections for National Citizens" (handwritten copy), ECS-LC; *HWS,* 3:80–94; *80Y,* 319; ECS to SBA, 14 Jan. 1878, ECS-LC.

67. ECS to SBA, Nov. 1878, TS-DL.

68. ECS to ESM, 26 March 1879, and ECS to SBA, 4 May 1879, TS-DL.

10. WRITING AND WIDOWHOOD, 1880–88

1. ECS diary, 15 Nov. 1880, *Letters,* 179.

2. SBA to Mrs. Spencer, [winter 1880], Harper, *Anthony,* 2:516; ECS to SBA, 18 Aug. 1880, TS-DL.

3. ECS to SBA, 20 Aug. 1880, TS-DL; ECS to Mrs. Spofford, 18 Jan. 1881, Harper, *Anthony,* 2:526.

4. *80Y,* 335.

5. ECS diary (quoting Robert Browning's "Rabbi Ben Ezra"), 12 Nov. 1880, *Letters,* 171; ECS to Harriot and Theodore Stanton, 12 Nov. 1880, *Letters,* 171–73.

6. ECS diary, 12 Nov. 1880, *Letters,* 171. ECS need not have worried about her children's devotion. Margaret remembered that "she always seemed to have plenty of time for fun and frolic with us young people, for a game of whist or chess, of which she was very fond and a good player. She was ever ready to sing to us, and play for us to dance, or go for a drive or walk. She was the companion of which

we children were most fond, as she entered into all our joys and sorrows, and was always sympathetic. Her sons and daughters confessed all their sins to her, she knew their lives as she did the pages of a well read book; we trusted her with our very souls." Lawrence, "Sketch," 84.

7. ECS to SBA, [summer 1877?], TS-DL.

8. ECS to Harriet Cady Eaton, 21 Dec. 1871, TS-DL; ECS diary, 2 March 1891, *Letters,* 272: "This is Neil's birthday. . . . I dreamed of him last night. We seemed to be on the piazza at Tenafly, talking to Bob. I said, 'Why, Danny, they told me you were dead.' 'Ah, no,' he said with a sweet voice, 'not to you, dear mother.' . . . It was but a dream, a pleasant one. If he can come to me in dreams with sweet messages of love, I shall sleep with new pleasure."

9. Will of Daniel Cady Stanton, 1887, probated 1891, County of New York, Surrogate's Court.

10. Henry Stanton, Jr., to GS, 6 March 1873, GSM-SU; obituary, *New York Times,* 6 Dec. 1903. Although closer to his father than to ECS, Henry, Jr. always defended her. In 1870 he threatened to "cowhide" Greeley. ECS to SBA, n.d., TS-DL..

11. ECS to SBA, 4 May 1879, TS-DL; obituary, *New York Times,* 25 April 1927; Archives, CU.

12. ECS to Elizabeth B. Harbert, [1885], Harbert MSS, HEHL; *80Y,* 331.

13. ECS to Joseph Pulitzer, 29 Dec. 1885, Pulitzer MSS, CU. To another publisher she wrote, "Contrasting him with my four other sons (though as good as the general run of young men), he seems to me as near perfection as a young man can be." ECS to Mr. Underwood (editor of the *Index*), 19 Oct. 1886, AL-VC.

14. Obituary, *New York Times,* 2 March 1925; Alumni Office, Cornell University, Ithaca, N.Y.

15. ECS to Margaret Stanton, 16 May 1877, *Letters,* 151–53. Margaret's copy of *In the Kitchen,* AL-VC. ECS's inscription reads: "When we remember that the intellectual and moral ambition of a man depends on the food he eats, we appreciate the dignity and responsibility of those who feed the human family."

16. Lawrence, "As a Mother," 322; Lawrence to Robert B. Stanton, 11 Nov. 1890, R. B. Stanton MSS, NYPL; clipping files, JPL; Alumnae Office, VC. Her sister found Maggie "by nature a character, an efficient, patient, even-tempered woman." *CY,* 17–18.

17. ECS to Elizabeth B. Harbert, [1885], Harbert MSS, HEHL; *CY,* 4.

18. In addition to *CY,* see obituary, *New York Times,* 21 Nov. 1840; Alumnae Office, VC.

19. Obituary, *New York Times,* 26 Feb. 1920; Alumni Office, Cornell University; Archives, CU; R. B. Stanton MSS, NYPL.

20. Lucretia Mott died 11 Nov. 1880. ECS diary, 13 and Nov. 14 1880, *Letters,* 177–79; ECS to Mott children, 14 Nov. 1880, LM-FHS.

21. *HWS,* 1:419, 407–431; 3:187–89.

22. Partnership agreement, Harper MSS, HEHL.

23. For Gage see *NAW* article by Elizabeth Warbasse; *HWS,* 1:465–66.

24. ECS diary, 27 Dec. 1880, *Letters,* 181.

25. *80Y,* 433. As part of the *History* project, SBA hired a young woman to paste her clippings into account books. Eventually they amounted to thirty-two scrapbooks and were deposited in SBA-LC.

26. SBA to Rachel Foster, 19 Dec. 1880, SBA-LC; Lawrence, "As a Mother," 323.

27. Lawrence, "As a Mother," 323.

28. ECS to SBA, 10 Jan. 1880, *Letters*, 163–65.

29. ECS to SBA, [May 1881], Harper, *Anthony*, 2:531–32.

30. *CE*, 248; G. S. Stanton, "Aged Housekeeper"; ECS to Mrs. Laura Brownell Collier, 21 Jan. 1886, AL-VC: "For several reasons I have lost my interest in Vassar College. First, because of its narrow sectarianism. I hear the liberal element has been slowly weeded out and Baptist professors installed. 2d, the last chair endowed was on the condition that no woman should fill it. 3d, I sent a copy of *The History of Woman Suffrage* as a gift to The Library, which has rejected it without thanks." See also SBA to ESM, 15 Feb. 1882, ESM-NYPL.

31. ECS to SBA, 26 July 1881, TS-DL; ECS and SBA held meetings in Mass., Conn., R.I., Maine, and N.H. As a result, New England women attended the 1882 National meeting as delegates for the first time. Harper, *Anthony*, 2:534; *HWS*, 3:222.

32. ECS diary, 28 Oct. 1881, *Letters*, 187, 184–85; SBA to [?], [Sept. 1881], and SBA diary, [Nov. 1881], Harper, *Anthony*, 2:537, 539.

33. Wendell Phillips to SBA, [Jan. 1882], Harper, *Anthony*, 2:360.

34. LS to ECS, 30 Aug. 1876, Harper MSS, HEHL; *HWS*, 2:756; *CY*, 62–63.

35. *80Y*, 336.

36. Ibid., 338–39.

37. Lawrence, "Sketch," 88; ECS diary, 20 July 1882, *Letters*, 191–93.

38. ECS to ESM, Nov. 1882, TS-DL.

39. ECS diary, 22 Nov. 1883, *Letters*, 213. In her diary, 10 Jan. 1895, *Letters*, 310, ECS revised her opinion: "I like the style and refinement of thought of all of [his] fiction. And then I am always drawn to him with affection because of his open advocacy of our political emancipation. The support of such men is a mighty aid in our uphill struggle."

40. *80Y*, 353; *Letters*, 200–209.

41. ECS to SBA, [Mar. 1883], Harper, *Anthony*, 2:553.

42. ECS diary, 7 Oct. and 15 Nov. 1883, *Letters*, 211–13.

43. *80Y*, 187.

44. ECS to SBA, [Jan. 1888], Harper, *Anthony*, 2:635; *CE*, 306.

45. *HWS*, 1:459, 456–57. Others offered their opinions of the partnership. Amelia Bloomer wrote, "without the push of Miss Anthony, Mrs. Stanton would probably never have gone abroad into active work or achieved half what she has done; and without the brain of Mrs. Stanton, Miss Anthony would never have been so largely known to the world by name and deeds." Bloomer, "Recollections," 339. Carrie Chapman Catt suggested the relationship was more sinister, writing to Alice Stone Blackwell, 18 Sept. 1930, Blackwell MSS, AES (courtesy of Ellen DuBois): "Miss Anthony always thought [ECS] could exceed anyone else in style and strength of her appeal and that is one reason she clung to her, but I see that it is just possible that there may have been other reasons. I always thought it strange that she was so under the influence of Mrs. Stanton. It always seemed to me that she thought and did things because Mrs. Stanton indicated that that was the way to do them."

46. ECS diary, 22 and 17 Nov. 1883, *Letters*, 213.

47. ECS to SBA, [Jan. and Feb. 1884], and 23 Feb. 1884, TS-DL.

48. SBA to ECS, [Jan. 1884], Harper, *Anthony*, 2:586.

49. Clipping files, JPL; *80Y*, 379; ECS diary entries, *Letters*, 216–19.

50. *HWS*, 4:58–60.

51. Ibid. For Colby see *NAW*, article by Norma Kidd Green.

52. ECS to ESM, 27 Jan. [1885], TS-DL; ECS to SBA, 29 Jan. 1885, *Letters*, 224.

53. ECS diary, 20 Feb. and 30 Sept. 1885, *Letters*, 225–27.

54. Stanton's intellectual debt to the British secularist Annie Besant is a theme of Ellen DuBois, "The Limitations of Sisterhood: Stanton's Political Leadership, 1875–1901" (paper presented at the Berkshire Conference of Women Historians, VC, June 1981).

55. Copies of articles in ECS-LC. See also ECS diary, 27 April 1886, *Letters*, 232.

56. HBS, *Recollections*, 3d ed., 68.

57. *80Y*, 385; Rice, "Henry Stanton," 471; ECS to Theodore Weld, 2 Feb. 1881, Weld-Grimké MSS, Clements Library. ECS had no photograph of her husband: "He was always averse to being photographed or painted and but one very poor picture of him is extant, which . . . does him great injustice. . . . He was a very handsome man in youth and very bright and youthful in age." ECS to [D. Phillips], 29 July 1896, AL-VC.

58. *80Y*, 385, 389. HBS comes and goes in ECS's diary and correspondence.

59. ECS to ESM, [1885], TS-DL; HBS to George W. Curtis, 22 March 1886, Curtis MSS, HH.

60. Call for celebration, *New Era* 1 (Oct. 1885):313.

61. *80Y*, 387; ECS to Elizabeth B. Harbert, [Nov. 1885], Harbert MSS, HEHL. For Lozier see *NAW* article by Milton Cantor; ECS entry in "In Memoriam: Mrs. Clemence Sophia Lozier, M.D." (1888), AES.

62. Obituary, *New York Times*, 15 Jan. 1887; ECS diary, 12 Jan. 1887, *Letters*, 236. The incorrect dating of the entry suggests that ECS wrote it long after the event or that she was too shaken to concentrate. She had also mistaken the date of their marriage.

63. HBS to Margaret Stanton, 16 Jan. 1857, ECS-LC: "Tell your mother that I have seen a throng of handsome ladies, but that I had rather see her than the whole of them; but I intend to cut her acquaintance unless she writes me a letter." Although she was flattered by the attention of male admirers, there is no indication that ECS had any extramarital affairs.

64. ECS to ESM, 30 June 1878, TS-DL.

65. ECS to R. L. Stanton, [May 1887], *CE*, 266; Lawrence, "Sketch," 107.

66. ECS diary, 27 Nov. and 6 March 1887, *Letters*, 242, 237; ECS to ESM, 5 March [1887], TS-DL.

11. SELF SOVEREIGN, 1889–1902

1. W. Andrew Achenbaum, "The Obsolescence of Old Age in America, 1865–1910," *Journal of Social History* 8 (Fall 1974):48–62.

2. Social learning theory confirms the important influence on development of an individual's "private vision of a future self." See Alice B. Rossi, "Feminist History in Perspective: Sociological Contributions to Biographic Analysis," in *A Sampler of Women's Studies*, ed. Dorothy McGuigan (Ann Arbor: Univ. of Michigan Press, 1973), 93.

3. *HWS*, 4:85–111; ECS diary, 12 Jan. 1887, *Letters*, 239; ECS to SBA, [Jan. 1888], Harper, *Anthony*, 2:635.

4. SBA diary, [Nov. 1887], *CE*, 268; SBA to ESM, 26 Jan. 1888, ESM-NYPL.

5. Harper, *Anthony*, 2:636; *80Y*, 413. ECS claimed to have been permitted a daily drive.

6. *HWS*, 4:125; Harper, *Anthony* 2:126.

7. *HWS*, 4:134.

8. *80Y*, 413.

9. ECS diary, 4 April 1888, *Letters*, 250–51.

10. ECS to Clara Colby, [1896?], *CE*, 296; ECS diary, 9 Jan. 1889, *Letters*, 254.

11. *80Y*, 414–17; ECS diary, 20 Aug. 1888 and 20 July 1889, *Letters*, 251–52, 259; ECS to ESM, 11 Sept. 1888, TS-DL.

12. *80Y*, 416; ECS to ESM, 11 Sept. 1888, TS-DL.

13. "Grand Old Woman of America," *New York American*, 1896, ECS-LC; *International Council of Women Report* (N.p., 1888), 339.

14. Douglas, *Feminization of American Culture*, 74.

15. *80Y*, 419. ECS chose the Dansville Sanitorium because she had known the senior Dr. Jackson, who had been a member of Gerrit Smith's Peterboro circle.

16. ECS to SBA, 1 March 1853, TS-DL; ECS to ESM, 24 June 1860, Autograph Collection, VC, courtesy of Ellen DuBois; ECS to ESM, 11 Sept. 1888, TS-DL.

17. Harper, *Anthony*, 2:659.

18. ECS to Wisconsin Woman's Suffrage Association [late 1889], *CE*, 277.

19. Harper, *Anthony*, 2:627.

20. ECS diary, 9 Jan. 1889, *Letters*, 253–54.

21. ECS diary, 2 Jan. 1890, ibid., 260; ECS to ESM, 12 Feb. 1890, AL-VC.

22. *HWS*, 4:158.

23. Harper, *Anthony*, 2:667, 951.

24. *Woman's Tribune*, 22 Feb. 1890; *CE*, 278–79; Harper, *Anthony*, 2:631.

25. *CE*, 281–82.

26. Ibid., 285; ECS to Clara Colby, 6 March 1890, Colby MSS, HEHL.

27. ECS diary, 25 Feb., 30 Aug., 4 Nov. 1890, *Letters*, 262, 264, 268; *80Y*, 421; ECS to ESM, 21 March [1890], TS-DL.

28. Delavan, "Stanton," 5; Hemon, "Stanton," 6; Lawrence, "Sketch," 38; ECS diary, 7 Oct. 1881, *Letters*, 186–87; ECS to ESM, 29 May 1890, TS-DL.

29. *80Y*, 426, 428–31; ECS to ESM, 31 July 1890, TS-DL; Harper, *Anthony*, 2:712.

30. SBA to ECS, [summer 1891?], and tribute to Anthony (paraphrasing Emerson), 15 Feb. 1890, Harper, *Anthony*, 2:712, 667.

31. *80Y*, 432.

32. Dolores Hayden, "Two Utopian Feminists and Their Campaign for Kitchenless Houses," *Signs* 4 (Winter 1978):274–90.

33. Lawrence, "Sketch," 116.

34. ECS diary, 3 Jan. 1891, *Letters*, 271; *HWS*, 4:176–78; "The Matriarchate," ECS-LC; ECS to SBA, [Jan. 1892], Harper, *Anthony*, 2:717.

35. *HWS*, 4:189–91. This section and subsequent quotations from the speech text.

36. Karlyn Kohrs Campbell, "Stanton's 'The Solitude of Self': A Rationale for Feminism," *Quarterly Journal of Speech* 66 (1980):304–12, provides an insightful analysis of the speech in terms of its lyric style and feminist content.

37. ECS to Olympia Brown, 8 May 1888, Brown MSS, AES.

38. ECS to Lillie Devereux Blake, 19 February 1901, Blake MSS, Missouri Historical Society, St. Louis, Mo.; ECS diary, 16 Feb. 1900, *Letters*, 348.

39. See Aileen S. Kraditor, ed., *The Ideas of the Woman Suffrage Movement*,

1890–1920 (New York: Doubleday, 1971), for a discussion of the righteousness argument.

40. *Letters,* 346.

41. Speeches in ECS-LC. Regarding the Spanish-American War, Stanton wrote: "I am strongly in favor of this new departure in American foreign policy. What would this continent have been if left to the Indians?" ECS to William Lloyd Garrison II, 27 July 1898, WLG-SSC.

42. ECS diary, 1 Nov. 1892, *Letters,* 289–90.

43. ECS to ESM, 18 Oct. [1892?], TS-DL; Robert Collyer to "Sweet Heart" (ECS), 9 May 1900, and others, ECS-LC; ECS to W. L. Garrison II, 6 Jan. 1896, WLG-SSC. On her seventy-eighth birthday, ECS described her daily routine: "A half dozen articles . . . have been written by me this month. I keep in good physical condition because I act rationally. Every pleasant day I take a drive in the park, and indulge in short naps thrown in between my reading and writing. I mingle good novels with other reading. The half dozen letters—there are sometimes more—which I write daily are disposed of at intervals during the day. A half hour before retiring for the night, I play a few games of backgammon." ECS diary, 12 Nov. 1893, *Letters,* 300.

44. ECS diary, 23 July 1893, *Letters,* 284–85.

45. SBA to ESM, 15 Feb. 1892, ESM-NYPL; ECS diary, 1 Aug. 1893, *Letters,* 293; Harper, *Anthony,* 2:712.

46. *80Y,* 441; ECS diary, 16 Oct. and 11 July 1893, and 29 Aug. 1897, *Letters,* 298, 293, 327.

47. Wills of Tryphena Cady Bayard and Daniel Cady Stanton, both probated 1891, County of New York, Surrogate's Court. No copy of Henry Stanton's will has been located. Robert Stanton published *80Y* because the publishing house with which ECS had contracted asked her to change one sentence and she refused. The sentence referred to William Jennings Bryan's campaign for the presidency in 1896: "I heard the clarion call of the coming revolution." Lawrence, "Sketch," 128–29.

48. ECS to Ellen Wright Osborne, 10 March [?], WLG-SSC; ECS diary, 17 Aug. 1894 and 23 Dec. 1893, *Letters,* 307–8, 301–2.

49. Delavan, "Stanton," 14–15; *CE,* 292; AL, *Anthony,* 293; Harper, *Anthony,* 2:847.

50. R. B. Stanton, "Reminiscences." Henry's nephew had never been an admirer of his aunt and may have purposely described a melancholy old woman rather than a triumphant feminist.

51. ECS to E. H. Slagle, 10 Dec. 1885, TS-DL; Elizabeth Cady Stanton and the Revising Committee, *The Woman's Bible* (Seattle: Coalition Task Force on Women and Religion, 1974), 7–13. Another useful reprint of *The Woman's Bible* is *The Original Feminist Attack on the Bible,* introd. Barbara Welter (New York: Arno, 1974).

52. ECS diary, 25 Nov. 1882, *Letters,* 198.

53. *80Y,* 382, 389–92; ECS diary, 31 Aug. 1886, 13 and 16 March 1895, *Letters,* 233, 312; *CE,* 302; Mary Gray Peck, *Carrie Chapman Catt: A Biography* (New York: H. W. Wilson, 1944), 87–88. For Catt see *NAW* article by Eleanor Flexner.

54. The others were Rev. Phebe Hanaford, Ellen B. Dietrich, Ursula Gestafield, Louisa Southworth, and Frances E. Burr; none were prominent either as feminists or as scholars.

55. ECS to Antoinette Brown Blackwell, 27 April 1896, Blackwell MSS, AES.

56. ECS to Clara Colby [Jan. 1896], *CE*, 302.

57. *HWS*, 4:263–64.

58. Harper, *Anthony*, 2:856; AL, *Anthony*, 280.

59. ECS to SBA, [July 1895], Harper, *Anthony*, 2:842.

60. ECS to SBA, [1897], ibid., 951–52. SBA to ECS, [Dec. 1897?], *Letters*, 328 (ECS wrote two of the requested speeches, see *HWS*, 4:316–18); ECS diary, 7 Feb. 1896, *Letters*, 321–22.

61. SBA to ESM, 12 March 1897, ESM-NYPL; ECS diary, 8 June 1901, *Letters*, 357–58; ECS to Ida Husted Harper, 30 Sept. 1902, Harper MSS, HEHL.

62. SBA to Clara Colby, 20 Nov. 1899, Harper MSS, HEHL. For Blake, see *NAW* article by William A. Taylor.

63. ECS to Lillie Devereux Blake, 12 June 1899, Blake MSS, Missouri Historical Society.

64. ECS to Elizabeth B. Harbert, 25 July 1901, Harbert MSS, HEHL.

65. ECS to Clara Colby [early 1895], *CE*, 297; *80Y*, 450; ECS diary, 3 Dec. 1900, *Letters*, 354. About playing chess, ECS wrote, "In my younger days, chess was thought to be a necessary accomplishment. But now you seldom meet a woman who knows the game. They all say it is too hard work as if thinking were not one of the pleasures of life." ECS to Grace Greenwood [Sarah J. Lippincott], 30 May 1873, *Letters*, 141–42.

66. ECS diary, 20 May 1896, *Letters*, 318; see also newspaper clippings, ECS-LC.

67. ECS diary, 25 Aug. 1901, *Letters*, 358.

68. ECS diary, 1 April 1897, *Letters*, 325. ECS's granddaughter, Nora Blatch Barney, also went blind in her old age. There were other shared family traits: Stanton's relatives and descendants were robust and rotund, had good teeth and low blood pressure. Several had weak knees and varicose veins in their left legs. Rhoda Barney Jenkins, telephone interview, 26 Feb. 1981. ECS asked visitors to read to her as well, but as each selected his own favorite book, the result was " 'mixed drinks,' as my menfolk would say, and I believe this is never good." ECS diary, 20 July 1896, *Letters*, 320.

69. ECS to Harriot Stanton Blatch, 20 Aug. 1880, TS-DL; ECS to Theodore Stanton, 25 Oct. 1896, ibid.: "There is nothing like work to heal all our sorrow." ECS to H. S. Blatch, 11 March 1877, *Letters*, 150–51; ECS diary, 4 Feb. 1899, *Letters*, 337.

70. ECS to Clara Colby, 12 Nov. 1900, ECS-LC; ECS diary, 12 Nov. 1900, *Letters*, 353–54. She also recalled that Henry had been terrified of dentists and would not have a tooth out "unless I was there to laugh at him." With only 4 percent of the population over age sixty-five in 1900, longevity made ECS statistically rare. Achenbaum, "Obsolescence of Old Age," 52.

71. SBA diary, [May 1902], *CE*, 317; ECS to Theodore Roosevelt, 22 Oct. 1902, and ECS to Edith K. Roosevelt, 25 Oct. 1902, reprinted in *Independent*, 6 Nov. 1902, ECS-LC.

72. H. S. Blatch to Helen Gardener, n.d., ECS-LC. See also Lawrence, "Sketch," 134.

73. Rhoda Barney Jenkins, telephone interview, 26 Feb. 1981; ECS diary, 20 Oct. 1901, *Letters*, 359–60.

74. SBA to ESM, 29 Dec. 1902, ESM-NYPL.

75. SBA to Ida Husted Harper, [Nov. 1902], Harper MSS, HEHL; SBA to Theodore Stanton, 18 May 1903, ECS-LC.

76. ECS diary, 9 Feb. 1895, *Letters*, 316. ECS is buried in lot 5421. Nearby are the graves of HBS; Henry, Jr., and his wife Mary; Theodore; Margaret Lawrence; Harriot Blatch; and Robert Stanton.

METHODOLOGICAL NOTE;

STANTON IN PSYCHOLOGICAL PERSPECTIVE

1. For discussion of the usefulness of the available theories, see Allan J. Lichtman and Valerie French, *Historians and the Living Past: The Theory and Practice of Historical Study* (Arlington Heights, Ill.: AHM, 1978), 128–39. Jacques Barzun, *Clio and the Doctors: Psycho-History, Quanto-History, and History* (Chicago: Univ. of Chicago Press, 1974), challenges the validity of psycho-historical endeavors on all counts.

2. Leon Edel, "The Figure under the Carpet," *Telling Lives*, 33–34.

3. Albert Bandura, *Social Learning Theory* (Engelwood Cliffs, N.J.: Prentice-Hall, 1977), vi–viii. See also Albert Bandura and Richard Walters, *Social Learning and Personality Development* (New York: Rinehart & Winston, 1963); Walter Mischel, "Toward a Cognitive Social Learning Reconceptualization of Personality," *Psychological Review* 80 (1973):252–83.

4. Albert Bandura, "Self-Efficacy: Toward a Unifying Theory of Behavioral Change," *Psychological Review* 84 (1977):191–215.

5. *80Y*, 1.

6. Jeanne J. Speizer, "Role Models, Mentors, and Sponsors: The Elusive Concepts," *Signs* 6 (Summer 1981):692–712.

7. Laura Curtis Bullard, "Elizabeth Cady Stanton," in *Our Famous Women*, ed. Bullard (Hartford, Conn.: Hartford, 1888), 604.

8. Lois Hoffman, "Early Childhood Experiences and Women's Achievement Motives," in *Women and Achievement: Social and Motivational Analyses*, ed. Sandra Schwartz Tangri et al. (Washington, D.C.: Hemisphere Publishing Co., 1975), 132–36.

9. *80Y*, 2; ECS diary, 23 May 1900, *Letters*, 350: "During the nine months of prenatal life, [mothers] are stamping every thought and feeling of their minds on the plastic beings to whom they are giving life and immortality." Stanton advised young mothers not to play euchre or drink cocktails, for fear of making gamblers or drunkards of the next generation.

10. See *Dictionary of Scientific Biography*, 1975 ed., article by Anthony A. Walsh; Justin Kaplan, "The Naked Self and Other Problems," in *Telling Lives*, 47–49.

11. ECS to Daniel Cady, 12 Jan. 1853, *Letters*, 46–47; "Phrenological Character of Mrs. Elizabeth C. Stanton," ECS-VC. Bump-reading was very popular in that era. George Combe studied Lucretia Mott's head when he visited Philadelphia in 1838 and found her temperament "nervous [and] bilious." Bacon, *Valiant Friend*, 67.

Index

Laura Fair trial. *See* Trials
Lawrence, Margaret Livingston Stanton (Mrs.
    Frank) (daughter), 2, 76, 78, 87, 161,
    174, 183, 195, 198, 201, 207
Liberty party, 15, 24, 32, 40, 42, 46
Lincoln, Abraham, 105, 110, 112, 113, 115,
    116-17
London, 1840. *See* World Anti-Slavery Con-
    vention
Lozier, Dr. Clemence, 187
Lyceum, 160-61, 169. *See also* Elizabeth Cady
    Stanton, lecturer

Married women's property rights, 92, 109-10,
    146; in New York, 7, 43, 49, 81-83, 92,
    97, 100-101
McClintock, Mary Ann, 51, 52
McMartin, Margaret Cady (Mrs. Duncan)
    (sister), 6, 8, 195
Medicine, 23, 87; women doctors, 65, 92,
    187. *See also* Graham, Sylvester; Home-
    opathy; Stanton, Elizabeth Cady, health
    care
Merger. *See* National American Women Suf-
    frage Association
Miller, Elizabeth Smith (Mrs. Charles)
    (cousin), xiv, 40, 49, 67, 75, 107n, 137,
    159, 223; in bloomers, 71-72; family, 24,
    68, 75; in old age, 183, 195, 201, 206,
    214
Minor v Happersett, 155-56
Mormon women, vii, 150, 199
Motherhood. *See* Stanton, Elizabeth Cady;
    image; motherhood
Mott, James, 38, 39
Mott, Lucretia Coffin, 116, 132, 135, 137,
    139, 169, 223; background, 37-38;
    death, 175-76; and economics, 53n;
    meeting attendance, 93, 125, 166; and
    religion, 41, 45, 210; as role model, 10,
    59, 62, 76, 175, 221; Seneca Falls, 50-
    54; Elizabeth Cady Stanton and, 60, 75-
    76, 96, 124. *See also* Abolition; Mott,
    James; Quakers; Seneca Falls conven-
    tion

Name, women's use of, xiii-xiv, 41, 90-91,
    127
National American Women Suffrage Associ-
    ation (NAWSA), ix, xii, 175, 202, 208,
    211; leadership, 199, 204-5, 214-15;
    merger, 142, 146, 193, 194-95, 197-98
National Woman Suffrage Association
    (NWSA), viii, 118, 119, 137, 140-41,
    145; leadership, 168, 171, 197; meet-
    ings, 141, 142, 149, 151, 168, 169, 176,
    184; and Elizabeth Cady Stanton role,
    165, 167-68, 187, 199
National Woman's Loyal League, 112-13
National Woman's party, ix, x, 175

National women's rights conventions. *See*
    Women's rights national conventions
Neall, Elizabeth, 35, 41
"New Departure." *See* Suffrage, woman's,
    "new departure"
New England Woman Suffrage Association,
    135, 146
New York Married Women's Property Act.
    See Married women's property rights

Oberlin College, 17n, 27, 65, 90n, 91, 92
Owen, Robert Dale, 123, 202

Parker, Theodore, 44, 45-46, 54, 210, 223
Phillips, Wendell, 35, 36, 92, 104, 122, 123,
    125, 128, 179, 194
Phrenology, 44, 96-97, 194, 224, 230-32
Pillsbury, Parker, 44, 92, 131, 132, 133, 144
Post, Amy, 59
Prohibition. *See* Temperance
Prostitution, 150-51, 160
Psychological methodology, 219-25. *See also*
    Biography

Quakers, 38, 51, 52, 59, 73, 154
"Queen" (as metaphor), vii, 10, 11, 18, 170,
    192, 195-96, 203, 207

Random Recollections (Henry Brewster
    Stanton autobiography), 115, 186
Reform, 14-15, 21-22, 28, 32, 44. *See also*
    Revival
Religion: Christian perfectionism, 45-46; role
    of women, 20, 22, 218. *See also* Re-
    vival; Stanton, Elizabeth Cady, religion
Republicans, 89, 105, 153; and reconstruc-
    tion, 118, 124, 129; and woman suf-
    frage, 124, 129, 134, 135, 171, 192. *See
    also* Lincoln, Abraham; Stanton, Henry
    Brewster, and politics
Revival, 19, 20, 22
Revolution, The, 131-33, 137, 155; debt, 133,
    144, 145, 162, 166
Role model, 13, 19, 62-63, 75, 86, 219-24.
    See also Mott, Lucretia; Social learning
    theory
Rose, Ernestine, 43, 104, 112, 137
Roosevelt, Theodore, 214, 217

Secret Six, 24, 98
"Self-sovereignty," xii, xiv, 203-4. *See also*
    "Queen" (as metaphor); Stanton, Eliza-
    beth Cady, feminist ideology
Seneca Falls, N.Y., ix, 7, 46-48, 107, 174
Seneca Falls convention, 39, 47, 51-60; an-
    niversaries, ix, 167, 169, 174, 192, 193.
    See also *Declaration of Rights and Sen-
    timents*
Shaw, Anna Howard, 204-13